In the Space of Theory

BORDERLINES

In the Space of Theory

Postfoundational Geographies
of the Nation-State

MATTHEW SPARKE

BORDERLINES, VOLUME 26

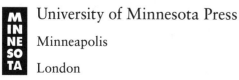

University of Minnesota Press

Minneapolis

London

The publication of this book was assisted by a bequest from Josiah H. Chase to honor his parents, Ellen Rankin Chase and Josiah Hook Chase, Minnesota territorial pioneers.

Two core sections of chapter 1 originally appeared as "A Map That Roared and an Original Atlas: Canada, Cartography, and the Narration of a Nation," *Annals of the Association of American Geographers* 88, no. 3 (1998): 464–95; reprinted with permission of the Association of American Geographers. Portions of chapter 2 were originally published as "Nature and Tradition at the Border: Landscaping the End of the Nation-State," in *The End of Tradition?* ed. Nezar AlSayyad (New York: Routledge, 2004), 155–78; reprinted with permission of Thomson Publishing Services.

Published by the University of Minnesota Press
111 Third Avenue South, Suite 290
Minneapolis, MN 55401-2520
http://www.upress.umn.edu

Library of Congress Cataloging-in-Publication Data

Sparke, Matthew.
    In the space of theory : postfoundational geographies of the nation-state / Matthew Sparke.
        p.   cm. — (Borderlines)
    Includes bibliographical references and index.
    ISBN 0-8166-3189-1 (hc : alk. paper) — ISBN 0-8166-3190-5 (pb : alk. paper)
    1. Boundaries. 2. Territory, national. 3. State, the. 4. Globalization.
    I. Sparke, Matthew. II. Title. III. Borderlines (Minneapolis, Minn.) ; v. 26.
    JC323.S72 2005
    320.1'2—dc22

                                                                        2005007122

Printed in the United States of America on acid-free paper

The University of Minnesota is an equal-opportunity educator and employer.

12 11 10 09 08 07 06 05   10 9 8 7 6 5 4 3 2 1

For Katharyne

BORDERLINES

Contents

Acknowledgments

My first, last, and biggest thanks are to Katharyne Mitchell. Her scholarly savvy, writer's wit, and editorial intelligence have much improved this book while her love and our wonderful times together have made the many years it has taken me to complete the manuscript the best years of my life.

The years of writing are now so numerous that my other debts have become discomfortingly extended. I need to thank at the start all of the people who made the geography department at the University of British Columbia such a brilliant place to learn. Trevor Barnes, Cole Harris, Dan Hiebert, David Ley, and Gerry Pratt were all wonderful guides, and Derek Gregory was and remains a very special intellectual inspiration. Among the student community I also owe big debts (although I hope not any outstanding book-borrowing arrears) to Alison Blunt, Sarah Bonnemaison, Bruce Braun, Noel Castree, Dan Clayton, David Demeritt, Robyn Dowling, Rhys Evans, Jennifer Hyndman, Debbie Leslie, Christine Macy, Suzie Reimer, Tim Solnick, and Anita Srivastava. In the years after UBC many people enabled me to build on my work. Gerard Toal and Donald Moore both gave generous gifts of critical feedback, and Nezar AlSayyad, Sanjay Chaturvedi, Eve Darian-Smith, David Harvey, J. P. Jones, Cindi Katz, Sallie Marston, Carrie Mullen, Alec Murphy, Deborah A. Oosterhouse, Allan Pred, Sue Roberts, Ananya Roy, Neil Smith, and Erik Swyngedouw all offered encouragement at vital moments.

At the University of Washington I have been well supported by David Hodge, Lucy Jarosz, Susan Jeffords, Reşat Kasab, Joel Migdal, Uta Poiger, Priscilla Wald, Kathleen Woodward, and, at the toughest times, by the guidance and friendship of Vicky Lawson. I am further thankful to many other colleagues and students, including Don Alper, Tani Barlow, Carlo Bonura, Michael Brown, Dominic Corva, Mark Ellis, Kim England, Amy Freeman, Bano Gokariksel, Steve Herbert, Rich Heyman, Chandan Reddy, Carolina Katz-Reid, Nikhil Singh, Matthew Sothern, and Jonathan Warren, all of whom gave me valuable revision, inspiration, and assistance. Inspiring me with their wonderful cooking along with their ideas and energy, I have also benefited greatly from the "food for thought" eaten with Sarah Stein, Fred Zimmerman, Walter Parker, Sheila Valencia, Jim Hanford, Linda Nash, Peggy and Marv Waterstone, and, for the longest time now, Gary and Eleanor Hamilton.

More formally I must note that the recent research represented in this book was funded by U.S. National Science Foundation Grants 9710957 and 9984250. Any opinions, findings, and conclusions or recommendations expressed in this material are mine and do not necessarily reflect the views of the National Science Foundation.

As the book has neared completion, other academics have provided me with wonderfully encouraging feedback. I am especially thankful to Simon Dalby, Gill Hart, Jamie Peck, James Sidaway, and Michael Shapiro for their scholarly support. At the end, though, I must also thank my daughters, Sage and Emma, who resolutely refuse to offer scholarly support. My childcare responsibilities are one of my main excuses for taking so long to finish this book, but over this period the girls have simultaneously taught me how to put my work on deterritorialization in its properly decentered place, and for this personal lesson in geographic deconstruction, and for all the joy Sage and Emma have brought to me and Katharyne, I could not be more grateful.

Introduction
The Space of Hyphen-Nation-States

What has happened to all the "deterritorialization" debates of the late twentieth century? Arguments that were animated by this theme once seemed as omnipresent as they were divergent in their implications. In popular discourse, in rhetoric about friction-free capitalism, and in advertising slogans about Geography becoming History, deterritorialization reflected often quite banal commercial interests in the touted end of the nation-state and the emergence of a supposedly borderless world. As an academic preoccupation, by comparison, deterritorialization instead described diverse postfoundational philosophical critiques of such metasubjects as the state, power, consciousness, identity, and even desire. In this context, deterritorialization meant unpacking the ways such subjects had previously been treated as containerized units or "spaces" of theoretical argument. The gap between these antiessentialist epistemological concerns and the ontological arguments about the death of distance was huge, and whether as a result of ignorance or care, it was a gap that was rarely bridged in subsequent discussion. By contrast, this book attempts to critique the arguments about deterritorialization on both levels at once. Countering the end of the nation-state rhetoric, it explores the changing geographical "ends" of two North American nation-states—Canada and the United States—addressing the contemporary rearticulations of nation and state that are implicated in their relations with one another and the world. But in doing so, the book also offers a sympathetic critique of a subset of postfoundational theoretical arguments that in one way or another have made assumptions about space in the context of deterritorializing other theoretical categories. The awkward neologism of hyphen-nation-states used in the title of this Introduction is useful in this respect because it opens up the space of theory that lies at the intersection of the book's two lines of critique. It does so because it highlights two hyphens that relate to both the ontological and epistemological aspects of deterritorialization at once. These hyphens, I argue, disclose critical geographies of displacement and disjuncture that discourses of deterritorialization dissemble.

The first hyphen is the one that ties "the nation" to "the state" in the conventional couplet of "the nation-state." The second is the equally established but usually hidden hyphen that lies latent in the word "geography" itself as a name (derived from the Greek words *geo* and *graphein*) for "earth-writing." Far from just indicating interesting etymological conventions, both hyphens point toward powerful world-making processes. The first aim in what follows is to try to make sense of these processes by using the hyphenated interpretation of geography as *geo-graphy* to unpack the increasingly unstable hyphenation of Canada and the United States as nation-states. The contextual construction and contemporary contestation of the space of *the* nation-state become more legible and, as such, more questionable in this way. And exploring the diverse geographies of the ends of Canada and the United States in such a fashion makes it possible to critique facile claims about *the* end of the nation-state. But more than this, the aim here in developing an argument about the inherently unfinished and multilayered "graphing of the geo" is also to problematize theories that assume some sort of end to geography too: doing so by critically graphing displacements and disjunctures to the hyphenated geo—the nation-state—that has provided the jargon of deterritorialization with one of its most commonly used but least carefully examined metaphors.

The hyphen in nation-state has traditionally symbolized the reciprocal consolidation of national homelands and state territories, a volatile and often violent two-way geographical dynamic that only really became stabilized in the mid-twentieth century at the same time as it was extended through anti-imperial independence movements across much of the world. As a text-spanning symbol of space-spanning phenomena, the hyphen in nation-state came to represent two mutually reinforcing geographical processes. On the one side were the diverse state practices such as border policing, migration control, and planning that regulated territorial belonging. On the other side were the modern space-producing social and cultural dynamics that, in generating taken-for-granted national landscapes, national monuments, national maps, and so on, gave state regulation its space and place of legitimacy. By the 1990s these never entirely convergent geographical reciprocities were beginning to fall apart more and more. State practices became increasingly mediated by transnational market dynamics, and the social, political, and legal flux created by intensified global interdependency also created new spaces for diverse postnational imaginings. The hyphen had often obscured struggles over who belonged to the nation-state and it had literally drawn a line through the possibility of state sovereignty for "internal" nations, but at the end of the millennium these inherent instabilities were exacerbated by the changes most commonly referred to (as well as unfortunately deferred to) as globalization. Alongside the smug homilies about the end of history, the end of the nation-state became in fact one of the main articles of faith in the deferential "globalization is inexorable" creed. Yet while such epitaphs proved premature and politically tendentious, their emergence and endurance nevertheless indicated the increasingly incongruent territorial "ends" of state and nation amid all the global changes. In this context, the hyphen, like the nation-state itself, did not disappear. It merely morphed into a symbol of displacement and disjuncture. No longer a metonym of consolidation, it remains instead a reminder of diverse and open-ended geographical struggles.

If critical reflection on the hyphen in nation-state discloses diverse geographical struggles, an awareness of the implicit hyphen in geography itself serves as a corrective against totalizing claims about the resulting geographical fallout. Such totalization can take many different forms. Most commonly it has consisted of assumptions about the death of distance and the complete relativization or smoothing of globally networked space. As we shall see, though, it can also take the more complex intellectual form of assuming that spatial reconfigurations of the nation-state are always unbounding and emancipatory or, more tacitly, that the nation-state remains, despite diverse reformulations of "the political," the sole container of politics. The point about geography as earth-writing need not in these contexts be limited to a writerly concern with the ways in which books, travel guides, poetry, and the like evoke and contribute to the construction of particular landscapes (interesting as such connections can be). The more radical and far-reaching implication of the argument that the "geo" is constantly being "graphed" is that any assumption about geography either as a result of or as a basis or container for other social relations always risks fetishizing a particular spatial arrangement and ignoring ongoing processes of spatial production, negotiation, and contestation. These claims are by no means new. As will become clear, they draw upon a host of earlier arguments by Marxist and feminist geographers, as well as on the geographically sensitive work of numerous other critical theorists. However, by developing these arguments here in conjunction with analyses of crises besetting the nation-state, the chapters that follow seek to bring the critique of geographical fetishism into the unlikely arena, or rather antiarena, of theoretical deterritorialization. The aim, in short, is to bring a postfoundational geographical sensitivity to a subset of postfoundational theories that relate to the displacements and disjunctures of the nation and state. These theories with their deterritorializing emphases on instability, decentering, openness, and antiessentialism (often dubbed post-structuralist, sometimes dismissed as postmodern, but really better bracketed as postfoundational) have proved to be especially well suited for coming to terms with the fin de siècle disruptions of the nation-state. The chapters that follow draw for these reasons on the particular works of the literary theorist Homi Bhabha, the cultural anthropologist Arjun Appadurai, the political scientist Timothy Mitchell, the political philosophers Chantal Mouffe and Ernesto Laclau, and the theorists of decentered global governmentality Michael Hardt and Antonio Negri. These scholars vary a great deal in their own epistemological and political outlooks, as well as in their substantive areas of interest. Some, most notably Hardt and Negri, use the vocabulary of decentering and deterritorialization while still making monolithic assumptions about the universal march of modern history; others, such as Mitchell, avoid much of the postmodern terminology while nevertheless making powerful critiques of modernist universalism. The purpose then in what follows is not to paint all these theorists with the same brush, nor to draw direct parallels between them, nor even to draw them into conversation with each other. Instead, in putting their particular arguments to work in a discrete set of investigations of worldly displacements of nation-states, the aim is to investigate their limits while also demonstrating their value as ways of making sense of some of the heterogeneous realignments of state hegemony and diverse rearticulations of nation in the contemporary world. The premise that guides this effort is that these theories have tended to make essentialist assumptions about space, or at least particular spatial conjunctions and disruptions, in the context of elaborating otherwise antiessentialist arguments about the state and nation. The recurring theoretical argument in the book rests in this way on an irony: that while the shifting geographical foundations of the hyphenated nation-state have created much need for postfoundational theorizing, this same theory has reproduced within itself foundationally fixed ideas about geography. Antiessentialist argumentation can be seen in this sense to fall prey to a geographical version of its own critique.

Insofar as each chapter that follows seeks to ground a particular postfoundational theory by using it to explore the shifting grounds of particular nation-states, both the theoretical question of grounds and the empirical problem of groundless national-statism are brought geographically together. The result is a critically deconstructive account of geography that draws most directly for its understanding of deconstruction on the inspiration of Gayatri Chakravorty Spivak's feminist, Marxist, and anticolonial reworkings of Jacques Derrida's writing. Spivak's dense, difficult, but critically responsible rereadings of cultural texts provide, I argue, a model for rereading geography *responsibly* as geo-graphy. Even in her first major publication on Derrida, Spivak was savvy to the question of geographical responsibility herself. There was, she said in her lengthy translator's preface, "a shadow of a geographical pattern" in Derrida's *Of Grammatology*.[1] In outlining this pattern (in which a global account of "phonocentrism" by Derrida contrasted with his occidentalist mapping of "logocentrism"), and in indicating the ways in which Derrida thereby repeated some of the same benevolent ethnocentrism that he was tracing in Lévi-Strauss, Spivak suggested how the philosopher fell prey to his own critique.[2] Far from an elitist form of esoteric wordplay for which it has subsequently been confused and misused, such a model of deconstructive rereading ultimately enables a worldly and nonmoralistic form of geographical critique: a spur to respond ethically to the erasures represented by any particular geography. Geography interpreted in this critically responsible way becomes, I will suggest, a call to map persistently without totalization or finalization *the fundamentally heterogeneous* graphing of the geo (always knowing we will fail, always subjecting that failure to the collective critique of others). Every geography, whether assumed or explicitly elaborated as such, every mapping, picturing, visualization, landscaping, theorization, and metaphorization of space becomes rereadable in this sense not just for what it includes, but also for what it overwrites and covers up in the moment of representing spatially the always already unfinished historical-geographical processes and power relations of its spatial production. Like the "White Mythologies" that Derrida deconstructed in one of his classic meditations on the repudiation of metaphor in the logocentric production of philosophical concepts, any supposedly fixed claim about the nature of space (including both monocausal claims about its production and ontological assumptions about its inherent disruptiveness) remains vulnerable in this way to the deconstructive point that it is at some level an *anemic geography*: a geography that, like white chalk on slate, conceals the complex geographical palimpsest over which it writes a singular and supposedly coherent geo.[3] Any geography, including one evoked or unconsciously reiterated in a postfoundational theory, can be examined in this way for the geographies it elides and yet also assumes and thus by which, at some deep level, it is written. In other words, the geo in geography is always being graphed by processes of spatial production that are tied to dynamics that, because they are operative at other scales or because they relate to far-off places, people, and ecologies or because they are ignored or tacitly assumed, remain never fully disclosed by the author of the geography in question. The deconstructive geographical responsibility I am invoking here consists therefore of ongoing attempts to open up and explore these unconnected connections that underwrite particular anemic geographies. These remain nevertheless all too ephemeral suggestions in the abstract, and the aim of this book is to steer a course away from the abyss of idealist abstraction as much as from the metaphysical rocks of supposedly real (for which read, transparently obvious, taken-for-granted, and fully finalized) geography. So to introduce a more substantive sense of the geographies that I seek to elaborate, I turn to a critical reformulation of mapping from another more obviously political critique of white mythologies by the African-American novelist Toni Morrison.

"I want to draw a map," Morrison says at the start of her book about whiteness, "of a critical geography and use that map to open as much space for discovery, intellectual adventure and close exploration as did the original charting of the New World—without the mandate for conquest."[4] It is again the so-called New World with all its vicious history of colonialism and white supremacism that forms the focus for the five chapters that follow. Like Morrison, my hope is also to remap this world without the original mandate for conquest, and this means, among other things, following examples such as Morrison's own and tracking the rearticulations of racism that commonly mediate and shape contemporary struggles over the nation-state in North America. The political stakes and transnational geographical ties of ethnic hyphenations such as African-American and Chinese-Canadian can also be disclosed in this way. But while I directly address issues of racist exclusion and its geographical mediation, the hyphenation of nationalized ethnic identities is not my focus here. Instead, I seek to explore how the anemic geographies of Canada and the United States *as hyphenated nation-states* can and must be rediscovered as sites of geographical displacement and disjuncture. It is by focusing thus on the recent and wide-ranging reterritorializations of the New World through First Nations' struggles, cross-border regionalization, free trade, constitutional reform, and U.S. imperialism that the book sets out to disclose a whole set of geographies for close exploration, geographies that are, I argue, of considerable significance for the contemporary politics of North America.

The notion of North America here remains just as freighted with imperial assumption and Eurocentric vision as the original earth-evacuating concept of the New World. It is, for example, not normally any more open to an encoding as Great Turtle Island—an ab-original name—than the national-state names of Canada and the United States of America. However, I prefer North America as a geographical bracket term because of the ways in which it rubs up against the nationalizing impulses of American studies and Canadian studies. Both academic fields provide valuable secondary sources, theoretical inspirations, and exemplary models for the work that follows. But both also, albeit in quite different dominant and subordinate ways, tend to assume the geo of each respective nation-state as the basis, container, or horizon for what counts as useful knowledge and study. This book aims to work instead in solidarity with those in each field who increasingly now seek to avoid such territorializing impulses. The efforts to "transnationalize" Canadian and American studies are inspirational in this respect, but here the focus is less on the political history of imperialism and diasporic ties (two of the main themes of the transnationalizing initiatives) and more on the reterritorialization of the basic lineaments of North America itself. As chapter 3 shows with its examination of the North American Free Trade Agreement, Mexico too is now encoded in official and accountable economic terms as part of North America: the white supremacism that traditionally obstructed its inclusion becoming trumped, at least in the sphere of political economy, by a powerful and quotidian form of reterritorialization. The reterritorialization with which the book begins, though, concerns First Nations' resistance against the national-state territorialization of the north of Great Turtle Island. Starting with this case, I now want to describe in more detail how I have sought to both use and critique postfoundational theory in the substantive studies.

Chapter 1 examines some direct challenges to "the original charting of the New World" by exploring the ways in which two Native or First Nations, the Gitxsan and Wet'suwet'en, took the governments of Canada and British Columbia to court in a trial that hinged predominantly on the ways in which all the nations involved, both native and colonial, mapped, which is to say cartographed, the geo of national territory. The chapter juxtaposes the maps used by the Gitxsan and Wet'suwet'en in the trial with an official, state-sponsored *Historical Atlas of Canada* in order to chart how they together disclose the political geographies (as well as the political stakes) of national origin stories. Edward Said's example of what he came to call "contrapuntal critique" is the underlying inspiration for the work of comparison and contrast in this chapter, but it is Homi Bhabha's examination of the "narration of nation" that provides the major theoretical focus. Bhabha's richly poetic account draws on deconstructive arguments about the disruptions wrought by supplementary performances in order to elucidate the ways in which performances of official national origin stories continually open up opportunities for rearticulations that resist and rework the exclusions, including racist and patriarchal exclusions, that have traditionally attended nationalism. Bhabha's attention to the politics of time and history is one of the many salutary features of his essay vis-à-vis coming to terms with the postcolonial politics of Canada. However, while his parallel treatment of space as the *con*text of disruptive performance speaks eloquently to the ways in which the Gitxsan and Wet'suwet'en disrupted the official space of the Canadian courtroom, it remains, I argue, strangely oblivious to the regulative geographies of nationalism that continue to contain and maintain the space and place of the national state. I suggest that this geographical blind spot in Bhabha's argument relates to a larger pattern of privileging space as automatically disruptive, a postfoundational argumentative privileging that rests in turn on a foundational elision of the ongoing regulative production of space.

Chapter 2 moves from the international political struggles created by First Nations' resistance to the transnational reterritorializations created by elite attempts to imagine and build business-friendly cross-border regions in contemporary North America. The case in question has been called Cascadia by its promoters, and while often presented as some sort of primordial precolonial space and while also mapped as inclusive of the disputed territories discussed in chapter 1, this imagined space of cross-border development opportunity has in fact much more in common with the kinds of colonial cartographies that charted the New World as "New." The newness of Cascadia as a cross-border region linking British Columbia with the American states of Washington and Oregon relates to the perceived benefits for capitalists of "cooperating regionally to compete globally" in a new world order of globalization. The fashioning of the Cascadian landscape as something real and economically tangible also recalls the original charting of North America insofar as the imagined space of newness betrays the preexisting ideologies held by the visionaries. In the Cascadian case the dominant ideology is that of neoliberalism, the belief that the capitalist market must be freed anew from the bureaucratic constraints imposed by the twentieth-century nation-state. For the region's promoters, then, a supposedly borderless Cascadia represents a real regional embodiment of the laissez-faire freedoms of the so-called borderless world. In practice, however, I show that this vision falls victim to all the inconsistencies of actual economic and political geographies (which remain still notably nationalized and bordered in the region) and so the visionaries are repeatedly forced back into reimagining or, as I call it, landscaping Cascadia as a natural place of development in the context of globalization. In order to unpack this process of landscaping, I turn to the work of Arjun Appadurai on the five "scapes" he famously associated with the globalizing imperatives of "modernity at large." Each of these "scapes"—which Appadurai called respectively *ethnoscapes, mediascapes, technoscapes, financescapes,* and *ideoscapes*—serves quite accurately to capture key aspects of the landscaping of a transborder and thus transnationalized Cascadia. However, while Appadurai only ever depicts his "scapes" as transnationalizing processes, and while he tends therefore to view them quite positively as antidotes to ethnicist nationalism, I argue this misses the ways in which the deterritorializations involve reterritorializations that are frequently only liberatory from the perspective of a neoliberal business elite. Cascadia, I argue, also makes manifest the political underbelly of this elite's "borderless world" vision, a neoliberal underbelly implying exclusions and exceptions just as glaring as those that scholars such as Uday Singh Mehta have traced in traditional liberalism.[5] To miss these political geographies by privileging a foundational story of global deterritorialization is again, I suggest, another blind spot in another postfoundational account of the nation-state's newly transformed "ends."

Chapter 3 proceeds to explore in much more detail the continental context of increasing free trade in which visions like Cascadia have been crafted. The passage of first CUFTA (the Canada–U.S. Free Trade Agreement) and second NAFTA (the North American Free Trade Agreement) were about much more than just reducing tariffs on commodities and restrictions on foreign investment, although the agreements were significant in these respects too. They and the politics surrounding their implementation need also to be understood as a systematic transformation of state practices in which the legitimacy of the national state was mobilized in order to put in place a set of transnational state effects that effectively extended and entrenched a neoliberal model of business-friendly government across transnational space. Theorizing the resulting transnational system of neoliberal governance as a congeries of state effects is made much easier, I suggest, by turning to Timothy Mitchell's cogent Foucauldian critique of traditional state theory. Mitchell's deterritorialization of the boxes into which political scientists have traditionally placed "the state"—the "functionalist" box, the "governing elite" box, and so on—makes it possible to examine how something as routinized as NAFTA's harmonization of nontariff barriers also can be viewed as a state "effect." Moreover, in doing so, this circulatory model of state power relations also makes it possible to describe how such state effects are effectively entrenched right across the transnational space of the free trade signatory countries. Mitchell's own account of state effects, however, remains couched at just the level of the *national* state. He assumes the state's hyphenation to nation as a prelude to deterritorializing the seemingly transcendental appearance of the state. The chapter therefore problematizes these limits while arguing that they still need not necessarily curtail a critical account of the production of *transnational* spaces of government that are also just as transcendental in their appearance and effects.

Chapter 4 also concerns a political theory that opens up a way of theorizing transnational politics only to return to reterritorialize internally the space of the nation-state as a container itself. The theory at issue here is Laclau and Mouffe's deterritorializing genealogy of the concept of hegemony. While this genealogy enables a retheorization of politics as an inherently plural, open-ended, and constantly recontested field of social relations, and while it makes possible a radical rereading of liberal democracy in terms of how hegemony shapes the tensional field between equality and liberty, I argue that ultimately Laclau and Mouffe themselves reterritorialize this "field" of hegemony by assuming that it is predicated on the space of the liberal nation-state. Not only do these assumptions impose unnecessary limits on any attempt to theorize transnational hegemonic struggles (like those over the transnational entrenchment of neoliberalism through free trade agreements), they also replay attempts by notable American and Canadian theorists to argue that their particular nation-state somehow embodies decentered, open-ended, and plural politics in a purified form. The chapter seeks to compare such claims (in particular those of the American intellectual historian David Hollinger and the Canadian political philosopher James Tully) with the actual hegemonic struggles over politics in both countries. It does so by examining the politics of constitutional reform in Canada and the quasi-constitutional politics of welfare reform in the United States. Using Laclau and Mouffe's theory of hegemony to come to terms with these specific Canadian and American struggles serves to disclose the elisions and erasures in the national narratives about inherent open-endedness. Hegemony, understood after Laclau and Mouffe as a process of politically reworking the inherent tensions of liberty and equality, helps in this sense to highlight the moments in which traditional political patterns of dominance have been resecured in the midst of all the supposedly decentered political struggles. However, in helping to highlight such moments and their complicities with the reproduction of national-state authority, the limits and costs of Laclau and Mouffe's own unexamined assumptions about the nation-state as a territorial container for politics are themselves made manifest too.

Chapter 5 in turn seeks to outline what a more transnational account of hegemony has to accomplish by examining the transnationalization of American state power in the context of the Iraq war. This particular moment of transnationalization, which I describe as an uncharacteristically unilateralist offshoot of informal American imperialism, has been attended by a violent reassertion of geopolitical rhetoric and affect. However, it has also been underpinned, I argue, by all kinds of economistic assumptions about globalization creating a global level playing field. I suggest that these assumptions comprise a form of geoeconomics, a hegemonic common sense about an emerging global system of market states. I show that advocates of the Iraq war collapsed the obvious contradictions between unilateralist geopolitics and multilateralist geoeconomics by arguing that America's manifest destiny now consists of enforcing and globally expanding the supposedly level capitalist playing field. In order to come to terms with this complicitous and contradictory articulation of geoeconomics with unilateralist American geopolitical assertion, I draw on what to many will seem the unlikely resource of Hardt and Negri's theory that globalization has created a wholly new kind of Empire. This is the only theory in the book that directly deploys the rhetoric of deterritorialization in *both* an ontological register (to describe Empire's eclipse of nation-states and their borders) and an epistemological register (to describe the theoretical need to abandon assumptions about territorialized government). By using Hardt and Negri's epistemological arguments about the need to come to terms with a new global regime of governmentality, a key goal of this chapter is to explore how globalist geoeconomic common sense emerging from the circuits of transnational business class commentary and business school training played a major role in determining, mediating, and legitimizing the geopolitical assault on Iraq. Business-class subjectivity formation understood as an instance of what Hardt and Negri call the "biopolitics of Empire" can be reinterpreted in this way as one of the important underpinnings of the geopolitically imperial campaign (a campaign that has elsewhere been largely interpreted as an unsettling departure from a more multilateral model of market-mediated global control). Using Hardt and Negri in this way to read Empire into American imperialism, the aim here is also to read *Empire* itself against the grain and critique the ways in which that book's sweeping vision of the "smooth space" of global deterritorialization elides the uneven development of a global capitalism defined today more than ever by the transnational asymmetries and contradictions of American state dominance.

From the critique of Bhabha to the critique of Hardt and Negri, the actual geographical dynamics and power relations that are foreclosed by the particular theories at issue in each chapter vary a great deal. Whereas Bhabha and Appadurai emphasize deterritorializing imperatives that dissemble powerful national and transnational geographies of regulation, Mitchell and Laclau and Mouffe make it possible to theorize the production and rearticulation of hegemonic regulatory space only to fall back themselves on accounts that assume the space of the nation-state as some sort of transcendental container. Differently again, Hardt and Negri write off (or rather graph over the geo of) the nation-state altogether but end up encrypting the particular national-state influence of America into the very heart of their argument. While the account of neoliberal governmentality they thereby produce helps to theorize the world-making force of business-class common sense, their own investment in the American worldview and its assumptions about a deterritorialized global destiny repeats at a theoretical level (albeit with very different political intentions) the ways neoconservatives surrounding President Bush argued that America's war making was all about the country's manifest destiny as the smoothing agent of global integration.

Given the variety of these geographical critiques, it needs noting that none of the theories at issue make geography an explicit central concern. Indeed, insofar as all of the chapters attempt to fashion geographical readings of work that is not explicitly concerned with questions of geography, the whole book might be accused of offering little more than the interested disciplinary readings of a geographer. Notwithstanding his locution of location, Bhabha is much more interested in displacing nationalist historicism; Appadurai is more preoccupied with critiquing the traditional anthropological fixation on the local; Mitchell, while attentive to the implicit spatial dualisms of modern political thought, is most keen to debunk top-down theories of the state; Laclau and Mouffe love to use spatial metaphors to describe "the political" but eschew particular political geographical concerns; and Hardt and Negri presume to move completely beyond geography by painting a picture of empire as a globalized, decentered, and radically borderless space worn smooth by deterritorializing networks. Nevertheless, against the criticism that my geographical readings are therefore in fact simply bad readings, I would like to submit two responses. The first is deconstructive and consists of arguing that the geographies are there already as geo-graphies in the works under consideration. All of them graph the geo of the nation-state in one way or another. All of them use spatial terms, names, and metaphors that carry geographical implications. And all of them are therefore open at some level to a geographical version of the classic deconstructive point about the "graphematic" structure of writing: namely, that an investigation of the various (geographical) underwritings discloses (spatial) ties, negotiations, and assumptions that are dissimulated in the original accounts. The second response is more critical and consists simply of arguing that the geographies at issue matter politically; that they also have significant implications for the theories developed by each of the theorists; and that, insofar as each of the chapters seeks to show how these particular theories supplement and enable critical geographies of displacement and disjuncture, the geographical limits of the theories are also of critical political import. The rest of this introduction seeks to develop the first of these responses—the argument about the graphematic structure of geography. The rest of the book seeks to demonstrate that the geographies matter.

GRAPHING THE GEO; OR, THE RESPONSIBILITIES OF GEOGRAPHY AS CATACHRESIS

Subsequent to her remarks about the shadow of a geographical pattern in *Of Grammatology*, Spivak has made a number of other arguments that usefully illustrate the possibilities of geographically responsible critique. It should be noted that she has never attempted to present herself as a geographer or to issue guidelines to the discipline of geography. Indeed, as those who have read her work know well, Spivak endeavors to map as carefully as possible the limits of her own authorial politics of location (including her disciplinary location) as a literary critic from a privileged Bengali background employed as a professor with an endowed chair at one of America's most elite universities in New York. Just like the French geographers who once interviewed Foucault about his geographical concept-metaphors, I do not therefore want to present Spivak as some sort of disciplinary mascot for geographers.[6] Nor do I want to suggest she is a metonym of marginality, and nor do I want to imply that I am adequately trained in continental philosophy to understand all the ins and outs of her sometimes frustratingly in-house engagements with the machinery of Derridean deconstruction. Instead, I only seek to identify some of the lines of argument in her writing that seem to me to triangulate a model of critical geographical responsibility.

The triangulation metaphor is precise insofar as there appear to be three main lines of geographical critique that Spivak's work brings together—albeit in a purposefully unstable assemblage. The first is her attention to the global geographies underwriting metropolitan theory, including most notably her critique of Foucault's spatial studies (of prisons, asylums, schools, hospitals, and so on) as "screen allegories that foreclose a reading of the broader narratives of imperialism."[7] Here the Freudian metaphor of the screen (and, by implication, all the Freudian arguments about the screening displacements through which dreams fashion disjunctive dream images) becomes for Spivak a critical geographical tool. She thus suggests that while Foucault was "a brilliant thinker of power-in-spacing" his accounts of disciplinary spaces screened out any direct attention to the larger geographical relations of imperialism in which disciplinary power developed. This screening out occurred, she suggests, while Foucault's actual approach to power screamed out, so to speak, for an analysis of the global geography of imperial ties in which the micromechanics of metropolitan discipline actually emerged.[8] Spivak rehearses this critique of Foucault in two essays where she also engages with the work of the Indian subaltern studies historians, and it is in these engagements that her second line of geographical critique can also be found. She seeks to do justice to the ways in which subaltern studies challenges elite historiography and graphs the subaltern (a generalized name for the excluded and marginalized) into Indian history. She notes in this respect the ways in which the geography of subalternity that emerges in the historians' writings relates disjunctively to the geography of India as a hyphenated postcolonial nation-state. But she also aims to respond critically by outlining the ways in which the geography of subaltern agency charted by the historians leaves unexamined the chronic influence of patriarchal discourses about women in the production of subaltern territoriality.[9] Tracing such unexamined geographies further herself, Spivak's third line of geographical argument relates in turn to how any particular geography of subalternity (and not just those of the dissident Indian historians) can subsume the particular and personal geographies of especially marginalized and oppressed subjects, most notably those of hyperexploited or brutally oppressed women. Various examples of such women are introduced by Spivak throughout her work, and, whether they are fictional figures such as Douloti the Bountiful from the stories of the Bengali author Mahasweta Devi, or whether they are anonymous women workers described by socialist-feminist scholars studying global commodity chains, Spivak remains persistently concerned with the ways in which the geographies of their worlds are subsumed by hegemonic geographies of power. Whether the latter take the form of imagined national communities or whether they take shape in illusory visions of a homogeneous global village, Spivak's concerns are with the ways in which the embodied spaces of subalternized women's lives and work are effaced from the geographies they underwrite and make possible. Ultimately, as with the case of Douloti who dies spitting up blood on a map of postcolonial India drawn in a school yard, Spivak is interested to mark moments when the elided and ignored actions of such women disrupt, if only momentarily and semiotically, the routinized reproduction of dominant geography.[10]

Spivak most commonly brings all three lines of geographical argument together at once, holding them in tension one with another. In this respect a recurring feature of her critical geographical arguments is a concern with the politics of metaphor. As she explains in discussing the metaphorical fate of Jashoda—another figure from the work of Mahasweta Devi—there is an important structural relationship between the *vehicle* and *tenor* in any particular metaphor, the tenor being the subject of the metaphor, and the vehicle being the object, idea, or person that is used to metaphorize the tenor.[11] For example, in the spatial metaphor "the field of political action" it is "political action" in all its diversity that is the tenor and "the field" that serves as the vehicle. Spivak's concern is with how the rhetorical organization of metaphor blocks attention to the worldly relations between tenor and vehicle and thereby necessarily underplays the "effect of the real" of the vehicle. Her immediate point is that when women like Jashoda are used as vehicles to metaphorize tenors such as the nation the actual relationships between women and nation are systematically downplayed such that the contributions, struggles, and oppressions of subaltern women in particular are ignored. It seems to me that this same argument can be usefully applied to much of the recent efflorescence of spatial metaphors in cultural studies writing. The more and more that space is used to metaphorize other things such as politics and identity—"the space of the political," "the terrain of identity," "mapping multiculturalism," and so on—the less and less are the geographical contexts of politics and identity adequately explored. Even though she does not directly make this point herself, an awareness of this danger seems to be part of what animates each of Spivak's critical geographical lines of argument. The concern about Foucault's spatial studies serving as screen allegories is partly a concern with how his diagrams of the power relations inside the prison, the asylum, the clinic, and the school function as geographical concept-metaphors that downplay the larger geography of imperial power in which they developed and by which they were shaped. The concern with the metaphorization of women in Indian history is that the subaltern studies historians ignore how such metaphorical discourse functions to consolidate subaltern territoriality both in practice and in their own historiographic discourse. And the concern with the wider instrumentalization of subalternized women leads to arguments that counterpoint the national and global geographies of their exploitation with their use as mute metaphorical vehicles in metanarratives of nation and globalization. A feminist attention to the politics of location and embodiment, including the possibilities and limits of transnational feminist solidarity, are clearly part of the background behind these concerns. So too, it seems, are Marxian emphases on the globality of capitalism and anti(neo)colonial critiques that Spivak makes of diverse nationalist and globalist erasures. Underwriting all these concerns, however, is also her abiding interest in what Derrida identified as graphematic structure. Reading Derrida via Spivak's critical attention to the worldly graphing of representation, I now want to introduce more directly my graphematic reading of geography.

Derrida's argument about graphematic structure dated from his early work in which he traced how traditional Western philosophers have tended to malign writing in the very same gestures that they have elevated speech as the closest expression of the immediacy and presence of pure thought. Reversing and displacing this marginalization of writing, Derrida proceeded to show that it betrays what are in fact systemic but forgotten features of speech and thought too. In his deconstruction of Austin's speech act theory, for example, Derrida notes that these features include the fact that speech, like *writing*, rests on prearranged systems of codes and customs; that these enable the speaker to be absent when the listener receives the message; and that they thus allow for a repetition of the original idea—itself dependent on convention and therefore a form of repetition—outside of its author's founding control.[12] Derrida shows that "[t]his essential drifting due to writing as an iterative structure cut off from absolute responsibility, from consciousness as the authority of the last analysis," carries a disruptive deconstructive force.[13] Pointing to the *underwriting* of a message, thought, or act thus leads in turn to an *undermining* of any "metaphysics of presence" that—like the one that reveres speech as an immediate presentation of consciousness—assumes either a fully comprehensible communication of meaning or a unique, original, and punctual moment of causality. Messages, or anything else subject to the same iterative structure, therefore become examinable as discontinuous from the controlling intentions of their authors or producers, cut off from an original context, causally overdetermined, and interminably dependent on unpredictable and uncontainable contexts of reading and experience. Context matters in this sense because, as Spivak explained in an interview, it takes us beyond the narrowness of the writerly text, articulating much wider geographies of contextuality.

> That's how one becomes an activist, I mean, to escape the text as you understand it—the verbal text. There are these various ways, in which you become "involved." But once you do that you won't get away from textuality. "The Text," in the sense we use it, is not just

books. It refers to the possibility that every socio-political, psycho-sexual phenomenon is organized by, woven by many, many strands that are discontinuous, that come from way off, that carry their histories within them, and that are not within our control.[14]

Interpreted following Spivak, Derrida's disclosure of the constitutive context outside of texts has an immediate parallel in the multiple and diffuse graphings that constitute the geo of a particular geography. When geographers and whomever else set out to describe a particular geography, and even more so, when they invoke geography and space metaphorically, there is a similar metaphysics of presence at work—what might be called a metaphysics of geopresence—that fixates on the "geo" of a particular spatial pattern or a particular poetics of location while simultaneously downplaying the geographic diversity of the constitutive processes that produced it. Every geography is thus, to use Spivak's phrase, "woven by many, many strands that are discontinuous, that come from way off, that carry their histories within them, and that are not within our control."[15] By using the notion of graphing the geo to address the limits of anemic geography, my concern is with how, because of this discontinuous graphing, critics have a responsibility persistently to ask about how heterogeneous graphings of the geo are dissembled in any particular geography. Understood as a representation of the dense complexity of spatial relationships, geography is often marginalized and, like writing in relation to speech, treated as secondary and supplemental. Understood as an effect, as a pattern, a particular inscription, or a map, by contrast, it is sometimes given special treatment and revered almost like a sacred text. But whether hallowed thus or not, it is still seen, enframed or invoked, as somehow cut off from the geographical or earth-writing processes that produced it.

Given the parallels with writing, it might not be surprising that Derrida himself employed the concept-metaphor of "spacing" (espacement), as another of his own supplementary antikey keywords. Like these other words such as *writing, trace,* and *différance,* and like *geography* too, spacing also works as a noun describing an effect, a particular spatial organization, and simultaneously as a verb describing a process, the act of organizing a spatial organization.[16] However, most of Derrida's discussion of the alterity of spacing was focused around his deconstruction of Freud's description of the psyche as a "space of writing." In this context, he says that "[s]pacing as writing is the becoming-absent and becoming-unconscious of the subject."[17] Ironically, the chief target of this deconstruction was the taken-for-granted universal quality of time (along with its codependence on a notion of a fully conscious centered subjectivity).[18] Thus, all the while Derrida used Freud's spacing of the mind to point toward the writtenness of time, he did not—as Spivak notes in her preface to *Of Grammatology*[19]—dwell in these early writings on what might be described as the more geographical spacing of Freud's *fort-da*.[20] To be sure, in the 1990s Derrida did directly address the question of the production of space. "I often talk about spacing," he said, "but this is not simply space as opposed to time, but a mode of producing space by temporalizing it."[21] Even here, though, he did not directly confront the production of the geography of his own writing, and it is the way in which space is related to temporalization that preoccupies his argument. In terms of tracing the graphing of the geo, then, it seems that, rather than his questioning of "spacing," it is instead Derrida's work on the responsibilities of writing that is ultimately most valuable.

The notion of constitutive conventions outside of direct reach rendered explicit in Derrida's deconstruction of writing may seem at first to indicate a form of absolution from "real" geographical responsibility, a way of exculpating an erroneously limited geographical description or reference by saying that this is always and everywhere predictable. Derrida's reference to *writing* as "an iterative structure cut off from absolute responsibility" may appear thus to sound the death knell of any responsible form of interrogation into a project that, like geography, can be said to be subject to the structure of *writing*. Yet such a gloomy prognosis would be missing the philosophical point.[22] Certainly the argument that identity is contingent on context and that determination is heterogeneous and sometimes concealed even as it works its effects disrupts humanist understandings of "absolute" responsibility that structurally assume a (normatively masculine) author's fully conscious capacity to know, see, and rationally describe a geography.[23] But at the same time, the deconstructive notions that highlight the writtenness of determination and geography do not liquidate "the subject" or, for that matter, "the geographer."[24] Instead, they serve to actually *widen* questions of responsibility by repeatedly remembering how geographical descriptions are heterogeneously centered in heterogeneous contexts, how contexts are thus contextualized, foundations founded, and grounds themselves diversely grounded. In proposing in this book to ground a subset of postfoundational theories, I am appealing to geography in precisely this deconstructive sense: a sense that suggests that the work of describing the graphing of the geo is never done; that a complete geography is, in the rigorous deconstructive sense, (im)possible; and that, as such, it is a reminder of a responsibility to examine other graphings, other geographies, that even avowedly antiessentialist work may have written out of the geo.

The critical implications of this argument about geographical responsibility can be illustrated by noting how the shadow of a geographical pattern described by Spivak in *Of Grammatology* came back in the 1990s to haunt Derrida's own ephemeral account of the *Specters of Marx*. "*Without this non-contemporaneity with itself of the living present,*" we might therefore ask with and of a now deceased Derrida,

> without this responsibility and this respect for justice concerning those who *are not here,* of those who are no longer or who are not yet *present and living,* what sense would there be to ask the question "where?"[25]

Here Derrida clearly does ask the question "where?" but downplays its significance by framing it in terms of temporality and following it with two antihistoricizing questions—"where tomorrow? whither?"[26] These questions only pull the argument back toward an interrogation of the ontologies of a *historical* materialism. Those who are "not here"—including all kinds of workers in the global south to whom metropolitan elites are connected by the "state of the [Third World] debt"—seem once again forgotten and left behind. The responsibility of an (im)possible geography of this "where?" was thus left unfulfilled by Derrida himself. To speak of the responsibility to the multiple and diverse graphings of the geo implicit in geography is not therefore a humanist position that assumes the geographer's or antiessentialist philosopher's ability to "choose" responsibility individualistically, nor is it a religious responsibility of moral duty. Instead it invites the careful labor of developing what Spivak geographically calls "the freedom to *acknowledge insertion* into responsibility."[27] It has to be said that in comparison with her critique of Foucault's Eurocentric "abdication" of responsibility, Spivak's acknowledgment of Derrida's insertion into more global responsibilities seems strangely muted.[28] Nevertheless, having challenged his misreadings of Marx as an ontologist of use value, and having marked his neglect for the dialectical formulation of labor power as abstract value as value in Marx's *Capital,* Spivak concludes her review by suggesting that Derrida's excavation of a "silly" youthful ontological Marx is overshadowed by the hauntings of subaltern women. To acknowledge responsibility to their "where?" she suggests, "*Specters of Marx* must travel in terrains that it seems not yet to know."[29]

The political charge Spivak gives to the question of geographical responsibility raises in its turn a series of questions concerning how a deconstructive approach to geography relates more generally to "politics." To be as clear as possible, I am not suggesting that an attention to the diverse graphing of the geo represents a new and all-encompassing political program for critical geography in general. To do so is to risk the "neutralizing anesthesia of a new theoreticism" that Derrida himself protested against, although perhaps too hauntingly much.[30] It also risks a global style of ideological crisis management common among contemporary business elites: elites like the manager of the Shell oil company recently quoted as saying that "we now have to be responsible for things we could never have imagined would be our responsibility."[31] Against such crisis management, and against theoreticism, I am suggesting that deconstruction "helps" politically because of its capacity, in Spivak's words, to "make founded political programs more useful by making their in-built problems more visible."[32] While deconstruction does not, or at least should not, therefore be allowed to found a political program itself, it does in this way offer a critical approach to thinking about political limits. By reconceiving of geography as *written,* as a conventional part of the general *social text,* it affords a means of subsequently monitoring how aspects of that con*textuality* are disavowed but yet used in the interests of writing and consolidating particular geographies. Through these means it services a general way of maintaining what, to adapt another of Spivak's antihumanist formulae, is a ceaseless "responsibility to the trace of the other in the [geographical] self."[33] This deconstructive persistence in responsibility to the radically heterogeneous becomes political, insofar as it obliges geographic analysis (along with other forms of critique) to be honest about the politics of encapsulating essentialism, including, not least of all, the essentialism of deterritorialization.

This book is by no means the first attempt to appropriate deconstructive arguments into a critical reflection on earth-writing. Among geographers, for example, Wolfgang Natter and John Paul Jones have argued that when positivist geography disavows its worldly location it "collapses any distance between the narrator and the narrated world, between the *graph*-ing and the *geo*."[34] Outside of the discipline, David Campbell led a responsible deconstructive way for dissident international relations theorists with his careful analyses of the territorializing earth-writing of U.S. security discourse.[35] And in a critique of the objectivity claimed specifically by the geopolitical theorists of statecraft, Gearoid Ó Tuathail (Gerard Toal) has pursued still further lexigraphic decouplings of geo-graphing. Indeed he has proposed writing a doubly hyphenated "geo-graph-y" as the name for both result and process of geographing. "Radicalizing our understanding of the 'graph' in this way," he says,

> encourages a resurrection of the deadened sense of geography as geo-graphing, an open-ended inscribing, delimiting, and engraving of the earth/globe/world. To study geo-graph-y, then, is to study the projection of geographs striving for signification; it is to study the graphing/weaving/writing of the geo/world/system. Geo-graphing can be viewed as an interminable tracing without ends or limits, a writing that never reaches closure, that never totally maps.[36]

I fully concur with the open-ended aims of these deconstructive projects, and Ó Tuathail's summary is especially valuable for a project that, like this book, aims to disclose multiple remappings of the displaced hyphen in nation-state. However, there is also a clear danger in producing quite such a hyperhyphenated study of "geo-graph-y," a danger of turning the "graphing/weaving/writing of the geo/world/system" into just another privileging of the written text. Ó Tuathail's own studies of geopolitical violence avoid this danger, but in less careful hands the textual play can begin to seem like the only displacement that matters. It is for this reason that I have sought in the chapters that follow to connect the geographies I read in the arguments and metaphors of the five postfoundational theories to worldly displacements of hyphen-nation-states. However, while this might serve as an answer to the charge of disconnected deconstructive theoreticism, where does it leave the question of interested and overly disciplinary reading with which I began?

By this point it should be clear that, instead of a disciplinary reading of postfoundational theory, what the following chapters seek to offer is an exploration of the relays of geographical responsibility into which the claims of the particular theorists can be inserted and mapped. These still remain remappings with inevitable elisions and limits, but in following the model of Spivak's worldly triangulations of deconstruction, my goal is to argue that there are significant geographical implications in this postfoundational work, implications that need to be unpacked and examined with a greater sensitivity to the heterogeneous graphing of the geo. The paleonymy, which is to say, the baggage carried by the words used in the theories, is itself quite revealing in this respect. Geographical concept-metaphors such as Bhabha's "location," Appadurai's "scapes," Hardt and Negri's "smooth space," and Laclau and Mouffe's "terrains," "fields," "areas," "frontiers," "boundaries," "planes," "surfaces," "positions," "regions," and so on, become rereadable thus as so many anemic geographies that cover over the palimpsest of unfinished and worldly geographical struggles. In suggesting this, however, the point here is not to imply that geography as a discipline holds some special key to graphing the geo. Indeed, the whole point about the heterogeneity of the processes that produce particular spatial arrangement is that it demands more thoroughly collaborative interdisciplinary enquiry. Nongeographers ranging from Miranda Joseph (a feminist and queer theorist of community) to Michael Shapiro (a critical international relations theorist) to Donald Moore, Jake Kosek, and Anand Pandian (three anthropological scholars of race and nature) have produced exemplary arguments in this geographical sense: arguments that model a persistent attention to the supplementary and yet frequently violent graphing of spaces of belonging.[37] The point then is not that postfoundational theory somehow lacks a geographical imagination. Nor is the argument that geographers have better access to some metaphor-free "real" space that has been ignored in the recent rush to metaphorize space in antiessentialist writing. It is true, as Cindi Katz and Neil Smith have argued, that this instrumentalization of space as a metaphorical vehicle in otherwise nongeographical arguments has often left space itself unproblematized.[38] Yet incorporating arguments from the discipline of geography may by no means prevent this, and may even promote more unproblematized usage if the incorporated arguments come from geographers who fetishize space and ignore all the lessons of Marxist and feminist work on the dynamic production of particular spatialities. Following the example of the feminist geographer Geraldine Pratt, we need instead to examine the *variety* of ways in which geography can be deployed as a concept-metaphor.[39] Rigorously pursued, such examination ultimately raises three ethico-political implications for all geographical descriptions, arguments, or assumptions, whether disciplinary or not: first, that at some level they deploy geography as a catachresis, a concept-metaphor without a singular literal referent; second, that the sheer variety of these deployments shows how mistaken it is to turn such catachreses into a catechism or transcendentalist claim to the ultimate ontological ground; and third, that it is therefore instead a responsibility of the critic-geographer to persistently examine the grounding of such catachrestic geographical grounds. This is what the following chapters seek to do in exploring critical geographies of displacement and disjuncture in North America—without a mandate for conquest.

1

Territories of Tradition: Cartographic Beginnings and the Narration of Nation

The boundary that marks the nation's selfhood interrupts the self-generating time of national production and disrupts the signification of the people as homogeneous. The problem is not simply the "selfhood" of the nation as opposed to the otherness of other nations. We are confronted with the nation split within itself, articulating the heterogeneity of its population. The barred Nation It/Self, alienated from its eternal self-generation, becomes a liminal signifying space that is internally marked by the discourses of minorities, the heterogeneous histories of contending peoples, antagonistic authorities, and tense locations of cultural difference.

—HOMI K. BHABHA, "DISSEMINATION"

In the late 1980s, at about the same time that Homi Bhabha was first publishing his essay "DissemiNation," the tense locations of cultural difference in the "Nation *It/Self*" became especially evident in Canada. In 1987 a trial over sovereignty and land rights had begun in the Supreme Court of British Columbia. The case had been brought by two First Nations—the Wet'suwet'en and the Gitxsan—against the federal government of Canada and the provincial government of British Columbia. Delgamuukw (Ken Muldoe), the chief whose Gitxsan name became the official abbreviation for all the plaintiffs making the case, concluded his opening address to the court by summarizing how the two First Nations did not view the trial as a simple appeal to the law of the land but rather as a political negotiation within the Canadian legal system. "The purpose of this case, then, is

1

to find a process to place Gitxsan and Wet'suwet'en ownership and jurisdiction within the context of Canada. We do not seek a decision as to whether our system might continue or not. It will continue."[1] As the year-long trial proceeded, the Wet'suwet'en and Gitxsan continued to affirm their traditions of self-government, educating the court and those members of the Canadian public who followed the immense trial ("The Mother of All Trials" as one virulently anti-native-land-rights writer later dubbed it) about their understandings of space, time, and territorial jurisdiction.[2] The trial transcripts are therefore filled with moments when "the heterogeneous histories of contending peoples" evoked by Bhabha come to the surface cartographically. One example, which will be a focus in what follows, concerns the disruptions signaled by the unfurling of Exhibit 102, a map showing the "Traditional Boundaries of the Gitxsan and Wet'suwet'en Territories."

25: THE COURT: We'll call it the map that roared

26: MR. PLANT: I beg your pardon

27: THE COURT: We'll call it the map that roared[3]

Later, in 1987, another rather different affirmation of nation emerged before the Canadian public in the more muted but institutionally privileged form of the first volume of a new historical atlas of Canada.[4] More than an academic exercise prosecuted solely for the purposes of historical and geographical research, the *Historical Atlas of Canada* was also a national project that narrated an origin story of Canada. National in production and funding as well as in organization and scope, the *Atlas* as a whole received over Can$6 million in public funds.[5] In the Foreword, Jean-Pierre Wallot, the so-called Dominion Archivist, tried to capture the scope of this national project in suitably sweeping terms. "An organized society," he said,

> tries to understand itself and its past, yet no easy determinism can explain how and why a complex society like ours has evolved progressively and sometimes unpredictably on this continent over hundreds, even thousands of years. The *Historical Atlas of Canada* has attempted to establish many of the relationships among the multitudinous factors . . . that together, as in a musical score, have shaped our past.[6]

Subsequently, reviewers acclaimed the *Atlas* as "public funding well spent,"[7] while others commented on how, with over forty authors, the *Atlas* seemed "a mega-project of Canadian intellectual endeavour."[8] Moreover, public reception of the *Atlas* was also successfully national and grand in scale. Initially published just in time for the Christmas commercial season, the attractive coffee table–sized volume—with 27,000 copies of the English edition sold by November 1993—found a much bigger audience than the one that was packed into the small Smithers courtroom on the opening day of *Delgamuukw v. the Queen.*[9]

There are many other obvious differences between these two examples of national narration. The court case took place in a legal setting whereas the *Atlas* was produced in a grant-maintained academic context and disseminated through commercial networks. More significantly, the court case involved a direct and necessarily adversarial conflict of colonialist with anticolonialist forces, whereas in the *Atlas* these antagonistic power relations found joint expression in a more interwoven and ambivalent national text. In addition, notwithstanding its own remarkable and novel attempts to represent the historical geography of everyday life—of home life, home building, and the quotidian routines of survival on the frontier of colonial contact—the literally textual character of the *Atlas* meant that it was less immediately related than the court case to the actual experiences of people. The court case, like the *Atlas,* involved a whole series of politicized representations of experience, but it also directly coordinated and controlled such experience within the confines of the court. Such differences notwithstanding, I concentrate in this chapter on how nevertheless, as coinheritors of overlapping historical-geographies, both these examples of national affirmation also shared a great deal as graphings or, more precisely, cartographic reworkings of space, territory, and state jurisdiction. Critical to both were maps of national space, and clearly evident in both was the paradoxical capacity of such cartography to function variously for and against the exercise of modern state power. Taken together the similarities of the two examples therefore provide a means for examining how mapping helps graph what I described in the introduction as the heterogeneously inscribed geo of the nation-state. While scholars such as Benedict Anderson have discussed the general *hegemonic* effect of national mapping—its role alongside the census and museum as colonial legacies turned hegemonic modes of postcolonial national imagination[10]—they have rarely addressed the *counterhegemonic* effect of cartographic negotiations, and it is precisely the tensions between the hegemonic and the counterhegemonic that the two case studies considered here help highlight. In juxtaposition, they illustrate an ambivalent potential in cartography that in turn points to a profound ambivalence in the very narration of the nation-state itself.

The paradoxical ambivalence of cartography and the wider overlap of historical geographies it reflects can be usefully examined in terms of what, following Edward Said, can be called "contrapuntal cartographies." The notion of contrapuntal reading that Said recommended had the goal of breaking down singularized and unidirectional understandings of the culture of imperialism.[11] Reading contrapuntally, he argued, involves "a simultaneous awareness both of the metropolitan history that is narrated and of those other histories against which (and together with which) the dominating discourse acts."[12] Said thus reworked the formal musical meaning of the term suggesting that a contrapuntal interpretation involves a strategic revoicing of a subtext to make it equal to the dominant text and thus to orchestrate an equality for strategic political purposes. In the two cases examined here this strategic contrapuntal orchestration that Said used to unpack largely aesthetic forms of colonial expression provides political purchase on what are at once both more state-related and overtly geographical forms of national narration. As case studies they in turn highlight how in a national struggle "to reclaim, rename and reinhabit the land," the impulse is indeed, as Said said, "cartographic."[13] In this way they also support some more nuanced distinctions about different forms of contrapuntal effect. In the court case, the dual histories of colonialism and anticolonialism, along with their respective geographies of oppression and survival, were more starkly, albeit not completely, set apart. In the case of the *Atlas*, by contrast, a contrapuntal duality is more difficult to discern. For the same reason, though, it is absolutely crucial to listen for its sounds. It demands a treatment of the maps and historical annotations in the *Atlas* that does justice to the ways in which they simultaneously record the dissonant as well as the harmonic chords of what, I will show, ultimately appeared to many readers as a form of cartographic national anthem.

The musical metaphor of the anthem brings me to the words of an official Canadian Archivist who compared the *Atlas* to a "musi-

cal score" primarily as a way of coming to terms with how it represented demographic, economic, cultural, governmental, and social
relationships altogether in the space of the nation-state. As a result of
such amalgamation, he wrote, "Canadians will have a better understanding of themselves, and, it is hoped, will be inspired to extend
the frontiers of knowledge even further."[14] Yet, as well as doing this,
I will argue here that the more radical and creative aspect of the
Atlas was to have provided a cartographic "musical score" that,
once given contrapuntal voicing, enabled its national Canadian audience to rethink the colonial frontiers of national knowledge itself.
By scrupulously mapping the supposed beginnings of the nation, the
Atlas subverted any punctual notion of a singular national origin,
displacing it with an invitation to readers to reevaluate the ways in
which the template of contemporary Canada is imposed proleptical-
ly on a heterogeneous past. Most particularly, it enabled Canadians
to reconsider the discontinuous positions of native peoples—their
positions quite literally in diverse geographies, on the continent, before the arrival of the English and French—as a disjunctive series
of national traditions at the ends of the frontier of Canada as nation. In the terms of Bhabha's more esoteric formulation, the *Atlas*
thus presents a case of a national narrative in which the nation is
alienated from "It/Self."[15] As such, I want to argue, its contrapuntal aspects exemplify the "liminal signifying space that is *internally*
marked by the discourses of minorities, the heterogeneous histories
of contending peoples, antagonistic authorities and tense locations
of cultural difference" ("DissemiNation," 148).

Still more tense were the differences in and over location evidenced in the court case. Like the *Atlas,* the contrapuntal dualities of
Delgamuukw v. the Queen made the *location* of national discourse
a contentious question through a repeated return to maps. Not only
were cartographic tools and arguments used by the defense (the B.C.
and federal governments), they were also a key component of the
Wet'suwet'en and Gitxsan peoples' own attempts to outline their sovereignty in a way the Canadian court might understand. They presented a wide range of maps that, with dense native namings of the
land and a great range of rubrics, documented First Nations' sovereignty (e.g., Map 1). It was one such map of native space (Exhibit 102)
that Chief Justice Allan McEachern was beginning to unfold when he
declared "We'll call it the map that roared." In the immediate context

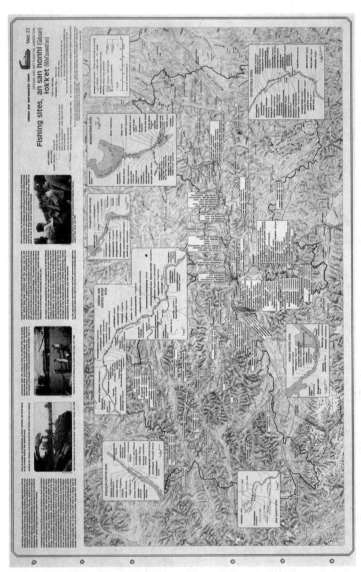

Map 1. One of many maps prepared for the trial, depicting Gitxsan and Wet'suwet'en names. Reprinted by permission of Don Ryan, Gitxsan Treaty Office.

of trying to open up a huge paper reproduction of the First Nations' map, his words appeared to refer to the colloquial notion of a "paper tiger."[16] They also may have been a reference to the 1959 Peter Sellars movie satirizing cold war geopolitics, *The Mouse that Roared*. As such, the comments might be interpreted as a derisory scripting of the plaintiffs as a ramshackle, anachronistic nation. However, as Don Monet, a cartoonist working for the Gitxsan and Wet'suwet'en, made clear, the chief justice's reference to a roaring map simultaneously evoked the resistance in the First Nations' remapping of the land: the cartography's roaring refusal of the orientation systems, the trap lines, the property lines, the electricity lines, the pipelines, the logging roads, the clear-cuts, and all the other accoutrements of Canadian colonialism on native land (Figure 1). As the trial judge, McEachern ultimately dismissed the Gitxsan and Wet'suwet'en's claims with a remarkably absolutist set of colonialist claims about the extinguishment of aboriginal rights.[17] In its original format, his judgment spanned almost four hundred pages and, in arguments ranging widely from the chief justice's colonialist view of First Nations societies to his narrow understanding of Canadian history, he systematically dismissed Gitxsan and Wet'suwet'en claims to ownership, jurisdiction, and damages for the loss of lands and resources since the establishment of the colony. Nevertheless, his comments on Exhibit 102, the map showing the "Traditional Boundaries of the Gitxsan and Wet'suwet'en Territories," would also appear to betray, albeit unconsciously, a real recognition of Gitxsan and Wet'suwet'en agency and territorial survival. That very same agency later recorded far more fulsome vindication when the Supreme Court of Canada handed down its decision overturning McEachern's judgment, thereby opening up the possibility of a new trial or at least greater bargaining leverage for the two First Nations with the provincial and federal governments.[18] This was a massive turnaround in native rights litigation more generally in Canada and, as well as making local news, was even reported on the front page of the *New York Times*.[19] At the time of editing this chapter for publication in 2003, the Web sites of both the Gitxsan and Wet'suwet'en nations still referred to the Supreme Court decision as a vindication of their struggles, a vindication against which the continuing resistance of the provincial government's treaty negotiators looks more and more egregiously unjust.[20] But before all this, the tensional clash of "antagonistic authorities" referred to by Bhabha as

Figure 1. "The Map That Roared." Reprinted by permission of Don Monet.

the internal mark of the nation space was already clear in the original courtroom discourse over cartography.

Of the two case studies I will begin first with the trial and proceed subsequently to the *Atlas* because the former case provides for a far more distinctly divided picture of the differences between colonial and anticolonial geographies of nation. These differences, I will then proceed to argue, come complexly together in the contrapuntal cartography of the *Atlas*. Ultimately, having explored such contrapuntal detail in both case studies, the argument of the chapter as a whole functions as a form of empirical inquiry into the ambivalence that Bhabha has so memorably located in the narration of nation. For him this psychoanalytically inflected notion of ambivalence serves as a form of theoretical counterweight to the muscular monologic of self-certain and unselfconscious discourses of singularized nationalism.[21] Monological nationalist teachings, he argues, typically turn "Territory into Tradition" ("DissemiNation," 149) while their actual processes of representing the space of the nation would seem to subvert the conscious certitude of Tradition with uncanny returns to the diversity of cultures located together in space. This ambivalent living together, this "obscure and ubiquitous form of living the *locality* of culture" (140), is therefore the way in which Bhabha would prefer to understand the nation. It is also one I work with here, and yet as I do so, I also seek to supplement Bhabha's own more general and ungrounded claims about the location of nation with some other, disruptive questions arising from the geography of the Canadian cartographies.[22] Before I can begin to outline this specificity and make the connections with national identity, though, it is first necessary to discuss some of the systematic links between mapping, the nation-state, First Nations' resistance, and the disjunctive doubleness that Bhabha finds in narratives of nation more generally.

MAPPING THE STATE AND GRAPHING THE NATION

Following the work of critical geographers such as Brian Harley, the connections between cartography and the consolidation of the European nation-state are now well understood.[23] Going far beyond the notion that maps simply represent nation-states in terms of exact borderlines and colorful contrasts, Harley documented how the relationship between map and nation-state has been reciprocal and constitutive. At one level, this dynamic has been cast as almost instrumental: most classically, for example, in J. R. Hale's axiom cited by Harley: "Without maps a man could not visualize the country to which he belonged."[24] At another level, the very instrumentality revealed in such axioms—the idea of men *using* maps in order to see in order to belong—can be recast as symptomatic of a far more subtle and decentered complex of modern, scopophilic, and masculinist power relations interconnecting the discourse of cartography with the imperial discourse of the modern European nation-state. To go beyond a simple symptomology, however, it is necessary to examine these interconnections geographically, and to that end I want to prepare the ground for my two case studies by moving from the argument that maps serve as instruments of the state toward the suggestion that, as technologies of spatial abstraction, they are indeed *constitutive* of the state. En route, I want to introduce some cartographic substance to Bhabha's locution of location and, in particular, to his provocative reading of landscape. "The recurrent metaphor of landscape as the inscape of national identity," he says, "emphasizes the quality of light, the question of social visibility, the power of the eye to naturalize the rhetoric of national affiliation and its forms of collective expression" ("DissemiNation," 143).

My initial point is that mapping as a powerful concept-metaphor of landscape illustrates why the scopic naturalization of national affiliation mentioned by Bhabha may work socially as well as rhetorically.

Clearly there are rhetorical aspects to the mapping of nations, and these have already been well documented by cartographic historians interested in specific cartographic genres, including the national atlas. Mark Monmonier, for example, has detailed how historically "the national atlas has been a symbol of national unity, scientific achievement, and political independence."[25] This is what he calls the atlas's "iconic function,"[26] and certainly national atlases like the *Historical Atlas of Canada* can have very marked symbolic effects. However, isolating such iconography from its broader social semiotic context ignores, or at least downplays, the far more powerful political implications of the links between cartography and the modern nation-state. Indeed, the isolation of the iconic is indicative of that very modern mode of spatial representation implicit in the notion that each single space (and, thus, each single nation-state) has its own singularized map whose rhetoric we simply read and interpret. As Henri Lefebvre once said: "The idea that a small number of maps or even a single (and singular) map might be sufficient can only apply in a specialized area of study whose own self-affirmation depends upon isolation from its context."[27] The modern nation-state is certainly one such specialized area of study, but given the need to examine what I have dubbed the graphing of the geo, it is precisely its isolation from context that needs to be called into question.

To better understand the production of the isolated, iconic space of the national map it is necessary to go back to the dynamic relation hidden by the hyphen in the "nation-state" and to consider the power relations running between state and nation. We need in this sense to address the reciprocal ways in which cartography has historically helped constitute the abstract space of the modern state itself. As Lefebvre has shown, this abstract space is "abstract" in the sense that it is decorporealized, bureaucratized, and commodified.[28] And yet, even in Lefebvre's *Production of Space,* where abstract space is depicted as "contemporaneous with the space of 'plans' and maps,"[29] there is no explicit mention of the production of abstract space through modern cartography: of the way in which such cartography enables abstraction away from bodies, social relations, and history. It is nonetheless just such abstraction that helps create the effect of the state as a reified apparatus. To come to terms with this state-constitutive aspect of cartography, it is useful to take a Foucauldian approach to theorizing power "as something which circulates, [as something that] is never localised here or there, never in anybody's hands, never appropriated as a commodity or piece of wealth."[30]

The reconceptualization of power as something exercised through networks of social relations remains one of Foucault's most radical reformulations, and yet it also seems to be one of the most repressed. While Harley, for instance, invoked the French philosopher's arguments about the intersections of power and knowledge in order to make his own claims about the power relations implicit within the scientific discourse of objective cartography, he also made a number of non-Foucauldian comments about states *holding* power through maps.[31] My criticism here is not a scholastic one. As Timothy Mitchell has shown and as I will discuss in further detail in chapter 3, abandoning a sovereign model of power has considerable implications for how we understand the state.[32] It is, after all, the sovereign model of power that supports a notion of the state as a singularized anthropomorphic actor capable of strategic action. By contrast, Foucault's ascending and relational analysis of power enables us to reexamine the state as a decentered complex of capillary and sometimes conflictual power relations that systematically create the larger *effect* that we call the state. Every time we fail to, in Foucault's terms, "behead the sovereign"[33] in our analysis of power, we make it harder to come to terms with the ways in which cartography contributes to the enframing of the abstract space around which this whole unstable complex of the state effect coheres. To ignore such cartographic enframing would be especially remiss because, as Denis Wood and John Fels have underlined, "outside the world of maps, states carry on a precarious existence; little of nature, they are much of maps, for to map a state is to assert its territorial expression, to leave it off to deny its existence."[34] Perhaps this overstates the case, but it nonetheless seems vital to recognize the way in which the enframing effect of cartography contributes to the concealment of the state's precariousness. It opens the possibility not just of a more nuanced understanding of the hegemonic effects of state mapping but also of counterhegemonic mapping.

The notion of "enframing" thus carries a very particular charge. Following Mitchell, who uses it to describe "the conjuring up [of] a neutral surface or volume called space" through the disciplinary routines of colonial society in Egypt,[35] I want to invoke both its practical and epistemological contribution to the production and deployment of abstract space through cartography. Practically, like the forms of modern planning instituted by colonialism, the discourse of modern cartography operates as part of a series of processes that exclude disorganized from organized space, the unplanned from the planned, the outside chaos from the disciplined state. Epistemologically, like the picture frame whose role in creating the larger effect of the picture is conventionally dissembled, this enframing work of cartography is effaced while the abstract state space it effects achieves hegemonic status.[36] Coming together, these twin dynamics effectively conceal the ways in which cartography is part of a reciprocal or, better, a *recursive* social process in which maps shape a world that in turn shapes its maps. They thus distract cartographic historians from the fact that cartography is more than a collection of map artifacts and mapping methods. The latter view is common even among critics who, like Harley, are skeptical about the objectivity of cartography as a mode of territorial description. What such critics tend to ignore is how the territorial abstraction implicit in such "objectivity" actually helps fashion the appearance of the state as a territorially defined actor in the first place. In other words, even before the state could be seen as an entity capable of using maps for the purposes of ideological justification and national self-definition, modern cartography had to be there to help lay the groundwork of spatial abstraction that was critical to the production of the modern, bureaucratic, and decorporealized effect we call the state.[37] There is, then, a profound ambivalence in the way cartography operates as a potentially disruptive "inscape of national identity." This in turn raises the question of how such compromise compromises Bhabha's own account of the national inscape.

The narration of nation, Bhabha insists, is deeply marked by ambivalence. On the one side, there is what he describes as the self-certain *pedagogy* of national discourse ("DissemiNation," esp. 145–48). Such pedagogy teaches among other things that the spaces of everyday life along with all "the people" can be abstracted into the nation space, all territory transformed into a new national tradition. On the other side of national discourse, argues Bhabha, is the supplementary *performance* of such teachings, the actual putting into practice and place of national pedagogy. It is in such performance, he suggests, that the political unity of the national narrative falls apart (split, in Bhabha's metaphorics, by the same displacement that Derrida—as was discussed in the introduction—elaborated in the supplementary structure of *writing*). The pedagogy has to be performed, put in place, and yet each time it is thereby supplemented it transforms homogeneity into heterogeneity. As a result, "the very act of the narrative performance interpellates a growing circle of national subjects" (145).

This canny articulation of national pedagogy displaced in performance is invaluable for coming to terms with the cartographic negotiation of nation-states. However, Bhabha himself, while he makes much of "location" in his essay and book, does not make any connections to the actual production of space, let alone to cartographic enframing. It would seem that for him space, location, and territory generally serve as metaphorized sites of performativity; they become the three spaces and, indeed, his idealized "Third Space," of displacement and difference, the space of hybridity, always already situated in between.[38] Much like Bhabha's (uncannily similar) arguments about ambivalence in colonial discourse, his claims about national narratives also therefore seem to be, in Robert Young's critical words, "offered as static concepts, curiously anthropomorphized so that they possess their own desire."[39] Bhabha offers no account of the historical production of abstract space, and he consequently ignores the possibility of how space can be operationalized pedagogically in attempts to convene and thereby potentially co-opt plural traditions and histories into the abstraction of the single territorial collectivity we call the state. This, I would suggest, is symptomatic of at least two more profound problems with his account: the first relating to how his rhetorical elevation of ambivalence abstracts away from the actual organization (and violence) of social power relations; and the second concerning his erasure of the state. As my preceding discussion of the state effects of cartographic power relations might suggest, I also regard these two problems as related. Thus as I go forward with the two case studies, and as I organize this account of cartographic struggle in terms of Bhabha's discussion of pedagogy and performance, I also want to show how the ambivalences I am addressing rest on very specific and geographical relations of power: relations in which the cartography of nation through maps takes place on the often violently abstracted terrain of modern state space.

THE TRIAL: PEDAGOGY POLICING PERFORMANCE

By entering into the Canadian legal process of the trial in the Supreme Court of British Columbia the Wet'suwet'en and Gitxsan peoples were insinuating their claims into the terms of reference of the dominant discourse. This is what Bhabha describes as the supplementary work of the *performance* of national narration.

> Insinuating itself into the terms of reference of the dominant discourse, the supplementary antagonizes the implicit power to generalize, to produce the sociological solidity. The questioning of the supplement is not a repetitive rhetoric of the "end" of society but a meditation on the disposition of space and time from which the narrative of nation must begin. ("DissemiNation," 155)

For the Wet'suwet'en and Gitxsan this was a contested and compromising entry, and while it did have a crucial antagonistic effect, it did not come with the same rhetorical ease with which Bhabha's account of "the supplementary" seems to spirit its way toward almost ontological conclusions. In fact, so dubious an ally was the Canadian law seen to be that many sympathetic commentators, from both within First Nations communities and without, criticized the chiefs for embarking on such a compromising strategy.[40] "A criticism we had to take," records Satsan, a Wet'suwet'en chief, "was that we were entering a game in which we had no involvement whatsoever with the putting together of that game, the making up of the rules, in the appointment of referees and umpires."[41] It was not simply that the Gitxsan and Wet'suwet'en had to deal with the adversarial protocols and far from sly spatiality of the courtroom. It was also that the actual arguments made by the two First Nations had to work within the framework of Canadian colonial law.[42] In order to make their claims, in other words, they had to turn the legal system, its archives, precedents, and process, against itself. This strategy, argues Satsan, was not a massive "sell-out" to the legal game but rather a massive challenge to the game itself.

> If we had chosen to play that game the way it was set out, I think that in the end we would more than likely have lost that which is so great to us. So we chose instead to challenge the whole bloody game, to say that this game is wrong, to say we don't agree with your referee and your umpire. This is a fixed game. We want to see a change.[43]

The lawsuit, then, was indeed an antagonistic supplementary action. But, as such, it amounted to more than just a "meditation" on the disposition of space and time from which the narrative of nation begins. The trial became instead a site of consequential struggle over the future political geography of Canada.

Coming into the Canadian court, the two First Nations had to attempt to insert their voices and speak their claims in a way that would successfully communicate their primarily oral knowledge and understanding of territorial jurisdiction to a white judge trained in the abstractions and textual formalities of the modern Western state. Like the Mashpee trial examined by the anthropologist James Clifford, the court case therefore represented a form of "borderline case" where cultural translations of different identities were very much in evidence.[44] However, in this case, the "powerful ways of looking" Clifford speaks of being thereby rendered problematic were nevertheless still hegemonic; they comprehensively structured the translation exercise. Thus the Gitxsan and Wet'suwet'en also had to negotiate the abstracting effect of the court itself: its rules, its norms of behavior, and its general distance from everyday life among the two First Nations. Central to all these courtroom abstractions was the removed, bureaucratized, and disembodied conception of abstract space that I have described as constitutive of the modern state effect. The Gitxsan and Wet'suwet'en were therefore obliged to negotiate with the structuring effects of this normalized abstract space—what might, following Bhabha, be called a pedagogic space of "the people"—at a number of different levels.

At the most microgeographical scale there was the actual spatial layout of the courtroom. The court's architecture, like that of courtrooms all over North America, reflected the adversarial and individualistic nature of courtroom exchange with an oppositional positioning of questioner and witness and an isolated, individualizing witness stand. As Timothy Solnick pointed out in an unfortunately unpublished master's thesis, this divisive courtroom arena was a very difficult space for the Gitxsan and Wet'suwet'en people to enter into as collective nations.[45] Some of the difficulties were created by the unilateral decision of McEachern to move the trial from Smithers, a small community in the heart of the claimed territory, to the city of Vancouver, over 1,200 kilometers away. The chief justice, working with a modern Western concept of justice applying equally everywhere within the abstract space of the state, was able to argue that Vancouver would be a more convenient location for the trial. His reasoning may have been predicated on his personal needs, but the abstract system provided his authority, and it was hard for the First Nations to contest the move within the rubrics of Canadian law. This meant that while the chief justice submitted that he was inconvenienced as a judge by the Smithers location—"I frankly admit that I do not have the endurance to continue a case as difficult as this one for any appreciable time outside Vancouver"[46]—he freely ignored the inconvenience and hardship imposed on the Gitxsan and Wet'suwet'en by moving the trial away from their own communities. Not only did all those testifying have to travel at great expense to a city far from their families and support networks, they also had to pay for places to stay in the city and negotiate the modernist monolith of the Vancouver courthouse. Far from Smithers, the location of this building, along with its alienating scale, its strictly monitored spaces, and its expensive environs, effectively barred the strong social support Gitxsan and Wet'suwet'en witnesses had received from the spectators' gallery in Smithers. It also made for a much more difficult place to have collective pre- and posttrial briefing sessions. Taken together, the spatial characteristics of the court and its location amounted in effect to a muted but colonial form of state-space-abstracting violence. It was with and in this same structure of violence that the Wet'suwet'en and Gitxsan chiefs knowingly decided to negotiate their national claims. As they did so, going one after the other through the witness stand, they were—within certain limitations—nevertheless able to subvert this space of the state effect.

One aspect of the First Nations' subversive courtroom performance was the repeated demonstration of the vitality and importance of their oral histories. Witnesses from both the Gitxsan and Wet'suwet'en sung ceremonial songs in court, among them the Wet'suwet'en *kungax* and the many Gitxsan *limx'ooy,* each of which evoked the *adaawk*—a form of historical geographic record—of particular Gitxsan Houses. There was a great deal of controversy in court about having such oral records accepted as legitimate evidence in exemption to the hearsay rule. In a Western juridical field that conventionally accepts only written and cartographic documentation of territory, such oral traditions were cast as illegitimate, and clearly the chief justice showed little respect both in court and in his written *Reasons for Judgment* for what he had heard in this way. When, for example, he was asked whether Antgulilibix (Mary Johnson) could sing a sacred song, McEachern exclaimed:

> Could it not be written out and asked if this is the wording? Really, we are on the verge of getting way off track here Mr. Grant. Again I don't want to be skeptical, but to have witnesses singing songs in

court is, in my respectful opinion, not the proper way to approach the problem.[47]

In making his judgment he ultimately reasoned that

> Except in a very few cases, the totality of the evidence raises serious doubts about the reliability of the adaawk and kungax as evidence of detailed history, or land ownership, use or occupation.[48]

Nevertheless, the very fact that the songs were sung at all subverted the hushed and sanitized sounds of normal legal procedure. Every time a First Nations' word was used it had to be interpreted and meticulously spelled out for the court records such that the cultural distinctiveness of the peoples as First Nations with disjunctive cultural histories was reaffirmed. The result was the complex cultural clash usefully documented by another of Don Monet's cartoons (Figure 2).

In addition to the formal spatiality of the court and its subversion, Monet's cartoon also highlights another more directly cartographic spatial theme. On the one side, he pictures Antgulilibix singing the *limx'ooy*. On the other is the chief justice surrounded by his written records and maps. The latter, with their Cartesian grid base and their orientation system organized by the north pole arrow, stand here as paradigmatic of the proper pedagogy of the courtroom. Monet uses them as both an indication of the rationalizations used by the government lawyers and examples of the "proper way to approach the problem" according to the chief justice. It was precisely the rules of this game played in abstract space with which the two First Nations had to negotiate. Given that ultimately they had to communicate their territorial knowledge to this judge in this court, they translated their oral knowledges into a series of maps. This produced, I think, one the clearest examples of Satsan's point about playing the game in order to change it. Through the medium of modern mapping they articulated their claim to their territories in a way the judge might understand. In the process, they were effectively cartographing their lands as First Nations within the abstract state space of Cartesian cartography. Simultaneously, they were supplementing the provincial and federal mapping of the land with maps based on Gitxsan and Wet'suwet'en oral knowledge. As such a repetition with a difference, a performance of the pedagogy of the place of the people, the maps served at once both to communicate in and to disrupt the cartographic conventions of the court.

Figure 2. "The Law vs. Ayook: Written vs. Oral History." Reprinted by permission of Don Monet.

Mapping had been closely allied with the strategy of going to trial since the 1960s when, as Medig'm (Neil Sterritt) reported, a map of the territories drawn by Chris Harris "began the court actions rolling."[49] Subsequently, Medig'm noted in court:

[T]here was a meeting in January 1975, it was a major meeting, and it was fully attended by the hereditary chiefs from all the villages and I believe the Wet'suwet'en as well, and this was in Kitwanga, and at that meeting the hereditary chiefs instructed three persons to put together a map and to go to work on land claims.[50]

At about this time other First Nations were also using maps in their negotiations with the government. Hugh Brody documents how in dealings with the Northern Pipeline Agency's 1979 hearings, map biographies were used to depict the extent of First Nations' occupancy and resource use.[51] This introduced complex questions about the intersection between the maps drawn up specifically for the hearings and the ancient maps of dreams and ceremony.[52] For the Gitxsan and Wet'suwet'en these questions of mapping and tradition were still more complexly interrelated insofar as the point of their maps produced as affidavits for the trial related to the project of translating the oral histories of the Houses into modern maps. Thus, unlike the land claims of the Labrador Inuit, the northern Ontario Cree and Ojibwa, and the northern Saskatchewan Chipewyan, the Gitxsan and Wet'suwet'en were not using map biographies of their occupancy and resource utilization in order to claim title on a resource tenure basis.[53] Instead, they presented the court with a series of maps that mapped their Houses and thus their territory over or rather, more accurately perhaps, *under* British Columbian provincial maps. Because such provincial maps had historically been imposed over the territory in a way that almost erased its precolonial spatiality, this cartographic representation of the Houses also served to chart the sheer density of the palimpsest produced by the whole series of precolonial, colonial, and postcolonial inscriptions. The process restored some meaning to spaces more usually covered by apparent emptiness on modern Canadian representations of the province (see, for example, the dense native toponymy in Map 1). Inscribing anticolonial names and places in the middle of the colonial coverage, it also addressed head-on what Bhabha describes as the "problem of signifying the interstitial passages and processes of cultural difference that are inscribed in the 'in-between'" ("DissemiNation," 217).

The abstract maps of Gitxsan and Wet'suwet'en territory showing the internal boundaries of the Houses—maps that also presented the paper tiger that McEachern had so much trouble unfolding—were perhaps the most obviously "in-between" of all the maps connected to the trial. As seemingly abstract national maps, they had a particularly marked ambivalence in their address (and, as such, found their way into both the chief justice's *Reasons for Judgment* and Monet and Skanu'u's critical report, *Colonialism On Trial*). The internal boundaries they indicated were abstracted from their oral, contextual, and embodied articulation in the songs of the First Nations' feasts and were represented instead in the silent, Cartesian, and decorporealized spatial codes of the modern Western state. They used national boundaries to isolate decontextualized spaces that were then subdivided according to what could very easily be understood as local jurisdictions. Yet the maps, while following these abstract rules of proper and stately cadastral procedure, nevertheless also transformed them by establishing a toponymy for the subdivisions with the names of the First Nations' Houses. In effect, they depicted the First Nations' territories as seemingly independent nation-states with their own internal boundaries. Ultimately, then, the maps did indeed begin to "roar." They successfully communicated the concept of First Nations' territorial jurisdiction while the audience in the theater of nation-state pedagogy witnessed a performance with a difference. But beyond the temporary disruptions to the orderliness of the court, the unfolding of specific First Nations' maps such as those charting the internal boundaries also evidenced a systematic recodification of the land. The territories that were repeatedly presented in the government maps as so many square miles of resources were thereby actively represented as a landscape rich with the historical geographies of Wet'suwet'en and Gitxsan names and meanings.

There was of course a number of risks attached to this cartographic strategy. The danger of publicizing First Nations' knowledge was among them.[54] However, the specific danger of the maps meeting with disrespect was similar to that relating to the singing of the songs in court and, as such, was knowingly subordinated by the Wet'suwet'en and Gitxsan to their wider project of educating Canadians and seeking recognition for self-government. But playing the court's cartographic game also opened up the plaintiffs' case to direct examination in the wider and usually opposing terms and assumptions of the court's conventions concerning abstract state space. For example, a lawyer representing the federal government is recorded as asserting the following:

> MR. MACAULEY: There is another matter that will come up when my friends, at last it is produced, that's his atlas of maps. The maps we received today. This comes as no surprise because we have seen

this kind of map before. The place names, the names of creeks rivers and hills and all the other features, are none of them geographic names, they are the Gitxsan names.[55]

The names on the government maps, the names of state, as it were, are held up here as the only real names, the "geographic names." The abstract effect of the state and the territorial homogeneity on which it is secured are thus flatly presented as admitting no alternatives. Rereading Macauley's disjointed words we can also perhaps detect signs of anxiety. The overbold assertion about Gitxsan names not being "geographic names" might thus be seen to point to how the Gitxsan and Wet'suwet'en maps had at least challenged the likes of Macauley to rethink Canada's official geography, the other national naming of the land, as an interested discourse. Yet in the context of the court such a rethink was obviously limited. The implication that the so-called geographic names were part of an abstract cartographic discourse that had erased the land's Gitxsan and Wet'suwet'en names was not examined. Instead, the project of erasure was reaffirmed against the looming threat of First Nations' displacements and recodifications of the state's abstract space.

Another more general risk of playing the court's cartographic game was of creating maps that simply reaffirmed the epistemic assumptions of colonialism and property rights jurisprudence. Ever since the recommendations of colonial surveyors, aboriginal space had always been targeted for recodification in the abstract terms of private property.[56] This was the disciplinary logic behind the whole reserve system, and as the following quotation from an anonymous surveyor in British Columbia makes clear, it was commonly seen as an effective means of controlling the colonially uncontrolled:

> A great stimulus will be given to the industrious Indian by giving him a tract of land and defining its boundaries within which he may recognize his own state. I know of no plan more calculated to discourage barbarous customs which tend to destroy individuality, or induce the improvement and general cultivation of their reserves. The first and distinguishing principles of civilization, no doubt, consist in the recognition and protection of private property rights.[57]

This was the violent system of spatial abstraction with which the Gitxsan and Wet'suwet'en inevitably had to negotiate in the trial. The language of the court was periodically just as oppressive, but the logic of property rights' spatial abstraction generally found reflection in more muted questions about the accuracy of the Wet'suwet'en and Gitxsan maps. Because the First Nations had made their claims in the cartographic terms of the dominant discourse, the colonial assumptions about native societies needing spatial reordering returned in uncanny appeals by the court to the importance of accuracy. Because of supposed *in*accuracy, the spaces represented in the House maps were said to fall short of the abstract standards of detail required by the court.

There were many moments when the accuracy of the Gitxsan and Wet'suwet'en map boundaries was challenged, not least in the chief justice's own reasoning. He complained that

> There are far too many inconsistencies in the plaintiffs' evidence to permit me to conclude that individual chiefs or Houses have discrete aboriginal rights or interests in the various territories defined by the internal boundaries. (*Reasons for Judgment*, 507)

The fact that the maps were translations of songs, and that such House songs of territory and history were unlikely to match up perfectly with discretely delineated blocks of territory in abstract space, was of little concern. Instead, the chief justice simply judged the cartographic affidavits by the standards of the colonial state. As a result, the evidence of House ownership presented by the Gitxsan and Wet'suwet'en was ultimately dismissed. Moreover, in his overall dismissal of the case, the chief justice not only measured the maps of the two First Nations in the terms of abstract state space, he also imposed the same distant and disembodied understanding of territory onto the whole question of life in the claimed territories. Despite all the work of the Gitxsan and Wet'suwet'en cartography, it did not seem to challenge the chief justice to reexamine this, his basic surveyor's view of the land.[58]

"I visited many parts of the territory which is the principal subject of this case during a three day helicopter and highway 'view' in June, 1988," McEachern reports (*Reasons for Judgment*, 200). This "view" it seemed, not unlike the colonial cartography of the "New World" that effectively depopulated the land of its older inhabitants, imposed a preconceived and abstract notion of emptiness on what the chief justice saw. He summarizes thus that

> These explorations were for the purpose of familiarizing myself, as best I could, with this beautiful, vast and almost empty part of the province. (200)

Whatever names and meaning the Gitxsan and Wet'suwet'en had sought to map back on to the landscape with their cartography was in such moments lost on the judge. For him, instead, the landscape was enframed as "beautiful, vast and almost empty." It might seem that these are just terms of innocent almost sublime reflection. And yet they are also terms of colonial conquest, terms that, with easy appeals to the abstractions of European aestheticism, serve to empty the landscape. Combined with the court's abstract cartographic conventions in the *Reasons for Judgment,* they explain a great deal of the chief justice's "proper way to approach the problem," and why, ultimately, he ruled in his abstract way to dismiss the suit. As Harley describes the enframing effect of colonial cartography, the chief justice's overall view might also be said to have dispossessed the Gitxsan and Wet'suwet'en "by engulfing them with blank spaces."[59]

In his *Reasons for Judgment* the chief justice also makes clear that, while he is in no doubt about his final conclusions, one specific section of evidence during the trial particularly exercised him. Notably, it did not concern Gitxsan and Wet'suwet'en maps, songs, or in fact their actual presence in the land at all. Instead it was about Europeans, their laws and maps.

> One of the most interesting parts of evidence and argument in this case concerned th[e] famous Proclamation which was issued by George III, on the advice of his Ministers, on October 7, 1763, following the completion of the Peace of Paris on February 10 of that year. (*Reasons for Judgment,* 287)

Ironically, it was in the terms of this same Proclamation that the Wet'suwet'en and Gitxsan lawyers advanced what was probably one of the plaintiffs' most powerful arguments in the trial. It was an argument that, had it not also been dismissed by the chief justice, would have overridden his arguments about the inadequacy of the map and song evidence of House ownership and jurisdiction. The major reason for this was that it was an appeal to colonial law itself, a very clear case of playing the colonial game against the colonial project. It did not turn on First Nations' cartography and instead hinged on historical argument about the contradictions in the colonial cartographic archive itself. Ultimately, the court arguments still enframed the appeal in abstract spatial terms that emptied it of content, but this case of pedagogy paradoxically meant that the government's arguments involved shrinking rather than expanding the spatial extent of claims to colonial control.

In issuing the Royal Proclamation, George III had declared that before any aboriginal lands could be taken by British subjects in the New World the colonizers should have the informed consent of the aboriginal inhabitants. Because there were no treaties ever made with the Gitxsan and Wet'suwet'en that gave such consent, their lawyers pleaded the following:

> 64. The Plaintiffs have enjoyed and still enjoy their aforementioned rights as recognized and confirmed by the Royal Proclamation made by his Majesty King George the Third on the 7th of October, 1763 (hereinafter called the "Royal Proclamation").
>
> 65. The Royal Proclamation applies to British Columbia and is part of the Constitution of Canada. The Plaintiffs' ownership and jurisdiction over the Territory thereby includes without restricting the generality of the foregoing:
>
> 1. A right that the Territory be reserved to the benefit of the Plaintiffs until by the Plaintiffs' informed consent the said rights are surrendered to the Imperial or Federal Crown.
>
> 2. A recognition of the Plaintiffs' aboriginal title, ownership and jurisdiction and the special relationship of the Plaintiffs as Indians to the Imperial or Federal Crown.
>
> 66. In the alternative, by virtue of the Royal Proclamation of 1763, the Plaintiffs enjoy the rights hereinafter set out:
>
> 1. A right to ownership of all lands with the Territory and to territorial waters and to the resources thereon and therein, and
>
> 2. A right to the jurisdiction over the Plaintiffs and the members of their Houses and all the land, territorial waters and resources within the Territory, and
>
> 3. A right to the Imperial or Federal Crown's protection in reserving the aforementioned rights to the benefit of the Plaintiffs until, through the informed consent of the Plaintiffs, the said rights are surrendered to the Imperial or Federal Crown. (*Reasons for Judgment*, 288)

The response of the government lawyers and subsequently the chief justice himself was contorted to say the least. They could not simply deny that any such rights existed as this would be a denial of Canadian law itself. Likewise, given the government's own records, they could not reasonably argue that the Gitxsan and Wet'suwet'en had ever given informed consent. Instead, they found themselves in the peculiar and superficially anticolonial position of arguing that the colonial law of the Royal Proclamation did *not* apply to British Columbia. Central to this contorted argument were colonial maps that were used to try and demonstrate that the province was not adequately known by the king and his ministers at the time of the Royal Proclamation. It was an argument, as it were, from cartographic ignorance, and as such served to thematize the power/knowledge links between European law and European spatial knowledge that served elsewhere in the trial—not least in the chief justice's denial of House ownership on the basis of cartographic inaccuracies—as the unstated common sense of reasoning. The Proclamation had no legal effect in British Columbia, the defense argued, because at the moment of its enunciation the area had not yet entered fully into the European epistemic empire. Precisely because *it had not been properly mapped,* it was not yet a transparent space of state power.[60]

The cartographic archive of the period is rich and does not easily lend itself to this narrow reading. Nevertheless, an effort was made in a brief from Albert Farley, a geographer and historian of cartography. Collecting together a chronological series of maps of North America from the period of the Royal Proclamation, he concluded that what is now British Columbia was not well known. "It is inconceivable," he wrote, "that the framers of the Proclamation in 1763 could have had access to more than a very rudimentary knowledge of this remote area."[61] In court he again reaffirmed this view:

> To set this in perspective, one could say that before the publication of the narrative associated with Cook's third and last voyage, publication dated 1784, before that, even the coastline of what is now British Columbia was remote from the known world.[62]

It is, I think, a telling irony that, in a court where the supremacy of colonial knowledge and colonial records was constantly upheld, and where the abstract space of Cartesian cartography was elevated as a paradigm of accuracy, the government case turned at one of its more desperate moments on a claim about the limits and inadequacies of colonial cartography. Maps of North America were said to be vague and inaccurate in their depictions of the northwest coast. The usual spatial arrogance of European imperialism assumed elsewhere by the government lawyers in arguments about extinguishing aboriginal rights was thus displaced. In its stead came a litany of caveats concerning the limits rather than the sweeping reach of

European spatial knowledge. As a result, lawyers for the Gitxsan and Wet'suwet'en had a relatively easy time criticizing the argument. They cast doubt on the claims about spatial ignorance by showing other maps that existed contemporaneously with the Proclamation. One of these was a map drawn up by the king's geographer Thomas Jeffreys in 1761 that showed the "North West Coast."

> Q: Now, Dr. Farley, can you agree with me that this is Thomas Jeffreys' map of 1761?
>
> A: Yes. . . .
>
> Q: Now, if you look, Dr. Farley, the title is "A Map of the Discoveries Made by the Russians on the North west Coast of America?"
>
> A: Yes. . . . I have seen the Jeffreys' map before.
>
> Q: You did not include it in your folio?
>
> A: No.
>
> Q: Is there any reason you did not?
>
> A: It seemed to me that the Muller map was the first derivative from the Russian information, and that was the appropriate one to include.
>
> Q: Clearly here Thomas Jeffreys, as Geographer for the King—I think you have agreed that he was—is stating that there is a northwest coast of America?
>
> A: It is portrayed on the map, yes.[63]

Yet, while it was easy enough to demonstrate the tendentiousness of the defense material, it was still the argument about inaccuracies and empty spaces that ultimately persuaded the chief justice. Even if the coast was there on the Jeffreys map, there was still no detailed knowledge of the interior, he reasoned, and hence the details of the law, of statutory power relations, were not yet effective.

> While the evidence is not conclusive, and I have no doubt Mr. Rush is right when he argues more was known on the ground, it is my conclusion that precious little was known by governments in Europe in 1763 about the western half of North America. . . . For these reasons it cannot be said that those vast areas were British possessions at the time of the Royal Proclamation, 1763. (Reasons for Judgment, 292–93)

The whole project of the defense and then the chief justice to limit the claims to European knowledge and expansion seemed to go quite against the grain of the usual norms of knowledge production in a modern nation-state like Canada. The conventional tendency, as I will show in the next section, is for the modern nation-state to push its beginnings and hence its geographical integrity as far back as possible into history. Nations, as it is commonly noted, tend thus to celebrate their supposed age rather than their remarkable youth. And yet here were the administrators and defenders of the nation-state trying to pull forward the space of the properly Canadian past so that a historic part of state law could *not* be judged to apply to what was nonetheless repeatedly referred to as "British Columbia." In short, with their supplementary appeal to the colonial law of the Royal Proclamation, the Gitxsan and Wet'suwet'en provoked a struggle over "the disposition of space and time from which the narrative of nation must begin." It was not the interstitial maps of their nations graphed over provincial maps that prevailed very far in this struggle, nor their singing of House songs in court. These more radically resistant courtroom performances were simply policed and cordoned off with bold disrespect. The map that roared, it seems, was caged: locked up and assessed within the abstract space of the state. By unhappy contrast, it was the direct appeal to colonial law that came closer to disrupting the abstractions of the state pedagogy. It forced a radical review of the limits of Canada's past in space. But even as it did so, this performance of George III's pedagogy was itself no equal to the court's colonial clasp on the dominant apparatus of power/knowledge in the present.

The Gitxsan and Wet'suwet'en did not come away with nothing for their grueling efforts. Although they also lost their appeal to the British Columbia Court of Appeals, in June 1994 they deferred an appeal to the Supreme Court of Canada when a more sympathetic provincial government opened up the possibility of direct political negotiations instead. This development may have in part reflected the educational victory that was claimed by many people in the First Nations. Indeed, even by the time of the 1992 Charlottetown constitutional referendum (discussed later in chapter 4), Canadian public interest in acknowledging the right of First Nations to self-government was very considerable. There was also a widespread renaissance of resistance and national pride among the Gitxsan and Wet'suwet'en themselves. The trial had been a catalyst for organization, and a sympathetic researcher reports Herb George saying that

The whole process of preparing the evidence and arguing the case had taken them back to who they really were . . . : as they argued, they began to live the way they were talking. They went off the reserves to confront loggers and government and assert their rights. They went into rivers and began fishing in defiance of government regulations. Refusing to get permits, their people started to go out on to their traditional territory, "to manage it again," in George's words.[64]

This renaissance and the related decline of ignorance among non-native Canadians cannot be dismissed. And yet McEachern's quite brutal dismissal of the Gitxsan and Wet'suwet'en case itself, after all the courtroom testimony, after all the cartographic contestation, and after the most complex negotiations with the involuted structures of colonial law, points to how in this case the disruptive performance of the pedagogy of the "proper way to approach the problem" was not enough.

Despite the fact that the Gitxsan and Wet'suwet'en had effectively inserted their claims into the terms of the dominant discourse, their performance was still one around which the chief justice could simply close the curtain. There was still a duality of the hegemonic and the counterhegemonic made manifest in the process, and the cartographic contentions in particular showed how the trial served to thematize the overlapping historical geographies of colonialism and First Nations' resistance. These overlaps were what the Wet'suwet'en and Gitxsan replayed to such performative effect. But yet this contrapuntal duality in the trial taken as a whole did not immediately change "the game" in the way First Nations leaders like Satsan hoped it would. The chief justice's *Reasons for Judgment* show that the pedagogy of the proper persisted, and all the performance, all the attempts at supplementary rearticulation, were finally policed within the spatial abstractions of the state. Such crisis management may well then seem to vindicate Audre Lorde's famous axiom about how the "master's tools will never dismantle the master's house."[65] Cartography, in particular, may in this sense only seem a tool that is always already co-opted. Yet, while such a suggestion, like the case of the trial itself, provides a sobering reminder of the difficulties involved in negotiating with structures of violence, and thus while it also points to the perhaps preemptive nature of Bhabha's ode to the displacing performance of pedagogy, it nevertheless seems to me to close off the possibilities of displacement too quickly. Thus as I turn next to the *Atlas,* and as I examine it too in terms of pedagogy and performance, I aim to show that moments of displacement are not always policed. There is not always the same theatrical spatiality that shaped events in the B.C. courtroom, not always a judge privileged as the supreme all-comprehending spectator, and not always the same reduction of complex overlapping historical geographies to a "vast, beautiful and almost empty" stage.

THE *ATLAS*: FROM THE PEDAGOGIC ROOT TO PERFORMATIVE ROUTES

Given the associations between Canadian national mapping and what I described in the last section as the proper pedagogy of the courtroom, it might seem that an atlas of Canada would offer little relief from the pattern of nationalist hegemony identified by Bhabha as the transformation of territory into tradition. "For the political unity of the nation," he says,

> consists in a continual displacement of the anxiety of its irredeemably plural modern space—representing the nation's modern territoriality is turned into the archaic, atavistic temporality of Traditionalism. The difference of Space returns as the sameness of time, turning territory into Tradition, turning the People into One. ("DissemiNation," 149)

But to argue that the *Atlas* merely turned territory into tradition would be an error. Certainly it can be read as a classic example of nationalist pedagogy. Through its powerful social status as a teaching tool, its traditional evolutionary narrative, and its imposition of modern Canadian names and shapes on the precolonial past, it might indeed seem to transform the nation's modern territoriality "into the archaic, atavistic temporality of Traditionalism." And yet, I will argue, the *Historical Atlas* does not so much "displace" anxiety about Canada's irredeemably plural modern space as actively celebrate it as the very stuff of Canadian tradition. This, I suggest, has a number of critical implications about Bhabha's arguments concerning space, and the links between space, performativity, and disruption. At a more practical level, though, the example of the *Atlas* shows how a seemingly hegemonic narrative of the nation can also function through its very rigor and ideals of comprehensiveness to open up spaces for counterhegemonic questioning. Overall my account of the *Atlas* testifies to what I see as the wisdom in José

Rabasa's words about Mercator's original atlas. Such an atlas, he argued, must be understood

> as simultaneously constituting a stock of information for a collection of memory and instituting a signaling tool for scrambling previous territorializations. Memory and systematic forgetfulness, fantastic allegories and geometric reason coexist in the Atlas with an apparent disparity.[66]

It is this simultaneity and coexistence of pedagogic stockpiling with performative scrambling that was barred in *Delgamuukw v. the Queen* by the court's strict divisions. Performance was policed so that turning the map into a signaling tool that might further First Nations' reterritorializations was severely curtailed. The court and the counsel for the defense pontificated with strident pedagogy while the Wet'suwet'en and Gitxsan struggled to have their cartographic performance even recognized as such. In the *Atlas,* by comparison, the hegemonic and counterhegemonic were far more closely intertwined. As such, they can usefully be compared with two different sets of entangled roots and routes. One set is the pedagogic national genesis story with its *singular root* marked by the biblical subtitle given to the English edition of the *Atlas* by the University of Toronto Press: namely, "From the Beginning to 1800." The other less sacred sounding set, the set made up of the *multiple routes* charted performatively in space in the *Atlas* itself, instead found its more plural reflection in the doubled-up sensitivity of the French edition's subtitle: "Des Origines à 1800."[67] In what follows, I track back and forth between these two root systems with the aim of showing how the plural routes of travel, contact, and interaction mapped out in the *Atlas* displace its chronological narrative's transcendental truth claims to a national root in the soil of North America.[68]

Perhaps the most obvious illustration of the *Atlas*'s pedagogic status was the way it was planned, packaged, and disseminated as a teaching and research tool. National atlases have long been regarded as having a crucial educational function, and even cartographers who have pondered the supposed "Mathematical Basis of National Atlases" acknowledge that the final role of such cartography is "cultural and educational."[69] The *Historical Atlas* was no exception to this pattern. Right from its inception, it was advanced before the national funding agency—the Social Sciences and Humanities Research Council of Canada—as addressing some of the nation's pressing teaching needs. William Dean, the project director of all three volumes, repeatedly advertised the work as providing Canadians with the same kind of prestigious and pedagogic national resource possessed by other modern nations. "[E]very major country in the world including many Third World countries now has published a major thematic historical atlas," he argued.[70] In a similar vein he concluded with James Walker that, despite the expense and difficulty, the ultimate "prize" would be

> a further step in the continuing realization of ourselves as a nation—a legacy to future generations. The atlas will be a worthwhile, long-awaited and needed national expression of the fascinatingly peculiar confederation of regions that we call Canada.[71]

In less labile terms, the project proposal itself made a more specific case about how the *Atlas* would become "a prolific source of fresh ideas which would both stimulate research and enhance the teaching resources of the major participants."[72] Bringing together scholars from all over Canada, the project was hoped to spur on academic endeavors at trans-Canadian collaboration more generally. In an attempt to ensure that the fruits of such collaboration would be represented and understood collaboratively too, the *Atlas* was also published in both official languages.

The teaching role of the *Atlas* was subsequently reaffirmed when, at a time when funds for the project were dwindling, the private telephone company Bell Canada bought a large number of copies so that they could be distributed free of charge to all Ontario schools. Such public-private partnership, involving a telephone company and the mass dissemination of national cartography for educational purposes, seemed to many to crystallize the form as well as the function of being Canadian. The *Atlas,* in this sense, came to represent Canada in more than maps. Its very organization and circulation were turned into metaphors of the nation-state. For example, in the foreword to the *Atlas* Dean writes:

> The enormous costs in time and money required to complete this work are, however, part of the cost of being Canadian. Few of us realize how much distance permeates our lives. . . . Canadians are, of necessity, communications specialists. From the beginnings of nationhood we have needed to bridge our spaces and to link our diverse regions together. The *Historical Atlas of Canada* is yet another illustration of Canadian strength and ingenuity in communications.[73]

This classically Canadian theme hymning both the difficulties and distinctions that come with the vastness of Canadian territory harked back in turn to the work of Marshall McLuhan and Harold Innis, two of Canada's most distinguished teachers and scholars of the country's territorial uniqueness and related communications expertise. Given a widespread acceptance, or at least unconscious understanding, of these general theses linking the distinctiveness of the land with that of the people, the metaphor of the *Atlas* as a message itself—as well as medium for mapped messages—became the dominant pedagogic model through which it was commonly reviewed and read.

"An atlas is a fitting symbol of Canada," began William Westfall's celebratory assessment.[74] He noted how this carried a particular pedagogic burden for the reviewer, arguing that

> To review the first volume of this historical atlas . . . is (as the subtitle suggests) much like reviewing the Book of Genesis.[75]

Likewise, Roger Hall, reviewing the *Atlas* for the national Toronto-based daily *The Globe and Mail,* foregrounded the same singular root theme in terms of Prime Minister Mackenzie King's famous 1936 quotation: "If some countries have too much history, we have too much geography." A historical atlas, Hall therefore reasoned, was a particularly appropriate way to come to terms with the country's foundation. "What *The Historical Atlas of Canada* attempts to do, with considerable success," he concluded, "is to knit our history and geography together."[76] Such commentaries on the *Atlas,* shaped as they were by the spatial pedagogy of the dominant national narrative, also carried over into more directly pedagogical implications when reviews were undertaken with schooling in mind. "Within a generation, as schools, libraries, universities and individuals acquire and become accustomed to the availability and utility of the 'Atlas' . . ., a transformation in the understanding of Canada in its entirety can be anticipated," argued Paul Robinson, while also emphasizing the importance of geography to Canadians' self understanding.[77] Another typical educationally oriented review in the *Canadian Library Journal* reported that the atlas would become "a part of the cultural heritage of future generations of Canadians and an essential purchase for the reference collections of academic, public and school libraries."[78] James Reaney, reviewing the *Atlas* for the popular magazine *Saturday Night,* saw a still more immediate value in the *Atlas* as a tool for preparing Canadians for national struggle.

> The Historical Atlas of Canada is the most important reference book to come out in Canada since Hurtig's *The Canadian Encyclopedia,* and if, after surmounting the ninety-five-dollar investment challenge, you have both at hand with some clever kids in the house, you might just make it through the cultural rapids ahead of us as the American giant tries yet again to make us officially into the fourteenth colony.[79]

Published at a time when Canadian national debate was filled with concern about the implications of the Canada–U.S. Free Trade Agreement (see chapter 3), Reaney's review sounded a typical clarion call to Canadians to ready themselves against U.S. assimilation by educating each other about their country's distinctive place in North America. In so doing, it also addressed directly what a number of other, more academic, reviews approached only circuitously: namely, the national hegemony–building potential of the *Atlas.*

Understood as a vital element in such national educational endeavors, it is hard to imagine a more "national-pedagogical" positioning of the *Atlas.* Acclaimed in the national press as a symbol of Canada, celebrated by academics as an empirically rich cartographic essay, and widely purchased by the public who could afford it, the *Atlas* as both medium and message seemed to reach almost anthemic as well as hegemonic status. Yet, even as it did so, the very lengths to which its creators went in order to chart the complex regional dynamics of Canadian history and to simultaneously make the work speak to audiences across the country also invited questions.

The French edition, which made the *Atlas* accessible to francophone readers (who quickly purchased all the available copies), notably led to criticism. To be sure, the *Atlas* was also widely praised in Québec for making a united Canada visible: "[u]n plaisir pour l'oeil et pour l'intelligence," declared Yvon Lamonde.[80] But, at the same time, some French-speaking readers attentive to the *Atlas*'s ideals of comprehensiveness and national inclusiveness nevertheless worried over whether the documentation of development dynamics had not been skewed by English Canadian interests. "La spécificité canadienne du régime français, et l'epopée de Jacques Cartier ne font pas l'objet d'un très long développement," complained Jean-Pierre

Bonhomme in *La Presse*.[81] Compared with the detailed cartographic description of the fur trade and contact dynamics in the northwest, he went on, early French-Canadian history had received short shrift. Given the substantial effort in the *Atlas* to represent the distinct historical geography of French North America, these did not seem very fair criticisms. That said, what I rather want to highlight here, though, is the way in which the wide address of the *Atlas* inevitably led some readers to question the adequacy of its coverage. The calls for comprehensiveness and inclusiveness that it simultaneously issued and answered with every massively detailed map also called forth demands for more specific details from particular constituencies. This form of invitation to critique and rethinking is I think one of the more interesting achievements of the *Atlas*, and it serves as such as a good example of Bhabha's notion of displacement through narrative performance. In order to bring the radical implications of such displacement more clearly into focus, I next turn to the question of how the *Atlas*'s Eurocentric chronology was itself displaced in the *Atlas* by the details demanded by the actual work of cartography. As scholarly maps, the *Atlas* plates were, as Dean's foreword emphasizes, "inexorably tyrannical taskmasters." That same tyranny, I argue, helped introduce a multiplicity of routes where there might otherwise have only been a simple historicist root.

The clearest expression of the singularizing root system in the *Atlas* is the way in which its narrative evolution anchors the "beginning" of Canada in time, or, to be more precise, in European historicist chronology. Following the temporal logos of this chronology, Plate 1 begins the "Prehistory" section of the *Atlas* with a map of "The Last Ice Sheets, 18,000–10,000 BC." Here, as it were, is Canada's ice-bound garden of Eden, a picture of the glacial past dated geologically, labeled with anachronistic but also seemingly objective geographic terms like "New Québec Ice," and mapped in such a way as to present under the gentle purple hue of the glaciers an apparently unified and non-American space of collective Canadian experience. There then follows, in linear evolutionary sequence, a careful charting of the so-called Indian arrival on the continent. Despite the pre-European context, the land is nevertheless still named "the New World" in another anachronistic application of modern Eurocentric labels. Plates drawn up by paleobotanists, glacial geologists, and archeologists proceed to map all the most recent scientific findings concerning native peoples, plotting their positions like so many specimens in the translucent and icily anemic geography of transparent state space.

Positioned as early arrivals in this New World space, the first peoples are collectively (re)described by the *Atlas* as "Canada's first immigrants," which is to say they are reduced to early arrivals in a national pageant of immigration. As such early immigrants these peoples—ranging from those identified as the "Fluted Point" people to the "Northern Interior Microblade" to the "Late Palaeo-Eskimo"—are brought in turn into the national narrative without compromising its unified, if icy, starting point eighteen thousand years BC. They are encapsulated thus not as an active history-making historical presence but rather as the prehistoric fabrications of modern archeological research. Included in these objectifying terms, these peoples become inscribed with the geological and paleobotanical material in such a way that they are instrumentalized as a seemingly natural national foundation. The proleptic implication of this chronological foundation work is the notion that if there was no real, written record of history before the Europeans, there was nonetheless a territory that was somehow unified by "natural history" as Canadian.

A less chronopolitical interpretation of the "Prehistory" section might see it as just an inclusive multicultural revision of the exclusivist "white settler colony" narrative of the nation. Certainly this was the hope of one of the section's main contributors and organizers, the archeologist J. V. Wright. In contrast to Eurocentric atlases of Canada that "ignore twelve thousand years of history of the native peoples," he argued, "the *Historical Atlas of Canada* is a notable exception . . . and should contribute to a heartening trend away from what can only be called an ethnocentric perception of history."[82] This was also indeed how the *Atlas* was often read by reviewers. "Qui sont ces chasseurs et leurs pointes cannelées?" asked Claude Tessier. "Qui sont les Planoans? Et les Martimiens? Et les Bouclériens? Et les Laurentiens? Il y a une résponse," he inclusively concludes, "tous sont les premiers vrais Canadiens!"[83]

"The first true Canadians" seems an anthemic interpretation, and yet one should also ask in whose interests such anthems are sung? Paul Carter finds the answer wanting in the Australian example.

When archeologists "push back" the date of first aboriginal settlement, who gains? To be sure our legal preoccupation with issues of
priority ensures each new date some political leverage. More profoundly, though, the increase in knowledge, increases our control.
For it is we Europeans who associate antiquity with a rich "cultural
heritage." In discovering the Aboriginal past, we demonstrate our
piety towards the household gods of our own history.[84]

In the Canadian context, this critical point has also been connected
to the disciplinary divisions of modern scholarship by Bruce Trigger,
a scholar who was also one of the major contributors to the later,
"historical" plates on the St. Lawrence region in the *Atlas*. Trigger
had previously complained that "the study of native people prior to
the arrival of Europeans is still viewed, not as a part of Canadian
history, but as the domain of prehistoric archeology."[85] He argued
that this marginalized and minimalized the social, economic, and
cultural complexity of native history. Yet despite the presence of
his own work later in the volume, this is what the "Prehistory" section in particular begins to do. Clearly this is not a straightforward
problem of exclusion. Aboriginal cultures are definitely assigned a
complex set of spatial positions on the maps. But because those positions are organized according to the historicist logic of archeological
chronology there is what Fabida Jara and Edmundo Magana call an
"evolutionist taxonomy"[86] at work in the map series, a taxonomy
that, with its disciplined and repeated reference to "diagnostic artifacts," "cultural sequences," and academic debates over "poor data,"
turns this first part of the *Atlas* into the cartographic equivalent of
a state-managed archeological museum. It is a museum packed with
artifacts, and alongside the mapping of habitation sites, burial pits,
and the like, there are innumerable graphic representations of arrow
heads, pendants, and even such objects as a turtle amulet and ivory
snow goggles (Plates 9 and 15). Yet even as these latter examples
might begin to dramatize some of the cultural complexities of the
pre-European inhabitants, this complexity is in turn instrumentalized. The way in which they are generally represented on national
maps that stretch the length and breadth of modern Canada reveals
this instrumental value of the "first immigrants" as artifacts of an
acquired ancient history for the modern multicultural nation-state.
Indeed, it is a telling irony (to which I will return) that, in addition
to the plates on the environment, the only maps in the *Atlas* pictur-

ing the whole of the outline of what is now Canada are the maps of aboriginal peoples. Through the trick of historicist chronology they become part of the naturalized and spatialized prehistoric root out of which stems the avowed coherency of the modern nation.

The chronology I have outlined thus far, and the way it turns the heterogeneous differences of pre-European geographies into the singular space of Canada's origin, may well seem akin to that described by Bhabha in which the "difference of Space returns as the sameness of time, turning territory into Tradition, turning the People into One." Following Bhabha's argument further, however, it is also possible to find numerous moments in the *Atlas* where the cartographic performance of the chronology brings this singularizing narrative of a nation rooted in time into question. Most immediately and powerfully, the chronology is disrupted by the maps in the subsequent sections that represent the changing geographies of aboriginal societies *after* the arrival of the Europeans. With the advent of Western history, it seems, aboriginal people are not at all banished from the scene. Instead, there are maps of trade and warfare in the St. Lawrence (Plate 33), depictions of Iroquois and Algonquian seasonal movements (Plate 34), and incredibly detailed maps—better described perhaps as cartographic monographs—by Conrad Heidenreich displaying the complex spatial histories of native groups in relation to the developing fur trade in the Great Lakes region (Plates 35, 37, 38, 39, and 40). In addition to all this, the development of the northwest is not told as the traditional heroic tale of colonial discovery but rather as a haphazard history of imperial competition, error, and negotiation: a spatial history that is itself punctured by Plate 59 showing the maps of a Chipewyan and two Blackfoot guides. Admittedly these latter maps were drawn at the request of explorers and the plate itself is entitled "Indian Maps," a terminological homogenization of first peoples that is also symptomatic of European epistemological imperialism. However, the reader of the *Atlas* can still find in such moments a vivid representation of the complexity of different aboriginal geographies and knowledges. (Plate 66, which maps language groups and trading relations among West Coast groups around 1800, is another prime example.) Certainly, Trigger's complaint that aboriginal histories are commonly confined by chronology to Canada's archeological prehistory finds a substantive rebuttal in the form of these later plates.

The maps they bring together, not least Trigger's own of the St. Lawrence valley in the sixteenth century (Plate 33), mark a native presence and movement in spaces that earlier atlases simply emptied of aboriginal people altogether.

The chronological ordering of the *Atlas* is also disrupted by certain of the maps in the "Prehistory" section itself that register some of the dynamic local geographies of native trade and migration (Plates 12, 13, and 14). Plate 13 (reproduced here in black and white as Map 2), in particular, would seem through the very rigor of its depiction of Coast Tsimshian movements around 1750 to restore a certain historicity to this pre-European period. By describing the seasonal routes taken by the Coast Tsimshian with bold arrows on a map replete with First Nations' names, the plate presents a radical alternative to the "Indians" turned archeological artifacts in other parts of this museumizing section. Moreover, the plate's annotations, which refer to the peoples' history as an ongoing rather than extinguished affair, produce a sense of continuity that, accompanied by the cartographic information itself, makes the map a potentially useful resource for the sort of legal struggles engaged in by the Wet'suwet'en and the Gitxsan (and indeed Gitxsan villages and trade routes are themselves recorded on the plate). Instead of the empty land and museumized culture that was so much part of the chief justice's vision in the trial, the plate presents a picture of vital lifeways. Consequently, as one reviewer enthused:

> It is possible to follow the Tsimshian as they move their whole winter villages in what is now the Prince Rupert area, up to the Nass River for eulachon fishing in early spring, then out to the western islands to gather seaweed in late spring and up the Skeena in summer and fall for trade and salmon fishing, before returning to their main homes for the season of socializing and ceremonial activities.[87]

The plate thus enables a lively spatial history to be retold, one that subverts more orthodox presentations of this region's emptiness and irrelevance prior to European exploration. As it does so, it also invites readers to reconsider the constructed quality of a term like Prehistory, and thus unsettle conventional assumptions about the national Canadian nature of native history. In fact some reviewers complained that because Plate 13 was not sufficiently contextualized, it was impossible to tell in what exact part of British Columbia,

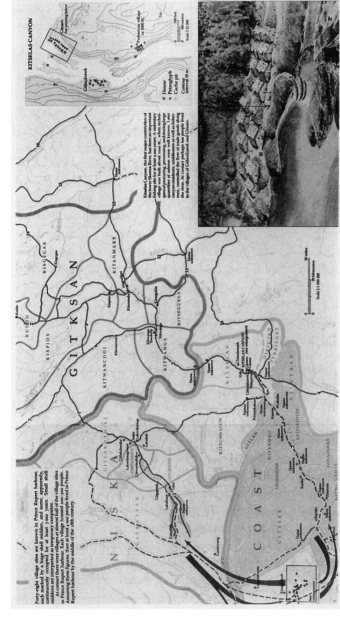

Map 2. A portion of the Coast Tsimshian map from R. Cole Harris, ed., Geoffrey J. Matthews, cartographic designer, Historical Atlas of Canada. Volume 1: From the Beginning to 1800 (Toronto: University of Toronto Press, 1987). Reprinted by permission of University of Toronto Press.

and hence modern Canada, the mapped movements of the Tsimshian took place. The alienating possibility that they constituted another First Nation was thereby opened up. In short, the plate makes possible a critique of chronology: a critique that, rather than being based upon critical academic arguments about the tendentious European root of evolutionary time,[88] stems from the mapped complexity of pre-European routes across the land.

At the other end of the *Atlas*, the final plate (Plate 69) in the volume also counters the evolutionary teleology set up in the "Prehistory" section with another return to the complexity and heterogeneity of aboriginal spatial movements, this time around the date 1820. In a recent restatement of his famous critique of Eurocentric chronologies, Johannes Fabian has argued that "[t]he important thing in [these] tales of evolution remains their ending."[89] Conventionally, of course, this ending is European, which is to say the tale is narrated such that European religion, social life, and political behavior—including the norm of the nation-state itself—are cast as the very pinnacle of civilization. By cartographically displacing such chronological convention, the *Atlas* valuably disrupts the evolutionist notion that after contact the only real history concerned the Europeans and their legacy. Instead, with the concluding Plate 69, the reader is made to consider how, despite all the colonial conflicts and interactions charted in the preceding plates, multiple aboriginal geographies were still extant, often transformed, but still in place, surviving, and continuing at the start of the nineteenth century. To be sure, the plate can be criticized for downplaying the full extent of the colonial impact at that time. The soft blue arrows marking the advance of "European settlement" visually dim the violence of displacement; the controlling effects of the developing reserve system are not explicitly marked; and some sections, like that representing the Beothuk movements on Newfoundland, miss the massive extent of the destruction already wrought by 1820.[90] Yet such arguments do not take away from the tremendous work made manifest in the plate of representing a surviving native geography in the context of and in the face of an advancing colonialism. Given the sort of evolutionary narratives of native subjugation put to work by the chief justice in *Delgamuukw v. the Queen*, this authoritative cartographic revision demonstrates the tremendous political potential in the *Atlas*'s performative tracing of aboriginal routes.

One of the reasons why the final plate in the *Atlas* carries authoritative weight as a rebuttal to national narratives of extinguishment is that it establishes an aboriginal presence in the terms of a conventional nation-state cartography. Plate 69's title is "Native Canada, ca 1820," and as such it claims comprehensive coverage of "Native" movements from sea to sea. The plate, in other words, negotiates with the abstractions of the modern Canadian nation-state. This, I think, is what bestows so much authority on the resulting cartographic product, and yet it also comes at a cost. As Cole Harris, the volume's editor, made quite clear in his preface, such abstractions in the *Atlas* present an inevitably limited perspective.

> We have tried to accord full place to native peoples while knowing, in the end, that we have not succeeded in doing so. The archival record and the research based on it focus on people of European background. More than good will is required to penetrate an Indian realm glimpsed through white eyes.[91]

In relation to Plate 69 we might thus note that the vision of "Native Canada, ca 1820" could never have been glimpsed through the diverse native eyes of the time. The people so carefully placed on the map did not see this coherent vision. It is a post hoc and indeed abstract reconstruction based largely on European records. Certainly it is a *re*vision, insofar as prior atlases of Canada rarely marked any place, let alone such a "full place," for native peoples. But, as a revision that abstracts the heterogeneous diversity of native geographies into one comprehensive map, the plate returns us to what Bhabha calls "the question of social visibility, the power of the eye to naturalize the rhetoric of national affiliation and its forms of collective expression." Considered in these terms, the collective vision of the plate seems to preemptively nationalize what were, and what sometimes remain, the nonnational or, at least, non-Canadian realities of native life.[92] The map as a technology of vision does indeed seem to naturalize this nationalization, concealing its abstracting work even as it turns the diversity of native geographies into a unifying common denominator for the whole of the territory of what is now Canada.

One limit Plate 69 could not reasonably be expected to prevent concerns how, despite installing a native presence in the conclusion of volume 1 of the *Atlas,* it is in turn eclipsed by the virtual native absence from the last volume of the *Atlas.* The *Historical Atlas,* volume 3, subtitled "Addressing the Twentieth Century," seems to have shared little of the commitment declared by Harris to according full place to native peoples.[93] As a result, the three-volume series as a whole retains a teleology that practically banishes native people from the present. This teleology, then, would seem to illustrate Bhabha's argument about how national narratives turn "the People into One" through an interested historicism. The diverse geographies that evidence the disjunction of plural aboriginal peoples from the oneness of Canadian nationality are put away as a problem of the past. However, here I want to keep the focus on the question of spatial nationalization made manifest in Plate 69. Following Bhabha's point about visibility, but *contra* his repeated suggestion that space operates as the performative other of pedagogical time, such maps show how spatial representation can itself also function as a pedagogical means for turning multiple traditions into national territory.

Like Plate 69, the earlier maps of the "Prehistory" section accomplish the same abstraction of aboriginal geographies onto a collective national stage. As I argued above, it also recoded them as "immigrants" following the conventional narrative of Canada as a multicultural New World nation-state. The recoding worked, I argued, by imposing the abstract template of modern Canada on the supposedly prehistoric past. It is this pedagogical deployment of abstract state space that makes the maps of native cultures, along with those of the ice sheets and ecological regions, the only maps in the *Atlas* to actually depict the whole of the outline of modern Canada. Harris notes in the preface that "We have not imposed the current shape of Canada on northern North America before that shape existed."[94] Yet, while many maps like those depicting the "Indian War and American Invasion" (Plate 44) remain true to this principle, the "Prehistory" plates do not. In particular the forty-ninth parallel secretes its way into Plates 5 through 9 (that is, into the maps describing the historical geography from 6,000 BC to the time of European arrival), as well as into the map of cosmological artifacts (Plate 13). In all these maps, as Ged Martin notes, "the future United States can be treated as a kind of 'Here Dragons Be' (or, in the more tactful formula of Plate 5, 'More Southerly Plano people are not shown')."[95] Clearly this is partly a product of the nationally organized nature of the archeological research that went into these plates and is not just a classic Canadian case of defining the nation-state against the United States; however, the effect of the abstracting work accomplished by these plates is nonetheless to enframe the modern Canadian state through the disciplined objectification of native peoples as part of the nation's naturally non-American landscape. To recall Helgerson's arguments about the cartographic consolidation of the state of Elizabethan England, we might similarly note that the *Atlas* presentation seems thus to make a constructed native landscape speak of Canada as a unified, non-American nation-state.

Martin suggests that this proleptic cartography creates a teleology the development of which inches slowly back toward the claim in the preface that "[t]he country's southern boundary is not a geographical absurdity."[96] This point is well taken, but it misses the more Innisian focus of the preface on the specific historical geographies of *Europeans* in northern North America.

> As Innis maintained, the pattern of Canada has been taking shape for almost 500 years and by New World standards is old. . . . From the beginning of the European encounter with North America, developments in the north, which led to Canada, were different from those further south, which led to the United States. The country's southern boundary is not a geographical absurdity.[97]

It is the attempt in the *Atlas* to cartographically document this *European* pattern of distinction that presents a second and different example of the national-pedagogical deployment of spatial abstraction.

Like the plates that nationalize native life, the maps doing the enframing work around Canada's European heritage represent the results of detailed empirical inquiry. At the same time, they also present a counterpoint to Bhabha's celebration of location and space as narrative disruptions because they employ spatial abstraction in the service of a national narrative. But they do so in a more complex way than the pedagogic vision of naturalized and nationalized non-American natives. Unlike Plate 69, for example, which convenes diverse native historical geographies on one single map, the other, European-focused plates from which the reader might infer Canada's distinctiveness from the United States are themselves very heterogeneous, and not one presents a picture of the country as a whole. Instead, by rigorously charting Canada's evolving geographical diversity they contribute to a national narrative in which it is diversity itself that is turned into the grounds of national distinction (a form of distinction that chapter 4 examines in more detail and compares directly with American arguments about embodying diversity). Most notably, and contrary to the reviews of more critical Québécois readers, the *Atlas* went to great lengths to chart the specificities of French as well as English exploration and settlement in what became Canada. From an attention to the French participation in the Atlantic fisheries (Plates 22, 23, 24, 25, and 28), through the maps dedicated to the Acadian experience (Plate 29) and the inland exploration of the French as well as the English (Plates 36 to 41), to the whole section of the *Atlas* devoted to the resettling of the St. Lawrence, there is a scrupulous concern for the specificity of French as well as English experience in North America. Clearly, that specificity is presented as part of the historical geography of Canada. Its many interrelationships with the English colonial experience are charted, and the *Atlas* does not annex the historical geography of Québec to a separate volume. Obviously, therefore, there is a general unifying impulse involved in terms of what is contained by the covers. "Published in both official languages, the atlas attempts to reconcile the frequently divergent French and English histories of Canada" was the interpretation of the *Globe and Mail*'s reviewer.[98] But my point is that this overall work of reconciliation did not translate into any systematic disavowal of geographical genealogies leading back to France. Indeed, in addition to the detailed research into the seigneuries (Plate 51), the St. Lawrence countryside (Plates 52 and 53), and the development of Montréal and Québec City (Plates 49 and 50), the *Atlas* also contains a whole double page dedicated to mapping "The French Origins of the Canadian Population, 1608–1759" (Plate 45). The *Atlas*, then, is by no means a monological (or monolingual) national narrative turning territory into an English-only tradition. Instead, it is better described as a project of charting the diverse territories of a doubled, English and French, foundational tradition. The end result is still a narrative of nation, but it is one in which it is the *duality* and, beyond this, the geographic *diversity* of regionalization that is abstracted into the nationalist project of interstate comparison. It is in the process of this abstraction-through-comparison that Canada's delineation in terms of nonsingularity comes to enframe and thus to ensure its distinction from a homogenized United States.

As well as addressing the French interrelations with the historical geography of English colonialism in Canada, the *Atlas* also breaks with a monological narrative through the attention paid to everyday life that runs through many of the plates. The big battles and their heroes are still recorded (for example, Plate 42 on the Seven Years' War, and Plate 43 on the battles for Québec), yet they come alongside a studied survey of the more quotidian aspects of life in the towns and countryside, including one plate devoted solely to the styles of wooden house construction along the St. Lawrence (Plate 56). Rather than an ultranationalist fascination with folk life, I read these mappings of everyday life as a form of practical engagement with a more Braudelian, spatially sensitive approach to history. This, I think, is why it irritated some reviewers trained in the orthodoxies of traditional history and who perhaps wanted to see more about specific people and their connections to specific place-names and colonial crises. "[L]ess than 2% of the cartography is devoted to the benchmarks of Canada's history," complained one more orthodox reviewer, concluding that "[t]his atlas is many things, but it is not fittingly described as a historical atlas of Canada."[99] Here too, then, as the voices of the traditionalists themselves testify, the *Atlas* by no means collapses territory into tradition. What we see with the focus on everyday life, as with the attention to divergent European routes into and across the continent, is rather a repeated, empirically informed effort to document how multiple traditions were actually reflected in a heterogeneous and regionalized geography. It is only this resulting geography, itself emphasized by the regionally organized sections of the *Atlas,* that subsequently becomes the stuff of the national narrative signposted in the preface, the section introductions, and the various annotations to the plates. As I have shown, it was certainly read by Canadian commentators as a form of national pedagogy, but clearly it also departed from the bold preaching of tradition that Bhabha depicts as the pedagogical heart of national narratives in general.

The fact that the *Atlas* as a geographical narrative does not quite fit Bhabha's general model could perhaps be itself taken as testimony to Canada's distinction as a unique nation-state. The story of Canadian distinction being rooted in diverse routes and regions is certainly not new. At least since the 1960s and J. M. S. Careless's canonical discussion of the "limited identities" of Canada's region-alized archipelago, the notion of Canada as a mosaic rather than a melting pot has proved the resilient core of endless nation-narrating contrasts with the United States.[100] The United States, in this nar-rative, would seem to be far closer to Bhabha's model of monologi-cal pedagogy. However, considered in its own turn, even the Great Republic is sometimes hegemonically narrated as a more complex, regionalized hybrid.[101] Like the hybridity that Robert Young finds instrumentalized in the racist narratives of a multicultural Britain, these cases remind us that the heterogeneity in space that Bhabha finds so performatively counterhegemonic can also sometimes serve hegemonic, nation-state-building ends.[102]

A good example of this is the Braudelian tradition of French schol-arship on everyday life and space that I have already suggested as an intellectual precursor to the *Atlas*. This tradition can be traced in part back to the geographer Vidal de le Blache whose own interest in the regions making up the geography of France as nation has recently been linked in turn by Derek Gregory to Michelet's famous *Tableau de France: Géographie physique, politique et morale*.[103] Here, in this foundational text of modern French history-and-geography, the peda-gogical potential of nationalization through regionalization crystal-lized out in a romantic vision of the nation. The process, said a sarcas-tic Roland Barthes, could be summarized in the terms of a chemical turned culinary experiment.

> The Tableau of France itself, which is ordinarily presented as the an-cestor of geographies, is in fact the account of a chemical experiment: its enumeration of the provinces is less a description than a methodical list of the materials, the substances necessary to the chemical elabora-tion of French generality. One might say it is something like the no-menclature put at the head of a good recipe: take a little Champagne, a little Picardie, a little Normandie, Anjou, and Beauce, stir them around a central core, the Ile-de-France, steep them in this negative pole, and you will have the superlative nation of Europe: France.[104]

I am not saying the *Atlas* amounts to such a comic attempt to cook up a nation-state. However, there are certainly some similarities between its charting of Canada as the superlatively diverse nation of North America and the proleptic enframing of regions Gregory depicts as carrying over from Michelet into Vidal's less romantic nationalism.

> Vidal contains [the contradictions, struggles, and tensions of France's modernizing regions] by the imposition of a national frame that projects historicism onto a geographical canvas and thereby provides his narrative with its meaning and orientation. This enables him to describe the production of regions as the progressive realization of potentialities that were inscribed within what he takes to be the *essence* of France.[105]

It is just such a progressive realization of a national essence that I have suggested stems from the *Atlas*'s account of varied European routes across the land. Like Vidal's geographical nationalism, it contains rather than denies the ensuing struggles and contradictions, ultimately narrating them as the contradictory core of the nation-state.

DISSEMINATING CONCLUSIONS

My critical point about Bhabha's thesis should now be clear. If national pedagogy is always linked with the timing of historicism while performance is always affiliated with the disruptive putting in place of such traditional teaching, where is there room for a critical account of the nation-enframing effects of spatial abstraction? Such abstraction may have immediately obvious homogenizing effects as I suggested were to be found in both the chief justice's comments in the trial and in the nationalizing collective vision of "Native Canada, ca 1820" in the *Atlas*. Alternatively, it may follow a more complex trajectory through the Gitxsan and Wet'suwet'en negotiations in the trial and the cartographies of spatial heterogeneity put to work in interstate comparisons of Canada with the United States in the *Atlas*. Bhabha's account provided some purchase on how such mapping can lead to disruptive performances, but his argument seems to me to remain hard pressed to explain whether such displacement can actually achieve very much: whether it can be used as a lever for resistance by those marginalized in the modern nation-state; or whether it can be simply internalized by a more geographically open-ended yet still hegemonic narrative of nation. Where is resistance located exactly, who articulates it, and what are its limits if it is always already found in the locution of location? These questions seem unanswerable in the terms of Bhabha's "DissemiNation." They relate back, I think, to his inattention to the state and power relations more generally, and it is by reexamining these limits that I will conclude.

Derrida's famous work on "dissemination"—from which Bhabha's essay draws its title and analysis of performativity—begins by drawing attention to the disruptive supplementarity of prefaces.[106] Each time a preface supplements an original piece of work, argued Derrida, it implicitly questions the originality and universality of that work.[107] At a philosophical level, there is clearly considerable disruptive potential in such a formula, particularly when considered in relation to a philosopher like Hegel whose work began to depend on the idealism of thought thinking itself pure and undefiled by worldly concerns. Derrida's disruptive point was that Hegel's prefaces illustrate moments when the worldliness of his own writing caught up with his universalist idealism, betraying the contingency of its context. This seems to be a good example of the (con)textualizing ethos of Derrida's own work. However, in Bhabha's reworking of this argument there is a way in which the Derridean gesture of persistent responsibility to the heterogeneous is sacrificed to a paean to heterogeneity in the abstract. Bhabha's transposition is not direct or singular, of course; it is itself supplemented by a host of other writings including the work of Claude Lefort on ideology. It is in fact by supplementing Derrida with Lefort's account of how ideology splits the representation of the rule from its operation that Bhabha develops his own thesis about a national pedagogy supplemented by seemingly separate performances.[108] In the disavowed dependency indicated by such supplementation Bhabha locates the spaces of disruption. One example of this, I think, is the way in which the Gitxsan and Wet'suwet'en forced the federal and provincial governments to supplement their sweeping narrative of nation with a rethink of the disposition of time and space of sovereignty at the time of the Royal Proclamation. Likewise, the mapping of the beginning of Canada in the *Atlas* revealed the contingency of its origin story with detailed cartographies like that of the Coast Tsimshian performing a valuable critique of a nationalized prehistoric past. What the trial and the *Atlas* both show, though, is that an account that finds disruption in any and every performance can too quickly neglect the power relations perpetuating nation-state pedagogy and policing.

In the case of the trial the active policing of performance was clear. Despite all their efforts to disrupt the game by playing it—by inserting their claims into the terms of the dominant discourse—the Wet'suwet'en and Gitxsan were finally rebuked and lectured by an umpire-judge who dredged up most of the more offensive Hobbesian images of natives as primitive children in the process. His was a form of paternalistic national pedagogy that could persist through evident performative contradictions: claiming Crown ownership of territory in a federal Canadian state at one moment while even denying Crown knowledge of territory in the next. Throughout, however, the spatial abstractions of the modern state were assumed, and while the two First Nations mapped their own claims into the terms of this dominant discourse their resistance was recoded as inaccurate and ungeographical. The roaring map depicted by Monet seemed to be thereby recaged. If there was a contrapuntal aspect to the trial, therefore, it was a very strange and strained kind of music the record of which was marked by resistant roars in the midst of the solemn sounds of legal proceduralism.

The *Atlas* by comparison sustained many dissonant chords in the course of a larger anthemic opus. My point about its limitation was not that it drowned out such dissonance but rather that it orchestrated it into the overall nation-state effect. Readers are certainly obliged to confront the colonial boundaries of the nation, but this confrontation also seems to serve as a prelude to the play of difference that the *Atlas* proceeds to present as the symphony of the Canadian state's self-realization in space. The ultimate irony of the *Atlas* is that the more readers examine the detailed mapping of diverging routes across the land, the more a monolithic picture of the nation fades, and the better is the state enframed as distinct from a homogenized United States. This may not be superstructural national ideology of the sort Bhabha, following Lefort, repudiates, but it does, I think, come peculiarly close to the gestures of the "new ideology" outlined at the close of Lefort's own text. This new ideology, he argues,

> does without capital letters; pretends to propagate information, pretends even to question and probe. It does not hold the other at a distance, but includes its representative in itself; it presents itself as an incessant dialogue and thus takes hold of the gap between the self and the other in order to make room for both within itself.[109]

The *Atlas,* it must be countered, does more than pretend. It does question and probe. And yet as it does so, it also carves out what must also be acknowledged is both a hegemonic and pedagogic national place for both "the self and the other" in northern North America.

My overall point about Bhabha's thesis has not been to disavow its value, but rather to question how the jump from Derridean "Dissemination" to "DissemiNation" can lead to the disavowal of context and power relations, a disavowal that can in turn efface the larger set of spatial effects around which the avowed coherency of the nation-state is secured. Having argued this, I do not want to neglect what seems to be the obvious and ongoing relevance of Bhabha's argument about how "the very act of the narrative performance interpellates a growing circle of national subjects." One small example of this is the inter-interpellation of the two case studies I have been discussing: the way in which they ultimately came to speak to each other.

During the trial the question of the *Historical Atlas of Canada* did come up, albeit momentarily during the evaluation of an expert witness. The witness concerned was Robert Galois, a historical geographer who was testifying for the Gitxsan and Wet'suwet'en and who had contributed to a number of plates, including the final plate, of volume 1 of the *Atlas*. Ironically, because of Galois's position in the court, it was the nontraditional and geographical aspect of the *Atlas* as a record of history that was registered by the legal policemen of pedagogy. The issue was Galois's credibility as an expert witness on First Nations' history. Macaulay, the lawyer for the federal government, sought to discredit this expertise by arguing that Galois was not a real historian. To this, the lawyer for the plaintiffs replied saying, "My Lord, that's not accurate. He [Galois] gave evidence that he has contributed to the 'Historical Atlas of Canada' beginning in 1881 [sic]."[110] Macauley retorted, "That's not a history, that's a geography with some notes on it, with not very profound comments in it, insofar as I could have looked at that Historical Atlas."[111] Such, it seems, was the ambivalence of the *Atlas* that it could not pass muster according to the orthodox abstractions of the courtroom. Perhaps in this pedagogic failure we can also diagnose a performative success, an acknowledgment, albeit in the negative, that by charting the diversity of the beginning of Canada the *Atlas* challenged the nation's traditional historical rooting with a detailed geography of colonial routes and contacts.

I argued before that ultimately, in volume 3, the *Atlas* as a trilogy curtailed the continuation of the coverage of contact geographies

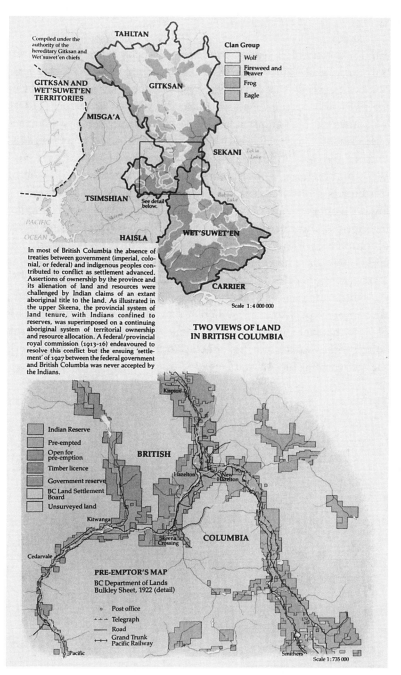

In most of British Columbia the absence of treaties between government (imperial, colonial, or federal) and indigenous peoples contributed to conflict as settlement advanced. Assertions of ownership by the province and its alienation of land and resources were challenged by Indian claims of an extant aboriginal title to the land. As illustrated in the upper Skeena, the provincial system of land tenure, with Indians confined to reserves, was superimposed on a continuing aboriginal system of territorial ownership and resource allocation. A federal/provincial royal commission (1913-16) endeavoured to resolve this conflict but the ensuing 'settlement' of 1927 between the federal government and British Columbia was never accepted by the Indians.

Compiled under the authority of the hereditary Gitksan and Wet'suwet'en chiefs

GITKSAN AND WET'SUWET'EN TERRITORIES

TAHLTAN

GITKSAN

MISGA'A

SEKANI

TSIMSHIAN See detail below.

HAISLA

WET'SUWET'EN

CARRIER

Clan Group

Wolf
Fireweed and Beaver
Frog
Eagle

Scale 1:4 000 000

TWO VIEWS OF LAND IN BRITISH COLUMBIA

PACIFIC OCEAN

Indian Reserve
Pre-empted
Open for pre-emption
Timber licence
Government reserve
BC Land Settlement Board
Unsurveyed land

BRITISH

COLUMBIA

Kispiox
Hazelton
New Hazelton
Kitwanga
Skeena Crossing
Cedarvale
Pacific
Smithers

PRE-EMPTOR'S MAP

BC Department of Lands
Bulkley Sheet, 1922 (detail)

○ Post office
⌐⌐⌐ Telegraph
——— Road
⊢⊢⊢ Grand Trunk Pacific Railway

Scale 1:735 000

Map 3. "Two Views of Land in British Columbia," from Donald Kerr and Deryck Holdsworth, eds., Historical Atlas of Canada. *Volume 3: Addressing the Twentieth Century, 1891–1961 (Toronto: University of Toronto Press, 1990). Reprinted by permission of University of Toronto Press.*

into the present. However, I could not say such geographies were totally banished because there is a moment of mapping in which a First Nations presence supplements the cartographic story of Canada in the twentieth century. Perhaps it should come as no surprise, after all I have argued about what the Gitxsan and Wet'suwet'en accomplished in the trial, that this splitting of the *Atlas*'s twentieth-century narrative address is forced by a map of the Gitxsan and Wet'suwet'en territories (Map 3). The plate invites a comparison of this First Nations' map with that of a colonial survey map thereby allowing readers to question the authority of the colonial cartographic inscription, and to consider the overwriting reterritorializing effect of national cartography more generally. The direct link to the trial, and the reason why volume 3 of the *Atlas* was supplemented in this way, was the work of Galois, who made the case for inclusion to the editors of volume 3. Beyond the individuals involved, though, we can perhaps also glimpse here a final disseminatory illustration of how the roaring cartography of the trial could burst out of the courtroom, roaring, in this contrapuntal case, into the anthem of the last verse of the *Atlas* it/self.

2

Reterritorializing Locality in Globality: Cascadia and the Landscaping of Cross-Border Regionalization

I have come to be convinced that the nation-state as a complex modern political form, is on its last legs. . . . The complexity of the current global economy has to do with certain fundamental disjunctures between economy, culture, and politics that we have only begun to theorize. I propose that an elementary framework for exploring such disjunctures is to look at the relationship among five dimensions of global cultural flows that can be termed (a) ethnoscapes, (b) mediascapes, (c) technoscapes, (d) financescapes, and (e) ideoscapes. The suffix -scape allows us to point to the fluid, irregular shapes of these landscapes, shapes that characterize international capital as deeply as they do international clothing styles.

—ARJUN APPADURAI, *MODERNITY AT LARGE*

While *Delgamuukw v. the Queen* illustrated how the hyphen in nation-state can be displaced by the struggle for statehood of subaltern nations, this chapter concerns instead the displacements sought by business elites eager to imagine new communities of capitalist belonging that can eclipse the boundaries of the hyphenated nation-state altogether. The case in question here has been called Cascadia by its promoters. They depict it as a vast cross-border region stretching across the forty-ninth parallel between the United States and Canada to include, in the most common mapping, all of British Columbia as well as the American states of Washington and Oregon. While Cascadia's promoters thereby arrogate into their region all of the territory contested in *Delgamuukw,* and while they also occasionally use native names in order to fashion some sort of prenational prehistory for their postnational development plans, their whole approach to naming and claiming the cross-border region has eschewed the formal forms of legal challenges taken up by the Wet'suwet'en and Gitxsan. Instead, the reterritorializing vision of Cascadia has been mainly pursued through economic and political channels in which the role of scrupulous cartographic history has been replaced by sweeping appeals to a future of burgeoning business opportunity. Inspirational in this regard, it seems, have been the bold arguments about the end of the nation-state issued by business gurus such as Kenichi Ohmae. "[T]he modern nation state," Ohmae famously argued, "has begun to crumble."

> Public debate may still be hostage to the outdated vocabulary of political borders, but the daily realities facing most people in the developed and developing worlds, both as citizens and consumers— speak a vastly different idiom. Theirs is a language of an increasingly borderless economy, a true marketplace. But the references we have—the maps and guides—to this new terrain are still largely drawn in political terms, . . . [and] in a borderless economy, the nation-focused maps we typically use to make sense of economic activity are woefully misleading. We must, managers and policy-makers alike, face up at last to the awkward and uncomfortable truth: the old cartography no longer works.[1]

Taking their imaginative cue from consultants such as Ohmae, the local governments, private think tanks, businesses, and chambers of commerce involved in promoting Cascadia have attempted in fact to suggest that, as a cross-border space with all kinds of cross-border synergies, the region actually embodies all the benefits of the borderless world. It follows, they have repeatedly suggested, that Cascadia is thereby poised for rapid development in a new world order of laissez-faire globalization. To some extent this vision of Cascadia represents just another local effort to attract inward investment and consumption spending, but from the late 1980s to the new millennium the consistent claim that the cross-border region embodies all the opportunities of borderless development has made it stand out as one of the more arrogant attempts globally to turn today's disjunctures of the nation-state into a place-promotional marketing scheme.

In order to come to terms with the production of Cascadia as a form of cross-border regionalization within globalization this chapter turns to the theoretical resources afforded by Arjun Appadurai's reflections on the disjunctive "landscapes" he sees as characterizing today's global cultural flows.[2] Appadurai's book-length treatment of these questions, *Modernity at Large: Cultural Dimensions of Globalization,* has been widely acclaimed, and is praised on the back cover by Sherry Ortner as "a work of sometimes dizzying brilliance." One of the main claims of the book is that electronic media and mass migration have now enabled the force fields of social and political imagination to cross borders and become radically transnationalized. While Appadurai is an anthropologist and cultural theorist, much of his account of these time-space-compressing force fields is filled with geographical references to space, locality, and context. Moreover, his attention to the "landscaping" of today's global flows would seem to offer exactly the kind of theoretical mapping of the "new world order" that Ohmae complains has been lacking in policy circles. Certainly, Appadurai is not afraid to throw away the old cartography of nation-focused maps. In this respect it should be noted that, like Ohmae, he announces many epitaphs to the nation-state in the course of his writing. While Appadurai is not at all a celebrant of deregulation, privatization, and free-market reforms, he does nonetheless share with Ohmae a certain optimism and excitement about the opportunities unleashed by the waning of the nation-state. Equally, while not championing (or even really discussing in any depth) transnational corporations and their space-spanning global webs, Appadurai also shares Ohmae's fascination with the supposedly borderless movements and postnational networks comprising globalization. For these reasons alone, his work speaks directly to the questions provoked by the production and promotion of a border-crossing region such as Cascadia. Furthermore, and in contrast to Ohmae's free-market boosterism, Appadurai approaches the problematic of "deterritorialization" with a cultural theorist's critical sensitivity to the power of imagination, image, and the media in the shaping of contemporary global flows. As well as bringing postcolonial concern with the power of colonizing epistemologies, and an area studies concern for the transnational impacts of migration, Appadurai's work is also distinguished by the particular attention he gives to the theme of *disjuncture.* Speaking of the breakup of the nation from state, he says that "the hyphen that links them is now less an icon of conjuncture than an index of disjuncture" (*Modernity,* 39). It is as an attempt to come to terms with the forces creating this disjuncture that Appadurai proposes his five "scapes": the ethnoscapes, mediascapes, technoscapes, financescapes, and ideoscapes that he argues are now themselves disjunctive one from another. These scapes are for Appadurai fundamentally about global flows, the flows of "people, machinery, money, images and ideas," and it is because these flows "now follow increasingly nonisomorphic paths" that they can in turn explain for Appadurai why the larger disjunctures between economy, culture, and politics can no longer be contained within the territorializing confines of the hyphenated nation-state (37).

It is Appadurai's sensitivity to the heterogeneity of disjuncture and the different modalities of postnational landscaping that makes his work so pertinent to this chapter's attempts to explain the multidimensional construction of Cascadia as a cross-border, postnational region. In fact, toward the end of his book, Appadurai even broaches the topic of postnational spaces, arguing that "transnational social forms may generate not only postnational yearnings but also actually existing postnational movements, organizations, and spaces" (177). Furthermore, he continues, in one of his more celebratory and sanguine segues, "[i]n these postnational spaces the incapacity of the nation-state to tolerate diversity . . . may perhaps be overcome" (177). More recently he has taken these already idealistic claims in a still more spatially utopian direction. "[O]ne positive force," he writes, "that encourages an emancipatory politics of globalization is the role of the imagination in social life. In particular, where the imagination as a social force itself works across national lines to produce locality as a spatial fact and sensibility, we see the beginnings of social forms without either the predatory mobility of unregulated capital or the predatory stability of many states."[3]

Exploring the production of Cascadia as a postnational "spatial fact" makes it possible to interrogate these sorts of idealistic claims. But, more than this, by bringing Appadurai's argument to bear on this very particular and spatialized example of postnational landscaping, this chapter also poses some searching questions about the cultural theorist's own more generally "deterritorialized" theorization and treatment of space. It is not that he ignores and obscures spatial themes and concepts altogether. Locality, landscape, context, and space are all frequently mentioned, and as such they would appear to evoke precisely the right balance of palpability and flexibility to provide his account with the combined forcefulness and generality it requires to make claims about modernity at large. And yet each time one of these spatial concept-metaphors is introduced by Appadurai, it is immediately deterritorialized and rendered aspatial. As a result, space seems at once present and absent in Appadurai's contexts, often evoked but rarely described as a material determinant of social action and imagination. Indeed, such is his inclination toward the themes and dynamics of deterritorialization that Appadurai's argument would seem to invoke space principally as a preliminary ahead of articulating its end. In this way geography is effectively presented as history, as always already history, an anemic geography of deterritorialization without reterritorialization.

Ironically Appadurai's style of anemic geography replays, at a theoretical level, a number of the more utilitarian but equally deterritorializing traits that comprise the landscaping of Cascadia by its business promoters. Borders, lines, and national territories are evoked again and again only to be all the more effectively dispatched into their discursive demise. Here, for example, is a typical millennial invocation of the region's raison d'être by Paul Schell (the onetime mayor of Seattle) and John Hamer (a fellow of the Discovery Institute, a conservative think tank based in Seattle and one of the leading institutional promoters of Cascadia on the U.S. side).

> The lines imposed over 100 years ago have simply been transcended by contemporary cultural and economic realities. . . . Cascadia is organizing itself around what will be the new realities of the next century—open borders, free trade, regional cooperation, and the instant transfer of information, money, and technology. The nineteenth- and twentieth-century realities of the nation-state, with guarded borders and nationalistic traditions, are giving way.[4]

It is the totemic power of these kinds of postnational appeals and borderless images with which Appadurai seems to try to come to terms. As we shall see, his attention to the deeply perspectival nature of the five flows-turned-scapes provides valuable purchase on the ways in which Cascadia's promoters imagine the region's future in these ways. In fact, in this regard Cascadia would seem to present especially poignant examples of Appadurai's argument "that the imagination in the postelectronic world plays a newly significant role" (5). Another, earlier statement about the *idea* of Cascadia by Schell and Hamer makes this very clear indeed.

> [Cascadia] is a shared notion, and one in active evolution. We're still inventing ourselves as a regional culture. Cascadia is a recognition of emerging realities, a way to celebrate commonality with diversity, a way to make the whole more than the sum of its parts. Cascadia is not a State, but a state of mind. But a state of mind can have important practical consequences.[5]

Not a State, but a state of mind with important practical consequences, Cascadia would thus seem to provide ample evidence underscoring Appadurai's argument about the newly transnationalized and materialized scope of the imagination in the context of globalization. Furthermore, it would also seem to illustrate his still more millennial claim that "[a]s the nation state enters a terminal crisis . . . the materials for a postnational imaginary must be around us already" (*Modernity,* 21). However, as Cascadia's promoters go about the business of imagining the future of their particular postnational construct, they also, in contrast to Appadurai, repeatedly imagine geographies for the region.

The geographical imaginations of Cascadia notably return to its supposedly natural landscape as a foundation for the various promotional ventures, and yet they relate to this landscape lightly and in passing, using it only when it suits to advance a particular kind of practical project of strategic partnering across the forty-ninth parallel. There are, as a result, a variety of different spatial scales at which Cascadia is mapped (see Map 4). At the smallest scale, the region is depicted as a "Corridor" for trade, high-tech development, and potentially a high-speed train between Vancouver, Seattle, and Portland. Wider mappings include all of the Canadian province of British Columbia and the U.S. states of Washington and Oregon. The most ambitious projects of all have been extended to include the whole of the so-called Pacific Northwest Economic Region, including Alaska, Alberta, Montana, and Idaho. Given the very variety of these mappings, it should be clear that they need to be seen as cartographic still shots of a much more dynamic, heterogeneous, and imaginative process of regional invention. Each instrumental map-

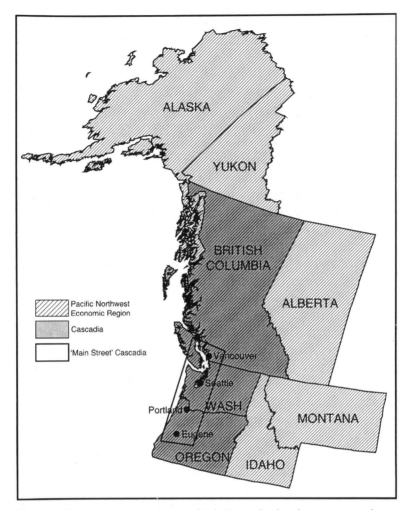

Map 4. The three main scales at which Cascadia has been imagined. Drawing by the author.

ping, taken on its own, represents only a thin and superficial geography of the region. But what nevertheless ties this whole project of Cascadian envisioning together is a repeated return to imagined geographies of reterritorialization, and it is precisely such attempts at advancing deterritorialization *through reterritorialization* that Appadurai's work leaves untheorized. In order then to demonstrate both the pertinence and limits of Appadurai's argument when applied to Cascadia, the main sections of this chapter examine the imagined geographies of Cascadian reterritorialization through the disjunctive rubrics of ethnoscapes, mediascapes, technoscapes, financescapes, and ideoscapes. Reversing the order of Appadurai's own argument, my account begins with the ideoscaping of the cross-border region and ends with the complex theme of Cascadia's ethnoscaping.

Other sympathetic readers of Appadurai's work have sought to supplement his five scapes with additions. The sociologist Martin Albrow, for example, questions the juxtaposition of the movement of tourists, refugees, and immigrants comprising Appadurai's ethnoscapes with what the argument suggests are the relatively stable communities through which the diasporas and travelers pass. "How stable," asks Albrow, "are these 'relative stabilities' and from the perspective of participants are they not equally 'scapes'?"[6] Answering his own question in the affirmative, Albrow argues that the five scapes presented by Appadurai need therefore to be supplemented by a sixth, which, predictably enough as a sociologist, he dubs "socioscapes." My own critical strategy is also supplementary, but while many other kinds of scape could clearly be conceptualized and added to the schema—enviroscapes, healthscapes, laborscapes, queerscapes, and protestscapes all come to mind—the strategy of supplementation I am taking here is, as in the rest of the book, geographical. Taking each mode of landscaping Cascadia at a time, I show how in each case the attempts to advance the project of cross-border *deterritorialization* operate through the geographical imagination of Cascadian *reterritorialization*. In each case I underline the utility of Appadurai's argument, but in each case too I highlight what it elides in terms of the production of locality in globality. To prepare the way for these main sections, and in order to do justice to the complex postdisciplinary scope of Appadurai's own project, a shorter theoretical section follows that addresses his approach to space in more detail.

APPADURAI IN SPACE

There is a profound ambivalence defining Appadurai's treatment of space. While most of the time he describes each scape as a flow, he does not shy away from activating the concept-metaphor's appeal to the more spatial connotations of landscape and the related notions of mapping and navigating one's way through space. "Indeed," he says, using the language of landscapes as a shorthand for the five scapes, "the individual actor is the last locus of this perspectival set of landscapes, for these landscapes are eventually navigated by agents who both experience and constitute larger formations, in part from their own sense of what these landscapes offer" (33). However, in these very moments when he would seem to be injecting the problematics of geography and the production of space into the heart of his argument, Appadurai immediately pulls back, reducing spatiality to the work of the imagination, accounting for it in terms of just the flux of the disjunctive flows, and thereby effectively essentializing the narrative of deterritorialization. It is in this way that he later goes on to argue after Deleuze and Guattari that

> The world we live in now seems rhizomic, even schizophrenic, calling for theories of rootlessness, alienation, and psychological distances between individuals and groups on the one hand, and fantasies (or nightmares) of electronic propinquity on the other. (33)

It is "here," concludes Appadurai that "we are close to the central problematic of cultural processes in today's world" (29).

Appadurai's "here" is not only deterritorialized in the more psychic senses outlined by Deleuze and Guattari.[7] It is also a "here" (as well as at once a "there") where territory in the more political and economic sense of the space of national sovereignty is also imagined to be at an end.

> In a world of people on the move, of global commoditization and states incapable of delivering basic rights even to their majority ethnic populations, territorial sovereignty is an increasingly difficult justification for those nation-states that are increasingly dependent on foreign labor, expertise, arms, or soldiers. (21)

To some extent Appadurai's eagerness to announce this end of the territorial nation-state can be traced to his profound concern with the ethnic absolutism that is so often proclaimed and defended in the name of nationalism. Later in the book he notes thus that the nation serves "[a]s an ideological alibi for the territorial state, it is the last refuge of ethnic totalitarianism" (159). Territorialized spaces, when seen from this perspective, would therefore appear to be produced only by closed minds and totalizing ethnicist imaginations of identity. Elsewhere through much of the book Appadurai seems to be of the view that spaces more generally are formed through the work of the imagination. It is in this strangely individualizing way that he further qualifies his initial account of the disjunctive scapes, noting that "these various flows [comprise] landscapes, from the stabilizing perspectives of any given imagined world" (46). In such moments Appadurai does allow for a certain sort of territorialization, but given his global and somewhat decontextualizing treatment of imagination at large, these moments are quickly superceded again by the metanarrative of deterritorialization. Thus we read that "[t]he link between the imagination and social life"—the very stabilizing force Appadurai purports to be the foundation of particular landscapes— "is increasingly a global and deterritorialized one" (55).

Appadurai does try himself to come to explicit terms with the ambivalence with which he treats space. As he introduces the disciplinary and academic milieu out of which he came to write the book, he notes vis-à-vis his use of Indian examples that he is "aware of the irony (even the contradiction) in having a nation-state be the anchoring referent of a book devoted to globalization and animated by a sense of the end of the era of the nation state" (18). Quite how much his actual treatment of Indian cricket and the colonial census constitutes an "anchoring referent" is another matter, but with these kinds of comments he does invoke a connection to area studies and to South Asian studies in particular as some sort of personal corrective to the "megalomania" he justly ascribes to abstract accounts of globalization. It is in this way too that he also applauds area studies as having "provided the major counterpoint to the delusions of the view from nowhere that underwrites much canonical social science" (16). However, almost in the same moment that he appeals thus to disciplinary traditions as a way of countering aspatial abstraction, Appadurai immediately begins to distance himself from the traditions' spatializing tendencies, arguing in particular that the way "anthropology and area studies predispose me by habit to the fixing of practices, spaces, and countries into a map of static differences" constitutes a "danger" from which his concern with diaspora and deterritorialization must necessarily take flight (18).

Clearly informing Appadurai's sense of danger are the valuable critiques—now well established in anthropology and growing in area studies—of the orientalist or otherwise containerizing and museumizing approaches Western academics have taken to mapping and packaging accounts of "the other." Elsewhere, he has further explained in this regard that "[a]s social scientists concerned with localities, circulation and comparison, we need to make a decisive shift away from what we may call 'trait' geographies to what we could call 'process' geographies" (232). It is partly as a way of attempting to make this shift, then, that Appadurai is so keen to be done with conjunctive concepts of territory. But, as he moves from this epistemological register to making bolder, more material claims about the nature of the globalized world, this same avoidance strategy turns into a more audacious ontology about the end of the nation-state in the context of deterritorialization. As Aiwha Ong, another anthropologist keenly attuned to the dangers of epistemic violence, points out, these reactive paeans to deterritorialization in the book end up obscuring as much about the power relations of the present as they make manifest. Appadurai, she concludes,

> ignores the fact that nations and states are still largely bound to each other, and he ignores the need to consider how the hyphen between the two has become reconfigured by capital mobility and migration. What are the structural tensions between a territorially based nation and a "deterritorialized" one?[8]

It is presumably as an attempt to answer questions about the localized reconfiguration of the hyphen in nation-state that the last chapter of *Modernity at Large* turns to theorize a process geography of the "production of locality." As he begins this final account of locality there is at least the promise of some relief from the metanarrative of deterritorialization, not least of all because he claims at the start of his argument that it is informed by Henri Lefebvre's geohistorical theses about the production of space. But it quickly becomes clear that Appadurai's "locality" is as thoroughly despatialized as his "territory." "I view locality," he says,

> as primarily relational and contextual rather than as scalar or spatial. I see it as a complex phenomenological quality, constituted by a series of links between the sense of social immediacy, the technologies of interactivity, and the relativity of contexts. (178)

Worried perhaps by the degree to which this formulation of locality as a structure of feeling deterritorializes space, he then introduces a supplementary term, "neighborhood," to refer "to the actually existing forms in which locality, as a dimension or value, is variously lived" (179). He further explains in a footnote that "[t]his sense of neighborhood can also accommodate images such as circuit and border zone" (204), which might make it seem especially appropriate to a localized transborder space such as Cascadia. However, just as with his landscapes stabilized by the particularities of discrete imagined worlds, and just as with locality transmuted into a complex phenomenological quality, so too does neighborhood ultimately fall prey to the deterritorializing gesture, as the notion of "virtual neighborhoods, no longer bounded by territory" (195) comes to dominate his discussion. Thus at the very close of the book locality comes to be defined more or less as a deterritorialized "structure of feeling" incompletely held together against the forces of dispersal and disjunction.

If Appadurai offers a process geography, then, it is one where the only processes allowed to be determinative are cultural ones concerning the flux of feelings. The overdetermining and equally dynamic processes of economic and political geographies thereby become occulted by his overweening account of the imagination. The arguments too quickly dodge the detailed material questions surrounding who precisely is enabled and who, by contrast, suffers as a consequence of all the deterritorializing dynamics. Even among the transnational migrants that form the core of his focus, Appadurai does not do much to distinguish between the transnationals moved to become refugees by violence and those who move in elite circles of wealth and privilege. Nor does he address the inequalities shaping the ability of these diversely positioned transnationals to consume the media products that connect them with the people and places they have left.[9] Instead, we are simply told that "where there is consumption there is pleasure, and where there is pleasure there is agency." Appadurai adds to this neoliberal claim a caveat to the effect that "Freedom, on the other hand, is a rather more elusive commodity" (7). But given that even freedom here is reduced to the commodity form, we are left with a profoundly market-based notion of political action that ironically ends up obscuring the violence of global capitalism as it embraces its metaphors. To cite Ong again, the result is an analysis that "ignores the political economy of time-space compression and gives the misleading impression that everyone can take equal advantage of mobility and modern communications and that transnationality has been liberatory, in both a spatial and a political sense, for all peoples." Against these universalizing tendencies, Ong concludes that "the analysis cries out for a sense of political economy and situated ethnography."[10]

It is a sensitivity to the situated dynamics of political-economic development that underpins my own approach to the disjunctive landscaping of Cascadia in what follows. But lest it seem that my own critique of Appadurai's deterritorialization metanarrative is reactively localist and descriptivist, I should emphasize that I wholly concur with his call to examine the production of locality *in* globality. His more recent argument to this effect seems especially cogent: viz "that the principal challenge that faces the study of regions and areas is that actors in different regions now have elaborate interests and capabilities in constructing world pictures whose very interaction affects global processes" (236). This is exactly what the development of Cascadia illustrates as the promoters go about the business of marketing the cross-border region in global circuits of investment and consumption.[11] Having noted this, though, it should still be remembered that Appadurai's account is offered as a more general statement about the scope of modernity at large. It is at this level, where the spatial concept-metaphors still fly fast and where "context" is repeatedly invoked only to be radically decontextualized, that I think his argument falls short. Ultimately, this leaves Appadurai unable to offer an adequate answer to his initial and important question: "what can locality mean in a world where spatial localization, quotidian interaction, and social scale are not always isomorphic?" (179). It is as a substantive attempt to answer this very question that the following sections seek to come to terms with the production of Cascadia as a disjunctive form of locality in globality.

IDEOSCAPING CASCADIA: CO-OPTING ECOPOLITICS
INTO THE ECONOMICS OF GLOBALIZATION

For Appadurai ideoscapes fundamentally concern the global movement and mediation of key political and ideological principles. They are

> concatenations of images [. . . that] are often directly political and frequently have to do with the ideologies of states and the counter ideologies of movements explicitly oriented to capturing state power or a piece of it. These ideoscapes are composed of elements of the

Enlightenment worldview, which consists of a chain of ideas, terms
and images, including *freedom, welfare, rights, sovereignty, representation,* and the master term *democracy.* (36)

The questions he is most keen to address in this way surround how
principles such as democracy and freedom are radically renegotiated
and reworked as they become articulated in new contexts or rearticulated in old contexts shaped by new flows of media images, capital,
and information. Context becomes centrally important in this regard,
of course, and it is in this way that Appadurai notes that "[t]he very
relationship of reading to hearing and seeing may vary in important
ways that determine the morphology of these different ideoscapes as
they shape themselves in different national and transnational contexts" (37). Such sensitivity to context notwithstanding, Appadurai
nevertheless does not engage here with the actual production of new
spatial contexts through the interactions of different ideoscapes and
engages less still with the ways contexts thus formed become determinative of further interactions. It is exactly this recursive and agonistic
production of context that is brought into focus by the ideoscaping of
Cascadia as a postnational reterritorialization of regional space.

As a postnational space conceived in terms of Ohmae's new "region-
states," Cascadia reflects more than anything else the transnational
potency of neoliberal ideology and the power of this ideology to
transform the meanings of concepts like freedom and democracy.
Developed in the context of North American free trade, imagined as
a borderless gateway on the Pacific Rim, and repeatedly represented
as a free west of high-tech business development unfettered from
east coast government, Cascadia is held up by its promoters as an
embodiment of the very best the free market has to offer. In his book
The End of the Nation-State, Ohmae himself only lists the U.S.
Pacific Northwest on his table of new region-states and therefore
does not present the region as transnational.[12] But for Cascadia's
promoters concerned with ideoscaping the region's border-spanning
scope, this has not stopped them from repeatedly reusing Ohmae's
argument that "[region-states] make such effective ports of entry
into the global economy because the very characteristics that define
them are shaped by the demands of that economy."[13] Thus to recall
again the quotation from Paul Schell and John Hamer, Cascadia is
said to be "organizing itself around what will be the new realities

of the next century—open borders, free trade, regional cooperation, and the instant transfer of information, money and technology." The promoters of Cascadia speculate in these terms that by virtue of being created as a borderless market in the very image of free trade, the region is destined for a privileged future of wealth and growth precisely because of its capacity to internalize the liberalized logic of the global marketplace. In this way too, the region's border-transcending position on the Pacific Rim is also interpreted as site for a grand neoliberal experiment in transforming the meaning of the very elemental keywords listed by Appadurai. Thus, freedom, welfare, rights, sovereignty, representation, and even democracy all have their neoliberal Cascadian resonances. However, ideoscaped as a *region*, Cascadia also illustrates the complicated ways in which this kind of production of locality in globality is also profoundly predicated on a sense of place and a related reterritorialization of space. The glossy appeals to Cascadia enable the promoters to side-step presenting clear-cut legal and political positions while entrenching neoliberal policy goals in the postnational landscape. For this reason we need to consider more closely the ways in which Cascadia as an ideoscape of natural history has been put to work in advancing a neoliberal natural future for the region, a natural future that, in turn, is imagined as a form of laissez-faire utopia where freedom, welfare, rights, sovereignty, representation, and democracy can all be rearticulated in terms of the free market.

The natural history roots of Cascadia go back to an earlier eco-topian vision of the cross-border region defined by the ecology of the Cascade mountains and their cascading waters, rainforests, and salmon. Within this polity bioregionalists envisaged a population of inhabitants that might one day live in harmony with the integrated cross-border ecosystem. Initially, as it was evoked as the site of environmentalist resistance in Ernest Callenbach's book *Ecotopia,* this vision only linked northern California with Oregon and Washington and was not transnational.[14] Later, with the publication of Joel Garreau's *The Nine Nations of North America,* a less literary and less politicized ecotopia became border-crossing in scope, stretching from Monterrey through western Canada to Alaska.[15] Subsequently, during the 1980s, this sweeping transnational region was painstakingly redrawn by Seattle-based bioregionalist David McCloskey who produced maps of a more ecologically grounded transnational region based on the watersheds of the Cascade mountains and their cascading rivers (see Map 5).[16] These relatively autonomous environmentalist imaginings of the region continue to spur both interest and activism. New bioregional visions are still produced too: there is ongoing discussion of plans to create a North Cascades cross-border international park; there are active transboundary environmentalist campaigns by groups such as The Georgia Strait Alliance and The People for Puget Sound; and there are a number of environmentalist Web sites such as *Cascadia Planet* devoted to the bioregional vision and its ecocentric politics.[17] However, it is these same ecological

CASCADIA

a great green land
on the northeast Pacific Rim

Map 5. "Cascadia: A Great Green Land." Reprinted by permission of David McCloskey.

roots that have also been rerouted into the *routes* to ports, gateways, and the promise of prosperity by the more recent promoters. As William Henkel noted in an early critique of the more business-oriented Cascadian constructions, the *eco-logics* of the bioregional visions were thus effectively appropriated into the *eco-nomics* of the neoliberal Cascadia. "It is strange," remarked Henkel with irony, "when fiscal conservatives start employing the language and labels once used by a dispersed group of radical bioregionalists, but if crossing the border is the goal, an evocative symbol like Cascadia may well be the ideal Trojan Horse."[18]

Once the contradictions between the ecological and economic visions of Cascadia are brought into view, it is easier to examine the ways in which the ideoscaping of the latter relates to the former. Most obviously, the economic promoters have seen great advantage in the border-crossing scope of the ecologically defined region. Using the same regional template, they nevertheless radically rearticulate its meaning. Bioregionalists like McCloskey see in the transboundary space a harmonious ecosystem that needs to be liberated from the disciplinary apparatus of two industrial nation-states and the "unnatural" boundary line (and associated pesticide use along the line) dividing them.[19] The promoters of the economic vision likewise see a harmonious region unnaturally divided by the border and a history of two sovereign governments, but for them, of course, the natural system crying out for liberation is the free market. This, for example, is the argument of two Canadian economists who, as they imagine the hidden harmony of Cascadian common interests, slip easily between the registers of economic and ecological nature.

> The national and state borders that cross the land between the Arctic Ocean and Oregon are simply political artifacts, hiding a harmony of interest and opportunities that makes Cascadia as meaningful an economic entity as California. Indeed, this region has much that is the envy of California including untapped water, bountiful power and room to breathe. As borders come down with free trade, the prospects for Cascadia are as endless as its magnificent shorelines on two great oceans, and its folding mountains stretching from the Pacific to the Plains.[20]

Much of these economists' actual argument is taken up with charting economies of scope and scale in the region, a process that is equally perspectival and to which I turn in the next section on financescapes.

Here, instead, my focus is on how this appeal to the hidden harmony of Cascadian nature takes more than just a naturalization of postnational space from the ecotopians. In addition, the promoters' ideoscapes just as often emphasize decentralization and freedom from faraway federal governments, emphases that also run through the bioregional literature and its calls for ecocentric governance. Predictably, however, the economic call for decentralized governance rearticulates the notion of freedom and local sovereignty in strictly neoliberal terms as freedom from government regulations, bureaucracy, and federal interference in local business. Bruce Agnew, for example, the director of the Cascadia Project at the Discovery Institute, puts it like this: "We are finding borders and national government policies increasingly irrelevant and even crippling."[21] In the same way, Alan Artibise, the founder of the Vancouver-based Cascadia Institute, argues that one of the visions that "Cascadians share" is a "certain bemused antipathy toward the two national capitals."[22] Or again, in the blunter words of David Johnson, U.S. Consul to Vancouver and a participant in some of the early 1990s meetings on Cascadian cooperation, the claim is that "[t]his area is unified by a common hatred of their central governments."[23] As a corollary, then, to the suggestion that Cascadia's eclipse of the forty-ninth parallel enables it to internalize and thereby capitalize on the benefits of free trade, this argument asserts that because British Columbia, Washington, and Oregon have all shared a supposedly similar experience of historical alienation from faraway federal capitals they are all also inclined toward a distrust of big government.

Broader arguments about the positioning of Cascadia equally reveal connected commonalities and contrasts between the economic and ecological ideoscapes of the region. In both visions Cascadia is viewed as a central place and meeting point, but for bioregionalists such as McCloskey this is a middle ground defined primarily by mental maps of the local ecology and its ancient history. "In this flying arc of landscapes," he says, "you can feel tremendous forces working, a tension or torque of powers in the sky above and the earth below, a curve of binding energy revealed in the shape of Cascadia herself."[24] The promoters, it appears, also feel an elemental energy in the land, but for them it is produced predictably enough from what James Gardner refers to as "The Competitive Advantage" of Cascadia's middle-ground position. According to Gardner:

[W]e are beginning to visualize the globe without the impediments of nationalistic blinders—and with the Northwest nicely centered between Europe and East Asia. From this perspective our verdant Cascadia does not only cling precariously to a distant shore of North America but instead occupies the epicenter of the interlinked global economy, midway between Brussels and Tokyo—the incontestable geographic heart of the mighty Asian-American-European economic triad.[25]

Here, clearly, the binding energy pumping through the heart that is "verdant Cascadia" is global capital. But it remains remarkable, all the same, that this imagined geography of the middle ground can be used so flexibly to articulate a neoliberal rationale for the region and its competitive advantage in the global economy. Such, it seems, is the potency of an ideoscape that is fundamentally predicated on a reterritorialized conception of locality in globality.

Other themes and gestures also link and divide the economic ideoscaping of the region from the ecological. While as a bioregionalist McCloskey expresses distrust of national government, this has not stopped him from fashioning a flag—that most banal symbol of national imagining—for Cascadia. Not to be outdone, perhaps, the business boosters have also created a Cascadian flag as part of their project of branding the region. Charles Kelly, the Canadian publisher of the now defunct promotional organ *The New Pacific,* ran a flag competition in the magazine, offering a $2,000 prize for the winning design. However, the uses this flag has now been put to have shared little with the local circulation of McCloskey's flag as a backpack and bumper sticker. Most notably the *New Pacific* Cascadian flag has done service as a banner above a booth for small "Cascadian" software firms at the Las Vegas Comdex show. Hardly the stuff of regional separatism, this is also not a typical nationalist use either. For the promoters the flag was never meant to fly above government buildings or become part of an official seal. Indeed, Kelly has written with a clear sense of the bioregionalists in the rearview mirror that "My view used to be that a regional flag posed the double danger of being hijacked by some looney separatist fringe group which sees Cascadia as a new nation, or become a rallying point for those who oppose economic integration. I do not hold those views anymore. What I have witnessed is a maturity and growth of enlightened self interest among business and political leaders."[26] For Kelly

such maturity clearly involves connecting the themes of decentralization and deregulation with the neoliberal critique of national government bureaucracy. "We're not talking about political union here," he
told one reporter; "we both have capitals 3,000 miles away that don't
consider our interests a priority."[27] Artibise, one of the more academic voices promoting Cascadia, also comes to the same neoliberal
conclusion, citing the Discovery Institute to the effect that "there is no
desire to unify the region politically, nor to homogenize the historic
cultures of either Canada or the US. What inspires is not a marriage,
but a partnership—the result of strengthening friendship, economic
and environmental ties."[28]

Artibise's claim about partnership is of further note for the way
it closes with another easy segue from the notion of economic partnering across the border to the topic of environmental ties. In this
and his many other essays about Cascadia, Artibise is able thus to
use his expertise as a scholar of planning and Canadian urban history to advance yet another nuance in the economic appropriation of
the ecological ideoscape.[29] It is a nuance expressed in the language
of "sustainable development," two weasel words that have been
transformed the world over from the liberal environmental security
themes of the Bruntland Report into a rhetorical cover for sustaining neoliberal business as usual.[30] As David Harvey notes in his
critique of sustainability rhetoric, the words can be rendered entirely
harmless to the process of capital accumulation by providing businesses with a patina of green PR. "No one, after all," notes Harvey,
"can be in favor of 'unsustainability.'"[31] It is this same hard-to-
oppose greenery that Artibise brings to the business of cross-border
regional boosterism. "Opportunities for Achieving Sustainability in
Cascadia" is a typical title of one of his essays on the subject, a title
that effectively abstracts away from the difficult questions concerning *what is to be sustained* all the while that it presents Cascadia as
an already existing object of planning and opportunity. Notably,
Artibise's rationale for the sustainable development of Cascadia replays not just the ecological thematics but also the localism and the
sense of local limits to growth articulated by the bioregionalists. Yet,
while for the ecotopians it is the particularity of the regional ecology
that inspires a localist pride, and while the resulting exclusivism is
aimed largely at the depredations of transnational capitalism, for
Artibise and the other promoters of sustainability in Cascadia the

problems stem from too much in-migration to the region and the solution lies in managed growth. In this way, Artibise reuses one of the paradigmatic ideological achievements of documents like the Bruntland Report to ideoscape Cascadia.

As Harvey points out, the foundational documents of global sustainability invoked the supposedly immutable laws and limits imposed by nature in such a way as to leave unquestioned the far more mutable laws and limits of capitalism and elite-class interest.[32] It is precisely the same trick that Artibise performs at the local level through an elaborate three-step that moves from an ecotopian-styled eulogy to the precious local landscape, to warnings about the risk posed by rapid urban growth, to an articulation of the managed growth, sustainability solution. First comes the spectacularization of the region's nature as unbounded and borderless:

> The Cascadia Region offers a spectacular array of natural and built environments, with wilderness coexisting in relative harmony with sophisticated urban centres. Its geography has few boundaries.[33]

Then there is the outline of a warning.

> The Region is increasingly attracting attention, for the quality of life and relative prosperity it offers. As a result, in-migration from other parts of North America and overseas is contributing to rapid urban growth.[34]

And then we come to the remarkable conclusion that, without even missing a beat, links a solution of "sustainability" back to the project of cross-border integration and economic development.

> As leaders throughout the Region increasingly interact across the border, their common interests become apparent and alliances begin to form. The main issues which drive this cooperation relate to sustainability and rapid urban growth, transportation, trade, tourism and economic development.[35]

Artibise's arguments bring the construction of Cascadia back full circle to the original ecotopian vision of the region. However, by the time this vision is rearticulated in the language of sustainability, the bioregional ideoscape has been washed away in a cascading set of arguments, questions, and planning initiatives that recenter projects of economic development through trade, transportation, and tourism. Key questions for Artibise then become

What is required to manage growth throughout the Region in the short term, and to establish mechanisms for managing the doubling of the Region's population over the next 20 years? . . .
What is the impact of regulatory and transportation constraints on current cross-border investment, trade and tourism, and what measures are required to fix these problems and plan for future growth? . . .
What are the sectors which offer opportunities for partnerships, supplier contracts, venture capital investment, and what are the mechanisms which could facilitate their achievement?[36]

Although I am only citing a few of the many planning questions listed by Artibise, the general flow of the argument from growth management to economic development is quite clear. Holding it together and creating its overarching premise is a basic appeal to the logic of cross-border reterritorialization. Other promoters turn to Ohmae as an authority for this premise, but for Artibise the reterritorialization imperatives are as natural as the roots turned routes of Cascadia itself. Blurring the ecology-economy distinction once again he thus writes that "[a]s nations have responded to the restructuring of the global economy, natural regional alliances have been stimulated."[37] It is this naturalization of reterritorialization that enables Artibise to make the argument for cross-border cooperation, and it is this argument that in turn serves for him and many other promoters as the preface to the project of promoting Cascadia in global circuits of investment and consumption. Presumably this end result is not the kind of postnational space in which Appadurai places his high hopes for a future free from the "predatory mobility of unregulated capital." If it is, then he and others will be sorely disappointed because the resulting reterritorialization of cross-border space has done more than allow the ideoscape of neoliberalism to win out over that of bioregionalism. Additionally, it has led to many more detailed proposals about how to finance and advance the interests of Cascadia as a locality amid global flows of predatory capital. In the next section, I turn to these more particular promotional projects through which the boosters of Cascadia have sought to explain the financial rationale for cross-border integration.

FINANCESCAPING CASCADIA: ENTREPRENEURIAL ENVISIONING AND COMPETITIVE POSITIONING

For Appadurai, financescapes are all about the destabilization wrought by the flows of global capital. "Thus," he says, it is useful to speak as well of *financescapes,* as the disposition of global capital is now a more mysterious, rapid and difficult landscape to follow than ever before, as currency markets, national stock exchanges, and commodity speculations move megamonies through national turnstiles at blinding speed, with vast, absolute implications for small differences in percentage points and time units. (*Modernity,* 34–35)

For him, it is the disjunctive quality of these flows vis-à-vis the movements of people and existing national governance structures that is of most note. As a result of such disjuncture not only is national sovereignty challenged fiscally, Appadurai argues it is also challenged politically and culturally as migrants and cultural commodities with their own autonomous financial backing create new ruptures in the meanings of citizenship and cultural belonging. I agree that these disjunctures and disruptions are profound. Indeed, it is arguable that the implications of deregulated global financial flows threaten far more instability than Appadurai even allows. The long-term stability of today's complex markets in currencies, bonds, equities, and derivatives seems highly questionable, and while they effectively contain and project present-day overaccumulation crises into a speculative future, that same future appears more and more like a bubble destined to burst (see chapter 5). But this crisis theory argument aside, another question that Appadurai leaves begging, even as he notes the impact of financescapes on the meaning of time, is their impact on space and place. Following my argument about the ideoscapes of reterritorialization, I argue in this section that the case of Cascadia also reveals how the production of locality in globality is profoundly linked with financescapes of reterritorialization. A crucial theoretical building block in this regard is the work of Harvey and other Marxist geographers on the interconnections between the circuits of finance capitalism and the production of space.[38]

Harvey famously argued in his treatise on *The Limits to Capital* that crises of overaccumulation in the production circuit of capitalism can be managed (albeit temporarily) through being financially rechanneled into various kinds of spatial fixes ranging from imperialism on the global stage to various redevelopment and urban renewal projects at more local and regional levels.[39] These spatial fixes, Harvey noted, effectively absorbed overcapacity by providing new economic opportunities for investment and speculation as well as often culturally and politically providing arenas for reestablishing elite authority. According to this argument, finance capitalism broadly understood creates a world wherein old spaces can be rescaled and refashioned, indeed where they *have* to be rescaled and refashioned, for the sake of financial stability and new rounds of interregional competition. In this way, new development strategies quite literally "take" place—remake it, remap it, and market it—in a global space of financial flows that is also a space of places.

Harvey's own historical work on the Hausmannization of Paris showed in great detail that the processes through which crises in the sphere of production were moved financially into the remaking of the built environment were highly mediated.[40] All kinds of political, cultural, and ideological dynamics came into play in the production, promotion, and management of the new spaces. No simple algorithm linking economic cause with spatial effect could therefore be used to explain the emergence of the resulting landscapes. The mediations were too complex and too interarticulated to admit such economistic accounts. In the case of mid-nineteenth-century Paris, the mediating dynamics ranged from the role of the state, the military, and the church to the painting and literature of modern urban life. In the case of late twentieth-century cities and regions, Harvey has suggested a quite different set of political and ideological mediations apply: mediations between the worlds of finance and the production of space that reflect the decline of the nationalized political economic regimes of mid-twentieth-century Fordism. Specifically, Harvey argued in 1985 that the new development strategies increasingly being explored by leaders of urban regions represented politically mediated attempts to answer the question: "How could urban regions blessed largely with a demand-side heritage adapt to a supply-side world?"[41] The hegemonic answer, he argued, came in four parts. Urban regions were obliged to compete in four spheres of ever more *international* competition for capital: first, the competition for a preferable position in the international division of labor (often amounting to competition for global investment capital); second, the competition for position in the global division of consumption; third, the competition for attracting key financial and governmental control functions; and fourth, the competition for a share of redistribution capital through both informal (e.g., charities) and formal (e.g., military spending) systems of transfer. Later, in 1989, Harvey further developed this argument, suggesting that the emerging regimes of urban and regional development that were premised on these competitive imperatives comprised a pattern of "entrepreneurial governance."[42] This pattern, he argued, looked set to become an increasingly dominant style of urban development in a world of neoliberal cutbacks, decentralization, and deregulation.

The neoliberal ideoscape of Cascadia would seem to represent a particularly acute form of entrepreneurial governance. What might be dubbed the financescaping of the region by the promoters is in essence all about the entrepreneurial promotion of Cascadia as a site for investment, consumption, and financial control. To be sure, Cascadia is distinct from the urban regions discussed by Harvey insofar as it has been promoted as a cross-border, binational region. The approach the promoters must take to attract major governmental functions into the binational region is therefore rather unique. Equally, attempts to attract more redistribution capital cannot be pursued in the normal way under the banner of Cascadia, although, as is illustrated by Washington State's dependency on Boeing and thus on the Pentagon, this does not prevent the component subregions from continuing to attract redistribution transfers from the national governments. At the same time, though, the border-transcending aspect of Cascadia's reterritorialization also opens up other opportunities for the promoters in terms of what Neil Smith refers to as scale-switching.[43] The ways in which the promoters act upon these opportunities call out for careful scrutiny because they blur the ideological with the economic. At first sight, the switch from the urban scale of entrepreneurial governance (which has been common to Vancouver, Seattle, and Portland from the mid-1980s onward) to a cross-border regional scale might be interpreted as a clear example of how the spatial fix has been denationalized, reterritorialized, and thereby rescaled in an age of NAFTA and increasing transnational interdependency. Using a different vocabulary, this is basically how the promoters themselves financescape Cascadia's natural future by arguing that the region somehow internalizes the freedoms and opportunities of free trade. But as they promote the region in this way it would be mistaken to view their efforts as a direct political relay of the actual economic imperatives unleashed by free trade in the local space. As I will explain further below, the profoundly disjunctive quality of Cascadia as a financescape lies in its notable *discontinuities* from the actual economic geographies of production and circulation in the region. Instead of being predicated on the activities of actual business supply chains and networks, Cascadia's financescape represents more of an attempt to anticipate and promote a cross-border economic geography where currently very little local economic integration actually exists. This is not to say that there is no economic determination behind the visioning of the region. Rather, in a local reenactment of global financial speculation, investments in the Cascadia idea and promotional venture deal in a certain sort of fictitious capital, a fictitious financescape of reterritorialization.

The promoters' vision of Cascadia puts great stock in the land itself. From the ecological outlines taken from the bioregionalists they proceed to find "gold" in the landscape by way of imagining a future of high-tech investment and growth. Here, for example, is a typical evocation of this natural history turned natural future from Doris Jones Yang, the Seattle-based Northwest bureau chief for *Business Week* magazine.

> Across the Pacific Northwest, from Burnaby to Boise, from Corvallis to Calgary, high-tech companies have sprouted up like mushrooms in a rain forest, emerging from the lush soils of the region and attracting an inflow of technical talent from across the continent. Cascadia is not yet the heart of the technology world. But as the glow in Silicon Valley fades, it's right where the high-tech sun is rising. And it has what many regions wish they could replicate: a natural environment where entrepreneurs thrive and techies long to live.[44]

The goal of writings like these, it would seem, is to evoke a set of entrepreneurial possibilities as rooted in the soil. The basic aim is to present Cascadia as the perfect place from which high-tech business can be conducted: perfect not just because of the position of the region, but also because it provides a postindustrial ludic landscape, filled with the environmental amenities that will enable the new masters of the high-tech universe to thrive. Seattle's Microsoft, Boeing, Amazon.com, and Targeted Genetics all loom large on this landscape, but so too do Portland's Tektronix and Vancouver's MacDonald Dettwiler. The founder of the latter company, John MacDonald, is reported by Jones as saying, "I'm very enthusiastic personally about the prospects for advanced technology industries in the whole of Cascadia."[45] So too it seems are actual investors, and so Cascadia, the name, has thus also come to brand a regional stock fund, the Cascadia Equity Fund, managed by the Aquila investment firm. The manager of the fund told a reporter that he did not just see the region as a picturesque landscape or as an accumulation of regional companies, but rather as a "geographically linked" combination of the two. "Some folks may just see trees, rugged mountain ranges, and a few famous companies like Boeing and Microsoft. But when Lacy Herrmann looks at the Pacific Northwest, he sees 'Cascadia,' a mythical but geographically linked region stretching from Nevada to Alaska."[46] The acknowledgment of mythmaking is frank here, but based on this financespace of appearances the fund manager nevertheless believes he can deliver real returns to investors in his fund.

The same double gesture—mixing geographic mythmaking with a vista of financial gain—seems to characterize the wider promotional attempts to position Cascadia in the global competition for investment capital. "The regional thrust," claims Artibise, in a typical appeal to the region's intangible potency, "has attracted the attention of analysts outside the region and has given Cascadia growing advantages in targeting investment from major financial centers."[47] When obliged by the very force of this kind of argument to further explain the basis of Cascadia's "regional thrust," Artibise and the other promoters tend to return to the imagined geography of reterritorialization, and specifically to the argument about the region's centrality in the global economy. In all of these appeals, British Columbia's, Washington's, and Oregon's previous positions as marginal corners of centralized national economies are reterritorialized and reframed in terms of Cascadia's centrality in a global economy of transnational finance and information flows. Thus Artibise and his colleagues can claim that

> Cascadia is strategically positioned on the Pacific Rim and, in fact, is geographically closer to major Asian markets than any other metropolitan region in North America. We're also in an ideal spot to broker international business between Asians, North Americans and Europeans. Cascadia is at the epicenter of the global economy, equidistant between Pacific Asia and the European Community.[48]

Likewise, Schell makes the same kind of argument, adding a certain historical finesse by comparing Cascadia to the old Mediterranean city-states that historians such as Braudel have seen as key nodes of political-economic development prior to the actual territorialization of the nation-state in the first place.

> As Venice once was to the Mediterranean economy, Seattle/Vancouver could become to the emerging New Pacific economy.[49]

Of course, anywhere on the globe can claim to be central. It all depends on how one draws the map. But with these deeply perspectival visions of centrality, Cascadia's promoters nevertheless seek to advance its status as a world-class region assured of fabulous financial prospects.

In addition to investors and promoters speculating on Cascadia's positioning as a financescape of high-tech, high-returns development, financial firms themselves have become caught up in the process of promoting the region on the global stage. "For financial services giant the Frank Russell Company the Pacific Corridor is more than just a nice place to live," begins another gushing article about the region as a place of wealth generation and financial opportunity.

> To George Russell, the Pacific Corridor is the best place in the world to be for a company involved in international finance. . . . Operating in Pacific time means that the working hours at the Russell headquarters include the close of financial dealings in Europe, all of the New York and Toronto trading days, and the opening of the next day's market in Tokyo.[50]

The article goes on to make the case yet again that the region is effectively at the center of the global economy, and in particular at the center of global finance. But more than this, it proceeds to connect the centrality and the Russell firm's significance as the funds manager for some of the world's biggest corporations (including GM, IBM, Boeing, AT&T, Xerox, Rolls Royce, Sainsbury's, Molson, Ford, and Daiche Life) with the CEO's love of mountain climbing and the local environment of Mt. Rainier and the Cascades. That same environment is also said to nourish a mode of living by the financial giant's staff that puts a special emphasis on the quality of life and good health. This is just one example, but again and again through the promotional columns and speeches about Cascadia there is the same repeated appeal linking the local landscape with a more sensitive, recreationally enriched, and thus supposedly more sustainable mode of business life. It is this way of life that is simultaneously offered up as the precious lure that comes together with the region's centrality to give Cascadia its especially competitive position as some sort of peak of privilege at the summit of the international division of labor.

There are two disjunctive aspects to this elite eco-aware finance-scape that need to be marked: the first relates to its radical discontinuity from the global circuits of production and exploitation that create the basis for financial capital in the first place; and second is the financescape's less obvious but no less discontinuous separation from the actual patterns of economic activity in the region itself. The first disjuncture from the dirty global business of production, pollution, and hard industrial work is explicitly celebrated by Cascadia's promoters who exhilarate in the region's postindustrialism. Obviously, they do not espouse a simplistic antiglobalism. Instead, they take pleasure in the vision of Cascadia as globally integrated in terms of investment at the same time as they find security in their view of the region as locally insulated in terms of lifestyle. Ultimately, this is an imagined geography of the region as a form of privileged gated community whose cosmopolitan citizens can enjoy the pleasures of nature, wealth, and direct flights to Asia and Europe while they are protected from the decline of living standards and increased insecurity brought about by the onslaught of neoliberalism in the world at large. Here, for example, is a description of what one sympathetic writer describes as the business "pilgrims" to the region.

> [Cascadians] have seen idealistic, if feckless, communism fall, sensible but uncaring capitalism triumph, and the dawning Information Revolution threaten to wreak as much social havoc in the twenty-first century as the Industrial Revolution did in the nineteenth. They know where they want to spend the next few decades of change, and it's the same sort of place that a lot of other smart people are starting to crave: a pleasantly isolated region rich with food, water and plenty of natural resources, where they can find a good job and a nice life. That's why, although compromises will be made and growing cities will sprawl alarmingly, the dominant ethic of this region will continue to revolve around environmentalism. The New Ecotopians have seen the rest of the world. In fact they help run it. And now they've moved to the suburbs—Cascadia, that is—they'll do whatever has to be done to keep its troubles away from their neighborhood.[51]

As the large coffee-table picture book in which Sutherland's comments appeared made clear, Cascadia conceived thus as an isolated postindustrial landscape makes for an appealing and environmentally diverse set of photo opportunities. Just like a suburban gated community, but writ large across a vast binational and heterogeneous landscape, the region is shown to possess all that the financially affluent need from high-tech business campuses to golf courses, ballparks, and expensive shopping malls to serene lakes and forests.[52] Picturing all this, the book contains page after page of glossy photos of the region, from the cities to the wilderness areas, each time playing up the similarities north and south of the border. This emphasis on the landscape's similarities *across* the border is a common one throughout the promotional literature, and it is especially significant because it serves in turn to conceal the second disjunctive aspect of the entrepreneurial representation of Cascadia: namely, the financescape's discontinuity from actual economic dynamics in the region.

According to Kelly, the publisher of the now defunct promotional magazine *The New Pacific*, the real rationale for Cascadia comes from the business community whose interactions across the border have necessitated the calls for policy harmonization and the regional integration of governance. People in the region, he says,

> are moving to establish some semblance of a regional order. Movement on the political scene represents a public realization that business is more and more looking to cross border opportunities. The shift, from business transactions to policy formation, makes official what many in industry and small business have known for some time—there must be greater cooperation if the region is to both compete in international markets and harmonize the area's sometimes conflicting and counter productive policies and regulations. The benefits in the long term are obvious. In all probability, the New Regional Order will have more staying power than the much hyped New World Order.[53]

Clearly the reference here to the New Regional Order hearkens back to Ohmae's arguments about region-states developing as key nodes of growth and prosperity in the wake of the nation-state. Just like Ohmae, Kelly also suggests in this passage that it has been cross-border business that has blazed the trail that the public and policy-makers must now follow. Unfortunately for his magazine as well as for his argument, though, Cascadia just does not possess the densely integrated input-output linkages that characterize Ohmae's other examples of region-state development. Indeed, the major reason for the demise of the *New Pacific* magazine was that there was not enough interest from businesses on either side of the border to pay for advertising that would be spread across a binational audience. Companies told the magazine that they preferred to advertise in outlets that could directly target a particular national market.[54] Thus, unlike the much studied agglomerative effects in regions like Hong Kong–Guangdong, Silicon Valley, Baden-Wurtenburg, and the Third Italy, Cascadia has a relatively disarticulated economy.[55] With the exception of the logging industry, which is busily logging the very forests that are supposed to give Cascadia its ecological integrity (Weyerhaeuser, a Washington-based wood and paper company, recently bought out British Columbia's MacMillan Bloedel), there is largely just disconnection. And in the postindustrial sectors that are the most frequently touted by Cascadia's boosters, the disconnect is especially marked. British Columbia's growing film industry (dubbed "Brollywood" because of the rain and its connection to Hollywood) has almost no connection to Washington and Oregon, while Microsoft, Adobe, Amazon.com, and other Seattle-based high-tech firms, not to mention Boeing, have few if any links with British Columbia.[56]

In the face of these disconnections, the promoters of Cascadia fall back on the locational centrality argument, often combining it with the claim that free trade will lead to new economies of scale and scope that will integrate the region. The economists Goldberg and Levi in fact see a particularly bright future for the local financial industry in the context of free trade. "A sector with particular potential for Cascadia," they say,

> is international finance. The West Coast of the United States lacks an international financial center of global importance. . . . There is a need for a financial and managerial center to fill the present gap in the Pacific time zone. Cascadia has a significant edge given its great circle route location (between North America and Asia) and other attributes relative to Asia. With reform of the US financial system imminent, and a free trade agreement that provides "national treatment" for financial institutions operating across the forty-ninth parallel . . . Vancouver (and possibly Seattle) has the potential to fill this niche. It could successfully exploit opportunities opened up by the US-Canadian Free Trade Agreement and the North American Free Trade Agreement. Encouraging Vancouver to build on its greater international financial expertise and take the lead for Cascadia might be the most sound strategy to follow. And it would provide Seattle with a close, and successful niche-oriented financial center. Both economies of scale and scope would be realized.[57]

These bold claims about the future of regional finance were made back in 1992, but even after a decade of free trade there is still little evidence at the time of writing that the industry in the region has filled the supposed West Coast niche. Most certainly there has been no integrated development of a single financial services hub with resulting cutbacks in duplication (e.g., the closing down of a bank in Seattle because the same services are offered in Vancouver). Real "economies of scale" demand precisely such cutbacks. This is where the economic efficiencies lauded by neoliberals are made. But they have not yet been made in Cascadia. More importantly perhaps, across the rest of the regional economy where Goldberg and Levi also pictured potential gains from free trade based on comparative advantages in complementary sectors there has been very little cross-border consolidation. NAFTA has certainly had an effect in increasing north–south flows, but these have by no means superceded the east–west flows internal to Canada and the United States. Thus while the volume of trade between the United States and Canada is now greater than that between any two countries in the world, and while in 1998 Canada imported $137 billion of goods from the United States, which was 68 percent of total Canadian merchandise imports and 22 percent of total U.S. merchandise exports, federal reserve bank economist Howard Wall notes that all this trade "is still small when compared with the level of trade between states or provinces within [either of the] countries."[58] To make his point Wall lists British Columbia's trade with various states and provinces as a percentage of their gross product (see Figure 3). The result is a table that also doubles as further documentation of the absence of north–south integration Cascadian style. Clearly the east–west links

Alberta	6.9	2.6	Washington
Manitoba	2.0	0.3	California
New Brunswick	2.3	0.2	Maine
Ontario	1.9	0.2	Ohio
Quebec	1.4	0.1	New York
Saskatchewan	2.4	1.0	Montana

Figure 3. Total trade with British Columbia as percent of gross product, 1996. From Howard Wall, "How Important Is the U.S.–Canada Border?" International Economic Trends (August 1999): 1.

with Alberta and other Canadian provinces are far more significant given their economic size and distance from British Columbia.[59]

The lack of local cross-border economic integration in Cascadia may seem to vindicate an approach such as Appadurai's that focuses solely on deterritorialization. However, to argue this would be to miss the ways in which the financescape of Cascadian integration nevertheless continues to be articulated even in the face of the economic disarticulation on the ground. A singular attention to deterritorialization would leave us unable to come to terms with the ways in which the promoters continue to seek to position the region as a competitor for outside investment and capital transfers through their entrepreneurial arguments about the ineluctable nature of cross-border regionalization. In order to see how these arguments might have real reterritorializing effects it is necessary to turn from the economic reports on local business activity to the policy-making environment in which the claims about a future of cross-border integration are far more effective.

In the policy arena the promoters' most effective slogan has been "Cooperate locally to compete globally."[60] The cooperation is necessary, they claim, partly because it will give Cascadia the necessary "critical mass" it requires in order to fight for international investment and government transfer payments. All this is in turn justified by repeated appeals to the regional logic of the new world order à la Ohmae. A *New Pacific* editorial entitled "The Power of One" put it like this:

> Border disputes, custom duties, punitive tariffs and inter-city rivalry will pale into insignificance in the cold, competitive light of the new world order. Co-operation will enable the Pacific Northwest to reach critical mass and be taken seriously in a world where trade will often amount to war by another means.[61]

Giving further elaboration on the meaning of such "critical mass," Artibise explained the need for reterritorialization as follows.

> In a North American context the Pacific Northwest/Alaska is a small player. If that regional market is expanded to include British Columbia and Alberta, however, it then ranks as one of the largest in North America. On an international scale the same principle applies. The two nations and the two regions can bring complementary strengths to the international marketplace.[62]

Such claims may seem absurd in the light of the local economic dis-connections, but they retain an ideological power to persuade. A re-porter from the *Chicago Tribune* hearing the discourse for the first time came away with the following impression:

> By marketing its assets—from high-tech industries to tourism—as a region, Cascadia hopes to expand its prosperity far better than it could through intra-Cascadian rivalry. "The idea is to have a larger pie where people can get larger slices," said Agnew [of the Discovery Institute]. The Cascadian pie is impressive. The regional gross do-mestic product totals $250 billion, almost equal to that of Australia. Led by Seattle-based Microsoft Corp, the region's combined high-tech industries rank as the sixth-largest such concentration in the world. "Separately, it is hard to attract meaningful investment," said Robson [of the Cascadia Institute in Vancouver]. "Together we have a lot more leverage."[63]

Running through this financescape of "critical mass" and "le-verage" is another notable form of disjuncture that would seem to legitimize Cascadia as based on the laws of nature while it com-pletely disconnects this nature from any local ecology. The actual terms "critical mass" and "leverage" are taken from physics, but displaced to the world of financial promotion they take on a more social form of naturalism that is more about place than space. Ul-timately it is about presenting Cascadia as a privileged "niche" in the global economy, and as such it amounts to a displaced form of social Darwinism. To achieve this elite niche the social Darwinian script suggests that Cascadia's leaders need to hang together and hang tough. The global economy is a harsh wilderness, the script seems to read, but by banding together across the border as some kind of binational regional wolf pack, Cascadians can beat off the competitors and win a larger slice of planetary resources.

The social Darwinian appeal to Cascadian basic instincts may seem very distant from the mundane details of local policy making. However, it is not hard to find the rhetoric being put to work in ex-actly these circles. Coming together with the arguments about global centrality, free trade harmonization, and sustainable development, it enables the promoters to make specific claims for government trans-fers as well as new bids for international investment. The net result is well illustrated in the following Cascadia Planning Group call to forge a Cascadia Corridor Corporation. "Co-operation in a corridor context has numerous, clear advantages," the document notes under the heading of "cooperating regionally to compete globally." It then proceeds to list the advantages as follows:

- It is an effective way to add leverage to investment strategies. The rationalization of functions corridor-wide and corridor-long can eliminate redundant activities and site them in the most cost-efficient, least disruptive locations.
- Corridor coalitions on border, trade and environmental issues can raise the Cascadia Region's profile as a competitor for funding. . . .
- A Corridor context can also create an idea sharing forum that offers leverage in innovative, comprehensive use of non-capital solutions: intelligent transportation systems, telecommuting, regulatory harmonization, work rules and hours of operation at key facilities.
- Corridor co-operation can create a larger, more secure financial base that allows access to funding under the most favorable conditions. The benefits include stronger credit ratings, use of the full range of current and evolving financial mechanisms and public-private partnerships, and the possibility of a distinctive Cascadia Corridor Corporation as a focal point for organizing the financial resources that support major investments.
- The result of corridor cooperation can make Cascadia one of the world's premier, cross-border regions, and define new economic, social and environmental realities for the 21st Century.[64]

This bulleted list clearly illustrates the practical connections that the visionaries see between their constructions and such financial matters as credit ratings. For them, therefore, there is no disjuncture between the financescape and actual future of funding regional development. Or at least, it is a disjuncture that they are as eagerly attempting to cross as the border itself. But more than this, the bulleted list also reveals another way in which the reterritorialization of Cascadia as a site for investment and capital transfers is actually *conjunctive* with the ideoscape of neoliberalism. The list is replete with telling references to all the most common neoliberal principles of entrepreneurial governance. From eliminating redundancy to increasing cost efficiency, regulatory harmonization, public-private partnerships, the neoliberal imperatives are written right into the heart of the regional policy goals. This is important to note in its own right, and it coincides quite comfortably, of course, with the gated-community vision of Cascadia as a protected place for the privileged, a premier resort, as it were, managed in the interests of management. But at the theoretical level too, this neat overlap of the ideoscape of neoliberalism with the financescape of attracting capital to Cascadia provides a cautionary lesson in the ways postnational spaces can be constructed that are driven less by disjuncture than by the coordinated conjunction of capitalist interests. This, it seems, is vital to note as a corrective to Appadurai's sanguine vision of postnational spaces providing freedom from predatory capitalism. It is also important to note as a starting point for understanding the landscape on which the technoscapes and mediascapes of Cascadia have been built. It is to these constructions that I now turn.

MEDIASCAPING AND TECHNOSCAPING CASCADIA: ALIENS IN SPACE

In Appadurai's attempt to rewrite Benedict Anderson's arguments about the nation as imagined community, the concepts of transnational technoscapes and mediascapes are crucial. *Technoscapes,* he says, refer to "the global configuration, also ever fluid, of technology and the fact that technology, both high and low, both mechanical and informational now moves at high speeds across various kinds of previously impervious boundaries" (*Modernity,* 35). *Mediascapes,* in turn, are meant to describe both "the distribution of the electronic capabilities to produce and disseminate information . . . [and] the images created by this media" (35). Thus while Anderson saw print capitalism as a technology and media that enabled the creation of national fellow feeling among citizens who would never meet one another, Appadurai sees contemporary electronic communications and media technologies as creating the same sorts of solidarity through deterritorialized webs (including the "World Wide Web") that span the globe. The resulting postnational spaces, he argues, not only blur the meanings of home and away and transform people's feelings of belonging, they also blur the distinction between the real and the imagined in ways that are radically transformative of how people act.

> The lines between the realistic and the fictional landscapes they see are blurred, so that the farther away these audiences are from the direct experiences of metropolitan life, the more likely they are to construct imagined worlds that are chimerical, aesthetic, even fantastic objects. (35)

Distance and space are still suggested to have an effect here, but it is an effect that unleashes the fantasies of the deterritorializing imagination, and with it, for Appadurai, the desired possibility of moving beyond exclusive nationalisms and their associated power structures. Clearly, it is these kinds of hopes that Cascadia calls into question. It does not diminish the importance of the search for post-national justice and freedom. But it reminds us that postnational spaces can also be put to work in the service of vested elite interests. Appadurai's observations about the blurring of image and reality are no less pertinent to this argument. In fact the mediascaping and technoscaping of Cascadia illustrate the degree to which the local promoters of neoliberal reterritorialization hope themselves to develop real revenues out of the fantastic objects of postnationalism.

Many media images have been made in the region or in reference to it, partly as a result of the growing film industry in Vancouver. Movies and television series ranging from *First Blood, Twin Peaks, Northern Exposure,* and the *X-Files* to *Frasier* and *Sleepless in Seattle* all play off aspects of the regional landscape celebrated by Cascadia's promoters (by contrast, of course, *The Battle in Seattle* of the anti-WTO protests did not). Besides these filmic representations, perhaps the best example of a mediascape in Appadurai's sense of the term, and one that has also been explicitly reterritorialized around the theme of Cascadia, has been the promoters' own concept of the Two Nation Vacation. The basic idea behind the Two Nation Vacation is that of cooperating regionally to compete globally. "By showcasing the region and bundling its three major airports, planners hope to attract more flights from overseas," noted the *Chicago Tribune* reporter in 1994.[65] Launched primarily at the instigation of the Port of Seattle with support from the Discovery Institute's Cascadia Project, the Two Nation Vacation was supported by B.C. tourism agencies and marketed to long-distance tourists from the United Kingdom, Germany, and Australia. The key purpose of the marketing concept is to twin the chimerical notion of a borderless Cascadia with the pocketbook notion that Cascadian tourists get two nations and all of their collective recreational diversity for the price of just one long-distance plane ride. The link between this "fantastic" mediascape and the more general financescape of entrepreneurial promotion now has quite a long history as a favorite concept of Cascadia's boosters. "[W]e are competing for tourists in a global market," Artibise explained in 1995. "To maintain our market share, and indeed increase it, we can do very well by marketing a region that crosses international borders."[66]

At a conference in June of 1996 at the new Port of Seattle conference center in Seattle, the Two Nation Vacation concept was revitalized once again with the unveiling of a glossy marketing poster and a magazine entitled *Cascadia: Your Two Nation Vacation Guide.* Examining the poster it is clear how the assembled images are used to evoke an ancient and enduring history and a seemingly sublime naturalness in Cascadia's contours as a region planted deep in the soil (see Figure 4). Here the whole panoply of iconic commodification has been put together with a map that lends a sense of objectivity and, in this version, a copper-plated sense of historicity to the reterritorialization of Cascadia. Native totems, waterfalls, forests, bears, eagles, salmon, trees, and orcas are all packaged into the advertisement. In this aestheticizing way, they are all also reduced to serving as objects of the long-distance touristic gaze. They form a mediascape that really does construct a fantastic imagined world to be viewed from afar, a world that links the entrepreneurial vision of the promoters with would-be vacationers' visions generated on the other side of the world. Thus, the serial elements comprising the Two Nation Vacation comprise a clear Cascadian example of how, just as Appadurai argues, mediascapes produce image-centered strips of reality linked to others living elsewhere. His exact words are that

> Media-scapes . . . tend to be image-centered, narrative-based accounts of strips of reality, and what they offer to those who experience and transform them is a series of elements . . . out of which scripts can be formed of imagined lives, their own as well as those of others living in other places. (*Modernity,* 35)

The imagined life of touring and spending money in Cascadia is the particular transformational experience the promoters hope the Two Nation Vacation advertising campaign will produce. While the poster only offered a sense of the separate elements that go into this touristic fantasy, the special promotional pamphlets later produced to be sent to tour agents also gave a sense of the kinds of scripts that the promoters hoped would be generated.

> Cascadia, gateway to the Pacific North-west and the Two-Nation Vacation, consists of the American states of Washington and Oregon

Figure 4. "Cascadia: The Two Nation Vacation." Reprinted by permission of the Port of Seattle.

and the Canadian province of British Columbia. It's an advantageous location of international tourism and trade; London and Europe's other great cities are as little as nine hours away by air, and a similar ease of access by land or sea puts the rest of North America and all of the Pacific Rim virtually at Cascadia's doorstep. There's something magnetic here for a certain kind of soul . . . one who appreciates natural beauty, limitless recreational opportunities, and the vibrant blend of international influences that have produced Cascadia's diverse culture and thriving economy. Many people have decided to call this region home which is a decision you'll understand once you see Cascadia for yourself. The merging of continent and ocean that defines Cascadia gives the region a diverse geographical climatic face. Waves that have traveled all the way from Asia crash on Pacific beaches, while inland—just beyond Cascadia's thousand-mile-long spine of snow-capped mountains—sun-kissed deserts and rolling farmlands are split by canyons carved during the greatest prehistoric floods in all of North America. The weather in Cascadia is as varied as the land and the people. It is entirely possible to sunbathe and snow-ski here in the course of one short visit, and today's gentle rain shower is almost guaranteed to lead to tomorrow's bluebird sky. Washington, Oregon and British Columbia. That's where Cascadia is. But once you've experienced this magical place, its going to be somewhere else as well. It'll be in your heart and on your mind . . . forever.[67]

Here there is a grand plan to script and disseminate the Cascadian "state of mind." Monied tourists, it would seem, with their own aestheticizing approach to nature, their love of "diversity," and their yearning for soul are envisioned in this material as constituting the practically perfect future Cascadian citizens. It is in every sense a postnational vision, and, as such, it is disjunctive from traditional and national appropriations of the local landscape icons. But reterritorialized for the purpose of increasing the region's capacity to attract consumption capital, the Two Nation Vacation sales campaign also attests to the far from emancipatory possibilities of postnational spaces. Indeed, the concept is obviously part and parcel of the overall entrepreneurial repackaging of the region, and as such it is also conjunctive with the narrowed circle of belonging imagined in the gated-community vision of Cascadia. Tourists in fact would seem to be the perfect neoliberal citizens of this landscape. Investing the region with their personal fantasies of recreation, they bring money, appreciation for objectified nature, and a desire that responds to price signals. Moreover, because they are only temporary visitors, they bring all this without the bothersome bureaucracy of democratic institutions, governments, courts, and welfare systems. At the same time, this mediascaping of the region also implies that alongside the wildlife and the forests, the region's oldest inhabitants, the native peoples of British Columbia, Washington, and Oregon are put to work semiotically as part of the regional "magic."

Like the mediascapes discussed by Appadurai, the Two Nation Vacation campaign also rests on a technoscape of transnationalism. In the Cascadian case this concerns more than just the global dissemination of the imagery of tourism, it also relates to the technological infrastructure of economic reterritorialization. Indeed, for some promoters such as Jim Miller, technological infrastructure, especially transportation infrastructure, ranks alongside trade as the most important integrating factor in the region, far surpassing the significance of Cascadia's environmental commonalities.

> Yes, there is a common climate along the Cascadia strip that fosters regionalism. . . . Yes, there is common geography. . . . Yes, we have a common appreciation of environment. Yes, we have an economy historically rooted in natural resources which has been moving increasingly to high technology. But none of these factors is as important as Pacific trade and transportation technology.[68]

Other promoters have shared Miller's keen interest in the technological advancement of Cascadia's competitive positioning. They have lobbied in this way for more investment in infrastructure to speed movement through the region. In particular, two of these practical technological attempts to "bulldoze the border"[69] are significant insofar as they are so clearly conceived as facilitating the wider projects of promoting Cascadia for high-tech investment and tourism: the first is a vision of a high-speed bullet train between Vancouver and Eugene; and the second is a transformation of customs and immigration processing at the border itself.

The concept of a Cascadian bullet train had its own origins in a now failed and largely forgotten effort to bring the Olympic games to the region. The idea was to promote the games as a unique binational event that would somehow embody the border-crossing international diversity of Olympic sport itself. Just like Olympic bids the world over, the idea was also to attract more government spending on regional infrastructure than otherwise might have been spent. Thus as both the ultimate goal of the bid, as well as part of selling the binational games as a viable concept, the promoters put forward the idea of a government-funded bullet train that would whisk spectators and reporters from events in Vancouver to others in Eugene, up and down mainstreet Cascadia. For Artibise, and some of the other promoters, high-speed rail was a particularly attractive technological fix to the problem of maintaining Cascadia's green image. Thus back in 1994 he noted that "there is significant interest in the Region in the future of high speed rail as an essential element of the regional transportation system and an efficient, environmentally sensitive alternative to highway and air travel."[70] Today, while the regional train service has been improved slightly with the augmentation of the Amtrak trains with faster, Spanish-made, rolling stock, bullet trains still seem a long way off. Yet neither this delay, nor the clear contradiction of seeking national government funding for the avowedly postnational project of Cascadian corridor development, has stopped the promoters from continuing to push for federal transportation funding. They have simply turned their focus more intently on the actual border itself, and on various attempts to expedite the movement of trucks, tourists, and business travelers across it. One sign of these efforts was the announcement in early 2000 that funding had been allocated to a cross-border commercial vehicle facilitation plan "to design and build a southbound information network for transmitting freight movement data to border inspection agencies for pre-arrival processing."[71]

Other technological initiatives that relate less to the transportation of goods and more to the movement of people have also been advanced by Cascadia's promoters in the hopes of reducing delays at the border. Most notably, in the early part of the 1990s they were successful in implementing expedited border-crossing lanes for frequent travelers crossing the border at the so-called Peace Arch. For traffic into the United States the "dedicated commuter lane" was called the PACE lane and for traffic into Canada it was called CANPASS. By the fall of 1992, the first year of the program, American officials had approved 19,000 PACE decals, and Canadian officials 27,500. These decals enabled drivers to line up in a dedicated fast lane at the border and move through with little questioning by the customs and immigration agents. The rapid passage of the cars with the PACE and CANPASS authorizations was ensured on the basis of preclearance data-management technologies that effectively meant that travelers who registered with the programs and who paid the required fees only had to answer the usual questions at the single moment of application. The initial success of the PACE and CANPASS lanes seemed to betoken the "bulldozing of the checkpoints" that Schell and Hamer had forecast when they lauded the program in their 1995 essay on Cascadia.[72] Of course, the "bulldozing" was only meaningful for a subset of frequent travelers across the border. This, after all, was a dual-track, two-tier border-processing technology that, by diverting resources to run the fast lanes, also reduced the ability of the border authorities to administer the other, ordinary lanes. Moreover, only Canadians and American citizens could apply, and only those who were able to pay the annual fee could actually assure themselves PACE and CANPASS membership. Such exclusivity was not something that overly worried Cascadia's promoters. Indeed, it was of a piece with their whole vision of the region as a neoliberal utopia, a kind of suburban country club writ large across binational space.[73] However, such comfortable assumptions about the border-crossing rights of cosmopolitan Cascadians were not to last. In 1996 another class of suburban interests—those represented in the U.S. House of Representatives by the Republican majority led by Newt Gingrich—were to bring all the fantasies of bulldozing the border to a sudden halt with the passage of a new border-hardening immigration control act. Only slowly were the promoters able to overcome this legislative threat to expedited border-crossing, and only one year after the PACE lane was given the reprieve they were seeking (in 2000) came the attacks of September 11, 2001, and another border clampdown. It is worth exploring in a little more detail these episodes of border hardening and their final high-tech solution because they reveal a great deal about the politics of the border-softening technologies pursued by Cascadia's promoters.

The threat to the Cascadian vision created by the Republican-drafted Illegal Immigrant Reform and Immigrant Responsibility Act of 1996 came from Section 110 of the act, which was chiefly targeted at what immigration control advocates regarded as the threat of "visa-overstays"—immigrants who enter the United States legally on visas but then overstay the specified time limit. The Section demanded that all "aliens" entering and exiting the United States would in the future have to file arrival *and* departure records thereby enabling the INS to keep track of the overstay problem. Although some politicians did not seem to realize this as they voted for the act, the wording "aliens" meant that the act would apply to Canadians, even if it was phobic fears about undocumented immigration from Mexico that was a driving force behind the legislation.[74] The promoters quickly realized that if all Canadians were asked to complete arrival and departure forms at the forty-ninth parallel it would create huge delays. They predicted that if Section 110 had ever been implemented the resulting traffic jams would have been so severe that it would have made it extremely difficult for anyone, whether they had PACE and CANPASS decals or not, to even get close to the border.[75] "It's more than a slap in the face," Artibise told a reporter. "It would bring business between Canada and the US to a grinding halt."[76] However, had Artibise and his fellow Cascadian visionaries paused to consider the technological reconfiguration of the border envisaged in Section 110 they would have noticed some startling similarities with the two-tier, dual-track system pioneered by the PACE lane itself. Indeed, in many ways Section 110 (along with a number of other key parts of the 1996 act) actually represented a form of congressional response to the techno-futuristic call Cascadia's promoters had been making for preclearance-based passport processing. Schell and Hamer, for example, made one such call themselves as they envisaged their ideal border-crossing scenario in 1995:

> Ideally, a continental North American clearance someday would make one-stop passport control available for overseas guests, and within the continent would make access between British Columbia and Washington, for example, as easy as access between Oregon and Washington today.[77]

Obviously, the predicted impact of Section 110 was the complete inverse for this vision. As Senator Patrick Leahy of Vermont critically put it: "This is not Checkpoint Charlie. This is the largest unguarded frontier in the world."[78] However, a closer look at the wording of the act itself reveals how it was actually built upon the same vision of technological facilitation, preclearance database management, and dual-tier processing that underpinned dedicated commuter lanes like PACE and CANPASS.

SEC 110. AUTOMATED ENTRY-EXIT CONTROL SYSTEM

(a) SYSTEM. Not later than 2 years after the date of the enactment of this Act, the Attorney General shall develop an automated entry and exit control system that will

(1) collect a record of departure for every alien departing the United States and match the records of departure with the record of the alien's arrival in the United States; and

(2) enable the Attorney General to identify, through on-line searching procedures, lawfully admitted nonimmigrants who remain in the United States beyond the period authorized by the Attorney General.[79]

Running through this section, as well as through the act more generally, was an emphasis on technological solutions. The entry and exit control system would be *automated,* the Section dictated. The technology, even though there was no budget to pay for it in the act, would somehow mitigate the danger of delays by creating a dual system for border crossers, thereby speeding up the movement of law-abiding travelers while enabling a foolproof process for identifying, detaining, and deporting the illegal. Collecting all departure records might in earlier times have created enormous problems, but another techno-futuristic part of the act—Section 104—saw this as easily addressed through new high-tech biometric systems. These systems, which were already being tested in 1996 at various U.S. airports, effectively represented a further technologization of the sort of preclearance system installed with PACE. According to a position paper by Ronald Hays, the assistant chief inspector of the INS in January of 1996, biometric systems would simply accelerate such dedicated commuter lanes by providing one-to-one automated inspections by machines at the border.[80] The machines would determine if the holder of a preclearance card actually was the person who had been precleared. A digitized handprint or voiceprint encoded on a chip on the card would be matched by the machine by a reading of the cardholder's hand or voice at the border. Automated in this way, the biometric systems promised to be extremely quick. Adding a further neoliberal gleam to this promise of technological efficiency and speed, Hays's description of INS planning also highlighted how the preclearance-lane cards and the automated checking machines would actually be owned and maintained by private companies. Reading his breathtaking description of this privatizing revolution in border processing technology, it is not hard to see why it appealed so much to the Gingrich Republicans.

> We have included in our design the necessary technological platforms to ensure that the card will have a useful life of approximately five years. Most importantly for commercial users today, it will sport the ubiquitous magnetic strip which the government will not use, making it completely available to the commercial sector. We have also included a microchip in the design as we will require some of the available storage space for automated inspections. We will make the remainder of the chip's storage available to our commercial partners. We think this is especially significant because of the recent announcement by Visa, MasterCard and Europay of their joint specification for chip-based credit cards. To further the appeal of this idea to the commercial sector, we will also allow cards prepared by our partners to display the logo of the partner. This would create in the mind of the card holder an instant link between our high technology application and the sponsoring corporation. Just think of the possibilities for a frequent traveler pulling out a card bearing the IBM or United Airlines logo, for example. Now potentiate that image by seeing the card as a charge card, an airline ticket, a medium by which you access telecommunications systems, an electronic bank, and/or any other card-based application you can conceive.[81]

"Potentiate" is probably the best word to describe what the Republican-controlled Congress did in the 1996 act as they proceeded to build on the existing practices of dual-tiered processing and preclearance with these sorts of futuristic visions of biometrics very much in mind. The particular vision of passports turned private credit cards turned high-tech deterritorialization devices was also not so very different from the one envisaged by many of Cascadia's promoters for whom public-private partnerships were and remain key, and for whom national citizenship more generally is eclipsed by the importance of postnational investment and consumption practices. However, as Cascadia's promoters themselves came to realize, the result of this whole techno-deterritorialization imperative once enacted promised to be profoundly reterritorializing. When considered from the perspective of border communities, the resulting legislative encoding of the futuristic vision seemed to promise only traffic snarls and frictions at the border. So, ironically, Cascadia's promoters were forced into joining a lobbying crusade against a section of an act of Congress that was predicated on the very kinds of border technoscaping they had been promoting locally. They were joined in this effort by other like-minded groups from northern border states across the United States whose equally two-tiered view of immigration included a view of Canadians as business partners not potential "illegal aliens."[82] A lobby group entitled Americans For Better Borders was also formed, supported chiefly by the big auto companies and other TNCs like Eastman Kodak, with vested interests in moving goods across the border. As a result of all these efforts, Section 110 was first put on hold, and then finally, in the early summer of 2000, rewritten so as to be completely harmless to the status quo.

For Cascadia's promoters the larger problem with the 1996 act was that it represented what the Gingrich Republicans themselves liked to call an "unfunded mandate." Had the costs for all the new bureaucratic technologies been budgeted into the act the probability of delays would have been considerably lessened. There would have been enough border agents and machines to make the arrival and departure processing of Canadians feasible. But as the business groups well understood, no such funding for an expansion of government services was ever likely to emerge from the Republican-dominated Congress. In this sense, the aftermath of September 11 was ultimately to prove a blessing in disguise for the advocates of high-tech dual-track border processing. Of course, initially, the response of the U.S. government to the terrorist attacks was to dramatically tighten border security. INS and Customs agents implemented Code Red antiterrorism operations that involved inspecting individually all private vehicles, trucks, and buses. Overnight this created monumental delays. Reporting on the resulting traffic jams, the *New York Times* noted that in some areas the wait times lasted nine hours or more.[83] Not surprisingly the PACE program was also shut down. By this time it had been expanded to more Washington/B.C. border checkpoints and had become the dedicated commuter lane with the largest number of enrollees in North America. Its closure therefore led to predictable complaints from the business community. "The PACE program was very beneficial to people and businesses, and I was one of them," said a local developer of a resort in Birch Bay to a reporter. "Our visitors are down 67%."[84] But in the wake of such protests, and in the context of constant calls for "economic security" to be made part of the new "national security," local representatives such as Washington State's Rick Larsen were able to persuade Congress and the Bush administration to pass the laws and budget the funds to make a high-tech replacement of the PACE lane finally viable.

The first step toward the new border technology was made on December 12, 2001, when Canada and the United States signed the "Smart Border Declaration." With this, the two governments declared their commitment "to collaborate in identifying and addressing security risks while efficiently and effectively expediting the legitimate flow of people and goods across the Canada-U.S. border."[85] The central aim of the declaration was thus to further entrench a dual-tiered approach to border management and thereby finesse the contradictions between the new emphasis on increased security and the ongoing concern with reducing frictions on business. John Manley, the Canadian minister of foreign affairs, made clear that from his perspective security and efficiency would thereby somehow become one. "We have agreed to an aggressive action plan that will allow the safest, most efficient passage of people and goods between our two countries, as part of our ongoing commitment to the creation of a Smart Border." Emphasizing the technological sophistication of the new plans, Manley went on, "[t]his action plan will enhance the technology, coordination and information sharing that are essential to safeguard our mutual security and strengthen cross-border commerce for the world's largest binational trading relationship."[86] Governor Tom Ridge, who had been appointed director of the new Office of Homeland Security shortly after 9/11, echoed the exact same mantra of combining efficiency and security with his own supporting comments on the declaration. "On behalf of President Bush," he said, "I was pleased to visit Canada to meet with Minister Manley and senior Canadian officials to discuss how to build a smart and secure border that allows the free flow of people and goods between our two countries. We look forward to working together to achieve real time real solutions as quickly as possible."[87] Five months later, President Bush himself repeated the same dual goals as he signed into law the Enhanced Border Security and Visa Entry Reform Act of 2002. "I'm honored today," he said, "to sign a bill that is an important step in an effort to secure our border, while promoting trade and commerce."[88]

As a result of the Smart Border Declaration, of the new law signed by President Bush, and of all the efforts surrounding them, the old PACE lane on the British Columbia–Washington State border came to be replaced on June 26, 2002, by the new so-called NEXUS system.[89] Visiting the NEXUS enrollment center on July 1, Representative Larsen explained in the now familiar dualistic "Smart Border" rhetoric that "NEXUS is going to help us insure a more secure border while insuring trade and tourism can continue."[90] Like the PACE and CANPASS systems, and yet joined together as a bureaucratic bridge between Canadian and U.S. governmental functions, NEXUS now allows for the same fast-track border-crossing experience with little of the normal customs and immigration questioning. It is also based on preclearance, but unlike the prior systems it operates on the basis of photo ID and biometric "proximity cards." NEXUS members crossing into the United States on the dedicated lane carry the card in their car, and as they approach the border it relays all their enrollment data—including finger prints, photo ID, name, date of birth, and so on—to an antenna and from there to a border guard's computer screen. This is by no means the complete apotheosis of automation and corporatization envisaged by Hays, but it clearly represents another step in that direction. It also very directly illustrates the ways in which the dual-track partitioning of cross-border traffic lives on after the PACE lane not just in terms of the dualistic "Smart Border" discourse, but also very practically in the new technoscape of border checkpoint policing. Thus, while the immediate impact of 9/11 was to interrupt the neoliberal dream of bulldozing the checkpoints, while it led to considerably increased federal attention on the border, this attention also led, in the end, to increased spending on technology and, through this, to the installation of a technical fix to the problem of combining neoliberal commercial freedoms with the heightened American emphasis on so-called homeland security.

One reason for documenting the developments of the border technologies advocated by Cascadia's visionaries is that they show how the visions of cross-border integration have had tangible outcomes. Even if they have been unable to secure bullet trains and deeper economic integration, the changes the promoters have demanded at the border itself have had real bureaucratic and disciplinary consequences. More than this, the technology of dual-track border processing that they have helped to put in place also shows how technoscapes of cross-border integration might more generally be reterritorializing as much as deterritorializing in their effects. The specific technoscapes represented by PACE, CANPASS, and NEXUS reveal in this sense a whole series of reterritorializing tendencies. There is the spatial separation of travelers into separate fast and slow lanes, a spatialization that makes explicit basic inequalities of access to the sorts of transnational movement celebrated by the likes of Appadurai. There is the fact that all the efforts at border bulldozing have remained fundamentally mediated by federal decision-making and changing visions of national security in Ottawa and, most especially, Washington, D.C. And there are the more general ways in which the dedicated commuter lanes have revealed that ideas about Cascadian identity are themselves as exclusive as they are cosmopolitan. In the next section I seek to explore the ethnic encoding of this exclusivity by exploring the construction of Cascadia as an ethnoscape.

ETHNOSCAPING CASCADIA: THE RETERRITORIALIZATION OF BELONGING

For Appadurai the anthropologist, ethnoscapes are the central feature of modernity at large. "By *ethnoscape*," he says,

> I mean the landscape of persons who constitute the shifting world in which we live: tourists, immigrants, refugees, exiles, guest workers, and other moving groups and individuals constitute an essential feature of the world and appear to affect the politics of (and between) nations to a hitherto unprecedented degree. (*Modernity*, 33)

Ethnoscapes thus are said to comprise the moving peoples who in turn constitute the core of the postnational public spheres he sees as so full of liberatory promise. This is not hard to understand perhaps when the foci are refugees and immigrants who by moving to new locales might escape experiences of ethnic absolutism or find new routes to agency (albeit sometimes ethnically absolutist agency) in the societies they have left behind. But notably Appadurai also includes tourists in his list of moving peoples, and, as I have already shown, the hegemonic tourist landscaping of Cascadia is hardly liberatory, or at least seems full only of narrowly neoliberal dreams of liberty. In what follows I suggest that other ethnoscapings of the region also reveal the limits of reterritorialized postnational belonging. Indeed, in stark contrast to Appadurai's idealized vision of postnational inclusiveness, the ethnoscaping of Cascadia illustrates all manner of regionalized racism and instrumental ethnicism. However, I also suggest at the end of the section that if there has been a more liberatory reterritorialization of the Cascadian ethnoscape it has been by native peoples: peoples who, far from being immigrants, refugees, or tourists, have instead been moving through the region for millennia and certainly from long before an international border was ever put in place. Their contemporary reterritorialization of regional space as a postcolonial borderless space does reveal emancipatory agency. However, somewhat against the grain of Appadurai's claims, its emancipatory possibilities stem less from a postnationalism than from a multinationalism, an insistence that as First Nations these peoples also have discrete, territorially defined claims to sovereignty that, in some cases, transcend today's international border and in all cases go back long before the Cartesian colonization of regional space by cadastral and national borders.

One of the most remarkably racist visions of the Cascadian landscape dates back to a much older, early twentieth-century attempt to promote the region's special destiny on the basis of its environment. Entitled *In the Zone of Filtered Sunshine: Why the Pacific Northwest Is Destined to Dominate the Commercial World,*[91] the vision took shape as a 1924 Seattle Chamber of Commerce promotional booklet. Although the author, Erwin Weber, did not use the name Cascadia, the booklet operationalized a very similar concept of regional space that, defined by supposedly natural features, is clearly shown in the image on the cover of the booklet as crossing the border and including much of western British Columbia all the way up to Alaska (see Figure 5). Much like today's promoters, Weber was particularly exercised by the region's location vis-à-vis Pacific Rim trade. "Seattle and Puget Sound," he says, "are the logical economical locations for the manufacture of all goods for which the raw materials are derived from the Orient, Oceania and Alaska, and for the manufacture of all goods to be marketed to those places."[92] However, much more crucial to his argument about the region's special commercial destiny was another kind of geographical claim about its natural future that rested on an environmentally determinist and racist vision of the region's climate. "Intense and prolonged sunshine," Weber explains, "is detrimental to the highest

Figure 5. Cover of pamphlet from Seattle Department of Commerce, 1924. Special Collections Division, University of Washington Libraries, Seattle, Washington, native UW17081.

human progress. . . . The most energetic human types and highest and most enduring civilizations have evolved in the cloudiest region of the world, Nordic Europe."[93] Extending this racialized model of environmental determinism to North America, Weber asserted that the Pacific Northwest with its limited sunshine was another of the earth's "few favored regions," a region "which possesses all the basic requirements necessary and desirable for the development of the most virile types of humanity, and the highest attainments of civilization."[94] Citing early twentieth-century environmental determinists such as Ellsworth Huntington as his authority, Weber then presented page after page of climatological data, all with a view to clinching his point that the region, thanks to its clouds and rainfall, had a special destiny as a white site, a "natural" base from which the white races could pursue their "natural" talents for conquering the commercial world.

Today, Weber's white supremacism lives on, but it would never be found in a Seattle Department of Commerce–sponsored booklet. Instead, it is marginal far-right groups in the region, in both British Columbia and the Pacific Northwest, that continue to reproduce versions of this environmentally determinist racist regionalism.[95] The so-called Northwest Kinsmen, for example, had a Web page that until recently introduced visitors with the following message:

> Welcome to the Northwest Patriot Gathering Place. This web site includes materials of political, religious or racial nature, and is designed to bring you information about various Christian Patriot groups and ideas. We advocate the "Northwest Territorial Imperative," which encourages the migration of White Christian Patriots to the Northwest five states in an effort to establish a regional power base.[96]

A link from the page went to an explanation of the "Northwest Territorial Imperative" from "Pastor" Robert Miles that returns to the region's "natural" mountainous geography to make the case for regionalism. Unlike the imagery that figures in the financescaping of Cascadia as a privileged peak at the epicenter of the international economy, here by contrast the mountains underpin a phobically isolationist outlook.

> America is not a free country. It is a land of sheep. . . . We who are the mountain rams understand. It is why we chose the high ground.

It is why we moved to the rocky peaks of the mountains. It is why we told our own to go to the northwest.[97]

In many ways this might seem an all-American ethnoscaping of the region. Certainly there is a virulent nationalism in the rhetoric.[98] However, in terms of the "white site" ethnoscape's binationalism it should be noted that British Columbia also has its white supremacist fringe groups such as the "Ku Klux Klan of the Pacific Realm" who make similar appeals to the "nature" of their racist regionalism.[99] Moreover, in 1996, the Royal Canadian Mounted Police seized a stash of weapons and survival gear that had been hidden by a U.S. militia group in British Columbia. The stash was found in a remote mountain area near Smithers and indicated cross-border organizing by U.S. militia groups quite far north into Canada.[100] Such cross-border activities by the far right are probably quite rare, but one development that has brought them together to collaborate openly and actively on either side of the border around a common cause has been the possible development of a North Cascades International Park. Ironically, the planning around this possible park represents an example of Cascadian environmentalism that goes deeper than the "sustainable development" sound bites of the promoters. There really have been attempts to turn British Columbia's Manning Park and Washington's Glacier Peak Wilderness into a common park for the purposes of better managing and protecting the area's unique transborder ecology. It has been these same attempts that have raised the ire of local far-right groups, including so-called Wise Use antienvironmentalism groups, leading them to make common cause across the border against the planning. According to David Neiwert, they saw the initiative as just the start of "a massive conspiracy to turn the North Cascades National Park into a United Nations enclave stocked with concentration camps, high-tech surveillance equipment and New World Order Ground Troops."[101] This paranoid vision only brought Canadian and American far-right groups together for a short time before other local issues came to the fore. But even as a brief concern, this paranoid imagined geography of the New World Order in local cross-border space mobilized the racist nationalists to network transnationally. As an example of reterritorialization, then, this example also reveals how reactive locality can be constructed in globality "in a world where spatial localization, quotidian interaction, and social scale are not always isomorphic."

Far from reactive, Cascadia's neoliberal boosters would no doubt be horrified by Weber's scientized racism and its farcical, if no less dangerous, return in the white supremacist fascination with a Northwest Territorial Imperative. Although the promotional vision of the region as some sort of environmentally insulated gated community might seem to resonate with a certain country-club white privilege, the promoters' keen interest in boosting Cascadia as a center of Pacific Rim trade explicitly leads to all kinds of declarations of the region's cultural diversity. Indeed, whereas Weber found license for his white supremacism in claims about the climate, the promoters of the Two Nation Vacation—to pick an example I have already cited—draw parallels between meteorology and their appeals to diversity. "The weather in Cascadia," the advertisement reads, "is as varied as the land and the people." More generally, these appeals to diversity are marked by the particular importance the promoters attach to the presence of local Asian-Americans and Asian-Canadians. Schell and Hamer, for example, put it like this:

> We also share an openness to Asian, as well as European, influences, perhaps as a result of lying equidistant between the two continents and having had a long history of exchange dating back to the early silk trade from China. Indeed, immigration—particularly of Asians, who have flooded into Vancouver, and to a lesser extent, Seattle and Portland in recent years—has become a major influence in Cascadia.[102]

In other scripts of Cascadian promotion, Asian-Americans and Asian-Canadians are also repeatedly instrumentalized and stereotyped as the "go-betweens" and "middlemen" that underpin the region's hopes of becoming a center of trans-Pacific trade. No matter that Japanese immigrants in both British Columbia and Washington were imprisoned in internment camps in World War II and that there is a long history of anti-Chinese racism in the region. These real commonalities north and south of the border can now be forgotten while "Asian-Cascadians" can be touted as part of the diversity that gives the region its special niche in a Pacific Rim future. As Gordon Price, a Vancouver City Council member and Cascadia sympathizer, told Robert Kaplan:

> Vancouver is attracting the young of the world's most dynamic middlemen minorities. . . . Look at these Asian kids—many of them are sent here to study by their families. For them, Vancouver must

be like Paris in the twenties—an earlier, modern capitalist culture, compared with the overnight glitz of the rest of the Pacific Rim.[103]

The instrumentalist ethnoscaping of Cascadia by the promoters is not limited to the stereotyping of local Asian populations as go-betweens for Pacific Rim trade and development. Native people are also made part of the cosmopolitan diversity. "Each of our urban cities," boast Schell and Hamer, "is rich in symphony, ballet, jazz, theater, fine arts, and native crafts."[104] Yet whereas the Asian influence is put to work in narratives about Cascadia and trade, the native presence is instrumentalized to explain Cascadians' touted ecosensibilities: "We have a love of the outdoors and a relatively high level of concern for the environment. The Native American regard for nature in Cascadia is a clearer influence than in the East."[105] All questions about the real concern for the environment aside, such clichéd stereotyping of native peoples as guardians of the earth also expresses a stunning disregard for the history of colonialism in the region. Less valuable than the environment, but often treated as equal to it in colonial management practices and discourse, the native peoples of British Columbia, Washington, and Oregon were famously left out of the initial nineteenth-century disputes between Britain and the United States over how the space that is now being reterritorialized should be territorialized in the first place. William Sturgis, an American critic of this disregard at the time, noted thus that the process that led to the inscription of the forty-ninth parallel as the dividing line between the two colonial interests also led to the erasure of the native presence.

> There is third party interested in this matter, of whom I have not spoken, and who have not been mentioned or even alluded to in the discussions and negotiations that have been going on, in relation to this territory. . . . The claims of this party do not depend on discovery, or exploration, or contiguity, but rest upon actual, undisturbed, undisputed possession—by themselves and their fathers from a period to which the history of this continent does not reach.[106]

Today in the context of reterritorialization there is no such lack of attention. In contrast to the events that led up to the creation of the border in the nineteenth century, the promoters of a borderless Cascadia do clearly allude to and mention the native presence frequently. But from the early modern moment of erasure and coloniza-

tion we have now come, it seems, to the postmodern moment of exposure and instrumentalization. The long histories of native peoples
in the region are therefore foregrounded all the better to be commodified and consumed. Thus in the Two Nation Vacation traveler
script, sandwiched between a section on "Art and Cultural Centers"
and another on "Dining in Cascadia," comes this lively consumer-
friendly celebration of Cascadia's "Native People."

> You may recognize some of their names: the Haida, Kwakiitl, Nez
> Perce, Chinook—all famous tribes of the Cascadia region. But more
> than 80 tribes, each with its unique language, stories, art and epic
> history live here today—many on the very land that their people have
> occupied for more than 10,000 years.[107]

To be sure, the long history of occupation (though not, it might be
noted, government) is highlighted here. But it is a history that is instrumentalized for the purposes of creating yet another natural history of Cascadia itself. Indeed, at a Two Nation Vacation planning
conference in Seattle, Bruce Chapman from the Discovery Institute
explained to a panel on native tourism that the reason he had wanted
to include the panel when he was helping to plan the conference was
because, in his mind, native peoples of the region were "the original
Cascadians."[108] In response, a Makah representative on the panel
took issue with Chapman's declaration. "*Ab*-original Cascadians,"
she said, making a profoundly disruptive point with the rhyming of
the words, "might be a better term." Moreover, she continued, "we
would prefer that instead of talking about a Two Nation Vacation
you would at least talk about a Three Nation Vacation."[109] This
insistence on native sovereignty as First Nations proceeded to animate much of the rest of the panel session. The native leaders who
were there all represented particular native tourism interests and
were certainly aware that they were involved in a certain sort of
capitalization of culture. But at the same time, they argued that if
anyone was going to be selling native culture and artifacts it should
be native peoples themselves. Moreover, they argued this had to be
done with care and on the basis of careful collaboration. As evidence of such work a tourist guidebook entitled *Native Peoples of
the Northwest: A Traveller's Guide to Land, Art and Culture* was
exhibited to the audience.[110]

In many different ways the guidebook presented at the conference represented a distinct departure from the general Two Nation Vacation campaign. Each section dealt in great detail with different First Nations' sites and their particular histories, often describing individuals with whom visitors can speak or from whom they can purchase services. The overall sense a potential traveler might receive therefore was far from a generic list of places to buy native artifacts, but a much more lively, heterogeneous set of what sometimes amounted to almost personal invitations to visit. Certainly the guidebook took the same regional template used for Cascadia by the promoters. But as a map of First Nations' sites that came with the guidebook showed, this Cascadian landscape was transformed, turned over on its side and reoriented (like the Gitxsan and Wet'suwet'en cartography discussed in chapter 1) with the up-river East at the top of the map. While for some native leaders even this kind of publication represents a dangerous dalliance with commercialization, the representatives at the panel in 1996 argued that putting native land on a map like this actually furthered the increasing recognition of First Nations' sovereignty and history. In terms of the ethnoscaping of reterritorialization the map was also significant, I think, as a sign of agency, a negotiation of a more meaningful representation of native localities within the structures of globality. By downplaying the border and reorienting the viewer's geographic imagination, the map also seemed to make a particularly telling postcolonial point, reworking the postnational Cascadian concept by recalling the precolonial native networks throughout the region. More recently, in 1999, a more deliberately political announcement of the same point was made in Vancouver at a special meeting of Canadian and U.S. native groups where illustrations of economic involvement in the global economy were combined with declarations about the importance of native peoples coming together across the border as a single people. "In a ceremony rich with religious pageantry, pride and hope," noted a local reporter,

> major native groups from the United States and Canada yesterday pledged to work in tandem to expand political rights and cultural values on both sides of the border. The "sacred document," as it was described by the groups' leaders, declares that while boundaries were drawn between the two countries by "others' hands," these arbitrary lines have not severed, and never will, the ties of kinship among our peoples.[111]

This declaration with its postnational-cum-multinational appeals to First Nations to work together across a border drawn by colonialists seems to me to reflect the most remarkable form of reterritorialization in the context of deterritorialization. It is a reterritorialization that moves beyond the nation-states of today not by creating a transnational ethnoscape of postcolonial movement, but by reclaiming an ethnoscape of precolonialism, an ethnoscape of native space that existed before the first round of modern territorialization even took place.

A DISJUNCTIVE CONCLUSION

For the promoters who have spent so much time landscaping Cascadia as a cross-border region there appears to be a solution to the disjunctures of deterritorialization. Ultimately it is a solution that seeks to reconcile globalism and regionalism by capitalizing on an arrogantly conjunctive series of ideoscapes, financescapes, technoscapes, mediascapes, and ethnoscapes of the region, all of them designed to present Cascadia as a premier global locale in which to make money, spend money, and manage the making of more money. After a short stay interviewing promoters and other commentators in the region, Robert Kaplan came away thinking that in this regard Cascadia was in fact the shape of things to come.

> Not only does Cascadia, with its high income professionals and growing Asian population, foreshadow a greater loyalty to the region and its landscape than to a state or nation, it also suggests a place of resident expatriates, of "rooted cosmopolitans," living in one place but intellectually and professionally inhabiting a larger world—the one across the Pacific and maybe beyond, as the old mass-production economy and the unified culture it spawned devolves into a customized production system with ties to no nation. Cascadia, in other words, is giving concrete expression to what is already beginning to happen in many other parts of the continent.[112]

For the same reasons that Kaplan evokes here, Appadurai's conceptualization of the disjunctive scapes of deterritorialization is not redundant in this context. It certainly helps us find useful ways for categorizing the different modalities of producing and promoting Cascadia's so-called competitive advantage. However, as I have tried to show throughout the chapter, Appadurai's single-minded focus on deterritorialization leaves us without a critical vocabulary for addressing the ways in which the production of locality in globality works through different forms of reterritorialization too. The production of new cross-border spaces is just one example of this, of course, but it provides us with a particularly useful antidote to the more hyperbolic announcements of a coming borderless world. Indeed, studying the promotion of a cross-border region enables us to see how claims about a borderless world can often be put to political-economic work in the service of advancing strategic neoliberal interests. It is important, though, to also qualify these critical conclusions about the limits of a deterritorialization metanarrative with a note about the ongoing significance of disjuncture. While I have shown the ways in which the neoliberal ideoscape of Cascadia effectively overdetermines the other promotional landscapings of the region, I would not like to leave the impression that this promotional effort has completely co-opted and erased other more radically disjunctive regional forces. Clearly the cross-border First Nations' networking is one example of this, but there are others too. While the economic boosters of Cascadia took their regional template from earlier ecological imaginings, the ecoregional and bioregional visions still persist. Many environmentalist groups continue thus to imagine other alliances and futures for the region. They too represent a challenge to national sovereignty on either side of the forty-ninth parallel, but they do so in a disjunctive way that cannot be easily remanaged through the rhetoric of Cascadian sustainable development. Ultimately then I would agree with Appadurai that there are fundamental disjunctures between economy, culture, and politics to which we need to attend. Doing so though, I would argue, should not distract us from the persistent task of examining how the foreclosures of hegemonic reterritorialization produce locality in globality.

3

An Almost Transcendental Level Playing Field: Free Trade and the Dehyphenation of the Nation-State

By establishing a territorial boundary and exercising absolute control over movement across it, state practices define and help constitute a national entity. Setting up and policing a frontier involves a variety of fairly modern practices—continuous barbed-wire fencing, passports, immigration laws, inspections, currency control, and so on. These mundane arrangements, most of them unknown two hundred or even one hundred years ago, help manufacture an almost transcendental entity, the nation-state. This entity comes to seem something much more than the sum of the everyday activities that constitute it, appearing as a structure containing and giving order and meaning to people's lives.

—TIMOTHY MITCHELL, "THE LIMITS OF THE STATE"

Institutionalized with the Canada–U.S. Free Trade Agreement (CUFTA) in 1989 and then completely renegotiated and extended in 1994 to include Mexico with the implementation of the North American Free Trade Agreement (NAFTA), the development of continental free trade has radically troubled the hyphen-nation-states of North America. Not only has it created the context in which cross-border regional visions such as Cascadia have emerged, it has also led to an intense and profound series of debates and struggles over the future of Canada, Mexico, and the United States *as* nation-states. In their place the geography of economic integration that has been entrenched by CUFTA and NAFTA has begun to create a singular continental space across which a transnational institutionalization of neoliberal politics has been extended as an invisible but powerful regime of governance. This is a peculiarly uneven and open-ended space of governance: one in which national sovereignty is still enabled to block nonneoliberal policy goals, and one that, as the more recent negotiations over a Free Trade Area of the Americas (FTAA) show, appears indefinitely expandable too. As Subcomandante Marcos, the spokesperson of the indigenous Zapatista insurgency in Mexico, underlined, free trade therefore represents "a new war of conquest of territories."[1] However, most of the criticism of the actual agreements made at the time of their ratification rarely addressed the spatial organization of the developing free trade regime. Instead, it was mainly the architects of CUFTA and NAFTA who sought to name and explain the new space *as* a space. It was in this way that Prime Minister Mulroney most famously dubbed CUFTA a "level playing field"; that President Bush senior said NAFTA would "level the North American playing field"; and that President Salinas saw the agreements creating "the biggest free-trading area in the world."[2] When President Reagan used the same "level playing field" mantra himself, he also explained that the field was foundational, that free trade represented "a new economic constitution for North America."[3]

In contrast to these labile descriptions of the newness, vastness, and constitutionality of the free trade "level playing field," the dominant critical commentaries around CUFTA and NAFTA at the time of their negotiation and ratification were most often focused on the question of national sovereignty. This was scarcely surprising given the direct threats the free trade agreements posed to national social programs, national environmental standards, national food safety protections, national taxation policies, and national labor conditions. The nation-state was also central because there were many ways in which CUFTA and NAFTA as government-to-government agreements instrumentalized the imprimatur of national government even in the act of eviscerating key competencies of national governance. More than this, of course, CUFTA and NAFTA preserved potent national disciplinary powers including those governing migration. The United States in particular persistently refused the calls from the Mexican government to consider liberalizing transborder worker movements in tandem with the freeing up of trade and investment flows. For all these reasons, the struggles over and for North American free trade did not sound the death knell of the nation-state at all. However, the creation of the liberalized level playing field for business has nevertheless profoundly changed the meaning and force of the links between the nations and states of the continent. It is this complicated, uneven, and incomplete delinking process, or dehyphenation as I want to call it, that I examine in this chapter through the conceptual approach opened up by Timothy Mitchell's important postfoundationalist critique of state theory.

In the academic debate occasioned by Mitchell's essay in the *American Political Science Review,* it was not Mitchell himself nor any of the other more orthodox state theorists who raised the problematic of dehyphenation.[4] Instead, it was the respected Marxist dialectician Bertell Ollman who, without using this exact language, referred in passing to NAFTA's looming implications to underline the delinking of new forms of state making from national-state practices. "[W]hat we also have here," Ollman argued,

> is a preview of the next stage of the "American" capitalist state, with the national forms of the state being reduced to performing mainly repressive and socializing functions, while most of the help rendered to capitalists in their drive to accumulate and maximize their profits is provided at the world and regional state levels. If we were describing a European country, we would have to add still another level, the multinational level of the European Community, which does not yet exist in the case of the United States but may soon, as the new economic treaties with Canada and Mexico begin to take on a life of their own.[5]

Ollman thus invoked free trade in order to make two points simultaneously. On the one hand such an example appeared to illustrate his own more functionalist claims about the superstructural nature of state making as a relay of economic determinations—hence the "help" Ollman refers to as being given to capitalists. On the other hand, he was invoking the macropractices and macroconsequences of free trade as a direct counterpoint to Mitchell's own emphasis on a more micrological analysis of state practices. Mitchell's article had suggested that such analysis should concern itself with the sorts of "mundane arrangements" he included in the list cited above: "continuous barbed-wire fencing, passports, immigration laws, inspections, currency control, and so on." On the basis of such analysis, Mitchell argued, the state can be examined not as a stand-alone entity that holds power, but rather as an emergent effect that, while it comes to seem as if it operates above and beyond society, emerges like so many other aspects of modern life as a result of multiple micropractices of ordering and disciplining everyday activities. Not an external structure that controls society from the outside, nor merely an institutionalized bourgeois bluff concealing the instrumental economics of ruling-class rule, the state, Mitchell therefore suggested, is made to seem separate from society by various organizational routines and relations. "The state," he concluded, "should be addressed as an effect of detailed processes of spatial organization, temporal arrangement, functional specification, and supervision and surveillance, which create the appearance of a world fundamentally divided into state and society."[6] It was against this argument with its Foucauldian emphasis on micropractices that Ollman had wanted to point to the macropractices of transnational state-making, practices that he argued would fall outside the purview of Mitchell's own analysis.

Though neither Ollman nor Mitchell directly addressed the changing nature of the hyphen in nation-state in their exchange, the tension between their two positions offers a valuable way in to the problematic of dehyphenation in the context of free trade. In short, Ollman's intervention provides a lever with which to open the door to transnationalizing Mitchell's analytical approach. Once this displacing move is made, Mitchell's approach can provide critical purchase on the delinking and transnationalizing of state capacities that has happened in concert with the emergence of the so-called level playing field of trade liberalization. The almost transcendental qualities bestowed on this regime in the legal and political discourse of its instigators illustrate exactly the kind of "separation from society effect" that Mitchell argues is part and parcel of modern state effects more generally. At the same time, Mitchell's work can in another way also be brought to bear on the stubborn persistence of national state-making in the debates around the free trade agreements. Clearly, though, there is a fundamental geographical disjuncture between these two arenas of state effects, and it is by putting Mitchell's argument to work on the two levels in turn that I aim to follow Ollman's lead and displace Mitchell's theoretical consolidation of that "almost transcendental entity," the territorial nation-state. It is in this consolidation that I locate Mitchell's anemic geography. It is a geography that so closely yokes nation and state in the analysis that ultimately Mitchell only connects the quasi-transcendental qualities of state effects to the territorialized effects of the hyphenated nation-state. This is why Ollman's use of the transnational state-making example was effective as a line of criticism. Mitchell's yoking of state to nation would seem to foreclose attention to just such dehyphenating developments of new transnational state effects. Nevertheless, by here connecting Mitchell's approach to exactly these dynamics I will argue that a more compelling and critical geography of dehyphenation can be developed.

So why exactly do arguments about emergent state "effects" speak to the duality of dehyphenation in the context of CUFTA and NAFTA? First, on the question of the persistent national-state practices and discourses, Mitchell's sensitivity to the routinized consolidation of the nation-state provides a way of unpacking how the debates surrounding the impact of free trade repeatedly reproduced the state-society dualism in which the national state is conceived as an abstract entity disconnected from socioeconomic change. In other words, the debates repeatedly invoked the nation-state in a quasi-transcendental way, providing numerous examples of how the production of the hyphenated territorialized effect dissembles the socioeconomic milieu out of which it emerges. To use the language of Mitchell's earlier work (introduced in chapter 1), these debates over free trade effectively enframed Canada and the United States respectively as abstract spaces turned independent actors on the global stage. There were still many differences between the U.S. and Canadian debates, but their similarity as practices enframing the nation-state by reproducing the epistemological dualism of state and society provides the starting point for comparison. Second, on the other question of the new continental regime itself, Mitchell's account enables an examination of how the legal and administrative practices institutionalized by the free trade agreements entrenched transnational changes already under way. It was this act of locking in free-market reforms through disciplinary practices that enabled the abstraction of a new transnational state effect: the effect turned quasi-transcendental in the terms of the "level playing field." This transnational geographical effect cannot therefore be dismissed as merely a ghoulish metaphysics of market management. Instead, it has to be analyzed in terms of its production of a political-economic geography in which *non*neoliberal state practices (such as maintaining public health care or taxing business or punishing polluters) become increasingly impossible to implement. In an almost ghostly way, it seems to haunt the practice of policy making, and in such a context, Mitchell's arguments are especially well taken. "The task of a critique of the state," he says, "is not just to reject such metaphysics, but to explain how it is possible to produce this practical but ghost-like effect" ("Limits," 91). More than this, the level playing field effect has also opened up a new terrain of struggle by anticapitalist and reformist groups including environmentalists, labor activists, and feminist organizations. By adopting a more relational and circulatory model of power, Mitchell's account also helps us come to terms with these new transnational networks of resistance.

It should be emphasized from the start that the appearance of "state effects" as I am using the formula here involves much more than discursive framing. Keeping up appearances as national negotiators was hardly a challenge for the stately champions of free trade because most of their public statements and actions were also predestined by reason of routine and bureaucratic protocol to function as an embodiment of national-state agency. Even the econometric models they most commonly used to evaluate the likely outcomes of the agreements were predicated on deep disciplinary assumptions about using "the nation-state" as the fundamental unit of economic analysis.[7] Indeed, as Mitchell's more recent book on political-economic regulation (and deregulation) in modern Egypt has argued, the very concept of "the economy" was always closely intertwined with the formation of territorialized twentieth-century nation-states.[8] In the case of "the economies" considered in the long and complicated negotiation processes that led to CUFTA and NAFTA, the negotiators organized their deliberations on the basis of nation-to-nation diplomacy, and throughout these international negotiations, the more executive aspects of modern state politics were also constantly in play. Whether it was Canadian negotiators attempting to protect national cultural industries, U.S. negotiators seeking protection for sugar, citrus, and winter vegetable farmers, or Mexican negotiators insisting that PEMEX, the state-owned petroleum industry, be protected, the actions of the negotiating teams repeatedly illustrated how territorially circumscribed socioeconomic interests became re-presented as the interests of the nation-state itself. More conspicuously, the final signing ceremonies for CUFTA and NAFTA served to embody this executive articulation of nation and state with simultaneous pageantry and legal codification. The leaders' acts of shaking hands, signing papers, and cordially fraternizing thereby became metonyms of the nation-states joining in partnership. That these meetings represented the culmination of years and years of lobbying by business groups; that such lobbying reflected the systematic reorganization of capitalist production across the continent; that the leaders, like the watching populations, had little or no idea about the precise content of the tomes of trade and investment legalese being signed; and that this same legalese was going to affect millions and millions of day-to-day transactions across North America's borders, all this became eclipsed by the drama of statesmanship. In other words, the drama effectively concealed the far more heterogeneous but systemic set of links established by the increasing economic interdependencies of the negotiating countries. Instead of highlighting the interstitial ties of this new economic space and its encoding in the agreements, these final ceremonial moments of negotiation produced the appearance of constitutional actions by sovereign states.[9]

In what follows I therefore argue after Mitchell that, just like the signing ceremonies themselves, much of the actual struggle and debate over CUFTA and NAFTA in Canada and the United States can be viewed "as part of the much larger social process of generating the mysterious effect of the state, as a separate self-willed entity" ("Limits," 86). Of course, it was precisely the long-term feasibility of such self-willed action by the state that was threatened by the trade deals, and yet, as we shall see, even as critics argued this, they too often tended to obscure the transnational imperatives at work by repeatedly articulating their concerns about state transformation with more national fears about the territorial integrity of the nation. I begin with the Canadian criticisms of CUFTA partly because they came first, but also because they provide a useful corrective to the dismissive view that any concern for the nation-state amounts to mere complicity with ruling-class ideology. Many of the fiercest nationalist critics of CUFTA in Canada repeatedly underlined how the free trade initiative was the product of business-class politicking. They understood the class interests involved, and yet, at the same time, their fundamental argument still tended to concern how the trade agreements and their boosters were taking part in what political cartoons portrayed as a traitorous act of butchering the nation for consumption by Americans.[10] By contrast, the most dominant U.S. critics of free trade such as Ross Perot articulated a very different discourse of the nation-state at risk. These criticisms came later in the United States, being focused around NAFTA rather than CUFTA. They were also much more preoccupied with militaristic worries about the weakening of national independence and the softening of the nation's frontiers. These contrasts are telling, but what nevertheless was so remarkable about the dominant Canadian and U.S. criticisms of CUFTA and NAFTA was how, despite their many differences, they operated by articulating concerns about state transformation under free trade with spatialized fears about national dissolution. It is this process of articulation that requires analysis in terms of Mitchell's account.

The way the appeals to and restatements of the hyphenated nation-state effect emerged in the debates can be interpreted after Mitchell as symptoms of the much wider dynamics creating the appearance of a quasi-transcendental territorial state existing at a remove from socioeconomic life. One of Mitchell's points is that this dissembling of the socioeconomic can have all sorts of political and ideological effects, and, as he argued in a 1998 essay, one such hegemonic effect in the mid-twentieth century has been to help fabricate the other parallel commonsense abstraction of a singular "national economy." "In the form of the nation-state," he notes, the production of the effect of a state apparatus simultaneously "establishes the spatial boundaries of the economy, creating the currency, the customs barriers and geographical borders that appear to separate one economy from the next."[11] Yet it was precisely such establishment economic features of the nation-state that free trade reterritorialized, and it was in turn this reterritorialization that the critics were contesting. As they did so they therefore exposed the geographical mismatch between the older territorialized nation-state effect (to which they wished to cling all the more tightly) and the newly reterritorializing transnational economic order. No longer could the dissembling abstraction of "the nation-state" be so coherently mapped on to the equally dissembling abstraction of "the economy," and one set of symptoms of this profound political and representational crisis was the increasingly desperate invocations of the nation-state as an embattled community at risk.

CUFTA, CANADA, AND THE LIMITS OF THE WELFARE STATE

In Canada the drama of negotiating CUFTA basically began in 1984 when Brian Mulroney's Progressive Conservatives beat Pierre Trudeau's Liberals in the general election, and the new prime minister abruptly abandoned prior pledges against free trade. Shortly after the election he departed to give a speech in New York in which he declared Canada was now "open for business."[12] Leaving behind the protectionism of his 1983 leadership campaign speech, he had become a fervent booster of free trade. In 1985 he was further enabled to set about negotiating an actual free trade agreement with the United States when a Royal Commission on Canada's economic future—a Commission that had been appointed by the Liberals and that therefore had the authority of seeming impartiality—finally laid out its recommendations.[13] Most notably, the Commission recommended that Canada abandon the protectionism of Trudeau's National Energy Policy, abandon government "frictions" on business such as the Foreign Investment Review Agency, and go forward with what was called "a leap of faith" into a new agreement on liberalized trading relations with the United States.[14] The commissioner, Donald Macdonald, summarized these findings as follows:

> My conclusion after nearly three years as a commissioner was that Canadians did not suffer from a failure of will, they were suffocating from failure in policy. As a result, among other recommendations the Commission made was the decision to seek free trade with the United States. Without secure access to a large market, infant Canadian industries will remain infants. Although the US is already our largest trading partner—two-way trade now totals $150 billion a year—we cannot count on continued growth. . . . Free trade is no sellout, it is a sales tool. Canada's gross national product would grow by an estimated three to eight percent over the next 10 years. That kind of growth would be worth from $12–$24 billion to the Canadian economy or up to $4,000 for the average Canadian family.[15]

Not only did these recommendations serve Mulroney's new pro–free trade project well, they also created the appearance that such a policy could be easily implemented by the state and improve the country's economic well-being. Free trade was in this sense proffered as a policy *choice* that would be taken by the state in order to change the shape of the Canadian economy. It was going to be an act of leadership and statesmanship, even an act of salesmanship too, but certainly not an act of selling out. The possibility that such a course of action might be a necessary outcome of already sweeping economic changes was not mentioned as such, and the economic determinations at work were thus downplayed. Canada's industries were metaphorized as "infants" that would only grow up if the paterfamilias of the state released them from the suffocating policies of fatherly protection. In this way, free trade was cast as a matter of the state needing to make a brave parental choice of trusting the infant individuals under its care to go off and play on what the state would ensure was a fairly leveled playing field. The benefits of this economic oedipal drama would then finally return, of course, to the Canadian family: the "average" family whose stereotypical relationships provided the hierarchical and decisionist model for the commissioner's whole discourse. To be sure, the report itself did note the trend toward interdependency in the global economy, and this was connected repeatedly, if sometimes confusingly, to the need for free trade. "In an interdependent world, Canada has many competitors. It can no longer, as it has in the past, fight back or forge ahead from behind tariff walls."[16] However, this fighting back and forging ahead were not advanced as a belated attempt to adapt policy so that it followed the continentalism of contemporary Canadian business organization. It was instead articulated as a bold "leap of faith": an audacious, albeit risky, act of global "leadership" by a hopeful, trusting, and, thus, thoroughly anthropomorphized state.[17] Overall, the whole Commission discourse was written as if the "leap of faith" was going to be made by a singular family patriarch, a separate, self-willed structural effect, otherwise known as the Canadian state.

As many critics noted, the lobbying of the Macdonald Commission told another story.[18] It was a story of business elites inundating hearings with complaints about the frictions posed to cross-border capitalism by tariff and nontariff barriers. These were the same groups that in another era had been energized to save the protectionist legacy of Canada's First National Policy from the Laurier government's attempts to establish "reciprocity" in trade with the United States.[19] By the 1980s, however, the investments in fixed capital and market development by Canadian corporations had become far more continental in character, and the owners and managers of this capital were therefore no longer committed to protecting the circuits of Canadian capital from foreign competition. Indeed, Canadian transnational corporations led, and in many cases continue to lead, the trend toward the transnational organization of North American production that followed in the wake of the 1970s crises of Fordist accumulation.[20] Even as early as 1981 the annual flow of Canadian investment into the United States was dwarfing the reverse flow, overturning the traditional *dependista* depiction of Canada as a victim of U.S. branchplant colonialism.[21] More recently, the ratio of Canadian foreign direct investment in the United States to U.S. foreign direct investment in Canada has continued to climb precipitously, leading at least some more critical Canadian commentators to locate the country among the top tier of neoimperial powers.[22]

If the Commission's analyses and recommendations tidily glossed over the business lobby's investment in continentalization, the next step of the journey toward the state-led promotion of free trade was the formal handover of the campaign to the career politicians. This movement of the initiative into the realm of political leadership is similar to the more disciplinary processes identified by Mitchell as constitutive of state effects, processes in which struggles taking place among key social actors are abstracted out of their societal context and into the seemingly separate sphere of the state. In other words, the political abstraction of the free trade debate dramatized the dualism of state and society, while its actual mechanics betrayed the embeddedness of political discourse in the dynamics of social struggle and socioeconomic change. As well as highlighting its long history, Frederick Engels's summary of the "edifying squabbles" and "lobby intrigues" arising from the fight over free trade in America in the 1880s captures the abstracting nature of this political pattern quite well.

> Then ensues a long and obstinate fight between Free Traders and Protectionists; a fight where, on both sides, the leadership soon passes out of the hands of the people directly interested into those of professional politicians, the wire-pullers of the traditional political parties, whose interest is, not a settlement of the question, but its being kept open forever; and the result of an immense loss of time, energy and money is a series of compromises favoring now one side, now the other side, and drifting slowly though not majestically in the direction of Free Trade.[23]

In Canada in the 1980s this pattern was repeated again, with the Progressive Conservatives lauding free trade and the Liberals—once the traditional party of Canadian capital—reading from the older script of Canada's protectionist past. In terms of the popular presentation of the struggle, however, this drama did not reflect a contest between different factions of capital and even less the crisis of Canadian Fordism.[24] Instead, the battle Canadians saw in the media came across as a clash of statesmen fighting over the future of the nation-state.

I use the everyday sexist language of "statesmanship" advisedly because it hints at how the sexualization of the political drama also contributed to the construction of the Canadian state as a seemingly separate self-willed entity.[25] As the Canadian feminist critics of free trade in the National Action Committee on the Status of Women (NAC) pointed out, Mulroney made a notably "macho" argument for the free trade leap of faith.[26] According to this argument, it was not only the brave thing to do, it was a manly move that only true patriots who believed in the capacity of Canadians to compete continentally could understand. Those who were against free trade were, following this masculinist-cum-Darwinist logic, emasculated pretenders to the patrimony of "true patriot love" (the "love" commanded of Canada's "sons" by the national anthem). Groups like NAC rejected this call to patriotic neoliberalism, and as we shall see, they have since questioned the embrace of what might be called "filial territorialism" too. However, other Canadian critics took up the gauntlet of Mulroney's patriot games with gusto. Most notably it was John Turner, a professional politician and the leader of the Liberal Party, who established himself as the figurehead of the anti–free trade campaign. Arguing that it was far more patriotic to be against free trade, Turner helped keep the mass-media focus on the questions of leadership, patriotism, and country.

The questions of economic patriotism therefore became the stuff of the 1988 general election. It was an election that consequently became transformed into a national referendum (itself a nation-state-reproducing practice) on free trade. Other issues in the election were ignored or transmuted into the questions of trade and patriotism. One result of this was that the left-leaning New Democratic Party (NDP) lost support in the election because its analysis and argument against CUFTA coincided with Turner's.[27] The head-to-head between Turner and Mulroney over the patriotism of free trade effectively eclipsed most other arguments about good government, thereby diminishing the significance of differences between anti–free trade positions and leading many working-class voters to turn to the Liberal Party as an ally. The result in immediate electoral terms was the NDP's poor showing with only 18.6 percent of the popular vote.[28] More than all this, though, what must also be underlined about the head-to-head confrontation over the patriotism of free trade was the way in which it created the effect of a leadership battle for control of the state. The actual rituals of the television debates therefore came together with the "leap of faith" script presented by the Macdonald Commission and effectively dissembled the transnational economic imperatives driving the free trade initiative forward. With Mulroney and Turner arguing about loyalty and leadership, and with each side proclaiming the other unpatriotic, free trade came to seem an issue of sovereign, if not entirely majestic, decision making. It became an "either-or" question, and whether it was to be a leap of faith or a leap into the arms of the great republic, it remained accordingly a clear-cut choice for the leaders of a sovereign, self-willed state to make.

The symptomatic state effects produced by the 1988 Canadian free trade debate and the political contentions of the November general election may now be clearer, but the connections between these effects and the forms of disciplinary practices that, in Mitchell's words, "define and help constitute a national entity" went further than the process of political abstraction. To be sure, the ritualized drama of television exchanges between leading politicians is a quite quotidian example of how the mechanics of the modern media contribute to the production of the appearance of national governance.[29] But the disciplinary enframing of the free trade debate went deeper than this. There were other more "mundane arrangements" helping, as it were, to hyphenate the nation-state: making it seem "a structure containing and giving order and meaning to people's lives" ("Limits," 94). First, there was the rather routine way in which both the free trade and anti–free trade sides proceeded to make their arguments by turning to the forms of data that detailed the so-called health of the national economy. Second, there were the more complex and profound ways through which such disciplined statistical surveys were then articulated with the fate of the nation.

Using figures on GDP, currency fluctuations, the balance of payments, per capita income, and national unemployment to summarize the impact of liberalized trade with the United States, both sides debated from a perspective that was already deeply shaped by a taken-for-granted "methodological nationalism."[30] In this case the specific method was that of the national institutions of data gathering, including Statistics Canada, which highlighted the disciplinary genealogy of *stat*istics. The mandate of the data-gathering institutions was and continues to be framed by borders that, through the course of calculating numerous statistics, they entrench, thereby turning the enframed object, the hyphenated nation-state, into an almost transcendental entity. When their statistical output was invoked like an incantation in the free trade debates it contributed to an extremely forceful effect. This enframing of the nation-state was further reinforced in the debates themselves by the way in which the statistics were articulated with discourses depicting Canada's national destiny: discourses concerning the future permeability of the country's borders, the integrity of its diverse regions, and the meaningfulness of its citizens' passports. Through this process of repeatedly articulating state and nation it became possible for commentators to discuss not only the "life" of the nation-state, but also, for those who were critical, to indicate what they saw as the imminent possibility of its death.

The pro–free trade side countered these doomsday descriptions with their own economic forecasts. Further nationalizing the anthropomorphization of the state found in the Macdonald report, they argued that the freedom of free trade would thereby enable the nation-state to become somehow fitter for the future. "Free trade, Free Canada," was the equation thereby drawn in the title of a representative book of boosterist speeches whose subtitle put it still more directly: "how free trade will make Canada stronger."[31]

All the abundant freedom unleashed by free trade, it was argued, would ultimately liberate everything and anything. It ultimately freed the nation-state itself: hence "Free Canada." This fetishization of "freedom" was and is banal. Yet while hobbled by its own hyperbole, it serves as another example of the articulation of the nation-state as a quasi-transcendental agent. The notion of freeing Canada from its protectionist past assumes thus that the agent so liberated can somehow realize its full transcendental potential. The critics of

CUFTA, of course, rejected this rhetoric of liberation, but by arguing that it was precisely the same transcendental destiny of Canada that was threatened, they nevertheless took part in equal measure in the process of enframing.

The anti–free trade arguments about the threats to Canada represented the condensation point of two main discourses, both of them conjoining and enframing the nation-state in the course of anticipating its imminent end. First, there were the arguments about how free trade represented an attack on the institutions and traditions of welfare-state intervention in Canada. This line of critique was aligned with an argument about the nation-state at risk because of the real and well-understood links in Canada between redistributive state practices and the overall integrity of such a regionalized country. From the time of the First National Policy and the building of the trans-Canada railroad to the postwar investment in regional redistribution and the concomitant commitments to trans-Canadian equality in welfare, health care, and education provision, Canada has been geographically contained through interventions by the federal government.[32] For many critics (who have since been vindicated by events) the privatization policies that were to be entrenched by CUFTA directly threatened such nation-consolidating state practices.[33] The threat was in fact seen as doubly dangerous in this case, though, because of the second source of concern about the death of the nation-state: namely that free trade with the United States also represented a further advance in the Americanization of Canada. Given the othering of American identity that is so much part of the traditional narration of Canadian nationality, this fear of Americanization repeatedly served to link the threats to state practices with the notion of national demise. The comparisons of Canadian communitarian traditions with American individualism, of "peace, order, and good government" with "life, liberty, and the pursuit of happiness," meant that the pursuit of the particular forms of life and liberty implicit in free trade appeared especially threatening (not to mention unpeaceful, disorderly, and bad) to the continued survival of Canada as an independent nation-state north of the forty-ninth parallel.

Though it is as much a political ideology as a product of actual disciplinary practices, the "un-American, welfare state" vision of Canada was and remains effective in Mitchell's terms at "containing and giving order and meaning to people's lives." Certainly, in the anti–free trade struggle it attracted a broad spectrum of support as an inclusive counterhegemonic discourse.[34] The coalition of CUFTA's critics thus ranged widely from the Council of Catholic Bishops and popular national writers like Pierre Berton and Margaret Atwood, to the Liberals and NDP, to the labor movement, environmentalists, and the feminists in NAC. This heterogeneous grouping, which later became formalized as the Pro Canada Network (and later still as the Action Canada Network), may not have agreed on much else, but their view of Canada as an imperiled, un-American society united by a welfare state ultimately meant that their discourse became collectively disciplined—in the sense of being simultaneously enabled and constrained—by the welfare statism of liberal Keynesianism. In fact some of CUFTA's critics keenly cited Keynes's famous 1933 article "National Self-Sufficiency" with its appeal to "let goods be homespun whenever it is reasonably and conveniently possible, and, above all, let finance be purely national."[35] This is significant because historically, as Mitchell has highlighted, it was just such Keynesian discourse that helped consolidate and territorialize the notion of independent measurable "national economies" in the first place. "The idea of the national economy was not theorized," notes Mitchell, commenting on the influence of Keynes's work in the 1930s, "but introduced as a commonsense construct providing the boundaries within which the new averages and aggregates could be measured."[36] Contained by just such Keynesian common sense, the critiques of CUFTA still touched on free trade's nonnational implications, but in a way that was less concerned with their transnational reach than with their deleterious effects on the national economy and thus the nation-state itself. In this way, the critics called attention to how CUFTA would likely force the downward harmonization of labor and environmental standards, weaken regional development programs, reduce wages and increase unemployment while forcing cutbacks in the social safety net, and limit the ability of future provincial and federal governments to take privately provided services like day care and auto insurance back into the realms of public provision.[37] Even as they noted this neoliberal normalization through free trade, however, the liberal Keynesian vision of the critics meant that they rarely addressed the new free trade–led hegemony of neoliberalism as a transnational tendency. As a result, their critical arguments ended up proffering protectionism and anti-Americanism as the solution to complex transnational socioeconomic problems. The examples of the labor and feminist movements—the two most likely advocates of a more transnational critique—illustrate the limits of this nation-state-enframing approach.

The leadership of the Canadian labor movement defined its campaign against CUFTA as a "fight for a sovereign and independent Canada,"[38] a struggle for "the survival and independence of our nation."[39] It was an agenda closely tied to the Keynesian economic strategy of defending traditional "tools of national economic management."[40] Contained by the economic autarky of this Keynesian strategy, the labor movement's alternatives to CUFTA were thus generally articulated in terms of protectionism or, as one of the most influential documents of the anti–free trade Left entitled it, *Building Self-Reliance in Canada*.[41] The labor movement buttressed its protectionist solutions with the somewhat sanguine hope that the economically enclosed nation-state would somehow be able to win future confrontations with international capital. Such hopes and their whole nationalist logic were then further bolstered by a form of populism that led some on the Left to even target poor foreign workers as part of the rhetorical assault on free trade.[42]

The first consequence of this populist protectionism was the weak showing of the NDP in the 1988 election. Having aligned itself through the logic of liberal Keynesianism with the Liberals, the labor movement and its political representatives lost what had previously been seen as one of their best chances to take control of the government in years. The tactical alliance with the Liberals to "save Canada's sovereignty" ended in more than just defeat. It also led to breakdown in the labor movement's own tactical alliance across Canada, and most especially its tactic of building working-class solidarity across the English-French divide.[43] Support for CUFTA had been stronger in Québec, partly because of the shrinking appeal of Canadian nationalism in the province, but also because of the way in which free trade seemed to promise a scaling back of federal government intervention in provincial affairs. By the mid-1980s, the leadership and tenor of the separatist movement in Québec had, as Alain Gagnon and Mary Beth Montcalm underline, shifted to the neoliberal right.[44] Consequently, the English-Canadian labor movement's call to Keynesianism clashed in Québec with a state effect framed not by the Fordist formulae of protectionism but by the project of protecting a language and culture through the neoliberal scaling back of federal Fordism. These splits and losses were devastating to the Canadian Left, and the NDP, in particular, has found it hard to recover.

The feminist critique of free trade was somewhat different and certainly led to different consequences in defeat. Indeed, the free trade issue served to bring feminists from Québec and the rest of Canada together. A report drafted by the then vice president of NAC, Marjorie Cohen, showed that one of the groups most vulnerable to the forms of free trade–driven restructuring were women working in the low value-added clothing, textile, footwear, and food processing sectors of the Québec economy.[45] These sorts of workers both in Québec and elsewhere, along with women working in the services sector across Canada, were going to bear the brunt of what the free trade boosters preferred to call "adjustment costs."[46] Cohen also pointed out that women were unlikely to benefit from the retraining programs proffered as a palliative by the government because their ability to move was often limited by the patriarchal division of labor and decision-making in the home.[47]

In NAC's public news releases and television interviews, Cohen and her colleagues rearticulated these more detailed points in broader statements about the future of the economy and the country in general. The argument that they most often reiterated was that this was not just a trade agreement. It was in these ways that NAC adopted the disciplined Keynesian discourse, arguing that free trade ultimately represented a threat to the national integrity, identity, and security of Canada. In their *Women Against Free Trade* manifesto, representatives from NAC along with other women's groups argued that to say "[t]he Mulroney trade deal was only about trade" was a myth.[48] In reality, they countered,

> This deal is a Trojan Horse that will bring Reagonomics to Canada. The trade deal is more about importing a set of economic, social and political policies than it is about changing the conditions of trade. In fact a number of important sections of the proposed deal have nothing to do with trade barriers. A closer look shows that "harmonization" means virtual economic integration with the United States. And economic integration means much more. Let's look at what Reagonomics has done for the US: A military budget of a trillion dollars and more homeless people than at any time in American

history. Hardship and destitution for families facing illness as a result of no public medical insurance. A crisis in farming unparalleled since the Great Depression. A steady decline in working conditions and a decimation of organized labor. Aggressive campaigns against women's and minority rights. Cutbacks in social services—forcing 22% of Americans to live below the poverty line in the richest country on earth! A shameless disregard for the environment. [And v]icious bullying of the Third World.[49]

By arguing that whole traditions of Canadian social services and regional redistribution were under threat, and by combining this with a picture of a Reaganized America that symbolized all that Canada was not, NAC effectively affirmed a form of national imagining that countered the patriarchal picture of survivalism presented by the free trade proponents. Moreover, it did so in its anti–free trade manifesto by making connections with the day-to-day lives of women in Canada. It directly countered the survivalist picture of Canadian consumers winning new low prices in the global marketplace by pointing out how certain products like drugs would become *more* expensive because of the new patent restrictions on national generic drug production ushered in by free trade.[50] Yet, at the same time, the whole argument was consolidated by a Canada-first commitment to liberal Keynesianism. The enframing logic of this approach effectively contained the scope of NAC's critique, and while the manifesto usefully highlighted the transnational Trojan horse effect of CUFTA, NAC still positioned itself as a defender of the Canadian citadel: a Trojan, as it were, trying to close the protectionist gate on the problems of the Reaganized world beyond.

It should nonetheless be noted that by voicing concerns about the everyday lives of women, NAC's argument was more open to certain continental continuities than some other anti–free trade women's voices, including, most notably, that of Margaret Atwood. Following the nationalist themes found elsewhere in her work, Atwood made a trenchant polemic against the deal, invoking, in a far more rhetorical way than NAC, a poignant affinity between the status of women and the state of the Canadian nation.

> Canada as a separate but dominated country has done about as well under the United States as women worldwide have done under men; about the only position they've ever adopted toward us country to country has been the missionary position, and we were not on top.[51]

NAC, by contrast, maintained a consistently substantive attention to the practicalities of the trade deal. It did not mobilize grand tropes of Canada as nation as Woman, and as a result, it did not fall into the same dangers of reentrenching heterosexual gender stereotypes for which others have criticized Atwood.[52] Yet while NAC's practical argument that the negative consequences of CUFTA would disproportionately affect the lives of actual women avoided the inadequacies of Atwood's allusions, the organization's commitment to a Keynesian welfare statism meant that its argument was still ultimately disciplined by a similarly sovereigntist construction of Canada. While it did not anthropomorphize the country "as Woman," then, NAC still contributed to a discourse on free trade that assumed the coherence of the nation-state in the course of commenting on its likely breakup. In other contexts, NAC had been critical about the priorities set within Canadian welfare-statism, but advocating the virtues of the Keynesian welfare state in the free trade debate as an alternative to neoliberalism carried some costs. For instance, when NAC again joined its anti-trade-liberalization voice to the chorus of nationalist dissent over NAFTA, the protectionist position it took met with internal criticism from representatives of immigrant women. In effect, these representatives complained that the nation-state-enframing argument simultaneously devalued skills learned by women outside of Canada.[53]

Despite enframing Canada as nation-state in the debate, NAC, the labor movement, and the rest of the Action Canada Network were ultimately unable to stop the Trojan horse of free trade. Moreover, they not only lost the struggle over CUFTA in immediate electoral terms, they also lost—at least for the time being—the wider hegemonic struggle. Thus while Mulroney won the 1988 election and implemented free trade, what is arguably more significant is that by the time the Liberals rallied and won the 1993 election, they had switched to being a pro–free trade party too. The new government of Jean Chrétien insisted on only the most cosmetic of changes in the final draft of NAFTA before expeditiously making it part of Canadian law and keenly maintaining it as such in the subsequent decade.[54] In the United States, by contrast, the attempts to articulate concerns about state restructuring with the territorial integrity of the nation were beginning to reach a crescendo.

NAFTA, THE UNITED STATES, AND THE LIMITS OF THE WARFARE STATE

In the mainstream U.S. debate over NAFTA the dominant focus of commentary and criticism was quite different from the critique of CUFTA made by Canadian feminists. Nevertheless, in the American context the trade agreement still functioned as a sticking point for innumerable concerns provoked by the integration of the nation-state into state-transforming economic interdependencies. In response there was also the same discursive pattern of rearticulating the nation and state, conjoining them and enframing them as an abstract structure containing a territorialized society. However, the debate over the future spatial integrity of the United States was not defined by a communitarian enframing of the nation as a country with a Keynesian *welfare state*. By contrast, the discourses enframing the United States as a nation-state at risk in the NAFTA debate ultimately came to be dominated by a defensive delineation of the nation-space, a militaristic fetishization of the abilities and boundaries of what was sometimes imagined more as a *warfare state*. To be sure there were concerns about free trade's implications for social welfare and equality raised by U.S. liberals and leftist critics. However, because most of these critiques tended to return to the theme of threatened American employment, they easily became subsumed into the larger fearful discourse about a looming loss of American jobs south of the border, or what Ross Perot dubbed with savvy simplicity "the giant sucking sound."[55] It was this nationalist anti-NAFTA discourse with its attendant, sometimes explicit, assumptions about Mexico and Mexicans as a drain on the American way of life that finally dominated the U.S. criticisms of NAFTA, sucking other less chauvinist critiques made by environmentalists, unions, and consumer rights groups into its vortex. To understand how this happened it is useful to examine the ways in which the buildup to the American debates was also characterized by the same kinds of bureaucratic and methodological nationalism that had shaped the direction of the CUFTA debates in Canada.

Just as was the case north of the border, the territorial consolidation of the nation-state as a central object of concern in the debates was underwritten by a scripting of the pro–free trade statesmen as father figures leading their nations into agreement. Again, the negotiation process itself helped to secure this effect by systematically

foregrounding the roles of the political leaders and downplaying corporate interests, pressures, and integration patterns. In fact it was
President Salinas of Mexico who first publicly initiated the process
of negotiating NAFTA at the World Economic Forum in Davos in
1990 when he approached the U.S. trade representative Carla Hills.
Her office then became interested when, after a review of key U.S.
economic sectors, they realized that "[t]raditional malcontents such
as steel, etc. wouldn't be opposed, [and that] there was a lot of interest in the investment community."[56] However, the public debate
and struggle in the United States at large only began when President
Bush senior followed the advice of Hills and asked Congress for
Fast Track negotiating authority in 1991. For Bush, NAFTA represented a positive engagement with what he had famously labeled
the New World Order. Subsequently, this was basically the same
theme that President Clinton went on to use—albeit in his own vocabulary of "embracing change"—as he proceeded where Bush had
left off, shepherding the almost finalized agreement along with two
side agreements on labor and the environment through Congress.
To this end Clinton not only enlisted the support of Bush, but also
Presidents Carter and Ford to highlight to the public and to recalci-
trant Democratic Representatives that this was an agreement that
really came with the fullest and highest executive endorsement imag-
inable. When even this show of leadership did not seem to assure
congressional approval, and when the day of the House vote drew
near, Clinton organized at the White House a gathering of some of
the most prominent U.S. state decision makers alive, including President Carter again, but also such classic representatives of executive
decision making as Henry Kissinger and James Baker. Here again
was a show of sovereign leadership. But it was more than a show;
it also provided one more opportunity for the promoters to make a
clear link between NAFTA and the seemingly sovereign ambitions
of American nationalism. Baker's own address to the gathering is
worth quoting because of its clear articulation of this ambition with
the cause of NAFTA.

> How we decide this issue and how we vote on NAFTA is really going
> to reveal a lot about what this nation is going to be in the future. Even
> more importantly, I think it's going to tell us what sort of people we
> are. I think this agreement marks a defining moment in American
> history, a moment that ranks with America's entry on to the world

stage in the 1940s, first to defeat Fascism and then to lead the great alliance of democracies that fought and won the Cold War. Then as now America faced a new era, an era full of opportunities, but also full of risks and perils. Then, as now, America had to choose between engagement on the one hand and isolationism on the other.[57]

Baker's geostrategic description of the NAFTA vote as an act of leadership invoked a whole history of U.S. internationalism in order to code the agreement as an embodiment of American agency on the world stage. Gone from this argument was any mention of the changing structure of U.S. capitalism, gone in fact were any explicitly economic rationales for the agreement at all. It had become an act of engaged statesmanship, and nothing less. This was not to say that economists were absent from the campaign for congressional approval. Indeed, there were a number of Nobel Prize winners for Economics in the East Room of the White House when Baker made his speech. However—just as had happened in Canada—their contribution to the debate had already been effectively territorialized by the methodological nationalism of their aggregate data calculations.

Given that the economists were also drawn into the debates to respond to the concerns raised by critics about American job losses, their public statements were all generally framed in terms of the national economy with a stress on national GDP, trade surpluses, net national job gains, and other similarly territorialized indices. For example, Gary Hufbauer, an especially influential economist in the promotional campaign, argued that the opening up of the Mexican market through NAFTA enabled him to predict job opportunity increases for Americans. Taking issue with the main union critique, he argued that NAFTA would in fact create a net gain of 170,000 U.S. jobs.[58] Such arguments proved somewhat vulnerable in the years that followed NAFTA's implementation, with the peso crisis and the resulting falloff in Mexican demand for U.S.-made products leading to claims that NAFTA had led to almost a million *lost* U.S. jobs twenty months after implementation.[59] Yet even during the debates over congressional ratification, the numbers war between such pro-NAFTA economists and the critics began to reveal the anachronism of the methodological nationalism on which the battling statistics were based. Predicting labor market changes from changes in national trade balances not only assumed that other factors such as currencies would remain stable (which they evidently did not), it also assumed that the continental labor market and production process itself could continue to be neatly divided up nation-state by nation-state. It was precisely this methodological national packaging that began to unravel as the debates between the predictors of job loss and job gain continued. In this "Numbers War," concluded Louis Uchitelle in a review article for the *New York Times*, "No One Can Count."[60] He asked if either side was right and, having underlined the decreasing pertinence of economic statistics collected and analyzed solely at the level of the nation-state, concluded that "[p]robably they are both wrong."[61]

Leaving aside until the next section the questions surrounding the continental leveling of the labor market, it is important to turn here to the critics' side of the debate over national job losses. Early on, during the struggle over President Bush's request for Fast Track authority to negotiate NAFTA, it had been the American Federation of Labor and Confederation of Industrial Organizations (AFL-CIO), the umbrella organization representing American unions, that had advanced the job-loss argument most ardently. The AFL-CIO's position in this regard was not only sovereigntist in terms of its rhetoric, it was also reflective of entrenched organizational interests at the national level. One indication of these, in fact, was the notable contrast with the AFL-CIO's previous approach to CUFTA. Unlike their Canadian counterparts, the U.S. union leadership had not fought a systematic campaign against CUFTA. In general terms the agreement had promised to bring more, not fewer, jobs to the United States, and it certainly did not create a significant hiatus in the circuits of U.S. capital. There was no grand split between domestic and internationalist investment aggravated by the agreement. CUFTA instead cheapened U.S. imports of Canadian staples, provided better access to the Canadian market, and consequently, allowed some U.S. branch plants to relocate from Canada to U.S. states with lower labor and tax costs. It was basically as a result of this net gain in employment opportunity that the U.S. labor movement retreated from solidarity with Canadian workers and, in large part, did not oppose the agreement.[62] In stark contrast to this, from 1991 to November 1993 when NAFTA was put before the U.S. Congress, the U.S. labor movement became radically mobilized against free trade in much the same way as the Canadian labor movement had before it.

Led by the AFL-CIO, the union campaign closely paralleled the campaign of Canadian workers against CUFTA in 1987–88. NAFTA was lambasted as a job-destroying, wage-reducing agreement that would work as a whipsaw to force wages along with environmental and health and safety standards down toward the lowest common continental denominators.[63] In practice, this open-ended critique was also simultaneously territorialized by the methodological nationalism of statistical aggregates and data gathering. Endeavoring to counter the administration's argument that the extension of CUFTA into NAFTA would create 175,000 new U.S. jobs, the labor movement turned with equally disciplined determination to the compilation and representation of national statistics.[64] AFL-CIO leaders cited studies by the union-supported Economic Policy Institute, which predicted 550,000 job losses in ten years, and by economists at the University of Massachusetts at Amherst, which predicted 490,000 job losses by the year 2000.[65] Individual unions such as the International Brotherhood of Electrical Workers (IBEW) and the Amalgamated Clothing and Textile Workers brought these abstractions home by publishing the names of factories that had already moved to Mexico and the number of union members thereby displaced.[66] Overall, the AFL-CIO argued that the "job-gutting Mexican trade pact [would] drain many thousands more US jobs across the border and exploit the poverty wages of Mexican workers."[67] They therefore pressured Democratic House representatives to vote against the agreement or risk losing the support of organized labor next election time.

Ironically, while the AFL-CIO campaign was widely articulated in terms of maintaining national jobs and national sovereignty, it was also significant insofar as it now brought U.S. unions together with their Canadian counterparts in a common shared struggle against the southerly movement of jobs. As we shall see in the next section, it was this sort of copositioning that led in turn to quite different transnational solidarity-building projects: some of them organized by the Canadian movement (which by 1993 was increasingly coming to terms with the transnational tendencies of continental capital), some of them initiated by the AFL-CIO itself, and some of them involving solidarity with Mexican workers too. However, little was heard of such transnational outreach in the national media, which focused with ritualized single-mindedness on the national job-loss versus national job-gain arguments. Moreover, when the AFL-CIO attempted to intervene directly in this media debate, most notably with a $3 million television commercial, it did so with a nationalist argument:

> In Washington, big corporations and lobbyists are spending millions making false claims about the NAFTA trade deal. . . . But people going to factories, to farms, to offices know NAFTA means jobs going South. Economists . . . say we could lose up to 500,000 jobs. . . . NAFTA: It's a bad deal for America, and Americans know it.[68]

The advantages of this nationalist framing were direct. It quickly created a popular, accessible hegemony-building discourse that could accommodate many different critical voices. Jesse Jackson, for example, joined the anti-NAFTA campaign on exactly the same register, arguing that "NAFTA is a shafta, shifting our jobs out of the country."[69] But by the very same token, this sovereigntist discourse against NAFTA also predictably proved the Achilles heel of radical critique because of the way in which it ceded so much control and ground to the conservative critics of the agreement. After all, if the loss of national jobs was the "issue," reporters needed only to turn to the author of the "great sucking sound" slogan, along with the rest of his readily repeatable calls to "ordinary Americans" to *Save Your Job, Save Your Country.*[70] Despite massive organizing efforts, therefore, the multiple voices of U.S. labor ultimately became drowned out by the single, albeit bombastic, voice of one very rich Texan. For Perot, the "giant sucking sound" came from outside the nation, from a Mexico depicted in terms of desperation and dependency, and it was this chauvinistic tendency to present the threat as coming from the outside that then allowed Perot's critiques to be wedded in the mainstream commentaries to Patrick Buchanan's still more reactionary nationalism.[71]

Perot's interventions also introduce the way the U.S. debate over NAFTA became politically abstracted into yet another clash of statesmen. Unlike the tussle between Turner and Mulroney, however, Perot entered the debate not as a traditional party politician but rather as a populist whose position was defined precisely as a critic of insider party politics. It was this seeming "outsider" status that had earlier catapulted Perot to national notoriety in his 1992 presidential bid. For pro–free trade organs like *The Economist,* this made the billionaire a cause for concern. "Ross Perot has aligned his wealth, his ambition and skill as a preacher of populist nonsense—all of them formidable—with the anti-NAFTA cause."[72] However, with his popularity declining, Perot made the perfect foil for the pro-NAFTA Clinton White House, and it became the administration's declared strategy not only to align him with the anti-NAFTA cause but to turn him into the very embodiment of NAFTA opposition.[73] The ultimate result was the staging of a television debate between Vice President Gore and Perot: a debate seemingly representing a straightforward head-to-head between pro-NAFTA and anti-NAFTA forces, but a debate that also dissembled the great variety of critiques ranged against the agreement. At the level of political strategy, therefore, the debate offered the Clinton administration a chance to avoid the more systematic critiques of organized labor and environmentalists while nevertheless appearing to rebut criticism of state policy. At the level of representations of the state, the resulting two-man "feud over Free Trade" further proved a tremendously powerful condensation point for the dynamics producing the effect of a sovereign nation-state. All the while Perot argued with Gore about his "outsider" credentials, his rhetoric only served to consolidate the idea that there was in fact an "inside" of decision making and state power. As a result, his debate with Gore was suffused with the imaginings of executive authority. It appeared that if one of the men "won" the debate they could simply implement their choice over free trade or autarky as a means to preserving the state's sovereignty.[74] Thus when Gore was said to have won, the rationale for ratifying NAFTA appeared not only superior but also a matter of stately decision making.

Having already marginalized the critiques coming from organized labor, environmentalists, and consumer groups like Public Citizen, the media focus switched from the Perot-Gore debate to the president's campaign of lobbying in the House of Representatives. Here the earlier embarrassment the administration experienced in being sued by environmentalists and consumer groups could be almost completely ignored.[75] Instead, all the hegemonic traditions of American presidentialism, along with the attendant fixation on the president as a Machiavellian fixer, came together with the construction of Capitol Hill as a powerful check on that same presidentialism to recreate another feud over the leadership of the state. Moreover, the administrative position of Clinton as president also enabled him to make a large number of behind-the-scenes deals with swing voters while simultaneously exerting sovereign force internationally (obliging the Mexicans to accept the last-minute changes to the agreement). When, on November 17, the House voted 234 to 200 for NAFTA, it was declared a "Major Victory for Clinton."[76] "President Emerges as a Tough Campaigner," "President as Deal Maker," "Clinton the Campaigner" were some of the typical headlines in the *New York Times*.[77] Clinton himself proclaimed the victory as "a defining moment for our nation." He went on:

> At a time when many of our people are hurting from the strains of this tough global economy we have chosen to compete, not retreat. Tonight I am proud to say: We have not flinched.[78]

The notion of a nation-state refusing to flinch, and the sound bite of choosing "to compete, not retreat," clearly reproduced the same anthropomorphization of the state as the Macdonald Commission's scripting of the Canadian state's "leap of faith." In the United States, however, this final articulation of a national "defining moment" took place against the backcloth of quite different and far more conservative oppositional discourses. In these NAFTA was commonly figured as a threat to the American warfare-state. Thus, all the while the proponents of the agreement recited the hymns to competition, and all the while they sidelined the critiques of unions and environmentalists with two toothless labor and environmental side accords, the oppositional narrative came to be dominated by a populist and paranoiac picture of the United States under threat.[79]

In a typical argument entitled "Keep Wealth in the North," Perot explained in detail that the "great sucking sound" that worried him most was the sound of *manufacturing* jobs being swallowed up by Mexico.[80] Other jobs could go, perhaps, but for Perot giving up manufacturing jobs was not unlike the act of self-emasculation imagined by Atwood in Canada, except for him it was not a joke. "We must have a large manufacturing base in the US for two reasons," he explained. "Manufacturing jobs are the best paying jobs and we cannot defend our country unless we manufacture here."[81] Warming to the theme of defending the warfare state he went on:

> We must never give up our ability to defend this great country. One of the primary reasons why we won World War II is that while our tanks, planes, ships and other weapons were being destroyed in war, we were able to outproduce our enemies with our ability to resupply our troops. If we move manufacturing to other countries and do not have the ability to make things here, we cannot defend our country.[82]

In *Save Your Job, Save Your Country,* which Perot coauthored with Pat Choate, these dramatic descriptions were given some more contemporary content with a discussion of how "[m]ore people in the US are now employed in federal, state and local government than in all manufacturing."[83] "By contrast," the narrative continued, recalling the old World War II enemies, "German and Japanese trade officials work to keep their manufacturing jobs at home. In 1965, manufacturing provided 36 percent of German jobs; today it's 32 percent. In 1965, 21 percent of Japanese jobs were in manufacturing; today, it's 25 percent."[84] This argument finally came down to the question of what constituted progress for the United States as a nation.

> It is just plain wrong to think that "progress" as a nation requires shifting from a manufacturing economy to a service economy. The fact that so many of our leaders support this concept explains why incomes and living standards are rising in Germany and Japan while they are falling in the United States.[85]

Not all of *Save Your Job, Save Your Country* turned on these themes of losing out to America's wartime enemies; many parts of the book made reasonable arguments about the transnational deregulatory impact of NAFTA. In fact, on the very first page readers were told that "the trade agreement will pit American and Mexican workers in a race to the bottom."[86] Just as in the debate with Gore, Perot also attempted to avoid accusations of racism—"The Fact that American workers don't want their jobs moved to Mexico is not 'racist'"[87]—by foregrounding his concerns about living and working conditions in Mexico. Equally, the book paid occasional attention to the continent-wide constitution-like effects of NAFTA.[88] Ultimately, however, these concerns for continental tendencies and inequalities were subsumed into the narrative of *Save Your Job, Save Your Country* through the argument that U.S. workers should simply not have to compete with Mexicans. In the end, the simple point was that "millions of Americans will lose their jobs."[89] Added to this dominant theme, Perot and Choate's argument was also punctuated with various criticisms of the Salinas regime's lobbying effort in Washington, a critical focus that linked Perot's populist concerns about lobbying in general with his fears about the loss of U.S. sovereignty through NAFTA. In a still more anti-Mexican gesture, the book also suggested that U.S. negotiators had been swindled by the Mexicans:

If you've travelled in Mexico and tried to buy anything, you quickly learned not to accept the first offer that someone gave you. Maybe the US negotiators didn't spend enough time in Mexico before they began negotiating.[90]

But this was the full extent of the book's manipulation of stereotypes. For Perot, it was the great sucking sound of manufacturing jobs being swallowed that most acutely threatened the national state's ability to defend itself. It was other critics, most notably Buchanan, who then turned this articulation of the warfare state under threat into a far more shrill, xenophobic nationalism.

It should by this point be clear that as a result of the debates over CUFTA, the nation-state in both Canada and the United States was rearticulated in exactly the normalized way described by Mitchell as "something much more than the sum of the everyday activities that constitute it, appearing as a structure containing and giving order and meaning to people's lives." But of course, at the same time, the free trade agreements themselves were introducing a new regime of governance that was profoundly changing some of the micropractices identified by Mitchell as constitutive of the quasi-transcendental hyphenation of nation-states in the first place. As became clear in the increasingly unreal numbers wars between critics and promoters, even the debates themselves began to show signs of this continent-wide process of transformation. The statistics might still have assumed the transcendental categories of nation-states containing coherent civil societies, but the debates' contradictions reflected the breakdown of this very containerization. It is to this process of breakdown that the next section turns directly as it examines the emergence of the quasi-transcendental level playing field entrenched by the agreements. While the reactions to CUFTA and NAFTA were crafted in terms that constructed "free trade" as the freeing-up of flows, the agreements themselves in fact represented the massive *reregulation* of flows. The central question of the next section concerns how this reregulation operated as a bureaucratic bulldozer leveling the space of continental capitalism.

FREE TRADE AND THE PRODUCTION OF THE LEVEL PLAYING FIELD

Paralleling his critique of "the state" at the start of the 1990s, much of Mitchell's published work in the subsequent decade developed a similar sort of argument against the singular taken-for-granted concept of "the economy." If the former argument had stressed the ways in which state effects emerge out of mundane economic and social practices, Mitchell's 1998 deconstruction of the fixing of "the economy" reciprocally addressed the ways in which national economies emerged as material, mappable, and contained conceptions during the mid-twentieth century under particular forms of state-framed analysis and management.[91] In 2002, in the shape of his new book on the *Rule of Experts,* this argument subsequently came together with Mitchell's brilliantly detailed investigations of the fixing and unfixing of one particular economy during the twentieth century: that of Egypt. This book begins with a notably geographical account of how modern state mapping has been coincident not only with the production of modern state effects but also with the production and management of modern economies. "The map," he says, referring to the archetypal modern state maps of colonies and metropoles alike, "can also be said to prefigure the work of twentieth-century economics, defining a contained geographical space to be organized later as a national economy, and addressing issues of statistical information that were to play a central role."[92] This is a quite substantive engagement in the geographical enframing of "the economy." However, despite his compellingly ethnographic account of what he subsequently shows have been Egypt's fundamentally unmappable and uneconomic economies, Mitchell moves by the end of the book to a much more metaphorical appeal to mapping and space. In an effort to make the broader point that "the economy" cannot and should not be preconceived as enclosed, coherent, and singular, he thus concludes: "The problem is that the frame or border of the economy is not a line on a map, but a horizon that at every point opens up into other territories."[93] The key question provoked by the cases of CUFTA and NAFTA is: what kind of territories?

Mitchell himself highlights territories that are not adequately addressed by orthodox economists, territories of social, cultural, and political life that he shows are intimately and inextricably bound up with formal forms of so-called market exchange and coordination. These are territories for him not merely in a metaphorical sense because all his examples of these sorts of extraeconomic economies are also scrupulously grounded in accounts of particular places and communities in Egypt. However, there is a way in which the cases of CUFTA and NAFTA also introduce a more practical form of transborder territorialization that undercuts Mitchell's parallel point that "the frame or border of the economy is not a line on a map." North American free trade, as we shall now see, has had a map: a two-country, then three-country map of the new so-called level playing field. To be sure, this map is at the time of writing being redrawn by the architects of the FTAA so as to open up to yet other territories in Latin America. But notwithstanding this open-endedness, there can be no doubting the practical, political, and not least of all, material economic consequences of the reterritorializations wrought by the North American level playing field map of free trade. It has in short fixed a new neoliberal economy across North America. This economy, as we shall see, has all kinds of political aspects to it that would not be normally counted as economic, and to this extent, Mitchell's epistemological arguments against the compartmentalization of economic affairs remains crucial to much of the following argument. But Mitchell himself, by combining his interest in the representational reterritorialization of "the economy" with an analysis of a single country, does not address the ways in which new transborder economic territories are today being fixed that have tremendous political import.[94] Here, by contrast, and by exploring this transborder fixing in the terms of the map of free trade's level playing field, the reciprocal and consequential state effects of economic reterritorialization can be made clearer. The level playing field, it should therefore be underlined, is not just a new disembedded mental map, although as we shall see later in chapter 5, it is infinitely adaptable to other global settings.[95] It also produces a powerful form of transnational state-making across the signatory countries to CUFTA and NAFTA. The quotidian regulatory practices put in place by the agreements have given this newly level playing field a quasi-transcendental state effect of its own.

Despite repetitive corporate visioning of the games to be played on the level playing field, the transnational state effect of free trade has not been complemented by the kinds of sociocultural routines and imaginings that have historically served to make nation-states become such important and meaningful abstractions. However, the level playing field is no less territorial in its scope and is therefore no less potent in activating "forces with a life of their own."[96] In order to come to terms with these forces it is necessary to avoid both idealism and economism. Without arguing it's all about political policies and without reducing the developments to the working out of simple class interests, it is necessary to come to terms with the transnational governance regime put in place by CUFTA and NAFTA. This is a regime of what Stephen Gill has usefully called "disciplinary neoliberalism," a new constitutionalism, as President Reagan well understood, of the market.[97] In this respect it is worth remembering a point that Antonio Gramsci underlined back in his *Prison Notebooks*: namely, that *"laissez-faire* too is a form of 'regulation.'"[98] The key to explaining the leveling of the level playing field, therefore, is to come to terms with how it represents a particular, market-driven, and therefore neoliberal form of transnational *reregulation,* and it is in moving toward this end that Mitchell's approach is invaluable.[99]

Approaching the level playing field through Mitchell makes it possible to develop three particular sorts of point. First of all, notwithstanding all the assumptions of the sovereigntist debates discussed above, CUFTA and NAFTA were not autonomous and self-contained projects. They *reflected* and *extended* already sweeping changes in the organization of North American capitalism. These were changes that were and remain part of the broader post-Fordist drive toward flexibility and outsourcing in production processes, and they centrally involve a new transnational as opposed to bi- or multinational form of corporate organization.[100] As Sidney Weintraub put it:

> [the] free-trade agreement, therefore, represents an extension of an industrial integration process that has been proceeding silently and steadily, for years.[101]

It should not be surprising, therefore, that corporate surveys made just ahead of NAFTA's implementation reported comments such as the following from a vice president of operations in a major paper firm. "Business is so far ahead of politicians on this one that it makes the agreement secondary. To many in our industry, NAFTA is a *fait accompli.*"[102]

The "secondary" quality of NAFTA points in turn to the second, more remarkable and yet commonly concealed state effect of the agreements: namely their legalistic *entrenchment* of trends already under way. It is this process of entrenchment that chiefly explains the rise of the level playing field mental map, but its more profound significance lies in the neoliberal reregulation of political and economic life that has made this mental map of transnational space meaningful. The reregulation relates in turn to what both nuanced critics and nuanced boosters of free trade characterized as its place at the core of an ongoing integration process.[103] At a time (the mid- to late 1980s and early 1990s) when governments in Canada, the United States, and Mexico were scaling back social-welfare interventions, privatizing public services, and making the market the standard tool and ideological fetish of most new policy making, economic interconnections were simultaneously making the relevant "markets" continental and global. Canadians and Americans in particular were coming to depend more and more on production processes in each other's countries for basic products and services (albeit asymmetrically because of the larger scale of the U.S. economy). The suppliers of these products and services who became dependent on the widened market also had a stake in its maintenance. More specifically, these transnational corporations had investment interests tied up in preserving their transnational market networks from possible deprivatization. For some of them, particularly in the increasingly privatized services sector, a major concern was the possibility that future governments might seek to reverse the neoliberal reforms and take a variety of privatized areas of resource allocation—health-care delivery, educational services, insurance provision, regional development initiatives, or as in the Mexican case, the newly marketized *ejido* land holdings—back into the realms of public control and public ownership.[104] The simultaneously mundane but hegemonic effect of the free trade agreements was to preempt such deprivatization by locking the privatized market system into place, and into transnational place at that.[105]

The third key aspect of the disciplinary neoliberalism entrenched by the agreements also concerns the preemption of future policy-making options insofar as the resulting level playing field has greatly increased the capacity of transnational businesses to play one location off against another. By accelerating the processes of economic integration and by simultaneously providing legal sanctions for businesses across the continent, CUFTA and NAFTA have made it still harder for governments to plan unilateral actions that might threaten the transnational investments of key corporate interests. Not only can certain government interventions such as bans on toxic substances be directly contested under free trade rules, but there is in addition the far more systematic risk of such action rebounding to the detriment of domestic capitalism and hence domestic employment. The result of this spiral of increasing interdependence, increasing competition, and increasing possibility of deregulatory litigation has been the further leveling downward of wages, local taxation rates, environmental regulations, and health and safety requirements to lower continental common denominators. The mental map of the resulting playing field does indeed therefore signify an almost transcendental effect. It creates an arena in which more redistributive and socially beneficial forms of government intervention in environmental and economic affairs become increasingly impossible to imagine, let alone implement. Ultimately, this means that considerable areas of governance have been taken outside of the sphere of democratically accountable decision making. Thus, as we shall now explore in more detail, the entrenchment of neoliberal reforms has also invisibly but effectively handcuffed the practices of national democracy.

In order to explain exactly how the trade agreements helped to entrench neoliberal reforms it is necessary to begin by dispelling the myth that they represented the complete deregulation of trade. This vision of the total freeing up of the market—supported in part by the humanistic view of freedom linked to the anthropomorphization of the nation-state—neglects how even the free marketeers are committed to some form of government intervention so long as it supports and preserves the market. More than this, the vision of complete deregulation also ignores what constituted the vast bulk of the agreements' written texts: namely the commodity by commodity, service by service, exception by exception recodification of tariff designations, along with their detailed timetables for implementation. These were accompanied by a whole range of new investment rules and, in NAFTA, the recodification of intellectual property rights too. In other words, yet another question missed by the "protectionism vs. free trade" scripting of the nationalized debates was the very managed nature of the trade legislated in the name of North American free trade. CUFTA and NAFTA remained basically *managed* trade agreements. They still therefore mandated customs checks, the sweeping surveillance of commodity and investment flows, and the complex computing of regional content requirements. Ironically, therefore, the level playing field effect remained founded in the management of the borders within and around North America.

A dramatic example of how much management NAFTA both

accommodated and demanded was afforded by the U.S. trade representative's office as Clinton campaigned to push the agreement's implementing legislation through the U.S. Congress in 1993. The agreement already signed by the three governments was, at this late stage, repeatedly rewritten in certain key areas, reducing or increasing tariffs like so many control knobs on a huge machine. As a concession to representatives from the farm states, for example, the president offered punitive barriers on Canadian wheat imports (which the U.S. trade representative argued were subsidized by Ottawa's provision of transport and marketing supports to Canadian producers—on which more shortly).[106] Similarly as a concession to representatives from Florida and Texas, the administration promised a new NAFTA rule stating that if Mexican shipments of orange juice increased and American prices fell the United States would impose steep tariffs on additional Mexican shipments.[107] The list continued affecting many other areas of trade and ultimately sounding like a shopping list: beef, peanut butter, bread, sugar, cucumbers, lettuce, and celery were all eventually affected. The irony was not lost on reporters. "To pass the trade deal that would eliminate taxes on imports from Mexico and Canada," commented Keith Bradsher, "the Clinton Administration . . . has agreed to impose taxes on imports from Mexico and Canada."[108] All these adjustments, however, facilitated the final passage of NAFTA into U.S. law. To this extent, they were a clear example of how much government intervention free trade's boosters were prepared to sustain (in Mexico and Canada as well as in the United States) so long as it supported the general opening and expansion of the market. Once in place, NAFTA guaranteed the more measured, routinized, and as such, largely unexamined management of trade across the emergent transnational, level playing field. In order to examine this emergent effect it is necessary to turn to the more disciplinary details of the agreement itself.

The sections specifying the derivation of "regional value content" in NAFTA illustrate how exacting and disciplinary the agreement's protocols are. These are the sections that underwrite the effect of so-called national treatment, which basically refers to treating foreign goods the same as national ones. If a commodity has the minimum regional value content for its category it can qualify for national treatment, which is to say, tariff-free entry into any of the three NAFTA countries. Since these sections defining regional value content thereby create the paradoxical effect of national treatment in transnational space, and since they bureaucratically consolidate the mental map of the level playing field, they are worth noting in their full mathematical specificity. Producers seeking to evaluate whether they qualify for "national treatment" under NAFTA are permitted to calculate regional value content according to one of either two equations, and these are given as follows:

$$RVC = \frac{TV - VNM}{TV} \times 100$$

where: RVC is regional value content expressed as a percentage; TV is the transaction value of the good adjusted to a F.O.B. basis; and VNM is the value of non-originating materials used by the producer in the production of the good.

$$RVC = \frac{NC - VNM}{NC} \times 100$$

where: RVC is regional value content expressed as a percentage; NC is the net cost of the good; and VNM is the value of non-originating materials used by the producer in the production of the good.[109]

While one equation uses the so-called transaction value of a commodity and the other "net cost," the more notable VNM, "value of non-originating materials," remains constant in both. Interpreted as the keystone of a huge and spatialized disciplinary project, VNM can thus be seen as a prime example of the dissembling dynamic Mitchell suggests is constitutive of state effects. VNM indicates in this sense a codified and, because of the equation's repeated use, constitutive assumption of territoriality. The notion of "non-originating" assumes as a matter of definition a space of origin, and the net effect of all the tabulations of nonoriginating components is thus to create by way of what is not excluded an original space of North America. The abstract territory thereby conjured up is clearly larger than the space of a single nation-state. All the while it qualifies North American producers for "national treatment," the dehyphenated state effect of this border-based management process nevertheless creates an arena for "national treatment" that is definitively *transnational* in scope.

It is important to underline again how these micropractices of customs management can be seen as just another modification of the "detailed processes of spatial organization, temporal arrangement, functional specification, and supervision and surveillance" that Mitchell characterizes as being constitutive of state effects. NAFTA has clearly not torn down the border in quite the dramatic fashion anticipated by Marx's famous declaration about capital tearing down all spatial barriers. The agreement actually demands more paperwork at the border. A U.S. Customs official told one reporter: "Some people think that customs is going to pack up and leave. But we're still going to be here."[110] Indeed, the same reporter found that in its first year of implementation NAFTA was actually snarling cross-border movement as Customs officials and import-export firms began the work of learning the new laws. This was itself a disciplinary process described by a number of those involved in pedagogical terms: "The first five months," said one exporter, "have been Agreement 101."[111] Corporations have also experienced the disciplinary impact, with the equations of regional value content being applied to every component, including the subcomponents of components supplied by subcontracted suppliers. The result has been a complex geographical genealogy for each final product crossing the border, a genealogy more often than not also affected by the multiple pages of special content requirements laid out in the Annex 302 (2) making up the vast bulk of volume 2 of NAFTA. It is out of this complex, inordinately detailed and particularized genealogy for every single border-crossing commodity that the *generalized* effect of a level, national-treatment-applicable, North American free trade playing field was produced.

If the regional value content formulae illustrate the micrological dynamics that have been constitutive of the free trade area as a level playing field, the sections of NAFTA relating to the deregulation of business provide a more profound sense of whose playing and whose freedom this "leveling" serves. These provisions provide for freedom of business from government-imposed performance requirements on foreign corporations (*NAFTA,* Articles 1106 and 1107); freedom to repatriate dividends and royalties (Article 1109); freedom from discriminatory expropriation and adequate compensation for measures that interfere with business in a way deemed tantamount to expropriation (Article 1110); freedom to move top management, professional, and technical personnel around at will (Chapter 16); and freedom to claim business ownership of knowledge through extended periods of monopoly protection for patents and other intellectual property instruments (Chapter 17). Clearly this list of freedoms amounts to a new constitution for business, a continental corporate bill of rites that is all the more potent given the powerful enforcement mechanisms with which NAFTA secured its protection (Articles 1115–37). Together with the transnational expansion of national treatment across all three nation-states through the codes and calculations imposed at the border, it is this legalistic form of bureaucracy that has effectively bulldozed the North America of "North American content" into being. Transnational corporations whose products qualify for "national treatment" within this space simply circumvent all the unevenness that was represented by government restrictions in the past. For them this form of border management does indeed level the playing field, but for democracy the leveling effect has quite different implications.

Perhaps the best metaphor for the effect the free trade agreements have had on democratic politics is that they have functioned as a hidden handcuffing of democracy: hidden in part because, like Adam Smith's "hidden hand," the disciplinary effect is market mediated; but also hidden because the reforms were not encoded as direct attacks on democracy at all, and only work incrementally like a ratchet that can get tighter but never looser, slowly closing down the possibilities for democratic governance over any market-mediated activity. Given that Canada entered into the free trade negotiations in the mid-1980s with the most extensive Keynesian welfare state apparatus on the continent, it provides a dramatic example of how this ratcheted handcuffing of democracy has taken constitutional effect. As Canadian critics such as Judith Darcy realized early on, the way free trade locked in neoliberalism related directly to the transcending effect of the level playing field itself. "Those who subscribe to the importance of a level playing field," she complained, "say our social programs are unacceptable subsidies and must be cut to bring Canada closer to the competitive level of the United States."[112] Indeed, many Canadian critics had highlighted the neoliberal handcuffing effect of the trade agreement when they first criticized CUFTA in the 1980s. The attorney general of Ontario, for example, argued:

> Free Trade will permanently alter the capacity to make economic and social policy in Canada, sometimes shifting it to the federal government, sometimes abandoning it for all governments. The dramatic change in the ability of governments to respond to the legitimate expectations of their populations amounts to a constitutional change.[113]

This, of course, was the same change toward a new economic constitution that Reagan had celebrated and that NAC in turn had caricatured as a "Trojan Horse" bringing Reaganomics into Canada.

As other Canadian critics of free trade have since pointed out, it is hard to overemphasize the scope of the neoliberal abdication turned transnational trade law turned almost transcendental effect. CUFTA established protocols governing sectors ranging from finance through transportation and telecommunications to agriculture, as well as introducing an intellectual property code and a harmonization of standards in professional qualifications, agricultural inspection, and health. Little of Canadian economic, social, or environmental policy was left unaffected. As Bruce Campbell argued, the agreement rendered redundant a whole host of policy tools that had previously held transnational business decision making accountable to national or provincial economic goals.[114] These included performance requirements to promote domestic value-added technology transfer; resource management tools, such as export taxes or quotas, to encourage domestic processing; agricultural supply management tools to balance supply and demand; compulsory licensing of patents to nurture home-grown technology; and many more. Other provisions of CUFTA prevented future Canadian (and American and Mexican) governments from adopting policies that would favor the development of domestically owned over foreign-owned businesses; and still others limited governments' abilities to meet policy objectives through public procurement policies.

Even before the victory of the Liberal Party in 1993, before NAFTA's passage into Canadian law, and before the message this sent about the irreversibility of the Mulroney reforms, CUFTA's entrenchment of neoliberalism was already clear. Any attempt to reinstitutionalize regional development grants, public review procedures, energy pricing, or resource conservation was halted by the possibility of prosecution by U.S. parties under the rules of CUFTA.[115] At the provincial level even so innocuous a policy as the Ontario government's attempt to introduce a public auto insurance scheme became unworkable because of the compensation rights U.S. private business could claim for lost market share under Article 1605. In addition, as well as creating downward pressures on Canadian wages through the combined effects of layoffs and capital flight to the United States, CUFTA also served to harmonize Canadian environmental standards downward: reducing federal pesticide restrictions and curbing attempts to halt acid rain.[116] All these tendencies have been further entrenched and further radicalized in NAFTA. By focusing on the specific provisions in NAFTA affecting public services, it is possible to highlight still more clearly the way in which the entrenchment and naturalization of the level playing field preempts future governments from moving in nonneoliberal directions.

The key provision of NAFTA affecting public services is the principle of "national treatment." In the chapter on services, the national treatment rule requires Canadian governments to give U.S. and Mexican service firms the same rights and privileges as Canadian service providers (*NAFTA*, Article 1202). In other words, governments are prevented from exercising policies that favor Canadian public or private service providers. NAFTA also prevents governments from requiring an American service provider to establish a "local presence." Services can thus be provided entirely from outside the country (Article 1205.1.4). This transnational freedom translates in turn into the transcendence of national, state, and provincial governance insofar as it comes together with provisions that specifically restrict the ability of governments to improve existing services or introduce new services. This is where the irreversibility and dedemocratization of the neoliberal entrenchment becomes most clear. Only such changes to social programs that open them to the contingency of the marketplace are permitted. Changes that would expand government involvement in service provision are by the same token rendered impossible. In this regard, NAFTA's procedure for grandparenting existing services that do not conform to the "national treatment" provision is more restrictive than that of CUFTA. Under NAFTA, governments can continue to provide exempted services only so long as they list them and only make changes to them that do "not decrease the conformity of the measure" with NAFTA rules, including "national treatment" (Article 1206.1.c). This means that national and local governments are unable to expand the public provision of existing services by shifting work back from private contractors to public sector workers (Article 1208). It is in such ways that democratically elected governments are disciplined by the marketized bulldozer logic of the level playing field.

These examples can be multiplied, but the point should be clear. The spiraling deregulation and privatization that lead to the level playing field effect have been locked in by CUFTA and NAFTA in such a way that the neoliberal reforms that they have put in place— literally so—have become increasingly difficult to reverse. More than difficult, in fact, the level playing field effect actually has a disciplinary force of its own just like that associated with Mitchell's "state effects." It thereby serves as an abstract container giving (neoliberal) meaning to the lives and plans of governments and their citizens. As well as affording a mental map for policy makers, it actually disciplines member governments in similar ways to the disciplining of citizens by modern states—including the use of self-monitoring and self-reporting requirements and legal sanctions for failures to perform. At the same time, the level playing field creates new rights for a select population of North American corporations. Unlike the state of traditional state theory, then, it is actually by transcending the territorial nation-state that the level playing field's own almost transcendental effect has been produced. Thus far I have only noted the resulting dedemocratizing tendency in relation to the disempowerment of democratically elected governments. What is perhaps more notable, however, as I now want to show, is that some of NAFTA's most fervent boosters in the United States and Mexico *also* emphasized the antidemocratic implications of the agreement, but in their case they saw these dedemocratizing imperatives as an *advantage*.

The antidemocracy discourse of the boosters became most evident in discussions over Mexico's future development. As Jesús Silva Herzog, Mexico's ambassador to the United States, put it in a diplomatic phrase, the trade agreement would allow Mexico "to pursue the permanence of the present economic strategy."[117] In other words, it would lock the neoliberal reforms of the Salinas regime in place—including the wholesale privatization of innumerable state services—irrespective of future rounds of elections in Mexico. John Bryan Jr., the president of the Sara Lee Corporation, viewed the agreement in exactly the same way. "[T]he most important reason to vote for NAFTA is to lock in [Mexico's] reforms."[118] Given the developments that have taken place since 1994—from the continuation of the Salinas reforms under Zedillo to the more recent election of the onetime Coca-Cola CEO, Vincente Fox, as president—it appears that these hopes for the short-circuiting of democracy have been largely fulfilled. Most notably, while the peso crisis led to a massive recession in Mexico, and the apparent failure of all the promises of NAFTA vis-à-vis Mexico's entry into first world wealth, it also illustrated all too clearly the hegemonic hold of neoliberalism secured through the trade agreement. President Zedillo's regime was forced overnight by its NAFTA partners to accept harsh austerity measures in exchange for $20 billion in loans and loan guarantees (known in the United States as the "Mexican bailout").[119] As a result the U.S. Treasury rather than the Mexican government came to have far more control over setting the fundamental macroeconomic policies in the country. Instead of the sovereignty that Salinas had trumpeted as a means of silencing calls for raised environmental and labor protections across the free trade area, NAFTA thus became another tool for suppressing domestic democratic accountability in Mexico.[120]

While Mexico affords an especially stark illustration, the disciplinary neoliberalism of the level playing field of free trade has in fact had antidemocratic implications throughout North America. As well as disciplining the Mexican government with more IMF-styled structural adjustment measures, and as well as securing the rollback of the Keynesian welfare state in Canada, the level playing field pits community against community across the continent in a race to attract capital. As was illustrated by the Cascadia case discussed in chapter 2, free trade has thus further unleashed and exacerbated the effects of continental competition vis-à-vis bringing inward investment to particular localities, and this competition only serves to further the process of leveling that made it necessary in the first place. If capital is attracted by low wages, low taxation regimes, low health and safety standards, and low environmental standards, and if it can move freely to wherever the best returns are available, these same low standards will increasingly set the generalized standard. It is a recursive process that, however incrementally, encroaches on the scope and meaningfulness of publicly accountable government. In short, the race to attract capital facilitated by the level playing field makes national and local democracy subject to what William Connolly calls the "globalization of contingency."[121] Connolly describes this process in a way that is perfectly coincident with the debate over the threatened nation-state discussed in the previous section.

> It puts the squeeze on the territorial ideal of democracy; it intensifies pressures to preserve the appearance of internal democracy by denying the significance of global issues that escape the terms of accountability in the territorial state.[122]

One of the more creative ways in which this pressure to preserve the appearance of internal accountability was manifested itself in the United States was in books like *The Work of Nations* authored by Clinton's first labor secretary, Robert Reich.[123] Unlike the would-be protectionists, Reich began by accepting the arrival of the level playing field as a mental map for policy making. He then argued that the employment policy most appropriate to the contemporary globalized economy was a policy predicated on creating highly trained citizens who can work and consume at the highest levels of labor and consumption:

> Well trained workers attract global corporations, which invest and give workers good jobs, the good jobs, in turn, generate additional training and experience. As skills move upward and experience accumulates, a nation's citizens add more and more value to the world—and command greater and greater compensation from the world, increasing the country's standard of living.[124]

This argument at least acknowledged some form of governmental responsibility and accountability to the voter-citizens, but as Stephen Cullenberg and George Demartino argue, it abstracted from the wider international context on which it depends.[125] As Reich's term in office went on to prove, this same context—including the influence of the bond markets and other global financial forces embodied in the decision making at the Federal Reserve—systematically blocked the implementation of most of his plans.[126] Such plans seemed doomed therefore because of the ways in which they bracketed the wider web of responsibilities created by the transnational networks in which workers create value. Even if they had been implemented, Reich's plans would never have worked with the same success *across* the level playing field. For this reason, the downward harmonization pressures would not have been suppressed. Instead, the high-tech symbolic analysts that Reich celebrates as the models for the future worker-citizen were still likely to become what they are now becoming, merely cosmopolitan coaches directing teams around the level playing field from on high.

The sporting analogy is relevant not only because of the level playing field metaphor itself, but also because of the visual order the abstraction of the level playing field sustains. Just as in the visual order that Mitchell argues was enframed by colonial government practices in Egypt, the complex neoliberal management systems of CUFTA and NAFTA enframe a field of symbolic display.[127] But rather than constituting this world as a giant and colorful museum-like exhibition, the free trade agreements enframe North America as a massive maquiladora: a duty-free, regulation-free level playing field of differentially distributed factor endowments. It is an abstraction that is clearly linked to the capitalist imperatives of speeding up turnover time, and yet it appears as something unconnected from the micropractices of border checkpoints and customs calculations. Instead, it seems almost transcendental and as such comes back to haunt state policy making, limiting and interrupting the possibility of government interventions in economic affairs even at the point of their initial conceptualization. Moreover, whereas the colonial enframing described by Mitchell dissembled the soldiers, missionaries, teachers, and bureaucrats that were busily assembling the colonized nation as a picture, so too does the process of neoliberal enframing occult the class interests of the symbolic analysts and business elites putting together the transnational econometrics of the level playing field.

In short, Reagan was right. CUFTA and NAFTA have created an economic constitution that, working like a written constitution, provides a sense of transcendental justice to what in reality are a routinized and quotidian set of procedures facilitating the development of continental free-market capitalism. The level playing field simply represents the net effect of these many and diverse practices but, as such, recursively regulates social, economic, and political life by entrenching neoliberalism across North America. In this sense, not only do the agreements represent, in Kathryn Kopinak's words, "the maquiladorization of the Mexican economy," they portend the maquiladorization of the whole continent.[128]

It can certainly be argued that American dominance is structured into this pattern of continentalized neoliberalism. In many ways, American patterns of decentralization, deregulation, and privatization have set the neoliberal standard, and it has been U.S. corporations who have dominated the newly opened markets. Moreover the U.S. government has still continued and even stepped up the quasi-imperial work of defending U.S. corporations by activating the trade sanctions put in place by CUFTA and NAFTA. However, this has by no means exempted U.S. citizens and states from the more generalized process of neoliberal handcuffing. On the question of U.S.

dominance it should also be noted that, while some commentators view the formation of the NAFTA regime as a U.S.-led attempt to create its own continental trade bloc in response to the European Union, the level playing field represents a notably open-ended form of territoriality. Neither a trade bloc with a high external tariff wall, nor a power-sharing alliance, NAFTA does not stand for the North American Free Trade Area (as some influential writers have misconstrued the acronym).[129] It likewise has less to do with the old imperial notion of fortifying the American "backyard" than with simply expanding the opportunities of corporate interests across the continent. That these opportunities are further extended by other regimes including APEC and MERCOSUR does not impinge on the level playing field at all, and instead only expands its neoliberal embrace.

If the level playing field has rather indeterminate edges, it nevertheless creates a regime of increasing political and ideological consistency within. Thus throughout Canada, the United States, and Mexico, policy making is increasingly driven by an ideology of economic Darwinism: survival of the fittest, or to be more precise, survival of the most attractive to capital. This is sometimes expressed in a frank language of making communities viable in the competitions over positioning in the international divisions of labor and consumption. In other moments, they are expressed through more complex metaphorical systems. For example David Mulford, a U.S. trade official and paradigmatic symbolic analyst of the level playing field, glossed its implications in the following masculinist terms:

> The countries that do not make themselves attractive will not get investors' attention. . . . This is like a girl trying to get a boyfriend. She has to go out, have her [hair] done up, wear make up.[130]

If this brutish caricature of national governance represents the nadir of democratic decline on the level playing field, it is nonetheless a useful example insofar as it introduces the significance of a new group of feminist, socialist, and union critics who, in rejecting this anthropomorphized and patriarchal portrayal of national agency, have begun to rework the level playing field itself into a space of radical democratic organization.

CONTESTING NEOLIBERALISM ACROSS THE PLAYING FIELD

Not large in number, but one of the more notable examples of the new modes of organizing across the level playing field are the transnational outreach efforts of women's groups in Canada, Mexico, and the United States. Organizations such as Mujer à Mujer, for instance, have linked women working in common economic sectors in all three countries in order to develop cooperative analyses and shared strategies for change.[131] Insofar as such groups are responding to the level playing field as a form of neoliberal state effect, Mitchell's comments on the implications of state effects for resistance usefully describe the way in which such feminist interventions attempt to reoccupy and re-present the new organizational space. Mitchell's contention against more romantic and libertarian visions of resistance is that

> Political subjects and their modes of resistance are formed as much within the organizational terrain we call the state, rather than in some wholly exterior social space. ("Limits," 93)

In the NAFTA case, the resistant political subjects represented by the new trinational feminist alliances can be understood thus as being formed as transnational networks within the organizational terrain of the level playing field. This is not to say, however, that they are uniquely or completely determined by this terrain. Instead, the emergent state effect of disciplinary neoliberalism forms a field of commonality into which other articulations of difference still enter and affect the debate. By no means are all of these post-NAFTA organizational efforts focused on free trade per se, and the many differences between women in each of the three countries very definitely inform the debates.[132] For example, Mexican women's groups representing women who have experienced the long-term effects of IMF structural adjustment have focused less on the trade agreements and more on how to address neoliberalism as a transnational process of neocolonial and often patriarchal violence. Christina Gabriel and Laura Macdonald suggest that this in turn "has helped women in Canada and the United States understand the underlying logic of current processes of trade liberalization which ignore the effects on women."[133] It was this form of dialogue that subsequently led a group such as NAC to move from its more nationalist position in the CUFTA campaign toward exploring different models of transnational development.

Union groups have also increasingly embraced transnational solidarity building and planning. Indeed, some member groups of the AFL-CIO and other union spokespeople did so quite actively in the U.S. debate over NAFTA only to see their "not this NAFTA" campaign become drowned out by Perot's "giant sucking sound." For example, Kim Moody and Mary McGinn of the *Labor Notes* progressive union paper, framed the problem as being clearly continental in scope:

> The North American Free Trade Agreement is not about the commerce of nations. This treaty that binds the United States, Canada and Mexico in economic union is more about corporate profits than about trade. It is about letting private businesses reorganize the North American economy without the checks and balances once provided by unions, social movements, or governments. The North American Free Trade Agreement (NAFTA) would roll back a hundred years of controls and restrictions that were placed on private business in the interests of the majority of the people.[134]

Likewise, Joe Farley, a president of a Teamsters local in Watsonville, California, exemplifies how many union leaders on the ground were spurred by the economics of continentalization toward new visions of transnational organization. "Corporations already make plans and build alliances as though national boundaries were not even there," he said, speaking about the workers in his local who had lost their jobs when Green Giant moved a food-packing operation to a nonunion plant in Mexico. "Labor," he continued, "has a long way to go to catch up."[135] It was this exercise in catching up that many of the "not this NAFTA" campaigns initiated. When, for example, the Teamsters took to the roads of California with their "Economic Earthquake Express," Raúl Márquez, the leader of the dissident Authentic Workers Front (Frente Auténtico de los Trabajadores, or FAT), was on board. His message about Mexican workers was clear. "We don't want to be used as international scabs. We want to work with you to win good jobs for everyone. . . . They don't want to raise our wages in Mexico. They want to lower yours."[136] Subsequently, other cases of cross-border solidarity have included the Farm Labor Organizing Committee development of a transnational project to help organize Campbell's farm workers, the United Auto Workers building of the MEXUSCAN trinational coalition in solidarity with the struggle of Mexican workers at Ford-Cuatitlán, the Communication Workers of America (CWA) development of closer ties with the Mexican telephone workers (STRM), and the International Longshore Workers Union (ILWU) provision of support for a struggle fought by the Mexico city bus drivers in 1996.[137]

Most of the above examples are illustrative of a broader trend that has involved initiatives led by U.S. labor groups directed at organizing efforts in Mexico. There have been at least two main difficulties in this regard. The first have been the frustrating experiences of attempting to activate the limited worker protections of the so-called labor side accord, the North American Agreement on Labor Cooperation (NAALC). This accord was never designed to provide a charter for equal worker rights across the NAFTA region. Indeed, back when they were negotiating the accord, Clinton's team had been told in clear-cut sovereigntist terms that they would lose Republican support for NAFTA if either side agreement created sanctionable trinational rights. As a result, the labor side accord basically only provides a transnational disputes management process for complainants contesting domestic infractions of domestic laws in each of the three countries. Thus while American unions such as the United Electrical Radio and Machine Workers (UE) have appealed through the NAALC mechanisms about labor rights infractions in Mexico, they have systematically met with obstacles and, ultimately, inaction because of the toothless and nationally compartmentalizing nature of the side accord. For example, in the UE case brought against a Honeywell plant in Chihuahua (which was a petition that the UE made jointly with the Teamsters), the U.S. National Administration Office (NAO) concluded that, while the timing of dismissals at the plant coincided with an independent union's organizing drive, it could not recommend any remedies.[138] More recently a UE appeal to the U.S. NAO about the violation of the organizing rights of another independent Mexican union led to an even more serious disappointment. The union in question, called "October 6," had attempted to organize workers at the Han Young plant in Tijuana. The NAO again found the claims about rights violations to be justified, but only saw fit to respond by coordinating with the Mexican authorities to arrange a seminar near the plant to educate workers about their rights under Mexican law to organize trade unions. Even this feeble response turned to failure when, after protesting their rights at this seminar, members of the October 6 union were physically brutalized in front of the Mexican social welfare secretary and the acting director of the U.S. NAO by men from the CROC, one of Mexico's principal government-affiliated unions. Nevertheless, this has not stopped the UE from continuing to organize joint projects with their Mexican alliance partners, the FAT, including the establishment of a small worker education center, Centro de Estudios y Taller Laboral (CETLAC), in Ciudad Juárez (which was jointly funded by Québec unions too).

The fact that it has been the UE, a progressive non-AFL-CIO-affiliated union, that has been at the forefront of the transnational efforts points to a second and still larger obstacle frustrating the development of widespread cross-border worker solidarity: namely, the combined effect in the AFL-CIO of America-first nationalism and the legacies of the cold war. There have been clear signs that this nationalistic effect is waning. In 1995 Lane Kirkland was replaced by John Sweeney of the Service Employees International Union (SEIU) at the head of the federation, ushering in a somewhat more internationalist agenda. The following year, the International Affairs Committee of the AFL-CIO made a move to replace the old cold war, State Department–sponsored foreign activities offices of the federation with a so-called American Center for Labor Solidarity.[139] Yet such developments notwithstanding, there remains a tendency within the federation and among its affiliates to return to a narrow focus on the loss of American jobs to low-wage competition from countries such as Mexico. Just as in the anti-NAFTA campaign, this allows for various forms of populist and jingoist co-optation of the union message. But more than this, as labor scholars such as Rebecca Johns point out, it also makes it much harder to make systematic moves toward *transformative* cross-border labor solidarity.[140] This ongoing Americocentrism among U.S. unions overshadows what limited examples of cross-border solidarity actually have occurred. This is because it tends to support a view of the United States as a role model turned hero in organizing efforts south of the border. Noting this danger of American paternalism, Bob Carr, a researcher focusing on labor internationalism under NAFTA, has nevertheless pointed to some countervailing examples. Most notably, he underscores the significance of a post-NAFTA 1995 effort by the Mexican telephone-workers union STRM to intervene through the NAALC mechanisms over the firing of more than two hundred U.S. workers by a Sprint Corporation subsidiary in San Francisco.[141] Not only was this a case of Mexican workers contesting the treatment of U.S. workers on behalf of a U.S. union (in this case, the CWA). It also represented an action based on a prior trinational union agreement between STRM, the CWA, and the Communications, Energy and Paperworkers Union of Canada. In other words, it directly countered the paternalism tendency by illustrating how meaningful forms of continental exchange and joint training can really lead to a two-way street of transnational solidarity.

It is out of a commitment to grassroots exchange and communication across the border that the UE and FAT have continued to build a north–south strategic alliance, notwithstanding the setbacks to their NAALC challenges. This alliance has also showed signs of being a two-way street where the FAT assisted the UE in an organizing drive in Milwaukee, Wisconsin.[142] They did so by sending a Mexican organizer from the FAT metal-workers union to support the recruitment of undocumented Mexican immigrant workers at the American company called AceCo. These workers had been afraid to join the union for fear of deportation, but with the help of the FAT collaboration these fears were overcome and the organizing drive was successful. Another indication of the depth of this north–south solidarity is the stress it has placed on rank-and-file education about conditions on the other side of the border. As radical labor commentators such as Kim Moody underline, these sorts of opportunities have sprung in part from a social-movement unionism that is welcoming of and cooperative with other lines of social struggle including feminism.[143] This is a point that is further illustrated and stressed by other groups such as the Mexican anti–free trade coalition, the Red Mexicana de Acción frente al Libre Comercio (RMALC). This group has been notably focused on challenging the hegemonic project of transnational disciplinary neoliberalism by building a diverse, multifaceted, counterhegemonic project. Writing about this struggle, Ximena Bedregal and Norma Mogrovejo argue that anti-NAFTA organizing must thereby learn from how feminists have sought democratically to recuperate voices shut down by patriarchy.

> As a civilizing project [democracy] has sought to recuperate the diverse knowledges of women which the patriarchal system has made invisible. The alternative to NAFTA thus must emerge by drawing out each specific aspect of the deal: the urban, the environmental, the cultural, the productive, the symbolic, the economic . . . to counterpose them in a creative fashion to the unitary logic imposed by the new order. It is necessary to understand that NAFTA is not just an economic project, but a specific route to a new totalizing social project which signals one single path toward a supposed development.[144]

It is this form of theorization—one that unpacks the unitary logic of the level playing field in order to fashion multiple strategies of resistance—that seems best fit to tackle the almost transcendental implications of the continentalized neoliberal state effect. If, as I have argued, we need to understand CUFTA and NAFTA as disciplinary agreements that lock neoliberalism into transnational place, then it is proposals to reenliven counterhegemonic democratic struggle on a transnational basis that offer the best hope for turning the power relations underwriting the level playing field into the basis of resistance. Analyses predicated on the nation-state can document the leveling of national democracy, but they are left bereft of tools for renegotiating resistance in this transnational way. If, by comparison, the level playing field is understood as an almost transcendental state effect and, as such, a site of disciplinary and circulatory power relations, these same power relations can be seen as a uniting rather than a dividing force among the multiple voices of resistance on the continent. In all this, however, analyses that present the nation-state as the paramount structural effect of the modern world create a certain obstacle, and it is with the questions about Mitchell's own argument provoked by this concern that the last section now concludes.

THE REINSCRIBED GEOGRAPHY OF THE ALMOST TRANSCENDENTAL

Using the work of Mitchell to examine the state effects surrounding the implementation of North American free trade, this chapter has focused on both the transnationalization of state formation and the nation-fixated debates it provoked in order to examine the substantive implications of dehyphenation. The central discontinuity between the two main concerns of this chapter—the discontinuity between the repeated, often reactive, rearticulations of the territorialized nation-state on the one hand and the neoliberal transnationalizing of the state on the other—represents one of the defining problematics of globalization. As such it has elsewhere been conceptualized in many different registers: as a sign of the growing disjuncture between the terrain of democratic politics and the spaces of economic coordination;[145] as a manifestation of the fundamental displacement of national economic governance;[146] or as another geographical indication of the seesawing uneven development of capitalism, a form of development that, as both David Harvey and Neil Smith have famously argued, creates stabilized forms of territorialization only then to displace them in the ceaseless search for ongoing growth.[147] Here I have sought to add a substantive focus on the state effects that are produced in the context of these displacements and disjunctures. This not only seems to represent a useful way out of the sterile yet exaggerated debates over the touted end of the nation-state. In addition, it raises a whole series of questions about the changing territoriality of state making.

Clearly in using Mitchell's account to theorize the level playing field and its discontents, my analysis has not been critical of his central argument. Indeed, my focus on the notion of state effects has stemmed from what I see as the tremendous value of Mitchell's deconstruction of the distorting distinctions between state and society, and politics and economics. It is precisely because Mitchell underlines the need to theorize the appearance of a separate state—a state understood as existing separately from socioeconomic processes and change—that his work speaks so effectively to the blinkered nature of the nation-fixated debates that took place over CUFTA and NAFTA. Again and again these debates obscured the formative influence of continental capitalist restructuring by fixating on the apparent executive authority of the state, by deploying methodological nationalism at every step, and by assuming that the core community of political action remained territorially bounded by the nation. By the same token, Mitchell's concern with the ways in which disciplinary dynamics create the seemingly overarching effect of state power provided a framework for examining the emerging potency of the level playing field itself as a transnational neoliberal regime of governance. As such, the level playing field illustrates perfectly how a fundamentally unbounded set of power relations begins to accrue an object status and, as such, an apparently almost transcendental identity and force. Constituted by the mundane management practices governing trade and investment under the agreement, and reflecting the increasing transnational interconnectedness of the North American economy, it has developed the almost transcendental force of a transnational constitution. Meanwhile, its existence ironically rests on a routine set of day-to-day practices, most of them surrounding the movement of commodities and finance capital, and many of them exercised at or around the borders of the NAFTA nations. Free trade's management protocols thus seem to illustrate exactly the state effect Mitchell speaks of "whereby methods of organization and control internal to the social processes they

govern create the effect of a state structure external to those processes" ("Limits," 77). However, by putting the argument about state
effects to work on this scale as well as at the national scale, my empirical investigations have also led to a question here about the limiting
spatial assumptions embedded in Mitchell's original account. In other
words, by counterpointing the transnational level playing field to the
sovereigntist appeals to the nation-state that were articulated against
it, I have sought to show how an account of state effects in the context
of free trade needs to come to terms with at least two quite distinct
scales of geographical consolidation. Insofar as Mitchell's rereading
of state theory retains a focus on only the nation-state as the almost
transcendental territorial arrangement of modernity, this forecloses
attention of the transnationalization of the state.

One of the weaker moments in Mitchell's original essay concerns
his somewhat functionalist explanation for why the state-society split
is sustained. "The appearance that state and society are separate
things," he says, "is part of the way a given financial and economic
order is maintained" (90). This claim, with its echo of the whole
base-superstructure genre of ideology critique that Mitchell otherwise avoids, may nevertheless seem to make sense when the "given
financial and economic order" in question is a form of Fordist national capitalism or the neocolonial capitalism Mitchell has analyzed
as enframing Egypt in development discourse. In these contexts, it
may well be vital that the state seem above and beyond the day-to-
day interests of capitalists—although to elevate this "function" as an
explanation of the state-society split still occludes the significance of
the disciplinary practices involved. However, Mitchell's formulation
breaks down when a more transnational order is involved. Indeed,
when the state effect that seems separate is no longer coincident with
national society, when, in other words, it is transnational in scope,
the result may in fact be profoundly *destabilizing* for a certain financial and economic order. The rise of Perot's populist anti–free
trade movement in the United States, and all the coeval Buchananite
concerns about free trade and so-called world government, obviously
testify to this destabilizing implication. To be sure, the level playing
field serves capitalist interests with a vengeance; that has been my
whole point about its entrenching of neoliberalism. However, its
seeming *transnational* transcendental separateness threatens the
stability of national-state capitalism to the extent that it presents a

disjuncture of state and nation. This has been much more strongly felt as an effect within the smaller economies of Canada and Mexico, and insofar as the United States has both modeled and championed neoliberalism, its structural dominance within the level playing field has largely hidden the impacts within the nation. Nevertheless, those impacts have still been felt (see also chapter 5 for an analysis of the resulting geopolitical contradictions). They range from the expanded whipsaw threats to U.S. workers to the importation of food grown using previously banned pesticides to the locking in of a mode of political-economic governance that will preempt any New Deal–type national economic policies for the foreseeable future. All of these developments represent a profound disruption to the territorial congruence of politics, economics, and democratic accountability that was once signaled (if never fully secured) by the hyphen in the American nation-state. Noting these dehyphenating tendencies also leads me to note again that Mitchell's own argument depends on an assumption about the spatial coincidence of state and nation that is difficult to sustain in the context of today's transnationalizing capitalism.

It might well be protested that the dissembling of the transnational is a symptom of the metaphysics of the nation-state itself. Given that Mitchell's project was aimed at highlighting and unpacking such metaphysics, it could be reasonably argued that it is sensible for him to maintain an analytical focus at this specific level. Moreover, Mitchell has more recently drawn specific attention to the ways in which political-economic imperatives are often excessive to the territorialized notion of a nation-state's "economy." He has written thus about how "economic powers and relations often extend beyond the geographical limit that represents the imaginary space of the economy."[148] This concern with displacing the metaphysics of the "national economy" would seem to clear the way for examining something like the level playing field of free trade. However, given that Mitchell's primary concern here is more with the epistemological indeterminacy of the economic, he only focuses on how the assumed edges of the national economy are artificially and representationally fixed. He does not explore what in a sense is the geographical corollary of this puzzle in the context of contemporary free trade: namely, how do dominant capitalist interests exploit and rework the indeterminacy of the edges of the economy in order to expand their field of opportunity? Perhaps these questions remain unasked because of the development-focused argument, but it might also be interpreted as a further indication of the limits of a deconstructive approach focused only on the nation-state. Certainly, back in his essay on the state the spatial specificity of Mitchell's national focus is itself never really addressed or problematized. Instead, his repeated references to the spatiality of disciplinary micropractices seem to create a show of geographical analysis at one scale that hides the lack of attention to geographical developments at the transnational scale. If, as Ollman argued, the language of disciplinary practices can itself become a contentless abstraction, then Mitchell's use of spatial language and his concern with the spatiality of disciplinary dynamics might be seen as witness to more materialist attempts to fill this void. Unfortunately, though, it is a spatial language that in his essay on the state actually ends up effacing the wider geographical questions. Not only is this different from Mitchell's attention to place-based dynamics in *Colonising Egypt*. It is also quite a marked contrast to his powerful analysis in *Rule of Experts* of the geographical fashioning of Egypt as a space of natural limits and American-led reconstruction.[149] Perhaps this difference can be explained by the fact that in his essay on the limits of the state Mitchell was taking on one of the most geographically blind discourses in the modern academy: viz, the discourse of the state in political science.

As numerous critics, including Mitchell, point out, political science state theory tends to be replete with all sorts of spatial assumptions about the territorial boundedness of the state. The problem is that the assumptions tend to remain tacit and unexamined and, as a result, often reifying, ahistorical, and objectifying. Indeed, out of these very objectifications, Mitchell argues, come the sweeping claims about the modern state's sovereign power. However, in critiquing these claims, and in doing so through an analysis of spatial-ordering micropractices, Mitchell's own account becomes entrapped by assumptions the orthodox state theorists make about macrospatial ordering. To see how this pattern unfolds we need only turn to Mitchell's critique of Theda Skocpol. Here he sets about showing how Skocpol's use of French history to demonstrate the power of the state instead actually illustrates how the state emerges as an effect of disciplinary power relations. In this way Mitchell introduces a characteristically Foucauldian phrase about space and order so as to provide a sense of the materiality of the disciplinary practices he sees as elemental to any account of the emergence of the French state. "The new bureaucratic and military strength of the French state was founded on powers generated out of the meticulous organization of space, movement, sequence and positions" ("Limits," 92). The argument is persuasive, and yet there is a sense in which the very meticulousness of the language makes up for a lack of a macrological geographical contextualization. In this case, such a contextualization might have addressed in more detail both the inter-European and interimperial struggles out of which the French state emerged. Clearly, such broader transnational spatial concerns are as effectively occluded by a focus on disciplinary microspaces as they are by a fixation on the executive authority of the territorially bounded state.

There is a parallel here with Spivak's critique of Foucault's screen allegories that was discussed in the Introduction. However, in contrast to Foucault, Mitchell's work, including his close study of colonialism in Egypt, has been informed by more than just an awareness of imperialism. In the case of his essay on the state, nonetheless, it is the topographical reinscriptions of contemporary transnational neoliberalism that would seem to be preemptively screened out. It is Mitchell's dissembling of the transnational that in turn leaves his account vulnerable to the charges leveled by Ollman about failing to theorize the transnationalization of state making under the new free trade agreements of Europe and North America. However, as I have shown in this chapter, such transnational reinscriptions can be productively examined in terms of the border disciplinary practices Mitchell connects with the appearance of the nation-state effect. Clearly, the level playing field also reminds us that in the case of managed free trade agreements like CUFTA and NAFTA, the disciplinary practices involved inscribe a new transnational geography that no amount of studies focused on disciplinary micropractices will explain if they do not simultaneously take account of the transnational geography of capitalist restructuring. Once a less anemic analysis of this geography is introduced, Mitchell's unpacking of state effects offers a valuable way of coming to terms with the almost transcendental transnational state effect that is the neoliberal level playing field.

4

The Haunting Ground of the Hyphen: Diversity, Hegemony, and the Spatiality of Democracy

Affirmation of a "ground" which lives only by negating its fundamental character; of an "order" which exists only as a partial limiting of disorder; of a "meaning" that is constructed only as excess and paradox in the face of meaninglessness—in other words, the field of the political as the space for a game which is never "zero-sum," because the rules and the players are never fully explicit. This game, which eludes the concept, does at least have a name: hegemony.

—ERNESTO LACLAU AND CHANTAL MOUFFE,
HEGEMONY AND SOCIALIST STRATEGY

During the same period that free trade began to be negotiated and implemented across North America, much academic debate was consumed with the questions raised by antiessentialist theories of politics and culture. Today too much of this debate tends to be referred to with simple, often dismissive references to the Culture Wars or Identity Politics, as if we no longer need be delayed by the huge questions that were and remain at stake. While many of the theoretical developments of this period can now be looked on in hindsight in terms of how they relayed their changing political and economic times, it remains important to reflect both on what lessons they still have for us as well as on how exactly they can help us make sense of the period in which they were debated. Of particular value in this regard, Ernesto Laclau and Chantal Mouffe's *Hegemony and Socialist Strategy* stands out as a paradigm-shifting intervention in political and cultural theory.[1]

Subtitled *Towards a Radical Democratic Politics* and published in 1985, it traversed a huge sweep of philosophical and political debate in order to connect a careful genealogy of the concept of hegemony to the strategic questions facing leftist politics in the context of the rising neoliberal assault. In doing so, the book issued a manifesto for an antiessentialist politics focused on articulating together diverse struggles of differentially oppressed and exploited groups in a plural and radically democratic hegemonic formation.[2] To explain why this was possible, Laclau and Mouffe outlined an open-ended and nego-tiated understanding of politics, arguing that the so-called political was foundationally without foundations and thus perpetually open to transformation through the process of hegemonic rearticulation. Only the two great pillars of the so-called democratic imaginary—*liberty* and *equality*—were presented as nonnegotiable, reimagined as hold-ing open the very tensional "ground" in which all other disputes be-come articulated and thereby made subject to constant rearticulation. Along the way, Antonio Gramsci's older battlefield concept-metaphors for hegemony were displaced by discursive concept-metaphors, the notion of a "war or position" being recontextualized in a "theoretical field dominated by the category of *articulation*" (*Hegemony*, 93).

One aspect of Laclau and Mouffe's manifesto that is especially remarkable in the North American context is the way in which its antiessentialist arguments have since chimed with strikingly similar claims made by national philosophers and thinkers in America and Canada during the late 1980s and 1990s. I use the phrase "national philosophers and thinkers" cautiously because in one way or an-other these writers have sought to *ground* postfoundational politics within their respective nation-states. Many examples of this national grounding pattern can be found. For instance, Laclau and Mouffe's emphasis on the unclosed and unfinished nature of politics has its echoes in claims by American liberals such as Michael Walzer that "America is still a radically unfinished society."[3] Likewise, the argu-ment in *Hegemony* that "[d]iscursive discontinuity becomes primary and constitutive" (191) is a common refrain of Canadian national-ists. Writing in the wake of a failure to agree on a new constitution for Canada, B. W. Powe tried with a typical Canadian gesture to make a national virtue of the resulting lack of closure. "I suggest," he writes, "that Canada has a discontinuous character. I mean that without a single purpose or predetermined goal—no violent creation and imposition of a political myth or ideology—Canadians have lived with, invited and responded to many stories, moods and visions, and many different kinds of people."[4] Such nationalizations of antiessentialism are clearly multiple and varied. As illustrated by Richard Rorty's notorious appeals to an American-first form of solidarity-indifference, this postfoundational approach to politics can sometimes be narrowly nationalist in tone. Rorty argued that American liberals should care about "the lives of young blacks" not because they were fellow human beings but because they were fellow Americans.[5] Such parochial provocations are not my concern here.[6] The particular national "groundings" that are my focus instead merely share a common gesture of framing the multiple negotiations, contestations, and affiliations of diversity within the terrain of the nation-state. My main Canadian example comes from the work of the political philosopher James Tully. Without directly engaging with the work of Laclau and Mouffe, Tully represented the same Canadian constitutional impasse described by Powe in terms that still more directly evoked an antiessentialist account of politics. Canadian federalism, thus argued Tully,

> consists of the continual negotiation, in terms of competing federation stories, on an intercultural middle ground that has been slowly woven together and worn smooth over centuries of criss-crossing and overlapping negotiations and interactions, from the first Huadenosaunee (Iroquois)-Canadien federal treaty at Trois-Rivières in 1645 to the Charlottetown Accord of 1992.[7]

This account, I suggest in what follows, can be usefully compared with the supposedly postethnic account of America promoted by the intellectual historian David Hollinger. Hollinger's nationalism is more populist and arrogant, but the effort to depict the nation-state as a ground for ceaseless political and cultural intermediations is no less marked.

> Both . . . today's middle-American Right and today's multiculturalist Left [have] tried to resolve the old American problem of "the one and the many" by relaxing it, by pushing toward either "one" or "many." A postethnic perspective is willing to live with this problem and to treat it as an opportunity rather than try to escape from it. A postethnic perspective invites critical engagement with the United States as a distinctive locus of social identity, mediating between the human

species and its varieties, and as a vital arena for political struggles the outcome of which determine the domestic and global use of a unique concentration of power.[8]

While the writings of Tully and Hollinger represent eloquent interventions that are both well regarded within their respective academic arenas, they are quite distinct from one another. Their contrasts are many. They include their disciplinary and thematic differences: Tully has a radical philosopher's interest in problematizing conventional constitutionalism whereas Hollinger has a liberal historian's concern with the changing face of American belonging. But they also extend to the question of national background itself. It is the latter question that is vital for this chapter. Bringing it into focus makes it possible to address the ways in which the two authors' approaches relate to the actual hegemonic struggles over the rearticulation of diversity in Canada and the United States during the late 1980s and 1990s. Tully's book *Strange Multiplicity,* unlike the article quoted from above, is not explicitly focused on Canada.[9] However, what he calls his "post-imperial" argument is filled with innumerable examples and concerns that spiral out of the complex struggles in Canada to develop a new national constitution in an age of hypermediatized politics and deeply contested norms of citizenship. Hollinger, who styles his work as a "postethnic" contribution to the American debates over multiculturalism, is by contrast concerned with a context overshadowed by right-wing attempts to alter particular aspects of the existing U.S. Constitution. These contrasting contexts have evolved in different ways. The Canadian struggles from the introduction of the Charter of Rights and Freedoms in 1982, to the failure of the Meech Lake Accord in 1989, to the demise of the Charlottetown Accord in 1992 have still yet, a decade or so later, to lead to a new constitutional document, but they have led along the way to a radical pluralization of constitutional politics with aboriginal representatives, feminists, and immigrants' rights groups entering the tensional field opened up by the attempts to address the ongoing alienation of Québec. By contrast, while the actual *Contract with America* and Newt Gingrich's dominance in U.S. politics have diminished in significance since the heady days of the midterm elections in 1994, their legacy has been long and powerful in narrowing the space of political discourse, leading to the conservative constitutional revisions that were embedded in the welfare-reform, anti-immigration, and anti-terrorism legislation of 1996, as well as the more recent conservative legislative initiatives (such as the Patriot Act) in the wake of 9/11. Notwithstanding these contrasting contexts, both Hollinger's and Tully's work must also be seen as taking shape against the backcloth of the continent-wide implementation of free trade, a transnational backcloth that neither text addresses substantively, and yet that, as the previous chapter and this one together show, raises difficult questions for any national framing of postfoundational politics.

By using Tully and Hollinger as a way into the divergent struggles over diversity on "the ground" in Canada and the United States, I will not be presenting the two scholars themselves as representative samplings of the divergent Canadian and American experiences. However, I do want to compare them in this contextual way in order to show how their groundings of antiessentialism reflect quite different spaces of emergence. At the same time, I also turn to them here as my main counterpoints to Laclau and Mouffe because their writings share one important commonality as intellectual efforts to chart the possibilities for national democracy in the context of multiplying struggles over cultural and political diversity. They both connect the logic of antiessentialism (albeit using different formulae) to the classic liberal problematic of combining the imperative of equality with diversifying demands for liberty, which is to say political freedom. This is exactly the same problematic that Laclau and Mouffe seek to resituate in the field of hegemony in the last chapter of their book. Neither Tully nor Hollinger uses the term "articulation," and as I seek to show in detail, neither addresses struggles over hegemony as such, but the tension between equality and liberty that Laclau and Mouffe locate at the heart of the democratic imaginary nevertheless animates both accounts. It is in the practical working out of this tension that they each—in their own nationally framed ways—find an antiessentialist essence for postfoundational politics.

Hollinger calls it the "diversification of diversity" and Tully uses the phrase "strange multiplicity," but both are profoundly exercised by the consequences of the rearticulation of diversity for national democracy. Their common concern with making antiessentialist political sense of this multiplying diversity—Hollinger's keenness to preserve the tension of "the one and many," and Tully's search for the middle ground at the heart of "criss-crossing and overlapping negotiations and interactions"—is what resonates so strongly with Laclau and Mouffe's emphasis on developing both the plural and egalitarian impulses of democracy together. However, where the American and Canadian theorists turn to the nation-state as the primary field in which these twin impulses can be set to democratizing work, Laclau and Mouffe turn to hegemony itself, describing it in their final paragraph as "the field of the political as the space for a game which is never 'zero-sum.'" It is this parallel-turned-contrast between Tully and Hollinger on the one side and Laclau and Mouffe on the other that provides the starting point for this chapter. As such it is a starting point that leads in two directions. On the one hand, the way Hollinger and Tully ground postfoundationalism in the nation-state raises a number of questions about the "'ground' which lives only by negating its fundamental character" in *Hegemony*. On the other hand, by drawing out the theoretical similarities between *Postethnic America, Strange Multiplicity,* and the arguments of *Hegemony* it becomes possible to introduce the question of hegemony into a reading of the works of Hollinger and Tully. This in turn opens an analytical opportunity to investigate how their Canadian and American groundings of antiessentialism relate to the actual political struggles over the grounds of hegemony in Canada and the United States. All these "grounds," I argue, remain haunted by the hyphen in nation-state. All of them assume, either explicitly or implicitly, a bounded territorial arena in which the flux and unfinished negotiations of postfoundational politics can be played out. And, as a result, all of them can be argued to have a certain built-in incapacity to register the changing geographical terrains of politics in the context of the sorts of political-economic transformations of nation-state territoriality discussed in chapter 3.

To begin with it is necessary to explore at greater length the dissembled "ground" of space in Laclau and Mouffe's own writing. Haunted by the hyphen in nation-state and thereby bounded by an implicit territoriality, this "ground," I suggest, comprises another anemic geography. Investigating why their argument seems to be dependent on such an unexamined geography also makes it possible to clarify how Laclau and Mouffe develop the concept of hegemony in relation to the fundamental tension between equality and liberty. I suggest that they ultimately hold this tension together through a radically pluralized notion of citizenship, a notion that assumes a decentered space of democracy that *as* a space, however complexly structured and unfinished it may be, brings the normative nation-state outlines of their geography of hegemony into clearer focus.[10] Having traced this theoretical argument, the chapter turns to the work of Tully and Hollinger, beginning with a comparison of their different approaches, and moving on to discuss the specificity of their accounts of diversity vis-à-vis the political-cultural contexts out of which they are written. Examining in detail the hegemonic politics that shapes these contexts, I show how their antiessentialist arguments can be usefully supplemented by Laclau and Mouffe's own attention to hegemony. In this way I argue that an approach to diversity that comprehends it in terms of a decentered struggle over hegemony provides a more rigorous sensitivity to the relations of force that persist even in the context of postfoundational politics. Having made this point about the utility of Laclau and Mouffe's argument, I then proceed to explore the reverse questions about what Tully's and Hollinger's national groundings might mean for an approach to hegemony that fails to interrogate the concept's geographical grounds. I do not suggest that the concept of hegemony will always and everywhere remain haunted by the unthought-of nation-state territoriality. However, I do make the case that, without a persistent attention to the geography of hegemony, scholars of radical and plural democracy may find their framework has a built-in obsolescence in the context of transnational state formations and various other challenges to nation-state norms.[11]

THE ANEMIC GEOGRAPHY OF *HEGEMONY*

What is the "ground" that Laclau and Mouffe speak of when they describe hegemony? The quotation used as the epigraph at the start of this chapter contains its own elusive but telling answer. It is an "[a]ffirmation of a 'ground,'" they say, "which lives only by negating its fundamental character." This may well sound today like an eerie premonition of the often verbless doublespeak of Third Way politicians. Make the affirmations less technical and prolix, and it is not hard to imagine the empty sound bite: "Yes to community, opportunity, and democratic choice, no to bureaucracy, regulation, and partisan politics." However, Laclau and Mouffe's serious and far from reactionary theorization of hegemony moved in a more radical direction.[12] Indeed, issued as a critique of what monological political rhetoric displaces, one of their primary concerns was to come to terms theoretically with the multiplicity of struggles against oppression. These concerns led to their reuse of the Freudian-turned-Athusserian notion of overdetermination as a term to describe how political "meaning" is constructed through condensation and displacement "as excess and paradox in the face of meaninglessness." This they then combined with the psychoanalytic-turned-linguistic theories of the "symbolic" developed by Jacques Lacan, and the result was a theory of hegemony as overdetermined by the ceaseless and axiomatically impossible search to fill a fundamental lack of fullness in the symbolic order. Thus when they spoke of the "ground" of hegemony as that "which lives only by negating its fundamental character" their concerns were fundamentally epistemological and political: the ground autonegates because of the Lacanian-inspired assertion of an essential lack defining the symbolic and hence, for Laclau and Mouffe, the political. Geography, it seems, was not what they were talking about. And yet, I want to argue, the geography of their "ground" returns to haunt much of their argument. Thus while Third Way triangulations and hyperdetermined sound bites may sound like the ghostly echoes of *Hegemony*'s articulation and overdetermination, it is a very different structure of haunting that concerns me here: the return of the repressed geography of hegemony.

The scare quotes around "ground" are warranted because *Hegemony* is remarkably full of other spatial concept-metaphors that have a strangely ghostly, autonegating geographic reference. "Locations," "terrains," "fields," "areas," "frontiers," "boundaries," "planes," "surfaces," "positions," "regions," "topographies," even a "no-man's-land," fill the book, and references to "space" and "spaces" themselves are ubiquitous. Yet despite this haunting omnipresence, whenever the consequential geographies of these concept-metaphors might seem to be almost tangible they slip away into a fog of symbolic indeterminacy. This ephemeral aspect of the geographic terminology might seem hardly surprising to those who read Laclau and Mouffe as hopelessly idealist thinkers lost in clouds of discursive determinism.[13] However, it is not necessary to adopt Norman Geras's unreconstructed base-superstructure reductionism to notice how Laclau and Mouffe's spatial concept-metaphors are transformed by their commitment to a theory of discursive overdetermination. If all politics and all struggle is reconceptualized in terms of the indeterminancy of meaning in symbolic regimes, then analyses of anything so seemingly material as national frontiers and territories would appear to be remote. This then frees up such words to be used in more metaphorical ways. Frontiers, for example, are reused in *Hegemony* to name the dividing lines in "the field of articulatory practices" and thus become redesignated as "essentially ambiguous and unstable, subject to constant displacements" (134). This observation may only seem to be about semantics (and not, for example, transfrontier visions such as Cascadia), but more is at stake here insofar as Laclau and Mouffe's spatial metaphorics is intricately bound up with the flattening effect of their symbolically reductionist abstractions such as "the political" and "the social." The flattening is brought about by their theoretical determination (one might even call it *over*determination) to reduce the vastly heterogeneous *processes* of social life and political struggle to the antiessentialist bottom line of symbolic indeterminacy (a flattening effect, incidentally, that is marked in the book by the particular use to which the spatial metaphor "field" is put). Here my argument is guided by the work of theorists such as Bob Jessop (who has critiqued what he calls Laclau and Mouffe's "empty realism"[14]), Nicos Mouzelis (who has found fault with the "institutional vacuum" at the heart of their analysis[15]), and Donna Landry and Gerald MacLean (who have most brilliantly deconstructed the work's "abstractionism"[16]). All of these critics highlight the decontextualizing tendencies of *Hegemony,* connecting them to Laclau and Mouffe's dependence on a flattening account of discursive politics. Building on these critiques, I want to suggest that the authors turn to the spatial concept-metaphors as a way of providing some sort of relief—in both senses of the word—to counterbalance the flattening effect of what they bulldozingly label as the "field of overdetermination" (*Hegemony,* 111): the "theoretical field dominated by the category of *articulation*" (93).

The story of *Hegemony* begins with two sets of spatial metaphors used to evoke the direction and nature of the journey ahead. The first is the metaphor that Laclau and Mouffe take from Descartes about moving in a straight line through a forest when lost (*Hegemony,* 2). This metaphor basically serves to describe their single-track focus on how the open-ended political possibilities of the concept of hegemony can be retrieved from the closures that have marked its development. Moving on from this, Laclau and Mouffe proceed to describe such closures with the metaphor "of a *fault*" that is invoked (they note in brackets) "in the geological sense" (7). This allows them to hold open the indeterminacy of the epistemological ground their genealogy moves through by suggesting that each instance of theoretical closure is in fact an impossible closure (the closures in question consisting of moments when hegemony is theorized in an ultimately reductive way as being determined by class struggle, the last instance of the economy, and so on). Recoded by the geologic metaphorization as a fault or "a fissure that had to be filled up" (7), such closures are discursively repositioned by Laclau and Mouffe in the field of overdetermination where the cover-up of their basal flux can be explored. This is what they then proceed to do as they turn to examine in detail the theorists and disputants of the Second International: Luxembourg, Kautsky, Bernstein, and Sorel.

When Laclau and Mouffe turn to what they next geomorphologically dub "The Gramscian Watershed," a more streamlined treatment (the metaphor is exact) of political topography develops. To begin with, Gramsci's own concern with the actual geography of the Risorgimento and what he called "The Southern Question" is quickly and assertively dismissed. Abstracted away into an account of how his categories "broadened the terrain of political recomposition and hegemony," Laclau and Mouffe insist they "should therefore be situated at the level of the general theory of Marxism, and cannot be referred to specific geographic contexts" (66). This radical decontextualization of Gramsci's own geographical sensitivities prepares the way (which is to say, flattens the field) for their subsequent argument later in the book that hegemony has no particular place. It is "quite simply," they say, "a *political type of relation, a form,* if one wishes, of politics; but not a determinable location within a topography of the social" (139). In order to get to this aspatial point, Gramsci's own spatial metaphorics of the battlefield have also to be radically reframed. "War of position," note Laclau and Mouffe, "supposes the division of the social space into two camps and presents the hegemonic articulation as a logic of mobility of the frontier separating them" (137). This assumption, they proceed to stipulate, "is illegitimate." In its place hegemonic articulation needs now to be understood as having multiple axes. "[I]n advanced capitalist social formations," they argue, the political arena is radically pluralized, and thus the old two-sided battlefield has been transformed into an articulatory field of multiple overlapping political spaces. The note about "advanced capitalist societies" gives a clue here to the reason why "the Gramscian view becomes unacceptable" (137). It is unacceptable for Laclau and Mouffe because, despite all their other stipulations against teleological argument, they have a developmentalist, which is to say, historicist view of modernity in which "the political" steadily becomes more and more complex over (Western) time. Gramsci's arguments might therefore have worked for older *"popular struggles,"* but Laclau and Mouffe want to speak about *"democratic struggles* where these imply a plurality of political spaces" (137).

Hegemony may not have a particular place in the political topography, then, but for Laclau and Mouffe it does appear to have a historical trajectory. Clearly there are very problematic Eurocentric assumptions about modernity and political development embedded in such a conceptual trajectory (i.e., *West is best is politically plural*).[17] Rather than rehearse a postcolonial critique of these here, however, I instead want to focus on how the resulting narrative of political modernity is haunted by the normative hyphenation that has defined the principles and scope of political community in modern European nation-states. In this important regard the haunting goes far beyond the fleeting outlines of the spatial metaphors I have described above. It extends to the fundamental shape of their argument and stems from the way in which this argument is developed within the structures and partially closed conclusions—the creaking timbers and leaky attics, if you will—of previous theorists' articulations of hegemony. Because Laclau and Mouffe seek to present their own claims as stemming from their radical genealogy of hegemony (rather than as a wholly new conceptual apparatus), they effectively inherit the spatial frameworks of the older articulations. This is not to argue that they are insensitive to the implications of hyphenation, only that their argument at some level still inhabits the same old haunted house of the hyphenated nation-state.

Laclau and Mouffe's sensitivity to the actual territorialization of the political within the nation-state becomes clearest in their treatment of Disraeli's politics. Disraeli, they say, wanted to go beyond the clear-cut dichotomies of political space into two camps, the two basic camps of "the people" and the dominant elite. To do so, he sought to rearticulate popular political positionings, delinking them

from the revolutionary peoples' camp and joining them to a wider
circle of belonging. In this, say Laclau and Mouffe, "[h]is formula
was clear: 'one nation'" (*Hegemony*, 130). Having hereby summarized Disraeli's hegemonic rearticulation of revolutionary identities
as national ones, Laclau and Mouffe proceed to note that "[t]his
constitution of a pure space of differences would be a tendential
line, which was later expanded and affirmed with the development
of the Welfare State." In other words, here they point to the transformation of nation-space into state-space, the very transformation
on which the hyphenation of the modern nation-state rests. Pointing
also to the related frontier effects, Laclau and Mouffe nevertheless
do *not* point to the obvious relevance of this tendential territorialization of the political to their own narrative of modern hegemony as
the emergence of a purified "space of differences" (albeit purified in
a far more modular and abstract sense) overlaying the older bipolar
battlefields of popular struggle. No doubt they would stipulate that
this is another illegitimate correspondence, and clearly, their own
abstract vision of a "ground" of interarticulated differences and
equivalences is not imagined in the identitarian terms of Disraeli's
"one nation" nationalism. Indeed, they renounce—to use their own
evangelical verb—what they call the "positivist illusion that the en-
semble of the social" can be presented like Disraeli's nation and the
Welfare State in fully bounded, essentialist ways. But, having issued
this and many other similar renunciations throughout, Laclau and
Mouffe return in the last chapter to explain that the contemporary
task of the Left "cannot be to renounce liberal-democratic ideology"
itself (176). It is when we come to this, their concluding attempts
to provide a leftist rearticulation of liberal democracy as "radical
and plural democracy," that their own limiting territorialization of
hegemony as a national space of differences finally becomes clear.
Looked at from the perspective of the haunting hyphen, the territorialization of this space appears like an unwanted and unexplained
holdover of hegemony's household ancestors: in other words, it results from the way *Hegemony* builds on the "ground" of the theories deconstructed in Laclau and Mouffe's genealogy.

Having said that Gramsci's vision of dichotomized political space
is too simple for advanced capitalist societies, and having argued
that the visions of society from Disraeli to the Welfare State are
too totalizing, Laclau and Mouffe are nevertheless obliged by their

commitment to rearticulating liberal democracy to maintain a fundamental engagement with the inherited grounds of democracy. The possibility for a hegemonic strategy on the Left, they argue, does not reside "in the abandonment of the democratic terrain, but, on the contrary, in the extension of the field of democratic struggles to the whole of civil society and the state" (137). It is in the inherited space of this democratic terrain stretching from civil society to the state that the territorialized legacy of hegemony's previous articulations makes itself felt. Laclau and Mouffe's references to civil society and the state throughout the book remain framed in distinctly national, territorial ways. Like Mitchell's, their account of the state is rigorously antiessentialist. In this way, they theorize the emergence of the state as a seemingly autonomous and separate political space produced through articulatory practices. Taking issue with Poulantzas, they therefore claim that "the autonomization of certain spheres is not the necessary structural effect of anything, but rather the result of precise articulatory practices constructing that autonomy" (140). However, such autonomization of the state seems only ever imagined in *Hegemony* in national, territorial ways. On the next page, for example, they use the case of how race and class politics overdetermine one another to point further to how national-state policy in a country like Britain overdetermines both. Moreover, toward the end of the book, when they discuss the challenges of changing societies in radical democratic ways, they note how such rearticulatory plans "will depend not only on the more or less democratic forces that pursue that strategy but also a set of structural limits established by other logics—at the level of state apparatuses, the economy and so on" (190). This strangely structuralist account—especially so, given their critique of Poulantzas—also reveals a tellingly singular conception of the state and its conventional national "logics" such as "the economy."[18] If the state seems thereby nationalized in *Hegemony,* the pattern of territorialization appears still clearer in the book's framing of civil society. While Laclau and Mouffe are keen to insist on "*the whole* of civil society," this seems only ever imagined in territorialized nation-state terms. To be sure, they emphasize the notion of civil society in order to stress how the sites of radical and plural democracy extend way beyond the state-sanctioned democratic space of the voting booth, but their list of other spaces—"of production, of citizenship, of neighborhood, of couples and so on"

(*Hegemony,* 185)—all seem contained within the larger space of differences that is the nation-state.

In addition to their conceptualizations of the state and civil society, it should also be noted that all of Laclau and Mouffe's examples of actual hegemonic struggles are, like the British one, situated in particular countries such as France, Italy, Nicaragua, and the United States. They do not refer to them as nation-states, preferring the less encumbered term "societies." But the references are always to singular societies that could otherwise be labeled nation-states. This problem of renaming is important to note because it seems to point to a real ambivalence between Laclau and Mouffe's antiessentialist commitment to problematizing bounded concepts (which drives their use of alternate terms like "societies" and "social formations") and their genealogical commitment to reexamining the preexisting examples and arguments that they have inherited along with the concept of hegemony. To put it another way, this might be called the problem of the "given ground." Describing Gramsci's notion of an organic crisis, they actually refer to a "given ground" themselves when they describe such a crisis as "a generalized weakening of the relational system defining the identities of a given social or political space" (136). However, when they explore the implications of such weakening in the radically antiessentialist terms of symbolic indeterminacy, their argument leads down the path of suggesting that any "given territory" (144) can never be said to coincide completely with a particular society or social formation. "Certain articulatory practices will make [national frontiers] coincide with the limits of the [social] formation," they say. But whether or not this happens "will depend on the multiple hegemonic articulations shaping a given space" (144). Here we loop back to "the given," but quite what is doing all the giving and how is left unclear while a kind of reverse chicken-and-egg question unfolds about which category—the given social formation or the given territory—will be dissolved last. This seems a lost opportunity because the notion of articulatory practices holding social formations and national frontiers in a state of partial coincidence could have led in far less obscure directions. It could have been usefully developed into a thorough analysis of the hegemonic territorialization of the nation-state. And in exactly the same way, it could have led to a more rigorous attention to the forms of social, political, and economic articulation that are *excessive* to "given" nation-states and that are therefore reterritorializing in their hegemonic effects.

Only once in the book do Laclau and Mouffe imply with a concrete example that the sorts of articulatory practices they are talking about can cross the borders of nation-states. The example in question consists of a reference to how the concepts of political liberty developed in the French Revolution crossed the Channel to inform English radicalism in the development of the Chartist movement. But here, as elsewhere, their primary concern is to point to how social and democratic imperatives overdetermined the workers' struggle. Nowhere do they address the obvious counterpoint to this, the way in which worldwide workers' struggles spread a politics of working-class resistance across borders from the mid-nineteenth century onward, rearticulating and thereby radicalizing numerous national democratic struggles in new ways. Had they considered these transnational kinds of counterhegemonic rearticulations at any length, the possibility of thinking radical and plural democracy in more transnational and less traditional liberal ways might have been developed. But even had they entertained such a possibility, another aspect of their explicit engagement with liberal-democratic ideology would no doubt still have kept them on haunted ground: namely, their central conceptualization of hegemony as developing in the tensional space between liberty and equality.

At the heart of their argument about the extension of radical and plural democracy to civil society and the state, Laclau and Mouffe place the utmost importance on maintaining the tension between what they call the "logics" of equivalence (equality) and difference (liberty). Sometimes—such as in their discussion of how feminism rearticulates women's subordination as oppression—they frame their discussion of this tension in terms of the space of citizenship: to paraphrase, women fighting for *liberty* as women through appeals to the *equality* of all citizens within the nation-state (159). In such cases the nation-state framing is clear, even if understated. But at other times, the abstraction of the argument is such that the territorial ground at stake becomes much more obscure. To examine how the nation-state still haunts this abstractionism, it is finally necessary to explore *Hegemony*'s account of the tension between liberty and equality in detail.

Following the antiessentialism of the rest of the book, Laclau and

Mouffe argue that both equality and liberty have totalizing implications. The principle of equality pursued in isolation can work to erase difference, while the principle of liberty elaborated on its own can lead to an essentialization of different identities as fixed and unchanging. On the one side, then, they see the threat of egalitarianism turned homogenization; on the other, the threat of difference turned identitarianism. In order therefore to mitigate these twin dangers and to maintain the space of democracy in a state of open-ended negotiation, Laclau and Mouffe argue for a conception of the political as a space of endless antagonism and contestation between the principles of equality and liberty. Equality allows for a radical democracy and liberty for a plural democracy, but only insofar as both can collide and disrupt the totalizing imperatives of the other can either be sustained democratically without a final moment of closure. "It is for this reason," they note,

> that the demand for *equality* is not sufficient, but needs to be balanced by the demand for *liberty,* which leads us to speak of a radical and *plural* democracy. A radical and non-plural democracy would be one which constituted one single space of equality on the basis of the unlimited operation of the logic of equivalence, and did not recognize the irreducible plurality of spaces. (184)

This terribly abstract account is subsequently fleshed out with the examples of plural sites of potentially radical hegemonic rearticulation noted above: the spaces "of production, of citizenship, of neighborhood, of couples and so on." (185). However, placed at this point in the argument, it becomes clear that these sites are not only territorialized in terms of their scale and inclusion in Laclau and Mouffe's bounded conceptions of the state and civil society. In addition, they are grounded in terms of a geographical matrix that only seems capable of producing spaces of politics framed by the nation-state. While the logic of equality and equivalence is earlier defined as "a logic of the simplification of political space" and the logic of liberty and difference as "a logic of its expansion and increasing complexity," that very expansion of political space to political spaces beyond the nation-state seems held in check by the need to articulate it with and in tension to the space of equality (130). Since the latter is systematically evoked in *Hegemony* in the language of citizenship and a national civil society, the whole abstract trigonometrics of the tension between liberty and equality seems to be grounded ultimately within the territorial confines of the nation-state. Despite the abstraction, but also in part because of it, Laclau and Mouffe's account never therefore completely leaves the national territorial grounds presupposed in the accounts of Gramsci and all the others whose arguments they seek to renovate.[19]

If the outlines of *Hegemony*'s anemic geography are now clear, its significance may not be. In engaging with the abstractions of Laclau and Mouffe's own account my argument has only hinted at the implications of their built-in territorialization of the political. In the next sections I want to show that this fundamental but ultimately unnecessary territorial limit matters a great deal when one comes to examine the actual hegemonic politics of America and Canada in the throes of constitutional debate. These examples and the work of Hollinger and Tully show again and in far less abstract ways how the unending tension between the principles of equality and liberty is conventionally upheld and reinterpreted as a defining feature of the nation-state. At the same time, insofar as such reinterpretations tend to exclude the political implications of transnational and post-national transformations, they also help underline the problematic limits of the anemic geography haunting *Hegemony*.

HOLLINGER AND TULLY: DEBATING DIVERSITY DIFFERENTLY

Insofar as they are both concerned with the need to maintain some sort of tension between the struggles for equality and the need for freedom for difference, Tully and Hollinger make for useful comparative entry points into the Canadian and U.S. debates over diversity. Moreover, insofar as they also both repudiate ethnic nationalisms and value civic nationalism, they would seem to share broadly similar inclinations. However, to any readers familiar with both their books, comparing Hollinger's and Tully's writings may seem to promise little but incommensurability. No doubt very few readers have actually read both books, and this itself is a symptom of their contrasting contexts and audiences. Too often the American literature on diversity is unthinkingly exceptionalist and simply ignorant of work by writers from other countries, even those so close as Canada. By the same token, Canadian commentary often tends to fixate on the totalized Canadian differences with "the republic next door" in such a way as to preempt engagement with the actual details and controversies internal to American debates. In fact, a classic gesture of the Canadian debates over diversity is to find national closure by claiming "we may not know who 'we' are, but we do know we're not American." Neither Hollinger nor Tully fits these stereotypes, and Tully departs from the conventional Canadian gestures altogether. Nevertheless, comparing the two books' treatments of diversity does demand a careful attention at the start to their divergent academic orientations and contexts. Only in this way can the subsequent analysis of what they share with Laclau and Mouffe become meaningful.

Tully's work departs from Canadian convention partly because he engages in depth with contemporary American exchanges between the likes of Richard Rorty and Clifford Geertz, and also because he addresses in detail such staples of U.S. debate as the tensions between federalist and anti-federalist traditions. He goes back in this way, for example, to explore the anti-federalist constitutional precedents adopted from the Iroquois Confederation by Jefferson in the 1778 Articles of Confederation (*Multiplicity*, 91–95). This is part of his more general postfoundational project of retrieving constitutional diversity from what he calls "the empire of uniformity." But it also effectively displaces the traditional territoriality of constitutional debate insofar as it recenters the precolonial territoriality of so-called Great Turtle Island as a continental space of debate. These displacing gestures appear to be somewhat reterritorialized when Tully turns to theorizing the given space of constitutionalism in the present. However, it needs only be noted that such examples illustrate how his book is not narrowly bound by the borders of contemporary Canada. Focused on the philosophical problematic of formulating postfoundational foundations for contemporary constitutionalism, he actually understates the Canadian roots of his concerns. This seems to be part of his deliberate postimperial strategy, and not a response to the way publishers say Canada sells poorly abroad. But the Canadian concerns are there all the same—including the focus on constitutionalism itself—and, for the same reason perhaps, Tully's book is not widely cited in American essays on diversity.

In contrast to Tully, Hollinger's postethnic concerns are classically American in their exceptionalist, albeit thoughtful and sometimes reflexive, assumption of the United States as the primary locus for mediations between the global and the local. The following is a typical, senatorially toned rendition of his argument:

> The national community of the United States—the "we" that corre-
> sponds to American citizenship—mediates more directly than most
> other national communities do between the species and the ethno-
> racial varieties of humankind. (*Postethnic,* 141)

Not only is this claim an exemplary piece of exceptionalism, it is also typically American in its focus on ethno-racial concerns as the center-piece for a debate over diversity. Unlike Tully with his Canadian focus on other parties to constitutional struggle, Hollinger is preoccupied with the fate of one distinct arena of state policy and sociocultural dispute, multiculturalism. To be sure, this key concern has immense constitutional and political implications, but it is a narrower focus. So while Tully engages with postcolonial literatures on aboriginal sovereignty and feminist literatures on the masculinist normativity of citizenship, Hollinger addresses diversity through the more singular focus of multicultural politics and the literatures on race, racism, and race formation.

Curiously at one point toward the end of his book Tully criticizes his own particularist outlook as including a "tendency to write as if all the world is America" (*Multiplicity,* 182). Perhaps this is a refer-ence again to his pan-American concern with the continental space of Great Turtle Island, but it is more likely that Tully here is seeking to underline how his engagement with U.S. debate tends toward a privileging of things American even when it reads them against the grain. In any event, this self-reflexive moment is immediately preced-ed by a more precise acknowledgment from Tully that his particular "borough" of ongoing constitutional concerns is Canada (176). The larger point in this respect is that in both these self-positionings Tully seeks to problematize the context out of which he writes. Hollinger is equally transparent about his provinciality, but unlike Tully, he prefers to justify his U.S. focus as simply important (as attentive to "a unique concentration of power," for example) rather than ask read-ers to add more global diversity to what Tully, by contrast, argues should be an "endless dialogue of humankind" (*Multiplicity,* 182). Tully's appeal for this dialogue may sound humanistically universal-izing, but this and any other residual Enlightenment ambition in the book is qualified throughout both by his postimperial political com-mitments and by the model of dialogical debate and language games that he borrows (along with the notion of the "borough" of one's self-positioning) from the later, postfoundationalist Wittgenstein. Hollinger, by contrast, is quite happy to applaud what he views as America's exceptional record as a bastion of Enlightenment universalisms. "The United States," he argues, "is unusual in the extent and passion with which its ideological spokespersons accept and defend the nation's negotiated, contingent character within a broad canopy of universalist abstractions derived from the Enlightenment" (*Postethnic,* 141). This claim also clearly illustrates the way in which Hollinger grounds a vision of negotiated, contingent politics within the nation-state. In this respect, he shares something with Tully as well as with Laclau and Mouffe's hyphen-haunted conceptualization of hegemony. However, unlike these others, Hollinger's understanding of negotiated, contingent politics does not stem from a close engagement with European post-structuralist writers such as Derrida. Rather he explains it in terms of a tendency toward "historicist and particularistic enthusiasms" within "American intellectual history," a tendency with which he expresses broad if somewhat aloof sympathy (66). This approach (which may merely reflect the popular and national audience targeted by *Postethnic America*) contrasts directly with Tully's much more engaged enthusiasm for Derrida's exploration of the "difference with itself" in European identity and metaphysics. Indeed, it is on the model of Derridean deconstruction that Tully offers his own vision of how "from the outset citizens are to some extent on a negotiated, intercultural and aspectival 'middle' or 'common' ground with some degree of cross-cultural conversation and understanding" (*Multiplicity,* 14).

It is out of a critique of European universalism that another of Tully's distinct contributions arises. More than just expressing post-imperial sympathies in the abstract, he seeks to illustrate his commitment to challenging ethnocentrism by foregrounding a need to learn to learn from the colonized other. This he does throughout through a number of strategies, including most notably his constant references back to a model of diverse constitutional politics he sees as embodied in a sculpture by the Haida artist Bill Reid. The sculpture of a black canoe occupied by various native figures is called *The Spirit of Haida Gwaii,* and Tully goes to considerable lengths to address the politics of its creation, Reid's own view of the artwork's meaning, as well as what can be read into and out of the piece as an instantiation of an intercultural middle ground. Obviously aboriginal art can be put to all sorts of political uses, including deeply reactionary ones. In Tully's hands the usage is more than an attempt to illustrate the notion of the intercultural middle ground. There is also a certain Canadian romanticism in the focus on a single piece of aboriginal art within a work of abstract political philosophy. He notes thus that his "greatest pleasure" as he presented the lectures comprising the book at the University of Cambridge was to place a large picture of *The Spirit of Haida Gwaii* beside himself so as "to point affectionately to the myth creatures from my childhood home." Such talk about home, pleasure, and myth creatures reads as the affect of a folkish national narration, and in this respect the gesture points to Tully's tacit national framing of diversity. However, as one reads on through the book it becomes clear that this is no idle, instrumental, or co-optive use of the artwork. Tully is very sensitive to the dangers of neocolonial appropriation and keeps reminding his political philosophy audience that they need to rethink their own provincial categories by learning to learn from the other. He never quite puts it in these Spivakian terms himself. Instead, he makes the point clear by repeatedly foregrounding what he describes as the sensitivity to diversity opened up by perspectives such as *The Spirit of Haida Gwaii*. "One of the central arguments of this book," he explains, "is that if constitutionalism is approached from the perspective of the struggles of aboriginal peoples, unnoticed aspects of its historical formation and current limitations can be brought to light" (4). Further buttressing these arguments with frequent appeals to the arguments of native and postcolonial scholars—including most centrally Said's critiques of normative imperial culture—Tully thereby makes a compelling case for addressing the politics of diversity in a diversely informed way.

Hollinger asks questions such as "How wide the circle of the 'we'?" (*Postethnic*, 68). And he is especially anxious to see the American "we" expanded postethnically through what he casts in legalistic jargon as a freedom "of affiliation by revocable consent" (13). But when it comes to learning to learn from the other, he does not attempt any of Tully's strategies and makes little obvious effort to see America other-wise. Indeed, two examples from the book point in the opposite direction. One of the most significant reterritorializations of the circle of the American "we" brought about over the last two decades has been the development of a Mexican-American culture with strong and ongoing affiliations with Mexico. Hollinger's reference to this transnational community of belonging, however, reads by turns as accusatory, perturbed, and dismissive: "Illegal immigrants from Mexico complicate the public services of California," he notes, "while prophets of 'postnationality' explain that the boundary between the United States and Mexico is an imperialist fiction" (2). This reference to prophets—far from Tully's talk about aboriginal wisdom—is not made with respect, let alone approval. It is a barb, and in this way coincides with Hollinger's later and more abrasive critique of a joke by Barbara Herrnstein Smith made at the expense of the conservative celebrant of American patriotism E. D. Hirsch. Smith had sought to paint Hirsch's American canon as shallow and facile.

> Wild applause; fireworks; music—*America the Beautiful*; all to-
> gether, now; Calvin Coolidge, Gunga Din, Peter Pan, spontaneous
> combustion. Hurrah for America and the national culture! Hurrah!
> (*Postethnic*, 158)

Hollinger interprets this as a naïve and "vitriolic attack" that dismisses the value of national solidarity. "It is doubtful," he goes on to argue, "that Smith would similarly parody the educational programs associated with Black History Month," and then—using the cover claim "[w]ere she to do so, it might sound like this"—he proceeds to take some writerly pleasure from offering the parody himself.

> Wild applause; fireworks; music—*We Shall Overcome*; all together,
> now; Father Divine, Ralph Bunche, Chicago Blues, NAACP, double
> consciousness. Hurrah, hurrah, for the African American culture!
> Hurrah! (158–59)

Hollinger's point here fits his more general and carefully articulated argument against any notion of prepackaged identity or enclaved ethnicity. However, his investment in the parody also reveals a privileged white male liberal's tendency to downplay power differentials under the guise of evenhandedness. As a result, we are treated to the dehistoricized couplet that equates one form of cultural formation with another that it historically subjugated and oppressed. This is especially unfortunate because Hollinger's earlier attempt to actually speak to such power relations comes off as at best genteel. "The damage the ethnic protonation of Anglo-Protestants—and later white Americans generally—inflicted on ethno-racial groups imperfectly protected by the civic nation endows the multiculturalism of our time with its political intensity" (136). Slavery, the Trail of Tears, Jim Crow, and all kinds of other racisms up to the recent mass incarceration of one in three African-American men (between the ages of eighteen and thirty-four) surely indicate something more than imperfect protection.[20] As numerous critics have argued, such terribly long lists reveal the racist normativity of the nation-state, notwithstanding the potential for civic protection therein. Quite distinct, then, from Tully's postcolonial critique of the normative force of dominant cultural expression, Hollinger would seem to survey intercultural disputes from the highest heights of universalizing yet exclusive liberal discretion.[21]

Hollinger's liberal gentility noted, there is nonetheless a fundamental similarity between the way he rejects notions of prepackaged cultural identities and the way in which Tully argues that cultures need to be seen as overlapping, interactive, and internally negotiated. Both scholars, just like Laclau and Mouffe, see no transcendental ground for group belonging, only an interarticulated middle ground where groups overlap and renegotiate identities in constantly shifting ways. To be sure, Tully's description of this middle ground is attentive to its sociality, unevenness, and historical-geographies of violence, whereas Hollinger, in another classic liberal gesture, conceptualizes the space in a voluntaristic way as a middle ground of personal "choice" and "preferences." He notes the Marxist point about not making choices within circumstances of one's own choosing, but proceeds to argue nonetheless that

> [t]he principle that ethno-racial affiliations should be subject to revocable consent is a modest choice-maximizing principle based on the presumption that people—especially Americans who can invoke the constitutional tradition of the United States—ought to be more free than they now are from social distinctions visited upon them by others. (*Postethnic*, 118)

This liberal and nationalist emphasis on "choice" noted, Hollinger's alternate focus on the overlapping middle ground of cultural formations shares much with Tully's, and as such introduces the larger area of similarities that both authors share with Laclau and Mouffe.

Like Laclau and Mouffe, who view all political and cultural formations only as temporary stabilizations of dynamic and ongoing articulatory practices, Hollinger and Tully seek to move the debate on diversity to a ground where inclusion and exclusion are not seen in terms of group identities frozen in essentialist ice. For Tully this is important as a way out of the empire of constitutional uniformity, and for Hollinger it is a solution for what he sees as the paralysis and vulnerability of bureaucratized multiculturalism. However, for both scholars the move is also made as a critique of traditional political liberalism. It is in this way that Tully critiques the imperialism of Rawls's Kantianism, and it is through some of the same sensitivities that Hollinger critiques Rorty's attempt to argue "that the exclusivity of the private club might be a crucial feature of an ideal world order."[22] Beyond these critical moments, both scholars also submit some sort of notion of an intercultural middle ground as a positive way of addressing the challenge of balancing liberty with equality while avoiding the traditional liberal binary of universalism versus relativism. Here, of course, we return to the tensional ground that Laclau and Mouffe seek to uphold in the name of radical and plural democracy. For Tully and Hollinger, though, the national territorial scope of this ground is clearer and the project and the terminology are different.

In Tully's Foucauldian terms the challenge is to combine the need to free oneself from oneself and the need to belong, or, in other words, the challenge of being free from one's defining culture and place while still being given equal rights of belonging within it. "The tension," he says, "between these two goods cannot be resolved or transcended, and it cannot be overcome by a rootless cosmopolitanism on one side or purified nationalism on the other" (*Multiplicity*, 32). Hollinger articulates the same tensional concept (with more angst about cosmopolitanism and far less concern about universalistic nationalism) in the bioethnic terms of *species* and *ethnos*. Species is invoked thus as a metonym for humanity and, as such, stands in for the notion of human equality. Ethnos, by turn, would seem to metaphorize the notion of group identity and hence the need for plural group freedoms. For Hollinger this tension between equality and plural belonging has its practical ramifications in the need to balance corrective action against inequality with the need for freedom of choice over group identifications. These then are the vocabularies and routes through which both scholars ultimately come to the same middle ground as Laclau and Mouffe, articulating political-philosophical positions that aim at holding open the fundamental tension between liberty and equality. However, while Laclau and

Mouffe explore this ground as the ground of hegemony in the abstract (with all the haunting assumptions of nation-state territoriality noted above), Tully and Hollinger turn directly to examples of the working out of this tension in the national spaces of Canada and the United States. Examining now how the two scholars' arguments relate to the contexts from which they take their examples, the next two sections allow for two sets of arguments. First, and following Laclau and Mouffe, I underline how the respective national contexts need to be considered in terms of struggles over hegemony. And second, by exploring them explicitly as national contexts, I also seek to show how the ground "given" by the hyphen in nation-state haunts the resulting hegemonic politics.

CANADA AND THE HEGEMONIC POLITICS OF *STRANGE MULTIPLICITY*

Tully ultimately comes to ground the tension between the two public goods of "strange multiplicity" in the middle ground metaphorized by Bill Reid's carving of the black canoe.

> The best evocation of this alternative play of the imagination is *The Spirit of Haida Gwaii*. If contemporary constitutionalism is imagined in the light of this wonderful sculpture, the two public goods it harbours come into sharp relief. . . . [T]hey are the critical freedom to question in thought and challenge in practice one's inherited cultural ways, on the one hand, and the aspiration to belong to a culture and place, and so to be at home in the world, on the other. The differences between these invaluable goods have been settled in the black canoe.

Tully goes on to explain that he has

> sought to outline both the philosophy and practice of constitutionalism informed by the spirit of mutual recognition and accommodation of cultural diversity. Both the philosophy and practice consist in the negotiation and mediation of claims to recognition and dialogue governed by the conventions of mutual recognition, continuity and consent. (*Multiplicity*, 209)

The Canadian ground of all this is understated to say the least. Moreover, as a boat floating on water there is a certain subversive quality to *The Spirit of Haida Gwaii*'s capacity to serve as a grounding example at all. But yet the romantic appeal to "this wonderful sculpture" betrays a latent Canadian nationalism, and when Tully approvingly cites Reid's own epigram, "the boat goes on forever anchored in the same place," it is only a small jump for readers who might share this nationalism to move to viewing the "place" in question as Canada itself with its endlessly unfinished constitutional struggles (202). It is not just that Haida Gwaii (the Queen Charlotte Islands) is in Canada, or that Reid's work has been exhibited widely and proudly as Canadian. It is also the whole way in which Tully's narrative works more generally with Canadian examples in the course of fleshing out what a new constitutionalism of strange multiplicity should look like in terms of nation-state politics. From occasional approving citations of the Canadian Supreme Court's decisions to careful references to Canadian scholarship that is rarely referenced abroad, the sensitivity to Canadian content and politics is clear. Moreover, early on Tully opens the way to connecting the metaphorical message of *The Spirit of Haida Gwaii* to such politics when he notes that "it evokes one final and immensely optimistic vision of cultural diversity. For all the celebration of diversity and vying for recognition [exemplified by the sculpture's myth creatures], the paddles are somehow in unison and they appear to be heading in one direction. The ship of state glides harmoniously into the dawn of the twenty-first century" (202). That the ship of state here is Canada (anchored to Canadian diversity, heading without sinking to a coherent Canadian future) is only inferred, but it is nevertheless an inference generously supported by Tully's many appeals—both critical and celebratory—to Canadian politics throughout.

The most obvious invocation of a Canadian case comes near the start of the book with Tully's extended reference to the struggles that led from the implementation of the Charter of Rights and Freedoms in 1982 to the Charlottetown Accord and its demise in a national referendum on constitutional reform in 1992. It is this same remarkable period that I seek to examine here in terms of the working out of hegemonic politics. As shall soon become clear, it was a period in which the whole hegemonic apparatus of the Canadian constitution and its associated discourses and practices was up for grabs. The Canadian government and other, increasingly diverse constitutional actors and parties became engaged in a serious attempt to write a new constitution for the country, and this at a time of late twentieth-century mass-media news coverage and almost instantaneous continent-wide communications. In Laclau and Mouffe's terms, it made for a period of especially frenetic and heterogeneous hegemonic rearticulation. Instead of framing his account in terms of hegemony, though, Tully represents this Canadian experience as a story of expanding constitutional diversity. He begins by saying he wants to illustrate the overlapping, interactive, and negotiated nature of cultural identities within such diversity "with an example from Canada." Then he proceeds to tell the story of Canada's constitutional crisis as a story of strange multiplicity becoming unleashed by debate and dispute.

> When the former prime minister of Canada, Pierre Trudeau, sought to recognise and affirm a unifying Canadian constitutional identity in the Canadian Charter of Rights and Freedoms, the ten provinces immediately claimed that it failed to recognise the political and legal cultures of the provinces and demanded a constitutional amendment. The government of Québec further argued that the Charter constituted an imperial yoke over Québec's distinctive French language and civil law culture, forged through centuries of interaction with English-language Canada, and that it needed to be amended to recognise Québec's cultural distinctiveness. The 633 Aboriginal First Nations of Canada protested that the Charter oppressed and failed to recognise their Aboriginal cultures: that is their forms of self-government, legal systems, languages and so on. (11–12)

Having outlined here just four of the major sectional parties to the constitutional struggle, Tully proceeds in the next two paragraphs to detail the further fissures of diversity evidenced by the unfolding dispute over the Charter. The constitutional differences between aboriginal people on reserves and those living off reserve are mentioned, as too are the concerns of Canada's French-speaking minorities outside of Québec and the English-speaking minority within Québec. Tully then introduces the disputes with the masculinism of the Charter brought forward by women's groups. Adding further nuance to this already complex picture of multiplicity, he goes on to underline the differences between the concerns of women in Québec and those in the rest of Canada, as well as the disputes among aboriginal women's groups over whether their rights as women could be better protected under the Charter or under First Nations self-government. "Finally," Tully finishes off his spiraling list of diverse disputants, "the multicultural groups and visible minorities of Canada demanded recognition of their cultural distinctiveness across each of these constitutional claims" (12).

Tully explains that the significance of this Canadian experience lies in how it makes manifest the "continuously contested, imagined and re-imagined, transformed and negotiated" qualities of strange multiplicity. "Cultural diversity," he concludes using a Foucauldian metaphor, "is a tangled labyrinth of intertwining cultural differences and similarities, not a panopticon of fixed, independent and incommensurable worldviews in which we are either prisoners or cosmopolitan spectators in the central tower" (11). It is this tangled labyrinth that remains Tully's central concern throughout. Exploring the controversies around the Charter is in this sense of a piece with his critique of how its framers "disregarded the language of diverse federalism" (163), an argument that in turn is part of the book's still larger aim of rediscovering and valuing the cultural diversity covered over by mental maps of constitutional uniformity around the world. Consequently, the Canadian examples are supplemented by numerous others, including many from the United States, as well as others from South Africa, New Zealand, the European Union, and even "Faustin Twagiramungu's negotiations towards multicultural rule in Rwanda" (13). Nevertheless, when attempting to find substantive examples of cultural diversity instantiated in constitutional debate, Tully most often comes back to his Canadian "borough." It is in this way that he returns to what was effectively the outcome of the diversifying disputes provoked by Trudeau's introduction of the Charter in 1982, the example of the Charlottetown negotiations that took place a decade later in 1992. These were negotiations that actually led to a new constitutional document—the Charlottetown Accord—a document that was agreed to by all the major constitutional parties, but that also went on to be discarded when the majority of Canadians voted in a national referendum against making it their new constitution. Tully's point about the Charlottetown negotiations is that they further evidenced the diversity of contemporary constitutional struggle, including most especially the multiplicity of aboriginal representation: "four Aboriginal negotiators (two women and two men), representing six hundred First Nations, the Métis, Inuit and Aboriginal people living off reserves, along with a national association of native women on the sidelines met ten provincial premiers, two territorial leaders and a prime minister, all on equal footing" (130). Clearly, this was significant constitutional diversity in action, and it is not surprising that

Tully concluded in his separate essay on the negotiations that their immediate result—the accord—could be interpreted as the most recent instance of an evolving intercultural Canadian middle ground "that has been slowly woven together and worn smooth over centuries of criss-crossing and overlapping negotiations and interactions, from the first Huadenosaunee (Iroquois)-Canadien federal treaty at Trois-Rivières in 1645 to the Charlottetown Accord of 1992."[23] This reading when put alongside Tully's attention to other expressions of Canadian constitutional diversity (such as those made by the nineteenth-century Québec jurist Thomas Loranger) provides a valuable antidote to the kinds of historicist and often ethnocentric accounts of modern constitutional evolution. However, as compelling as the notion of the middle ground may be, its "centuries of criss-crossing and overlapping negotiations and interactions" also obviously represent intense struggles over, in, and about power, struggles that the concept of hegemony helps elucidate but to which Tully himself does not directly turn.

Tully's general approach, it should be emphasized, is certainly not blind to power relations. In a more recent essay on the philosophical debates over recognition and distribution, he makes this quite clear. "[T]here are," he says, "always asymmetries in recognition and the distribution of power among those engaged in negotiations. Such asymmetries can scarcely be bracketed in the negotiations and their procedures of argumentation." Moreover, he adds, "[a]ll affected are not heard and those who are heard do not always gain a response, let alone a satisfactory one."[24] So while the philosophical style of Tully's writing—such as his occasional use of the "language games" concept-metaphors of Wittgenstein—has a somewhat depoliticizing tone, it should be underlined that his broader account of the evolving middle ground of "strange multiplicity" is more attuned to the practical experience of oppression and inequality than many other commentaries.[25] A brief consideration of some Canadian examples makes this clear.

The dominant scholarly commentaries made in the wake of the failed national referendum on the Charlottetown Accord tended to gloss over the power relations at the heart of constitutional politics with appeals to the nation and national ideology. Similar in some respects to Tully's account, such appeals made much of Canada's capacity to embrace and/or embody the decentered conversational ideals of postfoundationalist ethics. However, more idealist and presentist than Tully, they thereby also presumed to read the nation's essence and fate in the constitutional nonclosure. Thus on the one hand there were popular celebrants like Jeremy Webber who sought to make a national virtue out of the failure to ratify a new constitution, turning the very points of conflict and disagreement into a larger and happier story of national "conversational" diversity.[26] On the other hand, and also distinct from Tully's account, there were the more downcast treatments of the constitutional impasse that interpreted the crisis as somehow reflecting the nation's historical misfortune. The political scientist Janet Azjenstat's anguished assessment of the predicament was in this sense typical. "Canadians," she complained, "are attempting to remake a liberal democratic constitution at a time when the virtue has gone out of ideas such as universality, neutrality and objectivity, which are the enabling ideas of liberal democracy."[27] Ironically, for a scholar bemoaning the impact of postfoundationalist ideology critique, this nostalgic emphasis on the lost virtue of ideas was, like Webber's account, a rather idealist explanation of what was happening at Charlottetown. By contrast, Tully's account keeps the praxis of constitutional struggle much closer to the foreground. He does not explain the events in terms of either passing constitutional fashions or conversations in a rich and magnificent land. It is true that in his article on Charlottetown he formulates the problem in somewhat Hegelian terms, arguing that Canadian federation is "neither a unifying constitution nor a common vision, but the multiplicity of activities of multilateral negotiation itself."[28] However, it is this same emphasis on negotiation that also leads him in a more historical and materialist direction. Thus his book-length account of the "centuries of criss-crossing and overlapping negotiations and interactions" makes the postimperial case for arguing that even before colonial political history created national borders across North America there were preexisting constitutional conflicts and negotiations. For him, therefore, Charlottetown needs to be interpreted as the product of a long and bitter series of power struggles not all of which could even be properly called Canadian.

Tully's distinctions noted, it still can be argued that his approach to constitutional politics might be productively augmented with a closer attention to the question of hegemony and its grounds. One benefit of such augmentation is that it moves the discussion beyond the political conceit that the parties to the negotiations were on an "equal footing" by highlighting the uneven political and economic grounds on which they were standing. And a second benefit of an attention to hegemony is that, following Laclau and Mouffe, it directly introduces the question of the articulatory practices through which the preexisting constitutional norms were extended and reworked as they were connected to groups that were formerly unrecognized or actively misrecognized in prior rounds of constitutional struggle. In other words, the constitutional negotiation practices in question can be understood after Laclau and Mouffe in terms of the struggle to *articulate* hegemony: articulate, that is, in the double and never fully fixed meaning of establishing a political relation and representing an identity at once.[29] By now exploring in more detail the Canadian constitutional odyssey from the Charter's entrenchment to the Charlottetown Accord it is possible to show how such analytical reframing in terms of hegemonic articulation enables us to explore in more depth the grounds beneath Tully's "middle ground."

What do we find beneath the supposed "equal footing" of the parties to the Charlottetown negotiations? A sensitivity to hegemony highlights how, while it may have provided for a certain equality of recognition, it also ultimately included the newly "included voices" in a larger hegemonic regime in which the disempowering level playing field effect of transnational neoliberalism was also powerfully operative.[30] To be sure, the negotiations did indeed represent a high point of constitutional diversity and multidimensional contestation. Aboriginal leaders were sitting face to face with the leaders of all the provinces, including the premier of Québec, and there too was the prime minister himself. However, it was he, Brian Mulroney the representative of the Canadian federal state, who was also the prime mover in the negotiations. Far from resting on an equal footing he was setting the pace, the political rationale, and most significantly in terms of hegemony, the substantive emphasis that ran strongly through the accord on *constitutional decentralization*. At first impression, such a commitment to move governmental authority away from the central state may seem to fit well with the needs for constitutional diversity (providing most clearly more room for independent self-government by Québec as well as by native governments). To understand why such an emphasis also had hegemony-building implications it is necessary to step back and consider the political economy of Canadian federation.

From confederation in 1867 through the rapid development of the Canadian welfare state in the 1960s to today, there have always been economic imperatives impinging on the debate over how tightly the various parts of Canada should be bound together. Over time these imperatives have changed in the direction of their influence, systematically driving the consolidation of stronger unity and stronger central governance through the mid-twentieth century but, after the early 1970s, driving more and more in the opposite direction toward greater decentralization.[31] In order to come to terms with this switch, the Canadian political-economist Jane Jenson effectively argued in 1989 that much of the crisis of Canadian federalism needed to be understood as an outcome of a crisis in what she called "permeable Fordism." By this she meant a specifically Canadian regime of accumulation and social regulation in which the national coordination of mass production with mass consumption under the auspices of a Keynesian welfare state system was "permeated" by the effects of continental interdependence with the U.S. economy.[32] Such a permeating influence, she noted—in line with many other studies of Canadian political economy—led to the development of enormous interregional tensions within the country as a result of different regions having different types of economic ties (commonly characterized by the export of a particular raw material staple) to the United States. Jenson's critical suggestion was that, as a result of this peculiarly interdependent political economy, Canadian Fordism was dominated not so much by the politics of class conflict and class compromise (as, say, in the United Kingdom, the United States, and France), but rather by forms of regional conflict managed by a complex federal-provincial system of intrinsically geographical compromise.[33] From this argument it follows that when the economic underpinnings of Fordism fell away in Canada—as they did throughout Western capitalist nation-states after the "oil price" crises and the collapse of the formal Bretton Woods system in the early 1970s—so too did the federalist system of interregional compromise crumble in its turn. In this way the geographical fragmentation at the heart of the constitutional crisis is explained not as a reflection of Canada's inherently discontinuous character, and rather as a result of capitalist restructuring.

While this simplified summary of Jenson's already economistic explanation leaves little room for the role played by democratic negotiations in Canada's constitutional crisis, its readily appreciable emphasis on the context of negotiation underlines the importance of a political economic geography that much diversity discourse, including Tully's talk of a middle ground, obscures. It is within this geography that the supposed "equal footing" of the constitutional players needs to be reassessed. As chapter 3 showed in detail, this hegemonic ground of constitutional debate was increasingly influenced after the 1980s by the ever-more-powerful bulldozing effect of free trade. The equal footing at the bargaining table therefore has to be reappraised in part as equal footing on a descending and disempowering floor in which governmental authority however much decentralized was also increasingly eclipsed by the market. Moreover, just as the tendency toward constitutional decentralization complements the level playing field effect of free trade, so too does it go hand in hand with a neoliberal emphasis on a minimalist state within Canada. As many Canadian critics of neoliberalism have pointed out, therefore, it was precisely this hegemonic project of reducing the size and influence of the central state that the Mulroney government reframed in terms of constitutional decentralization.[34]

The basic means by which the Mulroney government attempted to articulate the constitutional negotiations with their more general neoliberal project was through what might be summarized as "laissez-faire osmosis." Rather than try, like Trudeau, to incorporate Québec though direct constitutional containment measures such as official bilingualism, the approach of the Conservatives was instead to actually invite the demands for more autonomy from Québec, using them as a spur for similar demands for equivalent autonomy from the other provinces. While this made for a spectacle of democratic negotiations among the provinces rather than acts of autocratic containment by the federal government, it also instigated a series of demands by provincial leaders calling for the federal government to relinquish more and more authority to the provinces. Given the neoliberal hegemonic project of shrinking federal governance, the Mulroney negotiators were eager to oblige. Thus, by repeatedly opening up the constitutional cleavages of Canada to negotiation, the very logic of the democratic discussion between the provinces ensured that equal rights would be demanded by all the parties, thereby allowing the osmotic spread of a federalism-dissolving neoliberalism. Key to this whole dynamic, ironically, were the very legacies of previous attempts to contain Canada as a nation-state via an array of statist-cum-constitutional projects. In a sense, the Conservatives simply reversed these earlier approaches, allowing the imperatives of increasingly multinational negotiations to undo the constitutional hyphenation of the nation-state and thereby undercut the rationale for federal state regulation. This reversal can be illustrated by reconsidering the significant constitutional events of the last two decades in terms of hegemony.

The Charter of Rights and Freedoms entrenched by the Trudeau government in 1982 laid the foundations for subsequent constitutional politics in two clearly separate ways. First and more practically, it was the conflict over the Charter's entrenchment that dictated the subsequent need for some form of constitutional reconciliation with Québec. It has generally been this moment of constitutional rupture and its reverberations in popular culture that has preoccupied commentaries.[35] More important from the perspective of the struggle over hegemony, though, is the second way through which the Charter served as a basis for subsequent negotiations: namely, its inauguration of the new form of equal rights national discourse organized around a supposedly pan-Canadian notion of legalized citizenship. In the language of Laclau and Mouffe, the Charter thereby entrenched and set loose a "logic of democratic equivalence" through which all future constitutional politics would have to be mediated. By both *judicializing politics* and *politicizing the judiciary* the Charter initiated a more individualized, contestable, and, ultimately, more sweepingly *national* model of citizenship. In short, it unleashed in Canada the spirit of democratic republicanism that Laclau and Mouffe trace back to the equal rights discourse of the French Revolution. It was subsequently also a version of this same equal rights discourse that underwrote both the radically democratizing initiatives celebrated by Tully and the process of neoliberal hegemony building.

The ambivalent implications of the Charter were quite evident in the circumstances surrounding its entrenchment. On the one side, its emphasis on equality rights existing throughout Canada irrespective of provincial location became so generalized that it even carried over into the language about the "equality of provinces" in the constitutional amending formula to which the Charter was yoked in the 1982 Constitution Act.[36] It was precisely this "equal individuals / equal provinces" logic of democratic equivalence that was to prove so valuable for the neoliberal project. More generally, it has been easy for the Conservatives to turn the Charter's language of individual equal rights into attacks on state governance of all kinds.[37] Indeed, this reworking has followed exactly the lines of the "new right" hegemonic project described by Laclau and Mouffe as the rearticulation of individual rights in the terms of possessive individualism (*Hegemony*, 171–75). Of course, as Tully and others underline, more progressive, diversity-expanding constitutional politics were also unleashed by the Charter. Women's representatives, native representatives, and minority representatives all started to rearticulate the tensional space of liberty and democracy opened up by the Charter.[38] But the context in which these bids for equal constitutional footing were made continued to be shaped by the simultaneous articulation of the equal rights logics with neoliberalism. Not surprisingly, the scope of this neoliberal hegemonic articulation process widened with the election of Mulroney's government.

Although Mulroney came to power in 1984 with a commitment to settling Canada's constitutional quarrels quickly, it was not until June of 1987 that his efforts led to a new constitutional accord. This accord was signed by all the provincial leaders at Meech Lake. Following the equality of the provinces logic that the Mulroney government fostered, this final version of the accord stood as a precarious attempt to placate all the provinces at once. The so-called Meech Lake Accord therefore included propositions that moved the division of powers toward the provinces; limited the use of federal spending power; constitutionalized the Supreme Court (reserving three seats for Québec justices); adopted a new constitutional amending formula giving Québec a limited veto; and, most significantly from the perspective of the resulting controversy, acknowledged Québec as constituting a "distinct society" within Canada. Announcing the accord, Mulroney declared it to be first and foremost a national achievement. "Tonight," he said, "Canada is whole again, the Canadian family is together again, and the nation is one again."[39] Yet all the while it was billed as a nation-building testament to Canadian skill in the art of compromise, the neoliberal state practices with which Meech had actually been articulated became increasingly apparent.[40] It seems, moreover, that the Mulroney-led negotiations were able to secure these significant neoliberal gains simply by allowing the debate between the provinces to play out along a logic of democratic equivalence. Of course this gave new governmental powers to the provinces, but given that these would soon be disciplined through the back door of a free trade agreement, the interprovincial negotiations served the neoliberal project well.

Unless this all seems too neat, it should also be noted that the cost for Conservatives of seeking to entrench neoliberal goals through the constitutional bargaining process was that they were also made subject to ongoing hegemonic rearticulation by other parties. For example, among the groups involved in the debate was the National Action Committee on the Status of Women, otherwise known as NAC. NAC was not opposed to the accord initially and began its campaign by arguing that Meech could be approved so long as Section 28 of the Charter was protected from amendment. This was in large part a concession to the principal liberal feminist group in Québec, the Fédération des Femmes du Québec, which supported the accord because of the seeming advance it presented for Québec autonomy. This compromise position, however, later broke down as other NAC member groups from the rest of Canada began to speak out more against the neoliberalism embedded in the accord. Thus, as well as raising concerns about how the "distinct society" proposition cast a shadow over equality rights and abortion rights in a traditionally pronatalist Québec, these other NAC member groups highlighted the threat to federal programs posed by the decentralizing implications of the accord. Still other NAC representatives underlined the problematic lack of attention in Meech to the constitutional situation of First Nations women and in this way articulated the feminist organization's opposition with the growing discord over the accord among First Nations more widely.[41] Such pluralization of the constitutional struggle was also ultimately reflected in the termination of Meech in June of 1990. This final failure of the accord occurred when, in another example of the democracy-deepening rearticulation, Elijah Harper, a Cree member of the Manitoba legislature, argued that First Nations had been excluded. He proceeded to use a procedural mechanism to prevent the legislature from ratifying the accord. Since unanimity was required, this poignant moment of First Nations' resistance simultaneously blocked the Mulroney government's neoliberal plans for the accord and sent a more general message about how any future constitutional negotiations would have to come to terms with the increasing demands for participation and the consequent pluralization of the democratic debate.

The failure of Meech was generally explained as a failure to recognize the depth of democratic desires for public participation, or how, in more popular terms, the accord had been negotiated by "eleven white men in a room."[42] The Mulroney government, which remained as keen as ever to pursue constitutional negotiations (and which instead dramatized the failure of the accord simply as a "rejection" of Québec), was therefore nevertheless obliged to widen the scope of its next series of attempts at bargaining. Meanwhile, separatist organizing in Québec itself also intensified the pluralizing pressure for constitutional change by forcing the premier of Québec, Robert Bourassa, to legislate a timetable whereby the government of the province was committed to calling a referendum on constitutional amendments or, failing that, on sovereignty itself by October 26, 1992. This effectively gave the federal government a deadline by which time they had to arrive at a new constitutional agreement on which Québec voters could vote. The machinery of constitutional debate was therefore restarted, this time with a still more involved and expectant public following the proceedings. It was this "Canada round" of negotiations that would lead to the signing of the accord by provincial premiers at Charlottetown and, following that, culminate with the Canada-wide referendum timed to coincide with the referendum in Québec. In the meantime, the negotiation process commenced with a peculiar combination of overt attempts at "national consultation" and prescriptive presentations of the government's own neoliberal agenda.

The main result of the huge public consultation project known as the Spicer Commission was a call for yet more public participation in the constitutional negotiation process.[43] "The People," concluded Keith Spicer, wanted to be involved through participatory mechanisms such as referenda and/or a so-called constituent assembly, a representative assembly of Canadians who would be given real authority to write a new constitution.[44] While the constituent assembly recommendation was never pursued, the fact that there was ultimately a referendum on the Charlottetown Accord showed how the federal government could not ignore this renewed call for equal participation by citizens, a call repeated this time with all the authority of a national commission. Nevertheless, in 1991 the Conservatives again attempted to make neoliberal notions of deregulated markets and scaled-back government the basic floor of the negotiations. This time they did so by drafting the proposals to be discussed in the newly planned public fora.

Neoliberalism was clearly etched into the government's 1991 proposals and became thematic in six main areas. The first of these was an audacious attempt to entrench property rights in the constitution as a basic addition to the rights guaranteed in the Charter. This was a clear attempt to rearticulate the liberal individualism of the Charter with the possessive individualism of neoliberalism and was all the more bold for its positioning in a "Shared Citizenship and Diversity" section.[45] The other main neoliberal proposals were included under the more appropriate, if euphemistic, title of "Preparing for a More Prosperous Future." Here the basic attempt to transform the constitutional impasse into the passage of neoliberal reform found reflection in a vocabulary of prosperity, competitiveness, and fiscal restraint. Thus the second main and overarching neoliberal proposal concerned the constitutionalization of competitiveness and free trade.[46] The third and more substantive set of neoliberal proposals continued this free trade theme by proposing to amend Section 121 of the existing constitution as a means of strengthening Canada's "Economic Union." The fourth area of proposals extended this amendment's logic into the realm of governance with a suggestion that a form of IMF-like "monitoring" institution be established within Canada in order to "harmonize" market deregulation.[47] Likewise, the fifth area of proposed change sought to restrict the Bank of Canada to a neoliberal focus solely on the monetarist mantra of price stability.[48] And finally, the sixth area of neoliberal reform was basically a continuation of the proposals for decentralization that had been previously advanced and then lost with Meech. These would again fit neatly with the equivalential dynamic that had led before to the other provinces demanding the same autonomy that Québec was demanding. It was for this reason that the decentralization arguments were to prove the only major area of the neoliberal proposals that would survive intact through the ensuing rounds of negotiation. The rest of the proposals, including others like Senate reform that were less directly tied to the neoliberal hegemonic project, were all to become the focus of intense debate and democratic struggle in the months ahead.

More than the Charter debates, more than the rejection of Meech, and more than the Spicer Commission, the response to the Conservative proposals of 1991 reflected a profound deepening and pluralization of the constitutional debate. The opportunities for this debate were ironically made available by what began as a Special Joint Committee of the House and the Senate on a Renewed Canada. This committee, which became known as the Beaudoin-Dobbie Committee after its parliamentary cochairs, left Ottawa and held over seventy-eight meetings across Canada, hearing testimony from seven hundred people and receiving three thousand written submissions before submitting its report in March 1992.[49] In the fall of 1991, with the committee suffering a number of organizational difficulties, the federal government also asked a number of research organizations to coordinate five constitutional conferences in order to facilitate further public input into the committee's report. Initially five of these "constitutional conferences" were held in January and February of 1992, and later a sixth was added with a mandate to examine aboriginal concerns. In fact, the addition of the sixth conference usefully attested to the way in which a form of disruptive democratic momentum developed in the preceding five. It was this unclosed and transformative form of debate that, in addition to legitimating a conference focused on First Nations self-government, also opened the possibilities for counterhegemonic questions more generally.

Each conference consisted of a "televised town-hall" meeting of around two hundred delegates. This was "strange multiplicity" indeed. Some of the participants were lawyers and academics specialized in the arcane details of amending formulae and constitutional history, while others were randomly selected "Ordinary Canadians" from among the many self-selected Canadians who had sent in applications. Put together with parliamentary representatives, they split into sections and engaged in wide-ranging debates that also had a huge audience in the country at large. The deepening of debate made possible by these arrangements was not just a reflection of the heterogeneity of the participants; it was also a result of the ad hoc and often undisciplined "middle ground" character of the meetings themselves. As a result, the process provided a forum in which the neoliberal proposals of the government could be contested and rearticulated along radically different political lines. The conference in Toronto that focused on "Identity, Rights and Values," for example, totally rejected the possibility of including property rights as a fundamental constitutional right. The heterogeneous criticisms of this property rights proposal usefully reveal the extent to which the heterogeneity of the participants—the copresence of planners,

feminists, aboriginal leaders, environmentalists, and labor representatives, among others—could be collectively articulated to counter
the neoliberal hegemony. Concerns about market forces were not
unanimous, though, nor did they extend into a wholesale rejection of
all the government's proposals. The general emphasis by the government on strengthening the economic union of Canada, for example,
was widely supported. Nevertheless, even in this case, conference
participants were critical of the government's approach to achieving the general goal.[50] Instead, many conferees took the neoliberal
apologetics of adjusting to globalization with economic reform and
reworked them into a justification for a series of more social-welfarist
policies. These policies were then advanced as a proposal to include a
"Social Charter" within the new constitution.[51] To understand how
the accord itself thus came to be written and debated, we must now
turn to the Charlottetown negotiations themselves.

Key representatives at Charlottetown, as at Meech Lake, were
the provincial leaders. This was because of the amending formula
that was set up with the Charter in 1982. It meant that, however
wide the public negotiations, the amendment of the Canadian constitution still remained an intergovernmental process involving the
provinces. Some of the provincial premiers arrived at the resulting
meetings advocating specific constitutional measures. These varied
agendas were themselves further complicated by the need to negotiate with First Nations leaders. Nevertheless, the nine provincial
premiers and Mulroney's team arrived at an agreement on July 7,
1992. On this basis Québec rejoined the constitutional negotiations
and on August 28, in Charlottetown, the federal government, all the
provinces, the representatives of the territories, and the First Nations
leaders reached an accord. At this point, the resulting document was
mainly discussed as Tully and others have also since discussed it
with reference to the radical steps the accord made toward both
acknowledging Québec as a distinct society and recognizing First
Nations self-government. At the same time, though, it stood as testimony to the complex struggle over neoliberal hegemony that had
evolved in the preceding years and months. Mulroney's government
had still been able to use the demands for equivalence from the provinces to further the decentralizing neoliberal project. Accordingly,
the Charlottetown Accord granted a vast sweep of new powers to
the provinces, acceding to the demands for autonomy by Québec

while using this as a lever to decentralize and scale back federal governance in general. Exclusive provincial jurisdiction was henceforth going to be recognized over Tourism, Mining, Housing, Recreation, Municipal and Urban Affairs, Forestry, and Culture.[52] In addition, federal spending power was to be constitutionally restrained.[53] This did not represent a complete abdication of federal spending authority, but it was designed to further enable the neoliberal erosion of federal powers.

The echoes of neoliberalism became far fainter in the effectively *counterhegemonic* Social and Economic Union clause. Here the government's hegemonic project of "strengthening the Canadian economic union" was rearticulated with and thereby subverted by the Social Charter themes that emerged from the Beaudoin-Dobbie constitutional conferences. Thus enclosed altogether in one "nonjusticiable" package, the notion of strengthening the "economic union" was articulated in turn with the "social union" policy objectives of providing quality health care, social services, housing, food, education, environmental protection, and worker rights and protections right across Canada.[54] This set of objectives was still only a wish list, but even as such it clearly served to give written legitimation to Keynesian rather than neoliberal policies. Coming together with the way in which the accord simply excluded the Conservatives' monetarist Bank of Canada proposals from consideration, it indicated a more systematic subversion of the neoliberal plans.

The other major form of counterhegemonic organizing evident in the accord was the struggle for the recognition of First Nations self-government. Trudeau's Constitution Act of 1982 had marginalized this struggle with largely unfulfilled promises of future constitutional meetings. The neoliberal consensus of Meech had similarly deferred the issue. And Spicer acknowledged that his commission had not heard enough from First Nations people. It was only with the opening afforded by the participatory momentum developed in the Beaudoin-Dobbie conferences that the voices of aboriginal leaders began to be taken seriously. Even then, they had to campaign for a sixth conference to deal directly with the question of native self-government. However, by the stage the provincial leaders began negotiating the details of the Charlottetown Accord in the summer of 1992, the First Nations' struggle had secured four seats for their leaders at the negotiating table. Their own hegemonic project of connecting the struggles of both on- and off-reserve natives with the Inuit and the Métis could not have been more different than that of the Conservatives. Yet having articulated their common demands for self-government in the terms of the increasing countrywide demands for democratic participation, their final mark on the accord itself was bold. Most notably the accord's proposed Canada Clause (the core of which comprised a series of amendments to the Charter) included the following, enormously significant declaration:

> The Aboriginal peoples of Canada, being the first peoples to govern this land, have the right to promote their languages, cultures and traditions and to ensure the integrity of their societies, and their governments constitute one of the three orders of government in Canada.[55]

Like the counterhegemonic victory implicit in the Social and Economic Union clause, this substantive First Nations victory also represented an articulation of equal rights discourse with an entirely different set of political goals to the possessive individualism articulated in neoliberal discourse. Indeed, far from possessive individualism, the deepening and pluralization of equality rights discourse in the constitutional debate thereby concluded in the accord with a significant recognition of First Nations *group* rights.

The deepening of democracy finally reached its apogee of democratic participation in the referendum on the Charlottetown Accord. This was also the moment when the full geographic scope of the middle ground came back to haunt the proceedings. What had seemed like an impressive accord uniting all the main constitutional parties in the negotiation forum in Charlottetown was suddenly being scrutinized the length and breadth of Canada with each concerned citizen interpreting the accord and discussing it through the lens of their own regional "common sense." The varied spaces, practices, and place-based discourses of everyday life comprising the heterogeneity of Canadian identity suddenly had to be articulated with the hegemonic attempt to describe the legal meaning of that identity in a single constitutional document that would apply universally to the whole nation-state. Such was the momentum of events that polls initially showed that the accord was popular enough to win a majority both in Québec and throughout the rest of the country. Thus without specifying exactly what sort of result was necessary for constitutional amendment, Mulroney's ministers agreed with the other parties to proceed with the referendum. The voting day was still the date set by the Québec legislation of October 26, and so, with little more than a month to go, the various parties to the accord confidently began the process of outlining what they saw as its merits. Their confidence was to prove short-lived. Having begun the campaign by hymning the "Canadian compromise" supposedly rendered incarnate at Charlottetown, advocates of the accord quickly found themselves defending it from a vast array of disparate local criticisms. Their responses to these criticisms necessarily had to speak to particularist concerns, and as soon as this began, the anthem of collective compromise was drowned out by the dissonant sounds of regionalized disagreements. Ironically, at this point, when an increasingly individualist articulation of equal rights began to dominate critiques of the accord, the federal government itself tried to advertise Charlottetown's two most popular and least neoliberal aspects—the Social and Economic Union clause and the agreement on First Nations self-government—in order to salvage a "Yes" majority. It was to no avail. Instead, on October 26, 54 percent of Canadians outside Québec, 57 percent of voters in Québec, and 62 percent of voters on official "Indian reserves" refused to give a mandate to their representatives to rewrite the constitution on the basis of the accord. In all, 74.9 percent of eligible Canadians exercised their democratic rights, and of these 55 percent signaled dissatisfaction with the proposed changes.

Insofar as the Charlottetown Accord never became a new constitution of Canada, it might well be argued that an analysis of its production as an outcome of layered hegemonic articulations counts for very little. However, as Tully and many others have pointed out, something substantive did come out of the process. More and more voices to the constitutional debate came to be meaningfully included, and the resulting "strange multiplicity" mapped out a middle ground in which any future constitutional settlement will still have to be made. Analysis in terms of hegemony helps us to understand how this result did not simply grow out of the soil of Canada like some diversely colored national flower. Instead, it was an outcome of ceaseless hegemonic articulations that only slowly led to the pluralization of debate, and that at the price of erosive neoliberal attacks on federal governance. Despite the failure of the accord at the polls, this process of neoliberal hegemony building has continued apace since 1992, expanded and entrenched by the implementation of NAFTA and by the rightward drift of policy making by the Liberal government that replaced the Conservatives in the 1993 elections. For these reasons alone it seems important to consider the unfolding of constitutional diversity in Canada in terms of hegemony. An account that only celebrates "the multiplicity of activities of multilateral negotiation itself" can all too quickly ignore the perils of associated political-economic initiatives, initiatives that the neoliberals persistently sought to make part, parcel, and final product of the Canadian constitutional negotiation process. In this respect the process did not so much reflect strange multiplicity as relentlessly normal capitalist singularity, and accounts that ignore this in the interests of discoursing on diversity do so at the cost of an unfortunate analytical discontinuity of their own. Introducing the question of hegemony is clearly a useful corrective in this regard because, without negating the vital question of recognizing difference, it keeps the meaning of and threats to democratic participation more directly in focus.

An approach that is attentive to hegemony does not negate the question of recognition precisely because it also points up the value of examining "strange multiplicity" in terms of the actual processes of equalizing and pluralizing hegemonic articulations. Indeed, it would seem hard to find a more perfect example of radical and plural democracy unfolding in practice (with all the attendant risks of liberal and neoliberal compromise). For all these reasons, then, a commitment such as Tully's to investigating the praxis of negotiation is further enhanced by the sensitivity to articulatory politics introduced by Laclau and Mouffe's approach to hegemony. Following Laclau and Mouffe, the final "No" vote on Charlottetown might even be interpreted in this way as an illustration of "an 'order' which exists only as a partial limiting of disorder; of a 'meaning' that is constructed only as excess and paradox in the face of meaninglessness" (*Hegemony*, 193). Certainly, this would coincide with other interpretations of the Canadian condition such as those of the legal discourse theorist Rosemary Coombe. "The original 'lack' (of meaning) which underpins the identity 'Canadian,'" Coombe says, "becomes the source and the site for hegemonic articulations."[56] Clearly, though, such an interpretation involves a certain nationalization of Laclau and Mouffe's argument. The unsutured space of the political becomes the unsutured space of the nation-state, and what I have argued is a tacit nation-state framing of hegemony in Laclau and Mouffe's own argument finally becomes explicit. It is in this respect that Tully's more straightforward approach to constitutionalism (with its clear acknowledgment of the roll of the state and legal infrastructure in facilitating multilateral negotiations) seems more useful. It does not project the notion of essential lack on to national space, but rather works in a much more materialist fashion to investigate the fundamental diversity of constitutional negotiation from the ground up. In this sense it takes the national grounds as a contingently given but far from necessary basis of the unfolding diversity. It is therefore arguably more supple in the context of dehyphenation where the nature of the negotiations becomes increasingly multinational and transnational in scope. From the perspective of many Canadian First Nations and separatists in Québec this is exactly what has been happening in Canada. Here, Tully's commitment to theorizing the federalist precedents of "deep diversity" all the way back to "the first Huadenosaunee (Iroquois)-Canadien federal treaty at Trois-Rivières in 1645" comes into its own. The danger with Laclau and Mouffe's own approach in this context is that it can obscure the multinational nature of the negotiations with preemptive albeit tacit historicist assumptions about the singularity of the modern nation-state as the ground in which articulatory practices unfold. Tully's account, by contrast, can account for the strange multiplicity of Canadian debate without assuming that it is fully contained by the singular ground of one national arena. What remains less clear, however, is how his account or others like it can come to terms with forms of multinational politics that are vectored through the invisible hand of market, which is to say with neoliberalism as a form of transnational hegemonic context for negotiations. It is to this question (and all the issues it raises about hegemony and democracy right across Tully's Great Turtle Island) that I turn at the very end of the chapter. Before this, I move now to the topic of how the notion of hegemony can further elucidate another account of political diversity, namely Hollinger's vision of a postethnic America.

THE UNITED STATES AND THE HEGEMONIC POLITICS
OF CIVIC NATIONALISM

Published in 1995, the same year as Tully's *Strange Multiplicity,* Hollinger's *Postethnic America* nevertheless emerged in a radically different political and cultural context. The early 1990s in the United

States were not a period of diversity-expanding reforms either con-stitutionally or otherwise. Indeed, America during this period wit-nessed a growing assault on a wide array of protections and initia-tives that had once enabled the development of a more inclusive and diverse civil society. From the antipoverty programs that dated back to the 1930s and the crisis management of Roosevelt's New Deal, to the expanded welfare-state provisions of Lyndon Johnson's Great Society, to the legacies of the civil rights movement such as affirma-tive action, all were suddenly under severe threat. Anti–affirmative action initiatives and propositions were passing in states across the country. Anti-immigration politics and organizations were also on the rise at the very same time as NAFTA was ratified by the U.S. Congress. Right-wing talk radio took off and, led by such celebrity conservatives as Rush Limbaugh, provided a venue for relentlessly racist and sexist innuendo on topics such as "welfare queens" and "dependent" immigrants. The "workfare state" was widely advo-cated in more polite policy-making discourse as the proper and time-ly alternative to the problems of dependency created by the welfare state. And in Washington, D.C., in 1994 a new, aggressively right-wing Congress was elected that for the first time in forty years was dominated by a Republican majority in both the Senate and the House. Claiming a mandate based on the so-called *Contract with America* of the new Speaker, Newt Gingrich, the House Republicans initi-ated a suite of legislative reforms ranging from the anti-immigration legislation discussed in chapter 2 to capital gains tax reductions for the wealthy to tax increases for the poor to so-called welfare reform itself, a massive quasi-constitutional piece of legislation that ended guaranteed federal entitlements for poor children and their parents while moving the residual responsibility of temporary support to the states. This destruction of what even Ronald Reagan had once sworn to protect as a "national safety net" was presented in the policy makers' populist jargon as a vital act of civic salvation, a rescue of ordinary Americans from a bloated federal bureaucracy. However, as was made clear in various, more coded ways, the law also rep-resented a targeted attack on the rights of African-Americans and immigrants of color. If this was still the work of Hollinger's civic nation-state, it was not one where the protection of basic rights and the provision of welfare were valued very highly; it was rather a civic nation in which the narrow normativity of the straight white man of property started to become explicit once again as the model of citizenship.

Embodying the disjunction between wide ideals of civic diversity and narrowed normative practice, the neoconservative assault took place in an America that, after 1992, had Bill Clinton as president, a president who had come to power promising a new injection of investment into America's educational, health-care, and welfare infrastructure, and a president who with his multicolored cabinet was widely thought to be one of the most concerned in the country's history with the fate of underrepresented minorities. With further telling irony, the political attacks on welfare and immigrant and minority rights also took place in an America where popular culture was increasingly enlivened by a new kind of nationalism that celebrated the multiculturalism of the United States, drawing attention to the nation's diversity as one of its most exceptional qualities. One paradigmatic reflection of the "multiculti" compensatory kind of cultural zeitgeist was the blockbuster movie *Independence Day*, filmed in 1995 and released in 1996, the same year as the welfare-reform legislation. As George Sánchez has pointed out in a brilliant commentary on the movie's central message, *Independence Day* crystallized the new-fashioned multicultural jingoism with dazzling success. "Once in the theatres," notes Sánchez, "audiences were treated to the vicarious pleasure of watching the outer space invaders defeated by a polyglot team of U.S. citizens, most conspicuously headed by an African American fighter pilot (played by actor/rapper Will Smith) and a Jewish electronics/mathematical genius (played by actor Jeff Goldblum), while the rest of the world's fighting forces combine across all historical and socio-political divides to back-up the American charge."[57] Reflecting on this battle, the actor playing the U.S. president (Bill Pullman) gives the following speech:

> Mankind—that word should have more meaning for us all today. We can't be consumed by our petty differences anymore. We will be united in our common interests. Perhaps it is fate that today is the Fourth of July and you will once again be fighting for freedom—not from tyranny, oppression, or persecution, but from annihilation. We are fighting for our right to live to exist. And should we win the day, the Fourth of July will no longer be known as an American holiday, but as the day when the world declared in one voice, "We will not go quietly into the night. We will not vanish without a fight." We

are going to live on. We are going to survive. Today we celebrate our Independence Day![58]

As Sánchez points out, this speech captures the whole multicultural nationalist essence of the movie. "Multiculturalism seemed to have emerged as a quintessential American value, marking the United States as a unique society among nations, while giving it alone the status to lead all nations to a new future devoid of interethnic strife."[59] For Sánchez *Independence Day* is just a symptom, and thus he also notes that the "cinematic fantasy—ahistoric as it may be—is also a central vision of some leading Americanists."[60]

Although he critiques Hollinger's erasure of power relations, Sánchez does not himself in so many words argue that Hollinger's book is simply an academic replay of the *Independence Day* fantasy. Nor is this my own argument here, but the resonances remain clear. "A postethnic perspective on American nationality," Hollinger argues,

> emphasizes the civic character of the American nation-state, in contrast to the ethnic character of most of the nationalism we read about today. A civic nation can mediate between the species and the ethnos in ways that an ethnic nation cannot. In the context of the worldwide resurgence of ethno-racial particularism, the transethnic solidarity of the American civic nation has much to recommend it. The United States, as a civic nation with an ethno-racially diverse population, mediates more directly than most nations do between the species and the varieties of humankind. I argue that the value of civic nation-states in protecting rights and providing basic welfare is undervalued by proponents of postnationality. (*Postethnic,* 14)

Hollinger's manifesto for a postethnic America with its focus on the touted American ability to mediate between "the one and the many" rests on a more sober historical assessment of the country as a civic nation. It also usefully cautions against "the dangerous conceit that [the United States] is a proto-world-state" (15)—a conceit I discuss at greater length in chapter 5. But ultimately its exceptionalist emphasis on America as the most diverse and time-tested ground of multicultural politics comes perilously close to the basic spirit of *Independence Day*. In this sense I follow Nikhil Singh's careful critique. "What is most brilliant about Hollinger's account," says Singh with discretely damning praise, "is that it effectively (re)presents the organic, ideological form that American national subjectivity has assumed during our epoch—namely the argument that America is universal—for our own more sceptical, multicultural times."[61]

Examining the context of hegemonic American politics in the 1990s, it fast becomes clear that as well as being intellectually skeptical multicultural times, they were also profoundly conservative times in terms of political and economic change. This is not to draw a merely ironic juxtaposition between Hollinger's high hopes and the neoconservative backlash of the *Contract*. Hollinger himself—in obvious contrast to a movie such as *Independence Day*—does much to reflect on the actual political and economic scene in which his call for postethnic politics is made. He cites David Harvey's critiques of post-Fordism and flexible capitalism, he ends the book with some passing reflections on increasing levels of poverty and imprisonment, and more significantly in terms of his argument, he directly describes America's political-economic turmoil as a major impediment blocking passage toward postethnic relations. He argues in this way that "the imprisoning of more and more of the population is an emblem for a complex of social and economic conditions that obstruct postethnicity" (*Postethnic*, 165–66). The obstruction happens in part, Hollinger contends, because it forces oppressed groups to turn to ethno-racial particularism as a mode of resistance. The actual causal ties are not fleshed out in this argument, but Hollinger's focus on how ethnic-racial identification may work in this way as a counterpoint to contemporary political-economic imperatives is a returning theme throughout the book. In this way, he argues that in a period of globalization when big business is abandoning the nation at the same time as lobbying for various forms of state entitlement, America's diverse ethnic communities risk doing something similar, demanding entitlement based on essentialized identities while simultaneously turning their backs on any notion of common nationality.

Clearly, Hollinger is profoundly exercised by the sundering of the hyphen in nation-state, or what I have described as the problematic of dehyphenation. He thus makes his argument for a postethnic America as a call for a renewed but antiessentialist hyphenation of nation and state, a rehyphenation that by constantly mediating between the one and the many can supposedly keep open the question of the national "we" indefinitely. Hollinger suggests this is especially vital in a context where what he calls the middle American Right is constantly attempting to narrow the circle of the national "we." "The ideological resources of the American nation-state," he says, "are too valuable to multiculturalists to be allowed to fall, by default, into the hands of [these . . .] Middle Americans, evangelical Christians, advocates of family values, and supporters of Newt Gingrich and of Rush Limbaugh" (14). However, having thus established the rationale for postethnic nationalism in what are in some senses counterhegemonic terms (as a struggle to rearticulate rather than abandon the national popular and as a struggle thereby to reclaim the nation from the Right), Hollinger does not really pursue the question of hegemony very much further at all. Thus, while his purpose in writing the book seems to be to carve out a new position for liberal multiculturalism so that it can take back the hegemonic ground from both a nationalist middle American Right and a transnational capitalist elite, and while his account, unlike Laclau and Mouffe's, clearly and indeed proudly identifies the national territorial scope of this ground, he does far less to explicate the relations of domination constituting the stuff of national hegemonic politics. Had he done so, I now want to argue, the prospects for challenging the middle American Right with the kinds of liberal appeals he makes to choice-maximizing individual ethnic self-ascription through revocable consent would probably have looked a little less compelling. Appeals to choice and individual opportunity, it turns out, were the very rhetorics that Newt Gingrich and other lawmakers adopted as they pushed the quasi-constitutional (and hard to revoke) reforms of the welfare-reform legislation into hegemonic place. Explained as a response to a national crisis, and legitimized in terms both of reducing the deficit and of enabling the diversity of devolution and state-by-state innovation to flourish, the act represented the hegemonic rearticulation of civic nationalism with a neoconservative assault on the rights and protections once provided by a national welfare state.

In many ways welfare reform would seem to confirm Hollinger's worst fears about the rise of the middle American Right. A nationalist ethnos of dominant whiteness, along with a whole panoply of associated assumptions concerning the ideal nature of the American family, was successfully yoked to a project of state transformation. However, by here exploring this transformation and rehyphenation of the nation-state in the explicit terms of hegemony it becomes possible to examine the plausibility of Hollinger's nationally framed postethnic politics and question its feasibility as a workable form of communal choice-maximization. Two main points are at issue in this regard. The first is one that perhaps Hollinger would himself support: namely, that the legislative events that took place after the publication of his book rearticulated discourses of individual choice and opportunity in such a way as to eradicate further the real choices and real options for consent available to the country's poorest and racially most oppressed citizens. The second is the point that this situation calls for strategies of counterhegemonic resistance that need necessarily to draw as much upon postnational solidarities as on strategies of national reclamation. Turning first to the erosion of opportunity and choice represented by the act, how can it be understood as part of a wider hegemonic project?

The Personal Responsibility and Work Opportunity Reconciliation Act (or PRWORA) abolished overnight the federal entitlement to aid that had originally grown out of the 1935 Social Security Act and that had finally become universal when expanded to African-American women in the 1960s. More than just "ending welfare as we know it," to use President Clinton's own unfortunate phrase, PRWORA might just as well be said to have ended welfare altogether by demanding that welfare recipients be made to work and thereby effectively making it impossible for poor women to be stay-at-home mothers. Reversing the development of a pannational, panracial safety net that had taken five decades to establish, the act's hegemonic achievements narrowed the circle of national belonging, effectively disenfranchising the long-term poor from the full freedoms of citizenship. Most significantly, it replaced the old federal support system known as Aid to Families with Dependent Children (AFDC), creating in its place a system of bloc grants to states to provide what the lawmakers purposively and tellingly dubbed Temporary Assistance for Needy Families (TANF). The support was thereby made temporary not enduring. It was devolved geographically to become the responsibility of the states. And it was also rearticulated as assistance to the "needy," no longer a right and pannationally guaranteed entitlement. Even this shift in terminology alludes to the act's hegemonic rearticulation of citizenship and belonging. As Nancy Fraser has underlined, shifts from rights-talk to needs-talk are always mediated by dominant social and cultural codes. They are shifts associated in particular with the imposition of patriarchal assumptions about men as normative citizen-subjects with rights and about women as secondary subjects with needs.[62]

In the case of PRWORA, the patriarchal ascription of need also came with an overriding concern about the problem of controlling poor women's bodies and behavior. Specifically, this concern was articulated in terms of reducing "out-of-wedlock births" and enforcing marriage. One does not have to search very far in the legislation to find articulations of this hegemonic patriarchy. Indeed, the preamble to PRWORA goes out of its way to note the following heavily freighted factoids as "Findings."

> (1) Marriage is the foundation of a successful society.[63]
> (5) The number of individuals receiving aid to families with dependent children . . . has more than tripled since 1965. More than two-thirds of these recipients are children. Eighty-nine percent of children receiving AFDC benefits now live in homes in which no father is present. (PRWORA, 2110)
> (5 C) The increase in the number of children receiving public assistance is closely related to the increase in births to unmarried women. (2110)
> (8 C) Children born out of wedlock are more likely to experience low verbal cognitive attainment, as well as more child abuse, and neglect. (2111)
> (10) Therefore, in light of this demonstration of the crisis in our Nation, it is the sense of this Congress that prevention of out-of-wedlock pregnancy and reduction in out-of-wedlock birth are very important Government interests. (2112)

As Gwendolyn Mink has highlighted, the net effect of these "Findings" when transformed into the legal code of the new welfare rules was a wholesale transformation of the meaning of citizenship for poor women. "When the [PRWORA] transformed welfare," she notes, "it also transformed citizenship. Flouting the ideal of universal citizenship the act distinguishes poor single mothers from other citizens and subjects them to a separate system of law."[64] Thus, despite all the proponents' talk of freeing citizens from dependency, providing opportunity, and liberating the civic nation from big government, the act's actual impact on poor women was overwhelmingly controlling and disciplinary. "Under the act," explains Mink, "government tells poor single mothers with whom to associate, under what conditions to have and raise children, and what kind of work is appropriate. These instructions invade poor single mothers' freedom of association and freedom of vocation. They curtail their fundamental rights—rights that are strictly guarded for everyone except mothers who need welfare."[65] In other words, then, this was a statutory and as such powerfully hegemonic rearticulation of the civic nation that deliberately and effectively thwarted the liberal vision articulated by Hollinger of "protecting rights and providing basic welfare."

Also hinted at in the "Findings" section but, much more significantly, emerging as a result of PRWORA's implementation were also a whole series of inequitous racial implications that overlaid the class and gender politics associated with the desire to put and keep poor women in waged work and heteronormative marriage. The act's call to tackle "the crisis in our Nation" and remake the United States as a "successful society" through enforced marriage was probably not what Hollinger had in mind when he commented in 1999 that "the United States is the most successful nationalist project in all of modern history."[66] His own nationalist multicultural vision of American success has more to do with the nation-state's "longevity, its absorption of a variety of peoples and its sheer power."[67] However, this paean to America's assimilative power and other statements like it in *Postethnic America* still seem wanting in light of PRWORA's powerfully racist ramifications. National success, the "Findings" section implies, also involves tackling the problem of inner cities.

(9 L) Neighborhoods with larger percentages of youth aged 12 through 20 and areas with higher percentages of single-parent households have higher rates of violent crime. (*PRWORA*, 2112)

This finding is conspicuously coded vis-à-vis race, but other statements by proponents leading up to the push for PRWORA left less to the imagination. Building on the hegemonic association of the ghetto with the alleged dysfunctions of what Senator Patrick Moynihan typecast in 1965 as "the Negro family," welfare reform advocates frequently used an interested moral mapping of the inner city to locate the problem.[68]

This attention to the geographical correlates of blackness and dependency was matched in the buildup to PRWORA by equally racializing assessments of the welfare-reform challenge in the *Contract with America* itself. "Today, one of every five white children and two of every three African-American children are born out of wedlock," notes the "Reducing Illegitimacy" section of the *Contract*'s "Welfare Reform" chapter, with a transparent hint to would-be voters that the cycles of dependency and delinquency targeted for reform were a much more serious problem for blacks than for whites (obviously the problems of corporate dependency and delinquency were not even at issue).[69] Insofar as such hints locked into and rearticulated more generalized hegemonic understandings, they need to be interpreted against the backcloth of a whole series of longstanding normative national notions of citizenship and belonging. As Dan Carter explains in his study of race in the conservative backlash, Newt Gingrich and his fellow revolutionaries were able in this sense to speak in a code that racialized welfare dependency without ever resorting to directly racist claims.[70]

Thus despite the professional appeals to geography and statistics, the politics of racial hegemony deployed by the reformers were not hard to see, and in many ways they simply reflected a more cautious rehash of the sort of *Heart of Darkness* perspective on the problem once made famous by Senator Orrin Hatch in his 1983 reference to "the deep, dark pit of welfare dependency."[71] It is because of such associations that we need, as Eileen Boris reminds us, "to understand reform in the 1990's as the triumph of a thirty-year reaction against the gains of the 1960's, after African American women finally shared AFDC and welfare became a right or entitlement."[72] This aspect of the hegemonic politics associated with welfare reform serves as a brutal corrective to the suggestion made by Hollinger at the end of his book that all that was happening in the early 1990s was "slow" progress. Reacting to critics who remain deeply skeptical about the value of civic nationalism, he writes that "[i]n our shared frustration over a rate of progress much slower than any of us want, we too often yield to the game of competitive disillusionment and are quick to accuse one another of being too optimistic" (*Postethnic*, 169). At the risk of being too quick to accuse here, it seems that at least in terms of welfare reform even the language of "progress" came to be misleading. This is not to compete with Hollinger over disillusionment (although one senses he is a chronic loser in this respect), but simply to draw attention to the hegemonic politics "mediating between ethnos and species" within the civic nation. As a legislative capstone to a thirty-year period of reaction and retrenchment, PRWORA marked a form of regress to a normatively white ethnos of civil citizenship.

Long it may have been in the making, welfare reform was nonetheless swift in unleashing racial inequality in practice. Implemented at the height of the long economic boom in the United States that ended in 2001, the immediate impact of the act was to begin drastically shrinking welfare rolls. By 2003 the number of people registered as on welfare had plunged from 12.2 million in 1996 to 5 million, a drop of 59 percent.[73] However, this process did not happen evenly across the diverse communities of America. Instead, after two years the decline in welfare rolls was largest among whites who, even before the reforms, comprised less than 40 percent of the national caseloads.[74] In other words, one direct result of the act was to increase the racial disparities in relation to work and welfare. Even as its proponents used geographical language to talk about race, PRWORA did nothing to tackle the uneven geography of job availability, let alone the equally uneven impacts of racism on hiring decisions and educational opportunity that have remained fundamental causes of unemployment among African-Americans. What the act did do, however, was to exacerbate drastically the geographical inequalities of welfare provision itself by devolving the responsibility for TANF support to the states.

The devolution of welfare policy making to the states had been widely heralded by policy makers as part of the hegemonic articulation of the reform effort with national American traditions of democratic freedom, diversity, and choice. "Revocable consent," it should nevertheless be noted, was not on offer for even states, and in fact PRWORA was a remarkably stringent act in terms of the way it allowed states to experiment *only* with variations in degrees of welfare *restriction*.[75] That said, Gingrich and the other house Republicans, along with Senate majority leader Robert Dole, repeatedly trumpeted the devolution in policy making as part of their civic commitment to states' rights, and the president, an ex-governor who maintained strong federalist commitments from his Arkansas background, argued that the states were closest to the problems of welfare and so were best suited to tailoring appropriate local responses (itself an argument that did conservative hegemonic work rearticulating welfare with local needs as opposed to federal rights).[76] The states, in this discourse, were portrayed as laboratories of democracy and diversity; they were to become sites of civic experimentation that would serve the larger national good. The problems with this hegemonic discourse concern both the dynamics it has set in motion between states and the ways in which states themselves have actually responded to their newfound ability to experiment with types of welfare restriction. In terms of interstate relations, like the push for provincial rights in Canada, states' rights rhetoric is clearly allied with a neoliberal vision of making states compete in a market-mediated race toward governmental cutbacks. As Sanford Schram explains in an excellent analysis of welfare politics, this neoliberal common sense informed the hegemonic idea that allowing states to experiment would successfully punish more generous states by turning them into so-called welfare magnets.[77] In practice, Schram shows, there is little evidence that welfare recipients do actually migrate to less punishing regimes, but among state legislators the discourse that says they do has remained hegemonic and this in turn has set the scene for a real race to the bottom: a bottom in this case of increasingly harsh welfare rollbacks as policy makers have sought to avoid allowing their own states to become seen as potential "welfare magnets."[78] Increasing numbers of restrictions have developed in states across the country, and now that the U.S. Supreme Court has outlawed discriminatory lower benefits to interstate migrants, Schram suggests that the future promises only more cycles of competitive cutbacks.[79]

Not surprisingly perhaps given the historic associations between white supremacy and states' rights discourse in the United States, the freedom states have acquired to experiment with welfare policy under PRWORA has also had systemically racist as well as neoliberal effects.[80] At the state level in the United States, policy making is generally less transparent to the national media and less likely to receive the sustained attention of national civil rights organizations. Amid such democratic deficits the so-called laboratories of democracy have mediated between species and ethnos in such a way as to produce markedly *non*postethnic results. As soon as they received their newfound freedom for policy innovation a number of states, most of them in the South with large and poor African-American populations, began the process of devising the harshest workfare rules allowed: rules with stricter work requirements; rules that set short time limits; rules refusing extra welfare support for women who become pregnant while on welfare; rules restricting access to welfare for recipients who make minor infractions such as missing a meeting with a caseworker; and rules that simply make it so complex and burdensome to apply for welfare that the bureaucracy becomes a barrier itself. Following from this perverse flowering of disciplinary diversity, a comprehensive quantitative study of the state-by-state impacts of the devolution revolution published in 2001 showed that one of the best predictors of a state developing punitive welfare rules was the percentage of African-American residents on its rolls. "We conclude," write the authors,

> that the "devolution revolution" has created openings for new forms of racial inequality that disadvantage African Americans in the U.S. welfare system. Because states with more black recipients have adopted stricter policy regimes, black families are now more likely to participate under the most punitive program conditions. Such disparities in TANF policy not only can produce inequalities in the distribution of resources, they also subject citizens from different social groups to systematically different treatment at the hands of government. Thus a black woman who conceives a child while receiving welfare is now less likely than a white woman to live in a state that offers additional aid to that child. Likewise, a black client who misses a meeting with a caseworker is now disproportionately likely to live in a state where his single infraction results in a termination of benefits for the full family. White clients are more likely to live in states that respond in a more lenient fashion.[81]

All this is obviously a long way from the transethnic solidarity of the American civic nation recommended by Hollinger.

In its effects, then, as well as in its promulgation as law, welfare reform has thus far proved to be the very obverse of postethnic. Hollinger would probably not quarrel with this claim, but it bears emphasizing that some of the aspects of American public life that he holds dear—including most notably the concept of personal choice—were hegemonically rearticulated by the Gingrich Republicans as they pushed through their reforms. With his own talk of choice, voluntary affiliation, and personal preference, Hollinger therefore not only tends toward a liberal neglect of the power relations in which and under which choices are made; he also shares in some of the same contractual common sense out of which welfare reform and the *Contract with America* were themselves crafted. This contractual common sense involves a legalistic individualism that abstracts away from the actual realities of peoples' lives and substitutes an interpretation of social relations based upon an entrepreneurial or at least juridical model of calculating and rule-bound rational choice. The hegemonic reinscriptions of choice and personal responsibility wrought by this discourse are best explained by Schram in his nuanced deconstruction of "Contracting America." "The Contract with America," he argues, "reinscribed the idea of social contract even as it rewrote it. In doing so, it reprivileged what might be called 'contractual persons'—those people who are in the right frame of mind, habit, and behavior to fulfil positions of responsibility in a contractual order."[82] If the parallels between this contractualism and Hollinger's discourse of "freedom of revocable consent" are not entirely clear, it bears noting that at one point in his book Hollinger makes the legalistic framing more explicit when he describes the American public working across lines of respected difference "the way juries work toward a common verdict without pretending to collapse the differences they bring to the task" (*Postethnic*, 156). Hollinger's point in using this jury metaphor is to provide an American example of how commonality can work in the face of difference. He thereby wants to critique certain feminist and postcolonial scholars who, he says, hold a "pathological fear of the common."[83] But what welfare reform showed in its design and practice was the hegemonic rearticulation of the civic nation's common interest by those with a pathological fear of others seen (for sexist and racist reasons) as incapable of joining the contractual order. According to Schram's study it "reinforced the idea that welfare recipients failed to meet the basic threshold requirement of personal responsibility expected of full citizens of the contractual order."[84] It is these sorts of exclusions stemming from a hegemonic rearticulation of citizenship in terms of contractual choice that Hollinger's own choice-preoccupied account of the civic nation misses.

When they later came to boast about their reforms, the advocates of PRWORA claimed that choice had in fact been increased for the poor and that their removal from the welfare rolls was indicative of their rising prosperity. Here, for example, are Gingrich's reflections in 1998:

> In 1994 we Republicans said we could balance the budget, cut taxes, reform welfare, help the poor move from welfare to work and thus from poverty to prosperity. . . . We can now say we kept that faith.[85]

The Republicans may well have kept their faith in individual choice maximization and entrepreneurial contractualism, but the claim that the poor had been moved from poverty into prosperity by PRWORA was and remains a complete falsehood. Welfare reform did reduce welfare rolls (although it should also be remembered that the numbers of unemployed were also reduced in the late 1990s by a booming economy and a booming incarceration rate, the latter being one of the few forms of state intervention that the *Contract with America* sought to roll out rather than roll back).[86] Notwithstanding the declining numbers of claimants, however, welfare reform has not reduced poverty, and in many ways it has exacerbated the misery of poor people by forcing them into low-skilled, dead-end jobs while reducing their ability to protect their children from similarly bleak futures.[87] Moreover, as Robert Reich, Clinton's first-term Labor secretary, explained in his memoirs, the fact that the workfare policy went into force at the same time that the U.S. Federal Reserve remained committed to a monetarist policy of keeping unemployment above 5 percent was hypocritical as well as brutally punitive.[88] Prosperity for the poor was and is never going to be an option under these circumstances.

Instead of prosperity came a newly disciplinary labor-market regime. As the economic geographer Jamie Peck argues in his comprehensive and rigorous critique, the "work opportunity" referred to in the act turned out thus to be mainly about putting the poor to work at a time of tight labor-market rigidities.

> Stripped down to its labor regulatory essence, workfare is not about creating jobs for people that don't have them; it is about creating workers for jobs that nobody wants. In a Foucauldian sense, it is seeking to make "docile bodies" for the new economy: flexible, self-reliant, and self-disciplining.[89]

In this sense welfare reform can be seen to have made over the contractualism of citizenship in the image of the capitalist labor-market contract: a not altogether surprising end point given that this is where the model for contractual common sense originally came from. Personal choice and responsibility are remade in this way too, of course, and the result, as Schram makes painfully clear, is devastating to the sorts of real choices that might once have nurtured more meaningful civic belonging.

> While personal responsibility may once have referred to someone who "kept a promise" (like a mother who promised her children she would take care of them), now it has been reduced to indicating

someone who can "hold a job" (like a mother forced to work in a low-wage dead-end job even though her children were being neglected).[90]

Hollinger would perhaps argue that this fundamental shift in the coding of personal responsibility and the resulting diminution of real civic choice simply underlines the importance of his original argument: namely, that liberals and leftists should be distracted neither by ethno-racial absolutism nor by newly fashionable postnational concerns and should rather come together to take back the civic nation from the middle American Right. But it must be noted in this respect that the hegemonic shift at work in welfare reform was by no means a uniquely American phenomenon.

Peck's analysis of workfare as what he calls a "fast-policy" regime shows that a fully adequate critique has to come to terms with how it is about both local hegemonic narratives and their interarticulation with a much more global pattern of neoliberal policy making, policy dissemination, and policy entrenchment. Workfare works hegemonically, he concludes, because

> as an ideological movement and as a regime of concrete reform measures, policy generics, and restructuring strategies [it] is increasingly assuming the character of a transnational regulatory project, particularly among neoliberal countries, where not only conservatives but most social and social democratic parties now embrace workfarism in some form or another. Workfare has become the cornerstone of the neoliberal regulatory "fix" advocated in international forums, such as G7 and the World Bank, where the United States is also—not entirely coincidentally—a dominating presence.[91]

As structurally consonant with global neoliberal entrenchment, welfare reform and indeed the whole package of other reforms that took shape in the wake of the *Contract with America* need to be addressed therefore in transnational as well as national terms. To be sure, America is in many moments the birthplace of some of the most radical neoliberal nostrums, but the ways in which these are turned into policy-making common sense and practice has, as Peck underlines, to be understood in terms of a whole series of transnational relays ranging from conservative think-tank cross-pollination to the basic ties of global political-economy itself. Thus, restricting counterhegemonic efforts to merely national efforts at rearticulation, as Hollinger's 1995 account advocated, would in this instance needlessly limit the critical project and possibly miss many of the transnational imperatives that would endure irrespective of any (highly unlikely) national transformations.

This argument about the needlessly restrictive ramifications of a focus on the nation as an arena for counterhegemonic struggle is further buttressed when we consider how the actual impact of American welfare reform has fallen disproportionately on immigrants. It should be noted in this respect that almost half the anticipated budgetary savings to "ordinary Americans" boasted about by the likes of Newt Gingrich as an achievement of welfare reform came through cuts to immigrant welfare claimants. Audrey Singer notes that of the $54.1 billion that was projected to be saved over the first six years, 44 percent or $23.8 billion came from cutting benefits to legal permanent residents.[92] Subsequent to the passage of PRWORA some of the cuts (specifically to Medicaid, food stamps, and Supplemental Security Income) have been reversed for migrants who were already green card holders in 1996. But all new "post-enactment" migrants remain ineligible for TANF and most other remaining assistance programs. Given that oftentimes such legal immigrants face particular challenges finding work because of language issues or prejudicial hiring practices, these restrictions seem especially perverse. However, such anti-immigrant outcomes should not be all that surprising given the clear insistence in the language of PRWORA on a profoundly conservative, albeit invented model of migrancy. Title IV "Restricting Welfare and Public Benefits for Aliens," for example, begins by claiming that "[s]elf sufficiency has been a basic principle of United States immigration law since the country's earliest immigration statutes" (PRWORA, 2260). Later on the section proceeds to insist that "aliens within the Nation's borders should not depend on public resources to meet their needs, but rather rely on their own capabilities and the resources of their families, their sponsors, and private organizations" (2260). Irrespective of the unrealistic assumptions underpinning these xenophobic statements, their legal impacts have been real. Thus, combined with the impact of the 1996 Illegal Immigrant Reform and Immigrant Responsibility Act that was itself spawned from the *Contract*, PRWORA successfully served to remake the civic nation by redrawing the boundary of the national "we." As Jaqueline Hagan and Nestor Rodriguez put it in their study of the Texas experience, "these laws restrict public services for immigrants, place new limitation on immigrant sponsors, and significantly expand immigration enforcement responsibilities of public and private service providers. In short, the two laws redefine the social membership of immigrants."[93] Hagan and Rodriguez's research further illustrates in painful and personal detail how such processes of redefinition have worked in practice to prevent even U.S.-born citizen children of noncitizen parents from being given Medicaid benefits to which they are legally entitled. This is just one illustrative example of where the processes of hegemonic rearticulation of civic nationalism went in the 1990s, but it raises an obvious question nonetheless about whether the "value of civic nation-states in protecting rights and providing basic welfare [really] is undervalued by proponents of postnationality."

The effects of the 1990s reforms show that serious and consequential forms of boundary drawing were going on. Hollinger's final sentences to the epilogue of *Postethnic America* seem all the more relevant in this regard. "Boundaries are necessary," he says. "A postethnic perspective understands this. Which boundaries, and where? We are all left with the responsibility for deciding where to try to draw what circles with whom, and around what" (*Postethnic,* 172). The promoters of the hegemonic project that spiraled out of the *Contract with America* clearly took such responsibility seriously, rearticulating the very notion of responsibility along the way with their contractual common sense about which kinds of people can make decisions and which others can be excluded from the national circle. Hollinger's own concerns about this right-wing hegemonic project therefore seem all the more valid in retrospect, and his argument that there are resources within the traditions of American nationalism that can be used to organize counterhegemonically remains important. But his skepticism about postnationalism, his tendency to consider racism more as a problem of personal attitudes, and his general liberal proclivity toward ignoring more systemic forms of power relations mean that his appeal to American civic nationalism comes off as ineffectual at best. It risks ignoring the ways in which the social relations and forms of democracy enabling the American nation to mediate between ethnos and species can be hegemonically reworked to narrow the circle of ethnic belonging even as the agents of hegemonic rearticulation employ the universalistic rhetoric of personal choice, responsibility, and opportunity to do so. At the same time, I hope it is also clear by this stage that Hollinger's nationalism further ignores the need for and critical insights made available by more transnational models of critical analysis and struggle. As Singh argues in his own critique of *Postethnic America,* "it fundamentally obscures the real universality of our planetary existence, thus inhibiting our imagination of the world-system as the necessary horizon of social transformation and political emancipation."[94] Having come to this point myself by exploring Hollinger's claims against the experience of hegemonic politics in America in the 1990s—including the transnational neoliberal policy-making circles that have enabled the anti-immigrant national circles to be drawn—I would now like to turn back briefly in conclusion to the question this same transnational problematic raises vis-à-vis Laclau and Mouffe's own original argument.

BEYOND CONCLUSIONS ABOUT THE SPACE OF HEGEMONY

If the basic problem with Laclau and Mouffe's theorization of hegemony was that it remained haunted by a tacit assumption of the nation-state as the spatial container of politics, my explorations of the actual grounds of hegemonic struggles in Canada and the United States have shown how more forthright attempts to ground the flux of democratic diversity in particular nation-states expose some of the dangers of preemptive territorialization. I have tried to show nonetheless how a theoretical approach guided by a sensitivity to processes of hegemonic rearticulation can help make these same dangers clearer. The original inspiration for making this doubled-up journey lay in an attempt to come to terms with the structural and poetic resonance between Laclau and Mouffe's account of democratic space as a "space for a game which is never 'zero-sum'" and other accounts like those of Tully and Hollinger that treat particular national spaces as exceptional embodiments of deep political diversity. The expectation that Tully's and Hollinger's accounts could help make the haunting "ground" of the nation-state in *Hegemony* thematic was therefore balanced by the hope that an examination of the Canadian and U.S. hegemonic politics would help dispel the nationalist conceit that any one nation-state can conclusively contain and sustain within itself all of the openness, unendingness, and inconclusiveness of politics. In short, to adapt some serendipitous words from the political theorist William Connolly, the purpose of these political geographies of Canada and the United States in the 1980s and 1990s was to illustrate how,

[b]y challenging the sufficiency of the territorial, democratic state with a multifarious spatialization of democratic energies, covert complementarities between nostalgic realism and nostalgic idealism might be contested more actively.[95]

Connolly's reference to realism here is chiefly to the political science and international relations theory orthodoxy that nation-states are the only important objects of analysis in a kind of Darwinian pool game model of competitive global politics. Similarly, his reference to idealism is to the more imaginative but no less problematic theories of liberal internationalists that commonly start out from a conception of nation-states as the principal actors in universalistic models of global governance. Clearly, the kinds of realism and idealism that are of issue in Tully's and Hollinger's works are quite different. Tully is certainly not an orthodox realist at all; indeed his whole approach to so-called strange multiplicity represents a sustained engagement with the kind of pluralization of pluralism advocated by Connolly in his book-length argument for an antiessentialist political ethic. That said, Tully's theorization of the intercultural middle ground he saw as embodied in the Canadian journey to the Charlottetown Accord exhibited a realist leaning toward the bracketing of transnational tendencies. Likewise, Hollinger is not an idealist in the international relations sense; in fact he is far less concerned with moving beyond the national than Tully. But he is an idealist in his exceptionalist American nationalism and in his tendency (like the German idealists famously critiqued by Marx and Engels in *The German Ideology*) to treat his homeland space as some specially unique embodiment of the best humans can hope for in politics. So what kinds of covert complementarities exist in the actual grounds I have explored here?

There is first of all the complementarity of spatial metaphorics, the frequent resort to terms like "middle ground," "distinctive locus," and "vital arena" as a way of somehow evoking the special national spatiality underpinning an essentially antiessentialist and diverse democracy. Beyond these symptomatic rhetorical devices, Tully and Hollinger also complement one another's tendencies toward an abstraction from the actual political geographies out of which they write. Most notably their accounts tend to abstract from and thereby minimize the systemic impacts of neoliberal entrenchment dynamics. Neither writer can be said to ignore the political-economic context of democratic struggle altogether, and clearly Hollinger's whole argument about the need to reclaim the civic nation represents an underlying concern with the postnationalism of globalizing corporate elites as well as with ethno-racial balkanization. But yet there is this shared tendency to downplay the ways in which neoliberalism structures the very same grounds that are so easily metaphorized as the middle ground of democratic diversity. Tully thereby does not attend to the ways in which the diversification of diversity that was part of the Canadian constitutional development process was simultaneously driven by a set of neoliberal imperatives toward decentralization and federal government austerity. Hollinger's account of how the one and the many can be held in perpetual tension by the American nation also tends toward the same bracketing of neoliberal hegemony building (including its entrenchment through a straitjacketed form of devolution). Moreover, his argument further compounds this danger with its liberal individualist emphasis on personal choice and opportunity, an emphasis, I suggested, that was shared and effectively rearticulated by the promoters of the Personal Responsibility and Work Opportunity Reconciliation Act.

I have indicated other complementarities and contrasts between Hollinger and Tully already, and here I want to conclude with some final remarks that bring the discussion back to Laclau and Mouffe themselves. In this sense, the covert complementarity that most interests me is the tendency that their abstract argument shares with Tully and Hollinger of territorializing the political. In their own hyperidealist fashion, however, this territorialization is mediated through a still more prodigious efflorescence of spatial metaphors. What the grounded complexities of Canadian and American hegemonic politics bring into clearer focus are the likely analytical costs of such preemptive territorialization. Three concerns in particular stand out. First, there is the danger highlighted in particular by the Canadian examples of assuming as an arena for politics a terrain that a significant number of the players *contest as the arena*. Seen from the perspective of separatist Québecers or many First Nations, the diversification of diversity in Canada may well create a middle ground, but it is not a middle ground they want to be part of, or even if they can tolerate still joining a skewed national democratic debate (as many First Nations try to do), it is a middle ground that often seems all too co-optive and destructive of deep constitutional diversity. Second, there is the danger of ignoring or at least downplaying the ways in which contemporary capitalist restructuring processes are shifting scales of both state-making and societal (including economic) inter-action. Neoliberal regimes of governance are thereby both eclipsing nation-states from above and undermining them from below, and in order to come to terms with these processes of reterritorialization it is vital to make the dominant spaces of politics thematic *and* track the processes through which they are being remade through a range of global, devolutionary, and microdisciplinary imperatives. Laclau and Mouffe fail to achieve the former, while they, like Tully and Hollinger, would also seem to foreclose the latter opportunity. Third, there is the danger that was highlighted best by a consideration of the plight of U.S. immigrants in the wake of welfare reform: the danger of theoretically reduplicating the gesture of right-wing national popu-lism and barring transnational subjects from even being considered as active agents in the politics of national hegemonic struggle. Even if they are somehow addressed despite the tacit theoretical boundary-drawing that militates against their acknowledgment as full parties to the flux of democratic debate, there remains the danger of ignoring the extranational democratic energies and resources such migrants draw on precisely because of their transnational lifeworlds.

All of these dangers of national foreclosure point to the need to retheorize how democracy is worked out at *and across* multiple spa-tial scales: liberty and equality, the one and the many, or even Tully's more plastic concept of the tension between belonging and the need to free oneself from oneself, all of these tensional grounds are worked out in actual geographies that are as often extranational, subnation-al, and nonnational as they are truly national in scope. Yet the chal-lenge of coming to terms with such plural and multiscalar political geographies need not be insurmountable for a theory of hegemony. As I indicated in my review of their original argument, Laclau and Mouffe do at one moment indicate how a theory of hegemonic ar-ticulation can actually be put to work to examine how the bounding of political space works through processes of hegemonic territoriali-zation. My point was simply that they did not pursue that theoretical possibility in *Hegemony* and therefore wrote an all too conclusive, albeit tacit, geography of the nation-state into their account of the inconclusive interplay of equality and liberty. The supplementary political geographies of hegemonic struggle I have sketched in this chapter point to the need to go beyond such preemptive closure. They represent in this sense a call for an inconclusive geography of hegemony, but one nonetheless that can carefully take account of how the rearticulations of hegemonic struggle actively produce new territories of the political, whether they be transnational, national, provincial, corporal, or anything in between. It bears underlining that some of these hegemonic territorializations are going to remain normatively national even amid the increasing globalizing pressures loosening the hyphen in nation-state. In particular that unique locus of concentrated world power heralded by Hollinger—the United States—stands out as a bastion of hegemonic territorialization, and yet the globalizing processes of political-economic interdependency that would seem to buttress this U.S. hegemony at the same time point to a wholly new kind of hyphen-nation-state comprising the complex overlaps of Americanization-Globalization. It is to the hegemonic and global struggles surrounding the associated disjunctures and displacements of this hyphen-nation-state that I turn next in chapter 5.

5

Empire's Geography: War, Globalization, and American Imperialism

We think it is important to note that what used to be conflict or competition among several imperialist powers has in important respects been replaced by the idea of a single power that overdetermines them all, structures them in a unitary way, and treats them under one common notion of right that is decidedly postcolonial and postimperialist. This is really the point of departure for our study of Empire.

— MICHAEL HARDT AND ANTONIO NEGRI, *EMPIRE*

The decentered global system of Empire that Hardt and Negri named with the title of their acclaimed book is not now the empire that scholars, pundits, and commentators of all kinds are discussing several years later. Notwithstanding the stunning academic success of *Empire* as one of the most widely read political theories of globalization, notwithstanding its ongoing salience as a critique of neoliberal governmentality, and notwithstanding its popularity among critics of global capitalism in venues such as the World Social Forum, it and its postnational arguments about the decentered power networks of an emergent "postcolonial" and "postimperialist" capitalist system have since been eclipsed by the recentered and reterritorializing forces of American hegemony.[1] There is clearly an "idea of a single power that overdetermines them all" at work in this respect, but it is an idea better evoked by writers such as Robert Kagan and William Kristol: two neoconservatives close to the Bush administration. "Today's international system," they say,

239

is built not around a balance of power but around American hegemony. The international financial institutions were fashioned by Americans and serve American interests. The international security structures are chiefly a collection of American-led alliances. What Americans like to call international "norms" are really reflections of American and West European principles. Since today's relatively benevolent international circumstances are the product of our hegemonic influence, any lessening of that influence will allow others to play a larger part in shaping the world to suit their needs. . . . American hegemony, then, must be actively maintained, just as it was actively obtained.[2]

As two ideological shock troops of American hegemony, then, Kagan and Kristol exemplify the very imperial arrogance that Hardt and Negri saw as transcended by the transnational entrenchment of neoliberal "biopolitics." Their neoconservative idea of a single *American* power that overdetermines all others represents a complete inverse of Hardt and Negri's view that "Empire is not American and the United States is not its center" (*Empire,* 384). Indeed, in some of the very networks of global governmentality that Hardt and Negri construed as the postnational "administrative machine"—global finance, multilateral alliances, and the norms of international politics—Kagan and Kristol saw the foundations of their Project for a New American Century. Their goal in pushing this boldly national "Project" in 2000 was not to dismantle "today's international system" but rather to tilt U.S. foreign policy away from Clinton's supposed multilateralism in order to maintain American dominance through more explicitly imperial policy measures. This geopolitical activism has since taken shape in the Bush administration's unilateral imperial practice, practice that, perhaps more successfully than even Kagan and Kristol would have thought possible, has made American global intervention synonymous with "empire." In the wake of two offensive wars, in the context of the ongoing occupation of Iraq, Afghanistan, and over a hundred military bases encircling the globe, and while also still maintaining all kinds of special privileges and authority in the institutions and agreements of global commerce and finance, it is now clearly this American empire that is the focus of debate and discontent around the world.

To be sure, the American influence over and in neoliberal globalization was often acknowledged before in terms such as "Coca-Colonization," "McDonaldization," and the "Washington Consensus." But with the Bush presidency, as the cultural colonization turned into unabashed occupation, as "ready to eat" military meals took over as the dominant American fast food across the Middle East, and as international consensus faltered, the dominative aspects of Washington's hegemony over global relations became much harder to ignore. In the American media itself talk of empire and imperialism was no longer eschewed. Against the grain of all the postcolonial national narratives about America's anti-imperial foundations, empire instead was suddenly all the rage. From lame liberal apologias for the wars as civilizing imperial missions, to crass conservative commentary about how to do empire "less reluctantly" like the British, to political satire about the imperial culture of the newly unilateral Washington consensus, the "modernizing" euphemisms, world-making slogans, and ambient colonial arrogance of empire became normal and commonplace.[3] "[W]hat word but 'empire' describes the awesome thing that America is becoming?" asked Michael Ignatieff, a Canadian liberal turned Harvard-based imperial apologist. Advocating the so-called rescue of Iraq, and claiming *contra* all the violent history of U.S. intervention in Latin America, South East Asia, and the Middle East that American imperialism brings "stability," Ignatieff urged war.[4] "Imperial powers," he lectured his *New York Times* audience, "do not have the luxury of timidity." Max Boot, a less contorted advocate of imperialism, made exactly the same point in plain prose. "We are going to be called an empire whatever we do," he argued. "We might as well be a successful empire."[5] And taking on the role of explaining exactly how to be successful, the British historian Niall Ferguson also won fame (and another place at Harvard) advising Americans about how the British Empire supposedly rescued the world from premodernity.[6]

Perhaps more significant than all the announcements of empire was the unconcealed imperial attitude brought to Washington by the Bush administration itself. Maureen Dowd, a columnist for the *New York Times,* chronicled this imperial attitude more deftly than most. "Why," she asked, during the buildup to the Iraq war,

> should former C.E.O.'s Cheney and Rummy settle for mere Jack Welch–style perks when they can have the perks of empire? They can restore civilization to the cradle of civilization. Lemon fizzes, cribbage and cricket by the Tower of Babel. A 36-hole golf course on the banks of the Tigris and Euphrates. Arab-Disney in the hanging

gardens of Babylon. Oil on tap at the Baghdad Hilton. Huge contracts for buddies in the defense and oil industries. Halliburton's Brown and Root construction company building a six-lane highway from Baghdad to Tel Aviv. How long can it be before the Empire strikes back?[7]

Dowd's question was a suggestive one, and not just because of its basic concern about imperial blowback. Her acknowledgment of the corporate culture of the Bush team combined with her allusions to the *Star Wars* mindset that some of them brought from their years working with Ronald Reagan also effectively broached a larger question about the political-economic ties between war mongering and corporate globalization. Were Cheney, Rumsfeld, et al. just managerial activists attempting to intervene like Luke Skywalker to protect America and the global system, or did they instead represent empire run amok, managers of the force who, having turned to the dark side, threatened the long-term reproduction of global capitalism? As the United States moved into the occupation phase of the Iraq war in the summer of 2003, even the *Economist* magazine could not seem to make up its usually dogmatic mind. It editorialized Ignatieff-style that American empire should be done with serious investment and not as "empire lite."[8] But in the very same issue, it presented a special report entitled "America and Empire" that argued that U.S. imperial practice in Iraq and Afghanistan would likely end up being nasty and brutish and "so it had better also be short." The play on Hobbes here effectively covered up an argumentative contradiction. "American empire passes the duck test," the report had noted; "it not only looks like a duck, it also walks like a duck and quacks like a duck"[9] (the three "ducks" here consisting of America's military capabilities, its economic influence, and its readiness "to sally forth and act"). But the report concluded contrarily by arguing that in the end a formal empire was unaffordable for America, that the financial capability was not there, and that the United States would therefore ultimately have to go back to promoting its aims in a more multilateral fashion.

In contrast to the rhetorical contradictions of neoliberal commentary, leftist critics addressed the problem of American empire in a way that, like Lenin in his early twentieth-century essay on interimperial rivalries, attempted to locate the contradictions in the tensions of imperialism itself.[10] These critiques therefore tended to underline the continuities with previous forms of American global hegemony, describing the contemporary moment more as a transition, in Perry Anderson's savvy Gramscian terms, from a hegemony of consensus to a hegemony of force.[11] If imperialism was invoked in such arguments, it was not used to register the newness of American empire so much as its new nakedness and, in some of the more cautionary accounts, its new vulnerabilities too. Arundhati Roy, for example, while making the case that the Bush aggressions were imperial in style, scope, and organization, simultaneously underlined that they only made manifest an empire that had traditionally been more carefully concealed. "Despite the pall of gloom that hangs over us today," she argued,

> I'd like to file a cautious plea for hope: in times of war, one wants one's weakest enemy as the helm of his forces. And President George W. Bush is certainly that. Any other even averagely intelligent US president would have probably done the very same things, but would have managed to smoke-up the glass and confuse the opposition. Perhaps even carry the UN with him. Bush's tactless imprudence and his brazen belief that he can run the world with his riot squad, has done the opposite. He has achieved what writers, activists and scholars have striven to achieve for decades. He has exposed the ducts. He has placed on full public view the working parts, the nuts and bolts of the American empire.[12]

Interpreting this moment of ideological demystification as a sign of weakness rather than strength, Roy also indirectly repeated a different caution made by others: namely, that critics needed to be careful about reproducing narcissistic narratives of national strength in their indictments of American imperialism. Such narratives were potent, suggested Thomas de Zengotita, because they functioned to construct a national "romance of empire." "Will we look back on these years," he asked in the mocking register of a love story,

> and say I remember when it all began? American Empire? Not the more covert beginnings during the reign of Bill the Benign, back when imperial force could masquerade as a natural process, an evolutionary stage called "globalization"—something that was just happening, you know, nobody actually responsible, myriad interests served and serving. No, I'm talking about Empire properly so called, intoxicated with images of its own might—unabashed, raw. I'm talking about the reign of Bush the Bold. Will we look back and say, That was when it all began?[13]

These ironic questions usefully disrupt the treatment of American empire as some sort of fetishized national love (or hate) object. Like Anderson's analysis and Roy's criticisms, they also pose the problem of historical continuities, but in doing so, they also raise all kinds of difficult theoretical questions about what exactly changed from the period when American elites did not so openly sport the badge of an imperial nationalism on their business suits. Was all the talk about "globalization" in the era of "Bill the Benign" merely a masquerade? How have arguments about globalization been tied to Bush's wars? How do the American aggressions actually relate to intensifying global interdependency and the entrenchment of neoliberal governmentality? And how, then, can we make sense of both the overlaps and disconnects between American empire and what Hardt and Negri chose to call, with deceptive simplicity, just Empire?

In attempting to answer these questions in what follows I am again, as in the previous chapters, taking a critical geographical approach. In this case I seek to explore the interconnections and contradictions of two imagined geographies that appear to confuse much of the contemporary debate about globalization and imperialism.[14] The first is the imagined geography of a decentered global space that underpins so many discussions of globalization and its deterritorializing imperatives.[15] Hardt and Negri's account is no exception, and their claim that economic globalization has taken us from the territorialized national imperialisms of the nineteenth century to a new regime of borderless global Empire is a claim that fundamentally rests on this deterritorialized imagined geography. "The realization of the world market and the real subsumption of global society under capital," they argue, "smooths over the striae of national boundaries" (*Empire*, 332). Turning this "end of the nation-state" thesis into an argument about subjectivity formation too, they insist that "[with] boundaries and difference suppressed or set aside, the Empire is a kind of smooth space across which subjectivities glide without substantial resistance" (198). It remains nonetheless, they argue, a space of capital: "a smooth space defined by uncoded flows, flexibility, continual modulation, and tendential equalization" (327). Insofar as this imagined geography of smooth space is intimately related to enframings of capitalist space such as "the level playing field" discussed in chapter 3, I argue here that it can be usefully conceptualized as a kind of *geoeconomics*, a globalist geoeconomics that both builds on and buttresses the metanarrative of globalization's integrative inexorability.[16]

By contrast, the second imagined geography I want to address consists of a much rougher-edged national-imperial *geopolitics,* an imagined geography of uneven and occupied space associated with ideas of an assertive and unilateralist American empire. Kagan and Kristol's hardened nationalistic view of American hegemony is a typical example. In debates over empire this geopolitical view is frequently made to clash with the geoeconomic one, and the contrasting imagined geographies often do a great deal of unexamined argumentative work. Imperialism is thus often only imagined in geopolitical terms as a system deliberately established by a metropolitan national power that holds and controls clearly demarcated foreign territories for a long period of time.[17] The uneven and haphazard historical geographies of actual imperial practices, including those of the British and French in the nineteenth century (sometimes administering every inch of imperial life, sometimes just gunboating from the coast) are thereby ignored. More significantly for current debates, the stark discontinuity between geopolitical visions of American empire and the geoeconomics of globalization elides the ways in which American hegemony has since at least the end of World War II comprised a form of *informal imperialism* operating in and through increasingly globalized networks. To describe the transnational hegemony of the United States in such terms is not to argue that American informal imperialism is unending, all-encompassing, and invulnerable to crisis and decline. American influence in the world will surely decline as has that of all other imperial systems of the past.[18] Moreover the speed of the decline will likely only be accelerated by the recent turn to more militaristic and unabashedly forceful attempts at imperial crisis management. But to insist, as I do here, that the dominant and much more continuous character of American influence is that of informal imperialism (and to point, as I do in what follows, to some of the symptomatic parallels between the eras of "Bill the Benign" and "Bush the Bold") is to reject the economistic view that American hegemony simply came to an abrupt end when the institutional arrangements of the post–World War II settlement—including the Bretton Woods dollar-gold peg and the dominance of the United States as the industrial workshop of the world—foundered in the early 1970s.[19] Rejecting such economism, I want to suggest, also involves debunking the geographic assumption that geoeconomics has simply eclipsed geopolitics.

The informality of American imperialism has not only allowed for exaggerated academic arguments about hegemonic decline. It has also traditionally enabled an exceptionalist American rhetoric of imperial denial. Notwithstanding the context of the post-9/11 war-mongering, it clearly remained enabling in this way for President Bush himself when he claimed at West Point in 2002 that "America has no empire to extend or utopia to establish."[20] Even despite the occupations of Iraq and Afghanistan, it was also still a dominant argument in 2003: America has not been and can never be an empire, the story went, because it does not occupy and control foreign territory in the direct and sustained long-distance manner of formal late nineteenth-century empires.[21] "America has no territorial ambitions," Bush reaffirmed at the White House. "We don't seek an empire."[22] In attempting to demystify such denials here I find Hardt and Negri's thesis a useful counterpoint. My aim is not to compare and contrast the arguments over American empire and *Empire* only in the abstract, however, but rather, as in the previous chapters, to ground them (and thereby explore them more critically) in the geographies of worldly political struggle. In this case, the specific political ground in question is that of the recent American war in Iraq: a war that has been widely interpreted as aggressive American empire-building, but a war too that has thematized and thereby also compromised the much more enduring and informal form of market-mediated American hegemony. By focusing in particular on two phases of the war—the legitimation work that led up to the military attacks, and then their prosecution and aftermath—the goal is to go beyond the imperial denial of geoeconomics without reconsolidating a simple geopolitical vision of American national empire-building. This means, I will seek to argue, paying particular attention to the *complicity* of geopolitical assertion and geoeconomic assumption in elite American and business-class opinion.

The violent asymmetry of the military action, the ways in which it played out the unilateral fantasies of national American dominance dreamed up by the likes of Kagan and Kristol, and the disturbance it thereby brought to all manner of multilateral conventions and agreements would seem at first sight to have vindicated geopolitical visions of American empire. To liberal critics and neoconservative celebrants alike, this was the moment of American empire unleashed. Here was the global hegemon casting aside the fuss of multilateral concord, throwing economic concerns about balanced budgets and the bond markets to the winds, and boldly sallying forth with unabashed military force. By contrast, the imagined geographies of geoeconomics—of smooth global space, of carefully coordinated planetary "police" actions, of deterritorialized networks of neoliberal governmentality, of in short, a decentered global Empire—seemed rendered as redundant as the United Nations itself was in the buildup to the bombing. But while the unilateralism of the war certainly upset many multilateral circuits of cosmopolitan capitalist convention and while the resulting disruption of geoeconomic visions was and remains clear, the offensive and occupation seem unlikely to prove geopolitical visions of American imperial dominance of lasting relevance. An understanding of the war as American empire unleashed may certainly have helped certain Bush administration officials to make their decisions, but analytically it misses the ways in which so many aspects of the war were predicated and dependent upon the assumptions, practices, technologies, and economic imperatives of neoliberal globalization, including, not least of all, the geoeconomic vision of a global level playing field. With its globally networked coordination (and the globally networked opposition that resisted it), its ideological justification in the corporate media, its private military contractors in the field, its commodified patriotism at home, its CEO-style promotion, its ties to a vision of free trade across the Middle East, its anticipation in global derivative markets, and its mediated relationship with oil economics, U.S. recession, and global overcapacity, the war is thus also analyzable as a symptom of what Hardt and Negri refer to in their book as "the passage to Empire." That, at least, is a key contention in the later part of this chapter.

It may seem strange to use the ideas of *Empire* to investigate the planning and prosecution of the Iraq war when Hardt and Negri themselves uncritically repeat so many of the geoeconomic assumptions that, as I seek to show, elide American dominance. But in putting their text to work in relation to a war that has made American hegemony synonymous with empire, it is possible to highlight the political-economic mediation of the militarism while also reading Hardt and Negri's own narrative against the grain. In other words, the theoretical aim here is to graph and thereby problematize *Empire*'s geoeconomic "geo" by using it to unpack the simple geopolitical vision of the war as American empire unleashed.[23] What ultimately makes this parallel debunking of geoeconomics and geopolitics possible is the one-sided approach that each vision creates of the peculiar hyphen-nation-state of American global hegemony. Neither vision can conceive of this hegemony as at once productive of, embedded in, and vulnerable to global interdependencies; and thus neither can adequately come to terms with the informal and deeply contradictory imperialism of U.S. hegemony *in* globalization. This mediated informal imperialism has effectively deterritorialized and reterritorialized the hyphen in the American nation-state, stretching American state authority in informal ways across national boundaries to create a hybrid and transnational hyphen-nation-state of market- as well as military-mediated dominance. It is the problems involved in describing this transnationally mediated informal imperialism in terms of empire that comprise the basic questions that drive the whole of this chapter. Rather than attempt to resolve them at the start, though, the goal is to use the geographical challenges they present as material tools with which to unpack the complicity of the simplified geopolitical and geoeconomic visions.

Set against the hyphen-nation-state of transnationally mediated American hegemony, the geopolitical visionaries produce a still territorialized form of nation-talk. They tend to anthropomorphize or at least overinvest in and overexaggerate the nation's "power," and thereby create a narrative of enduring, exceptional, and sometimes even absolute American national dominance on the global stage. Leftist critics sometimes replicate this geopolitical master narrative in their arguments against American foreign policy. But it is the agents of this foreign policy themselves, including most especially neoconservatives such as Kagan and Kristol, who are foundationally nationalistic as they return relentlessly to the fetish of "National Security." The muscular "realism" they propound is, I want to suggest, really better understood as a form of affected idealism, indeed an affect-loaded idealism of the nation as a coherent and anthropomorphic geopolitical agent.

In contrast to the neoconservatives, the predominant register of *Empire*'s argument is state-talk. One of Hardt and Negri's major accomplishments in their book is to outline the entrenchment of neoliberal capitalist practices and policies as a type of *transnational state-making*. Indeed, it is, I think, their sensitivity to the ways in which "state functions have effectively been displaced" from the national level and "integrated into the system of transnational command" that accounts for the book's appeal to so many scholars as an innovative political theory of globalization.[24] But in highlighting these emerging forms of transnational governmentality, and in describing their combined state effects in the terms of Empire, Hardt and Negri diminish two still significantly *national* forms of state power. First, they deny flat out the imperial hegemony of the United States. *"The United States does not,"* they emphasize in italics, *"form the center of an imperialist project"* (xiv).[25] Second, they fail to address the ways in which the extension and entrenchment of neoliberal practices has systematically depended not just on U.S. force, but also on the willing acceptance of free-market reforms by the national ruling classes of states outside of the United States. Ironically, however, Hardt and Negri compensate for this double denial of national-state power by arguing that specifically American national traditions of government provide the basic model for the new global regime of network-mediated governmentality. In a formulation that is emphasized even on the book's back cover, they argue thus that "today's Empire draws on elements of U.S. constitutionalism, with its traditions of hybrid identities and expanding frontiers." In other words, they inscribe American privilege right into the heart of their account of a postimperialist Empire even as their overarching "end of the nation-state" metanarrative makes it impossible to track the hyphen-nation-state of American hegemony. Moreover, they do so in a way that ultimately argues that this U.S.-based constitutional model will underwrite the long-term peace of Empire. These complicating claims (which, as we shall see, uncannily parallel the neoconservatives' nostrums about a new *Pax Americana*) seem especially absurd in light of the Iraq war and the spiral of hideous violence it has set in motion. But they also help highlight how geoeconomic visions of smooth global space encode assumptions about American influence even as they elide it. This means that before unpacking the geopolitical and geoeconomic visions of the war it is worth exploring the ways in which Hardt and Negri's own arguments elide American dominance while nevertheless encrypting America as a dominant model into their account. The next section takes up this challenge by way of simultaneously exploring what exactly the geoeconomic vision of deterritorialized global space entails and how it relates to American business-class *views* of globalization.

AMERICAN VISION IN *EMPIRE*

The underlying argument of *Empire* is a relatively simple retelling of the modern European story of modernity. Following the classic Marxist critique that capitalism digs its own grave, the core claim of the book is that the development of an ever more globalized capitalist system (including the late twentieth-century increase in global migration by workers) has created a "single supranational figure of power" (*Empire*, 9). Calling this power Empire, and depicting it in Foucauldian terms as a "biopolitical" administrative machine, Hardt and Negri argue that it carries within itself the immanent possibility of a global revolution by its subject population, the so-called multitude. This global multitude is supposed to be a heterogeneous category that takes us beyond the economism and singularity of having the global working class serve as the agent of history (as in *The Communist Manifesto*). It therefore supposedly encompasses rebellious subjects as diverse as women workers in the service sector, migrants, the International Workers of the World, the Chiapas rebels, and participants in the Palestinian Intafada (53–54). But the multitude is more commonly invoked by Hardt and Negri in an abstract, almost mystical way, and as such remains a singular category in what is ultimately a teleological narrative where its assigned role, following the supposedly protocommunist example of Saint Francis of Assisi, is to "push through Empire and come out the other side" (218).[26]

The notion of the multitude's push to "the other side" is not only symptomatic of the mystifying religious aura that overshadows *Empire,* it is also a strangely contradictory formulation of global revolution when one considers the totalizing spatial *vision* of the book. Empire, we are elsewhere repeatedly told, has no inside or outside, and no boundaries (*Empire,* xiv). It purportedly scrambles the regionalization of the First, Second, and Third worlds (xiii), it keeps centers and margins always on the move (39), and "its space is always open" (167). "In this smooth space of Empire, there is no *place* of power—it is both everywhere and nowhere. Empire is an *ou-topia*, or really a *non-place*" (190). From a critical geographical perspective, it is hard to see how this deterritorialization metanarrative can be reconciled with the appeal to a multitude that will push through to "the other side." It is true that *Empire* is attuned to David Harvey's argument that capitalist processes produce new spatial relations by constantly working to minimize the frictions of distance, but as Stuart Corbridge has underlined, the book's emphasis on the spatial equalization imperatives of time-space compression "neglects Harvey's more important point about the limits to capital that are imposed by the necessity of production and reproduction at fixed sites."[27] For Hardt and Negri, who seem more inspired by Deleuze and Guattari's totalizing nomadism in this respect, there are not even any temporarily fixed insides and outsides. Instead, in their all-encompassing "smooth world" vision even the outside is already somehow inside Empire. "Empire posits a regime that effectively encompasses the spatial totality," they assert, and because of this, and because it thereby takes us beyond older forms of imperialism with their rivalries over territory, it ultimately promises to bring peace (xv). This peace will be lasting, Hardt and Negri argue, when the creative forces of the multitude subvert Empire, creating a "real alternative" from the inside out. But yet this will only "take place on the imperial terrain itself" and is made possible by the ways in which Empire, while "continually bathed in blood," remains as a concept "always dedicated to peace—a perpetual and universal peace outside of history" (xv).

This compressed geographical summary of the argument does not do justice to Hardt and Negri's critical arguments about transnational governmentality and the disembedded force of market and informational networks (to which we will return). However, it does begin to explain how, in the year 2000 on the eve of George Bush's ascent to the presidency, they could be so sanguine about globalization bringing postimperial peace. In this respect *Empire*'s announcement of a new kind of postnational neoimperial order replays quite strikingly Karl Kautsky's similar argument about the emergence of a new "ultra-imperialism" in 1914. Kautsky's error was to argue on the eve of the most horrific nationalist war in history that a new transnational imperial system would somehow bring together all the world's imperialist powers in a singular and peaceful global concert of power, "a holy alliance of the imperialists."[28] As was pointed out by Lenin in his famously polemical critique, Kautsky's idealism may have allowed him to coin a clever new catchphrase in "ultra-imperialism," but it also blinded him to the deep contradictions between different factions of capital in different imperial spheres. One does not need to adopt Lenin's theory of financialization, nor his overly politicized approach to Kautsky (who, after all, was only arguing that socialists should prepare to struggle against the ultraimperialist concert of power as the new "enemy"), to learn from this critique.[29] *Empire*, it seems, also obscures the contradictions of the contemporary imperial order. But the problem today is not a disregard for the ways in which the convolutions of finance capital and global trade and production relations are intensifying interimperial rivalries. Instead, today's contradictions relate to how such tensions are mediated on a global scale by the unrivalled hegemony of the United States. As Leo Panitch and Sam Gindin argue in their sympathetic but rigorous Marxist review, it is the practical ways in which this hegemony works *through* globalization that are elided in *Empire*. "The distinction Hardt and Negri want to draw between today's new empire (and its 'imperial interest') and the old imperialism ('imperialist interest') is indeed very important," they say.

> But it can only be captured by an approach to contemporary capitalism which goes much further than Hardt and Negri are able to do in revealing those processes of economic, political and military globalization through which the American state specifically, and not the disembodied concept of "empire," . . . "casts its widely inclusive net to try to envelop all power relations within its world order."[30]

Rather than address the contradictory ways in which the American state has been implicated in varying forms of transnational hegemony, Hardt and Negri prefer to posit a simple and absolute historic break between U.S. "imperialist adventurism" and Empire. This break they date back with dubious precision to the Tet offensive of 1968 and the political defeat of the Johnson administration's policy in Vietnam (179). As Tarak Barkawi and Mark Laffey note in another useful critique of the resulting elisions, "it is hard to see how 1968 marks the 'irreversible' defeat of US imperialism. Not only is the inadequate nature of Hardt and Negri's historical analysis much in evidence here, it also becomes very difficult to locate the break at which US imperialism transforms into Empire." Barkawi and Laffey go on to argue that Hardt and Negri thereby miss the many ways in which the United States has continued to intervene globally since 1968, developing all kinds of complex patron-client relations as well as making diverse military interventions and setting up regional bases across the planet. "In our view," they sum up, "globalisation and many of the phenomena Hardt and Negri describe are better understood by reference to an international state dominated by the US."[31]

Even if they obscure and deny American dominance, Hardt and Negri do still acknowledge the "privileged position" of the United States within Empire. The problem is that, in line with the resolutely antiempirical approach of the whole text, they only address this privilege as an abstract effect of the U.S. Constitution and what they see, following Thomas Jefferson no less, as its innate appropriateness "for extensive empire and self-government" (160). The United States, they concede,

> does indeed occupy a privileged position in Empire, but this privilege derives not from its similarities to the old European imperialist powers, but from its differences. These differences can be recognized most clearly by focusing on the properly imperial (not imperialist) foundations of the United States constitution . . . [and the belief of the founders that] they were creating on the other side of the Atlantic a new Empire with open, expanding frontiers, where power would be effectively distributed in networks. This imperial idea has survived and matured throughout the history of the United States constitution and has emerged now on a global scale in its fully realized form. (xiv)[32]

It is out of this unfortunately "idea"-driven, neo-Hegelian argument that Hardt and Negri come to simultaneously deny ongoing American imperialism while encrypting American influence in the center of their account.[33] To do this all the complexity of American constitutional history has to be crammed into a four-stage narrative about the evolution of America's "constituent spirit": a process marked first by the development of the frontier, second by the closing of the frontier and the expansion of militarism overseas, third by the development of the cold war state and the struggle for civil rights, and fourth by the end of the cold war and the emergence of Empire as "a global project of network power" (179–80). For a moment they describe this fourth phase as "a new type of hegemonic initiative" (179), but the possibility that this may be an imperial initiative of the U.S. state is completely superceded by the postimperial zeitgeist metanarrative that we "are experiencing a first phase of the transformation of the global frontier into an open space of imperial sovereignty" (182). Thus, while the "idea of Empire" is said to be "born through the global expansion of the internal U.S. constitutional project" (182), the connection of that project to ongoing forms of specifically American state-making is ultimately severed. "It might appear as if the United States were the new Rome," they say, "or a cluster of new Romes: Washington (the bomb), New York (money), and Los Angeles (ether)." But having thereby made a list of useful starting points for any serious investigation of the scope and varied modalities of informal American imperialism, they proceed again to denial. "Any such territorial conception of imperial space, however, is continually destabilized by the fundamental flexibility, mobility, and deterritorialization at the core of the imperial apparatus" (347). This is an example of how the background binary opposition of geoeconomics to geopolitics becomes complicit in *Empire* with imperial denial.

While Hardt and Negri's own geoeconomic assumptions lead them to ignore the asymmetries and uneven development associated with American imperialism, and while their resulting vision of "smooth space" appears thus as a striking example of what I am calling globalist geoeconomics, their arguments about "biopolitical production" go some way to explaining the force of geoeconomics in actually shaping political and economic life. By biopolitical production they mean at base the production and reproduction of life under the conditions of market-mediated globalization. The category implies more than just this, though, because borrowed from Michel Foucault it comes with both a built-in theory of power and a historical narrative of change. The theory is underpinned by Foucault's emphasis on studying how power circulates, producing social subjects and objects that only retroactively appear as the powerful and powerless. The narrative of change that Hardt and Negri find, following Deleuze, in Foucault involves an account of another abrupt temporal break: in this case, from a "disciplinary society" (which they associate with the modern Fordist world of nation-states and the nationalized concept of "the people") to a so-called society of control (which they associate with the supranational relations of Empire and the emergence of the denationalized "multitude"). In an early chapter near the start of the book they thereby pose biopolitical production as a useful focus

through which to track "the material constitution of the new planetary order, the consolidation of its administrative machine, and the
production of new hierarchies of command over global space" (19).
By hereby combining arguments from Foucault, Marx, and Deleuze
and Guattari in a single argument that addresses the production of
global space, Hardt and Negri also provide a way of theorizing the
ways in which geoeconomics is consolidated and reproduced. The vision of smooth, decentered, and deterritorialized space can thus be
understood in their own theoretical terms as a panoptic "diagram" of
the capillary "biopolitics" defining the globalized free market's "anti-
architecture."

Interpreting the power of geoeconomics through the critical theory of biopolitics means understanding it as more than just an anti-
geography that obfuscates uneven geographical development. It means
examining how it simultaneously works as a profoundly *productive
and enabling* graphing of the geo that enframes a basic horizon of
planning and self-understanding among a certain set of global actors.
It would be obscenely ethnocentric to assume that such actors include
the whole of Hardt and Negri's supposed multitude. The arrogance of
geoeconomics and its dependency on an assumptive economistic view
of the world indicate that it only makes sense as a vision for a very
privileged community of biopolitical reproduction. For the majority of
the world's poor struggling to survive in peripheral communities they
cannot escape, and even for the majority of transnational migrants
who are poor, "gliding" across the "striae" of national borders is only
ever something that happens to the commodities that they labor to
make. It is not part of their own subjective experience. But elsewhere,
however, there is a much narrower community for whom such subjective feelings of smoothness and gliding come easily. Following the
sociologist Leslie Sklair again, this community can be usefully called
the "transnational capitalist class."[34] Sklair's own empirical analysis
of the transnational capitalist class in fact provides some corrobora-
tion of the idea that geoeconomics may in this way play a central role
in the training and subject formation of a new global elite. His survey of Global Fortune 500 annual reports, for example, shows that
businesses from around the world repeatedly use the smooth spatial
imagery of an abstract globe alongside rhetoric about global prospects to highlight their strategic visions and strengths to shareholders.
For such TNCs, it seems, the smooth space of the globe really does

enframe a level plain of boundless opportunity. The notion that there is easy mobility across the global plain also seems to be accepted as common sense by many of the global political elites with whom these TNCs deal as they play one locale off against another negotiating for tax holidays, regulatory relaxation, wage repression, and infrastructural support. It is true that the geoeconomic picture of boundaryless TNC behavior does not match the much more complex and uneven geographies of real world commodity chains, financing, corporate information exchange, and accounting systems.[35] And yet, even as he documents such complexities, the economic geographer Peter Dicken notes that corporate strategists themselves return repeatedly to the vision "that technological and regulatory developments in the world economy have created a 'global surface' on which a dominant organizational form [the global corporation] will develop and inexorably wipe out less efficient competitors who are no longer protected by national or local barriers."[36] What, then, explains the endurance and widespread influence of this geoeconomic vision?

Part of the reason for the hegemony of the vision is undoubtedly the intensity of the biopolitical training through which it is instilled. Hardt and Negri's theorization of biopolitics is again instructive. They make clear that they want to combine a traditional Marxist focus on production with a more open-ended attention to all the diversity of power relations in informational, cultural, and corporeal reproduction. They invoke in this way Deleuze and Guattari's antiessentialist activation of the notion of "social machines." They applaud how certain Italian Marxists have moved via biopolitics beyond a workerist analysis of capitalism. And, although it is in a footnote and although it is followed by what Lisa Rofel critiques as a masculinist recuperation of feminist theories of affective labor, they invoke Spivak's inspirational reworking of value theory to claim that "from a methodological point of view, we would say that the most profound and solid problematic complex that has yet been elaborated for the critique of biopolitics is found in feminist theory, particularly Marxist and socialist feminist theories that focus on women's work, affective labor and the production of biopower"(*Empire,* 423).[37] With regard to the biopolitical production of geoeconomics such an argument is borne out by the work of economic geographers such as Sue Roberts and Nigel Thrift.[38] They have shown that management-training programs create consequential combinations of governmentality and spatiality by training affectively in order to be effective. The programs thus create biopolitical regulation by linking lessons in the techniques of business efficiency with the cultivation of deeply personal and spatialized senses of self, including, as Roberts emphasizes, the masculinist sense of being able to stand over, see, and control sweeping vistas of global coordination.[39] Even if these globalist concepts of decontextualized sight are reworked (as much of the research shows they are) in their site-specific enactment, they would equally appear to be buttressed by the daily onslaught of globalist advertising and imagery (about friction-free networks, global villages, and so on) to which managerial trainees, along with the politicians and lawyers they proceed to work with, are also routinely exposed.[40] As a result, they are extremely entrenched and continue to circulate and reproduce in global networks of both corporate training and work. Geoeconomics therefore—as both by-product and coproducer of corporate governmentality among global elites—might well seem to exemplify Hardt and Negri's notion of biopolitical control extending "well outside the structured sites of social institutions through flexible and fluctuating networks" (23).

Another part of the reason for the persistence of geoeconomics, however, relates back to the capitalist organization of global space itself. As they do on many other key points of theoretical description, Hardt and Negri vacillate on whether to call this space an "architecture" or "anti-architecture." This vacillation fudges the problem of how they might reconcile their underlying assumption of a geoeconomic worldview with the uneven political, cultural, and economic geographies that make up the lived spatial architecture of life across the planet. Chief among these forms of uneven development is the asymmetry presented by the United States and the dominance it exercises in a vast array of global relations. One of the most unfortunate ironies of all in *Empire* is that, having explored how the American constitutional capacity for rule over flexible frontiers anticipates a newly global constitution, Hardt and Negri proceed to reproduce a geoeconomic discourse that elides ongoing and specifically American control over flexible frontiers *on a global scale*. It is still possible to draw on *Empire* in order to theorize the force of geoeconomics as a form of biopolitical worlding of the world in the context of heightened global interdependency. Moreover, it is possible to join this with Hardt and Negri's other argument about the specifically

American constitutional roots of the new global biopolitics. But a key reason for doing so involves going in the direction that *Empire* avoids: namely, examining how the geoeconomic vision of smoothed global space at once obscures and enables the privileges that accrue to the United States as the major structuring and steering influence of contemporary global capitalism.

Looking back on the early years of American constitutional history, Gindin and Panitch argue that

> Hardt and Negri were right to trace the pre-figuration of what they call "Empire" today back to the American constitution's incorporation of Madisonian "network power." . . . Yet far from anticipating the sort of decentred and amorphous power that Hardt and Negri imagine characterized the US historically (and characterizes "Empire" today), the constitutional framework of the new American state gave great powers to the central government to expand trade and make war.[41]

Coming forward to the present, it seems that the Madisonian model of network power has continued to give great powers to the central government to expand trade and make war. Now, though, the U.S. government lies at the center of a much more global and informal system, a system over which it has generally held hegemony through consensus. Today's war-making, argue Gindin and Panitch, is not necessarily indicative of a decline in this U.S. hegemony. Nor does it signal some return to interimperial rivalries. Instead, they suggest that the recent wars represent the heightened challenges of organizing an informal imperial system through the intermediaries of other national states. More specifically, the project of finding willing governments schooled in the vision of neoliberal globalization has, they argue, run up against the difficult challenge of incorporating the periphery—including so-called rogue states—into the system. This is a critical argument for the subsequent sections of this chapter because it explains why the smooth and decentered world visions of geoeconomics might be related to the development of the Iraq war. It opens the possibility, in other words, of investigating how geoeconomics not only obscures American imperialism, but also serves as a basic groundwork on which its contemporary builders have been (free)trading and making war. The resulting complicity of globalist geoeconomics with unilateralist geopolitics has been highly contradictory and unstable, and it is in an effort to unpack the resulting contradictions and instabilities that I turn now to examine the period of the buildup to war. This period, as we shall see, appears at first sight to have been shaped almost entirely by geopolitical assertion. However, after reviewing these geopolitical imperatives, I show how they were in turn underpinned and enframed by an array of geoeconomic assumptions. The resulting complicity of geopolitics with geoeconomics was extraordinarily influential, but as the war went on to show and as we shall explore in the later part of the chapter, it was also a contradictory complicity that was to prove extremely unstable in action.

PREPARING FOR WAR: THE INTERVENTION OF GEOPOLITICS

For many business commentators the "smooth space" geoeconomic worldview of the global village simply shattered on 9/11 when the planes crashed into the World Trade Center. Globalization gurus such as the *New York Times* columnist Thomas Friedman, for example, saw the events as nothing less than the start of World War III.[42] Indeed, in Friedman's case the attacks of 9/11 led to his clear shift in the months and years that followed from a transnational business-class neoliberal outlook toward a steadily more neoconservative and unilateralist prowar chauvinism. However, for the neoconservative masterminds behind the Project for a New American Century (PNAC), 9/11 was not so much a day of infamy as a geopolitical opportunity: a Pearl Harbor, perhaps, but a Pearl Harbor for which they had been waiting. In 2000 PNAC had published a report entitled *Rebuilding America's Defenses: Strategies, Forces and Resources for a New Century,* in which the authors noted that the expansion of America's military dominance that they were demanding would only happen slowly "absent some catastrophic and catalyzing event—like a new Pearl Harbor."[43] September 11 provided just such an event, and as such it gave the well-placed neoconservatives associated with PNAC much more leverage to force through their vision of a newly assertive American unilateralism, a geopolitical vision that they had effectively been airing ever since the fall of the Berlin Wall. Too often this geopolitical intervention by PNAC and its associates has been reported in scandalized tones as something of a secret conspiracy. The Scottish *Sunday Herald,* for example, thus described the reporter's discovery of the *Rebuilding America's Defenses* report in the language of a grand exposé. "A secret blueprint for US global domination," began the news article, reveals that President Bush and his cabinet were planning a premeditated attack on Iraq to secure "regime change" even before he took power in January 2001. The blueprint, uncovered by the *Sunday Herald,* for the creation of a "global Pax Americana" was drawn up for Dick Cheney (now vice-president), Donald Rumsfeld (defense secretary), Paul Wolfowitz (Rumsfeld's deputy), George W. Bush's younger brother Jeb and Lewis Libby (Cheney's chief of staff).[44]

Yet while the *Rebuilding America's Defenses* report was certainly audacious, and while it did indeed describe "the unresolved conflict with Iraq" as "the immediate justification" for increasing America's "force presence" in the Gulf,[45] the neoconservative luminaries that contributed to it were hardly a clandestine cabal. Moreover, their intervention was no sudden coup either. Many of them, for instance, had cosigned an open letter to President Clinton back in 1998 directly demanding "regime change" in Iraq. "Dear Mr. President," the letter began,

> We are writing you because we are convinced that current American policy toward Iraq is not succeeding, and that we may soon face a threat in the Middle East more serious than any we have known since the end of the Cold War. In your upcoming State of the Union Address, you have an opportunity to chart a clear and determined course for meeting this threat. We urge you to seize that opportunity, and to enunciate a new strategy that would secure the interests of the U.S. and our friends and allies around the world. That strategy should aim, above all, at the removal of Saddam Hussein's regime from power. We stand ready to offer our full support in this difficult but necessary endeavor. . . .
>
> Sincerely,
>
> Elliott Abrams, Richard L. Armitage, William J. Bennett, Jeffrey Bergner, John Bolton, Paula Dobriansky, Francis Fukuyama, Robert Kagan, Zalmay Khalilzad, William Kristol, Richard Perle, Peter W. Rodman, Donald Rumsfeld, William Schneider, Jr., Vin Weber, Paul Wolfowitz, R. James Woolsey, Robert B. Zoellick[46]

Putting their names to this public letter, the signatories may have been adopting Trotskyist tactics, but they were hardly acting like secretive conspirators. Moreover, the letter and the *Rebuilding America's Defenses* report have since remained well publicized on PNAC's Web site. They can easily be found there alongside the Project's 1997 founding call "to embrace the cause of American leadership." That founding call itself was far from a private PNAC pact. Hearkening back to the Reagan years as well as to Henry Luce's 1950s declaration of an American Century, it articulated as boldly as possible the neoconservatives' call for geopolitical activism with direct appeals to American principles and interests.

> As the 20th century draws to a close, the United States stands as the world's most preeminent power. Having led the West to victory in the Cold War, America faces an opportunity and a challenge: Does the United States have the vision to build upon the achievement of past decades? Does the United States have the resolve to shape a new century favorable to American principles and interests?[47]

Explaining in turn what such vision and resolve should entail, the PNAC founders declared in the name of the nation that

> [What we require is] a military that is strong and ready to meet both present and future challenges; a foreign policy that boldly and purposefully promotes American principles abroad; and national leadership that accepts the United States' global responsibilities.

Such views were widely shared beyond the circles of PNAC.[48] Other neoconservative organizations such as the American Enterprise Institute and the Center for Strategic and International Studies were just as involved in disseminating similar calls for geopolitical activism during the Clinton years, as too, it needs noting, were a number of "Bill the Benign's" own cabinet. Madeleine Albright, his second term secretary of state, famously extolled the virtues of America as the "indispenable nation,"[49] and Anthony Lake, Clinton's first national security advisor, had claimed that the fundamental feature of the post–cold war era was that "we are its dominant power. Those who say otherwise sell America short. . . . Around the world, America's power, authority and example provide unparalleled opportunities to lead."[50] Going back further in time, the narrower ideological roots of the new neoconservative geopolitics—at least its combined vision of militant American democracy and strategic independence—can be traced back via the cultural critic Allan Bloom, the Washington State senator Henry Jackson, and the older generation neoconservatives Irving Kristol and Norman Podheretz, to the antimodern philosophy of Leo Strauss and the antiestablishment nuclear doctrines of Albert Wohlstetter.[51] PNAC's geopolitical intervention, then, was by no means an overnight development, and notable signatories to its public statements such as Paul Wolfowitz, Richard Perle, and William Kristol (who all worked under Jackson's tutelage and took courses with Bloom at Chicago) had rehearsed their geopolitical outlook for years. Wolfowitz is especially notable in this regard because his public promotion of a unilateralist American geopolitics itself went back to the first Bush administration. Then, as undersecretary of Defense for Policy when Dick Cheney was Defense secretary, he supervised the drafting of a much discussed 1992 "Defense Planning Guidance" document advising that the United States should "prevent any hostile power from dominating a region whose resources would, under consolidated control, be sufficient to generate global power."[52] Obsessed, it seems, with the idea of deterring potential geopolitical rivals from developing a global role, the document had also noted with neoimperial candor that "the United States should be postured to act independently when collective action cannot be orchestrated." At the time, Wolfowitz's directness was questioned after leaks of the draft reached Congress, and Cheney had to supervise revisions to the text that downplayed the abandonment of multilateralism. But after ten years of public advocacy and after the forcing event of 9/11, Wolfowitz was to see basically the same censored vision (including its attention to maintaining U.S. access to key global resources in the Persian Gulf) articulated openly as official public policy in the build-up to the Iraq war. The key question in this regard concerns how. How did the geopolitical vision of unabashed U.S. imperialism that Senator Robert Byrd had once castigated as "myopic, shallow and disappointing" become the new Washington consensus and, as such, the basis for war?[53] Timing and ideology played a particular role, but so too, I will subsequently argue, did geoeconomic assumptions.

In the context of George W. Bush's presidency, 9/11 really did create a forcing event. Much is made in this regard of the opportunism of the PNAC geopoliticians. Most remarkable of all, Rumsfeld appears to have begun planning to use 9/11 as an excuse for attacking Saddam Hussein within hours of the attack on the Pentagon. CBS News reported that after returning from helping the injured on the outside of the Pentagon and hearing of the possible ties to Osama bin Laden, Rumsfeld noted at 2:40 p.m.: "best info fast. Judge whether good enough hit S.H. [Saddam Hussein] at the same time. Not only UBL [Osama bin Laden]. Go massive. Sweep it all up. Things related and not."[54] The staggering notion of sweeping "it all up" also illustrates the ideological work involved in promoting the Iraq war. Again and again the attacks of 9/11 were linked to Saddam Hussein, and from Bush's "Axis of Evil" State of the Union address to endless insinuations about Iraq's weapons of mass destruction and supposed links to Al Qaeda, the ideological legitimation for so-called regime change in Iraq did indeed "go massive." Such was the success of this campaign that long after the intelligence agencies had dismissed the stories of an Al Qaeda link, and even after the failure to find weapons of mass destruction after the war, nearly 70 percent of Americans still believed that Hussein had been personally involved in the 9/11 attacks.[55] As bumper stickers and front porch signs emphasized across America in 2003, the Iraq war was thus legitimized as a form of national retribution—"Remember 9/11: Support Our Troops." It was a geopolitical campaign that worked, argues Gerard Toal, "by the channeling of the public affect unleashed by 9/11."[56]

There are well-known dangers in trying to psychoanalyze a whole nation en masse, but Toal's own exploration of the instrumentalization of public affect in the buildup to the Iraq war avoids homogenizing a singular national psyche by focusing on the particular national narratives and symbols that the campaign for war deployed.[57] He notes in this respect how President Bush enacted an updated Jacksonian tradition of American geopolitical common sense, an affective as well as effective enactment that transformed the populist ideologies of individualism and self-reliance shared among Christian and gun-owning communities in America into a colonizing Manichaean geopolitics of "good versus evil" on the global stage. Other scholars of geopolitical scripting such as Michael Shapiro linked the initial "Wanted, Dead or Alive" approach Bush took to hunting down bin Laden to colonial collective imaginaries of the United States as a gunfighter nation.[58] And clearly the masculinism and white supremacism of a certain cowboy nationalism continued to animate much of the prowar lobbying throughout 2002 and 2003. But as Bush's hankering for a Wild West solution failed to turn up bin Laden either alive or dead, the affective resonance of 9/11 was recentered in 2002 amid wider foreign policy initiatives that went beyond the gunfighter nation set provided by Afghanistan's mountains and deserts. As a somatic marker, Toal argues, 9/11 thus became a more generalized domain of resentment and desire, the desire to avenge the symbolic castrating of America's power and profile on September 11, the desire to affirm that America "still stands tall," the desire to appear powerful, resolute and dominant amidst swirling questions of legitimacy (from Florida in 2000 to the Security Council in 2003), economic weakness (from the dot.com crash to corporate scandals and rising unemployment) and risk society (from airline safety to anthrax and nuclear proliferation).[59]

All of the complex anxieties surrounding such questions could thereby, Toal argues, be channeled through 9/11 into arguments supporting a war on Iraq. A week after the fall of Baghdad the popular country-and-western singer Darryl Worley was invited to sing a song to Pentagon personnel that said it all: "Some say this country's just out looking for a fight. After 9/11 man I'd have to say that's right." The words still seemed to speak powerfully to the assembled company, and, as Toal notes, the song even made Donald Rumsfeld cry.

Rumsfeld's tears give some indication of the ways in which a PNAC insider was himself swept up by the affective ties that came to link 9/11, the Iraq war, and a heroic vision of America's geopolitical mission. Things related and not, it seems, had gone massive for him too in September 2001, and it was perhaps not surprising that a year later, when Senator Mark Dayton of Minnesota asked Rumsfeld about what new developments necessitated the decision to attack Iraq, he sputtered, "What's different? What's different is 3,000 people were killed."[60] Against this "casuistry belli," as she called it, Maureen Dowd articulated the main liberal complaint: "The administration isn't targeting Iraq because of 9/11. It's exploiting 9/11 to target Iraq." To this, though, she added a critical nuance. "This new fight isn't logical—it's cultural. It is the latest chapter in the cultural wars, the conservative dream of restoring America's sense of Manifest Destiny."[61] These observations captured the cultural politics of the warmongering well, connecting them back to what, with Allan Bloom and Irving Kristol, had been the initial preoccupations of the neoconservative movement in the 1960s and 1970s. Her sensitivity to the masculinist self-imaging and posturing of the geopolitics also seemed right on the mark: "Bush is like a guy who reserves a hotel room and *then* asks you to the prom," she suggested.[62] But the warmongering was much more than cowboy cultural politics. It was, after all, not just their ideological outlook that the neoconservatives brought to office, but the political capacity to make it the new Washington consensus. In other words, the hegemony of their geopolitical outlook not only rested on their war of maneuver that linked an attack on Iraq with national desires for post 9/11 revenge, it also related to a war of position in D.C. that took the form of placing neoconservatives in key offices of authority.

Rumsfeld's position as Defense secretary was itself a good example of the new neoconservative influence. But because Cheney, another PNAC associate, worked as incoming vice president to control the Bush administration's transition into office, he was able to ensure that many other PNAC associates reached high-ranking jobs.[63] In addition to Rumsfeld, Wolfowitz and Douglas Feith were respectively given the number two and number three positions in the Pentagon, Elliot Abrams was put in charge of Middle-East policy at the National Security Council, James Woolsey and Richard Perle found influential positions on the Defense Policy Board, Lewis Libby became Cheney's chief of staff, and John Bolton became undersecretary of state.[64] To many mainstream critics such as Michael Lind, Cheney's success had produced a "weird" foreign policy executive and thus a weird geopolitics.[65] Explaining it to a U.K. audience as a "bizarre" outcome owing much to "happenstance and personality" he struggled to think of a suitable geopolitical parallel.

> For a British equivalent, one would have to imagine a Tory government, with Downing Street and Whitehall controlled by followers of Reverend Ian Paisley, extreme Eurosceptic, empire loyalists and Blimpish military types—all determined, for a variety of strategic reasons, to invade Egypt. Their aim would be to regain the Suez canal as the first step in a campaign to restore the British empire. Yes, it really is that weird.[66]

The problem with this view was that, like the conspiratorial picture of PNAC, it overstated the weirdness and underplayed the hegemonic achievement. To make his argument, Lind rightly highlighted the links of many of the PNAC associates to the viciously colonial outlook of the Likud Party in Israel. Yet while the strategic vision of creating a Hashemite kingdom stretching from Jordan to Iraq has hardly been a historic mainstay of American Middle East policy, and while two PNAC associates, Perle and Feith, were instrumental in developing this vision, the more basic overlaps between PNAC's geopolitics and Israeli colonialism are by no means unprecedented in

American foreign policy making.[67] As Melanie McAlister has documented with telling cultural nuance, the example of Israeli colonial militarism (including the preemptive strike of the so-called Six Days War) has long informed American informal imperialism both in the Middle East and domestically.[68] Moreover, as McAlister also shows, the other Israeli influence on the Bush White House—that of evangelical, often anti-Semitic, Christian Zionism—comprises a growing and far from Paisley-ite movement, weird though their "dispensationalist" visions of Jewish conversion to Christianity might make them as Israeli settlers' main American allies.[69] In other words, just as PNAC's call for an unabashed imperial approach by the United States to Iraq built upon much wider national narratives about militant self-defense and retribution, so too did the group's geopolitical affinities with Israeli colonialism resonate with more long-standing and more widely advocated objectives for American policy in the Middle East. The overall geopolitical vision that PNAC associates helped foster was thus to prove hegemonic, not weird.

Loaded with the affect of post-9/11 retribution and organized through orientalist scripts about Arabs only understanding force, the geopolitical arguments for unilateralism fashioned an anthropomorphic spectacle of the nation standing tall. War critics too became consumed with the fantasy of the United States being anthropomorphically assertive. "These are the days of empire," ran one typical tirade.

> Unrivalled and untrammeled, the United States bestrides the globe like a colossus. The President of the United States endowed with more power than Alexander the Great and Napoleon combined, can now wreak havoc at his whim and leisure. President Bush sits upon Zeus's throne and treats Congress, the United Nations and U.S. allies as mere vassals.[70]

When the critics joined the argument on this level, PNAC had already won the hegemonic struggle to script the Iraq intervention as assertive geopolitics. Combined with the dissemination capabilities afforded by Rupert Murdoch's media empire—including the *Weekly Standard* edited by PNAC cofounder Bill Kristol and the Fox cable channel that gave neoconservatives a mass-media bullhorn—the overall ideological hegemony of the neoconservative geopolitical vision therefore became unstoppable. All that was needed now for the war plans to proceed was an amendment of official American policy, and this is what happened in September 2002 with the release of a new *National Security Strategy.*

By this time, a year on from 9/11, more reluctant Republicans such as Colin Powell, Bush's secretary of state, and Richard Haas, Director of Policy and Planning at the State Department, were falling into unilateralist line, and Bush's national security advisor, Condoleezza Rice, spoke only of the United States needing "a coalition of the willing": a euphemism for Wolfowitz's older idea of "orchestrated" international consensus. When Rice finalized the *National Security Strategy,* it was clear that the geopolitical activism demanded for over a decade by Wolfowitz and PNAC's other associates had fully become the new Washington consensus. And while the plan for a unilateral, "preemptive" war on Iraq was not mentioned directly, its justification was now asserted as at once a national response to 9/11 and a new national policy. The text began by noting that

> The United States possesses unprecedented—and unequaled—strength and influence in the world. Sustained by faith in the principles of liberty, and the value of a free society, this position comes with unparalleled responsibilities, obligations, and opportunity.[71]

Here the echoes with PNAC's primacy "principles" were clear. Virtually cribbing from the *Rebuilding America's Defenses* report, moreover, the *National Security Strategy* proceeded to argue the case for preemption too:

> The gravest danger our Nation faces lies at the cross-roads of radicalism and technology. Our enemies have openly declared that they are seeking weapons of mass destruction, and evidence indicates that they are doing so with determination. The United States will not allow these efforts to succeed. . . . America will act against such emerging threats before they are fully formed.[72]

The connections drawn here went in three directions. They linked 9/11 (radicalism and technology) with weapons of mass destruction with a call for national preemptive action. Only later on in the text was Iraq placed in the center of the triangle. First came a supposed statement of fact:

> At the time of the Gulf War, we acquired irrefutable proof that Iraq's designs were not limited to the chemical weapons it had used against Iran and its own people, but also extended to the acquisition of nuclear weapons and biological agents.[73]

Next followed the statement of policy:

> Our comprehensive strategy to combat WMD includes: Proactive counterproliferation efforts. . . . We cannot let our enemies strike first. . . . The United States has long maintained the option of preemptive actions to counter a sufficient threat to our national security. The greater the threat, the greater is the risk of inaction.[74]

It only remained for the concocted evidence of Iraq's weapons of mass destruction to be presented to Congress and the "preemptive" war that PNAC had been proposing ever since the letter to Clinton could finally be declared on Iraq. The empire could now, in Dowd's punchy poetics, "strike first."[75] The United Nations became "irrelevant," french fries became freedom fries, stars and stripes fluttered like swastikas at the Berlin Olympics, protesters were deported, arrested, and ignored, and the president, who had long swept everything up in the affect of national retribution, declared that the war would "not be one of half-measures."[76]

Critics of the war plans argued that they were indeed unprecedented, but also unjust and, thus, ultimately, un-American. Joseph Cirincione, the director of the Non-Proliferation Project at the Carnegie Endowment for International Peace summed up this prevailing critical national sentiment when he described the assertive U.S. geopolitical unilateralism as a new colonialism.

> [W]hat they're planning is unprecedented in U.S. history. This will not just be our first pre-emptive war, but it will be followed by a massive, indefinite occupation. President Bush intends to send more than 200,000 American men and women to invade and occupy a large, complex nation of 24 million people half a world away. The last time any Western power did anything similar was before World War II. The last time any nation did this was the Soviet invasion of Afghanistan in 1979. As retired Gen. Wesley Clark, the former head of NATO forces, says, this war will "put us in a colonial position in the Middle East following Britain, following the Ottomans. It's a huge change for the American people and for what this country stands for." To the rest of the world it will indeed look like colonialism. With the best of intentions, and with surprisingly little public discussion, we are about to overthrow a government, appoint a U.S. military ruler, and, after several years of transition, install our hand-picked alternatives.[77]

These were criticisms that were echoed again and again by both liberals and leftists, Americans and non-Americans alike, all of them articulating in one way or another nostalgia for "Bill the Benign" and still older eras of American multilateralism. "Typically, in this perspective," noted Balakrishnan, in a critical review of the mainstream response, "Clinton's rule is looked back at longingly, as the halcyon days of a humane and responsible *Pax Americana,* whose abandonment since has been a brutal disappointment."[78] The limits of such nostalgic critiques—beyond the obvious denial of previous acts of aggressive American unilateralism in Panama, Grenada, Nicaragua, and, though much more arguably, Kosovo—were twofold. As Perry Anderson argued, they ignored the advances of American informal imperialism in the Clinton years themselves.[79] These included, in Anderson's assessment, the ways in which "[t]he USSR had been knocked out of the ring, Europe and Japan kept in check, China drawn into increasingly close trade relations, [and] the UN reduced to little more than a permissions office." Anderson himself adds that all this was accomplished in the Clinton era "to the tune of the most emollient of ideologies, whose every second word was international understanding and democratic good will."[80] It seems that it was precisely this emollient ideology that was abandoned by the Bush administration in its impatience with the fictions of "international community" and "multilateralism." And yet, as Anderson also notes, this was primarily a shift in style rather than in fundamental outlook, and to see it as the emergence or unleashing of a novel American imperialism was, I want to argue, another larger limitation of the nostalgic mode of critique. Neglecting the continuities from "Bill the Benign" to "Bush the Bold," critics rarely came to terms with how the war plans were predicated on a profoundly similar worlding of the world as an expanding level plain mediated through globalized networks. They ignored, in other words, the ways in which it was understood and articulated even by the war planners themselves in profoundly neoliberal ways. Here I return to the connections of the geopolitics with an underlying and enduring geoeconomics.

My suggestion in the next section is that the relationship between the geopolitical warmongering and the underlying geoeconomic assumptions was not of difference, distinction, or opposition, but rather one of complicity. While Bush enacted the role of virile national commander in chief, and while war critics and war fans inveighed against and invested in the image of an American geopolitical colossus reterritorializing the Middle East, the war planning remained paradoxically *dependent* on the deterritorialized worldview of geo-economics. As I suggested at the start of this section, a signal geo-political consequence of the martial mood was the enlistment of patriotic neoliberals such as Thomas Friedman to the hegemonic project of neoconservatives. But as I now want to argue in more de-tail, the reason why this enlistment lasted, the reason why it brought reluctant Republicans into line, and a key reason that it even worked abroad among transnational business-class opinion organs such as the *Economist* was due to the fact that the war planning was thor-oughly underpinned by the smoothing force of geoeconomics. It was possible to orchestrate (to use the Wolfowitz word) such a willing geopolitical coalition, I want to argue, because of the biopolitical force of the ideals of planar planetary space. America's geopoliti-cal intervention could thus make sense to someone such as Richard Haas (author of *The Reluctant Sheriff* and Wolfowitz's onetime contender as the Republicans' leading strategic thinker) because, as he explained to Nicholas Lemann in a distinction familiar to readers of *Empire,* there was "a big difference between being imperial and imperia*list.*"[81]

THE GEOECONOMIC GROUNDWORK

The very same *Strategy* that triangulated the geopolitical legitimation for the attack on Iraq and that hued so closely to PNAC's principles was also a text that was thoroughly underpinned by assumptions about globalization. "[T]he United States will use this moment of op-portunity," it declared, "to extend the benefits of freedom across the globe. We will actively work to bring the hope of democracy, devel-opment, free markets and free trade to every corner of the world."[82] Whole sections of the *Strategy* were thus devoted to the supposed security benefits of free markets, free trade, and global capitalist in-tegration, and the preface signed by President Bush began by claim-ing that there was now only one single sustainable model for national success: "freedom, democracy and free enterprise." To many observ-ers such as Robert Wright, the result was a completely contradic-tory strategic vision: global interdependency and American military supremacy could not be so easily made to coincide.[83] But such critics only read the *Strategy* through the traditional international relations opposition of idealism versus realism: global conventions versus na-tional power politics. They therefore overlooked the successful complicity of geopolitical assertion and geoeconomic assumption in the document: the way, to use Anderson's phrase, it sought to conjugate a specifically American form of dominance with a general task of coordinating global capitalism. "The U.S. national security strategy will be based on a distinctly American internationalism that reflects the union of our values and our national interests," the text asserted, before proceeding directly to describe those values and interests in the predictable terms of "political and economic freedom."[84] These prescriptions for a global *Pax Americana* were certainly explicit about the geopolitical importance of the U.S. in world affairs. Notwithstanding a nod to Wolfowitz's critics in the preface—"we do not use our strength to push for unilateral advantage"—the overall implication of the *Strategy* document was indeed an enunciation, in the geopolitical terms of U.S. primacy and preemption rights, of unilateral advantage. And yet this advantage was imagined as underpinned and as best maintained through free markets and free trade.

The complex combination of geopolitical assertion and geoeconomic assumption that organized the *Strategy* was to prove an elusive target of critique. A few critics noticed the geoeconomics.[85] But much more commonly, it was the geopolitical interpretations that dominated. From this perspective the vision of extending freedom through free markets was not an empire of decentered space but rather just an ideological cover for instrumental and specifically American-centered imperialism. Peter Gowan, for example, argued in this way against the hollowness of the U.S. rhetoric (as well as its continuities from Bush senior to Clinton to Bush junior). "For all the American ideological stress on free market capitalism and 'economic globalization,'" he concluded, "we find that the American state, backed by its business class elites, has been engaged . . . in increasingly feverish and increasingly militaristic geopolitical manoeuvers to reconstruct the inter-state system as a means to anchor the dominance of US capitalism in the twenty-first century."[86] From the neoconservative advocates of unilateralism themselves also came dismissals of the ideas propounded by capitalist cosmopolitans. Robert Kagan thus opined around the time of the *Strategy*'s release about "the unilateralist iron fist inside the multilateralist velvet glove."[87] However, this arrogant metaphor would seem to have belied a deeper dependency on a geoeconomic worldview that, as we shall see, even Kagan and his PNAC associates occasionally articulated themselves.

More than just an ideological cover or velvet glove, then, the bio-political force of geoeconomic discourse appears to have enframed the basic ground on which the plans for American intervention were developed. A review of some of the neoconservatives' engagements with a geoeconomic outlook (including Kagan's own) in the buildup to the Iraq war makes this clearer. Here the point is not to argue that they were actually engaged in a project of expanding a deterritorialized empire, but rather the more doubled-edged suggestion that they were conjugating their vision of American unilateralism using a geoeconomic grammar predicated on the sweeping MBA-style visions of deterritorialized global networks.

Rumsfeld, to pick perhaps the most extreme condensation point of prewar geopolitical affect, actually commissioned a private study after arriving at the Pentagon charged with investigating what the United States could learn as a global power from such ancient empires as those of Rome, the Mongols, the Chinese, and the Macedonians. At first blush this was an extraordinarily arrogant imperialist idea. But on closer inspection, the study was symptomatic of something closer to what Hardt and Negri call imperial biopolitics. Besides revealing the historical hubris of the Pentagon, the results of the supposed "research" also indicated the degree to which Rumsfeld and those he respected were profoundly engaged with the question of sustaining American dominance amid global networks. The authors of the study (including ex-Speaker Newt Gingrich and emeritus orientalist Bernard Lewis) noted: "Without strong political and economic institutions, the Mongols, and the Macedonians could not maintain extensive empires. What made the Roman Empire great was not just its military power but its 'franchise of empire.' What made the Chinese Empire great was not just its military power but the immense power and might of its culture."[88] For readers of *Empire,* it might not be hard to notice a certain symptomatic acknowledgment in this miserably reductionist and interested history of the decentering of power in global networks. However, while Hardt and Negri argue that their postmodern Empire has no Rome,[89] Rumsfeld's research squad came to a more instrumental and unsurprisingly American-centric conclusion. "If we can take any lesson from history it is this: For the United States to sustain predominance it must remain militarily dominant, but it must also maintain its pre-eminence across other pillars of power."[90]

Perhaps more significant than the study's conclusions about the limits of military imperialism was the fact that they were presented by the Office of Net Assessment and that the anti-Arab historical fantasist Lewis was partnered in the project with the antigovernment high-tech fantasist Gingrich.[91] Gingrich was a keen fan of the Tofflers (whose own 1990s arguments about a "third-wave" information war leading ultimately to "anti-war" bear a striking resemblance to some of Hardt and Negri's claims about Empire constituting the antiarchitecture of global peace).[92] Such enthusiasms made the ex-Speaker a good fit with the wider so-called revolution in military affairs that had already led to diverse revisionings of geopolitics at the Pentagon, and that Rumsfeld had sought to accelerate with plans to build a more flexible military alongside a continental missile shield.[93] Not surprisingly—given their long roots in neoconservative strategic thinking—it was these very same sorts of futurological ideas that also ran through much of PNAC's planning. The *Rebuilding America's Defenses* text itself is a good example, and the sections on future wars over outer space and the Internet are especially revealing of the market logics in which their own arguments for American primacy were being envisioned.

The PNAC report argues that

> space has become a new "international commons" where commercial and security interests are intertwined. 95 percent of current U.S. military communications are carried over commercial circuits, including commercial communications satellites. . . . [Consequently] national military forces, paramilitary units, terrorists, and any other potential adversaries will share the high ground of space with the United States and its allies.[94]

Here the geoeconomic conclusion is especially clear. "The space 'playing field' is leveling rapidly, so U.S. forces will be increasingly vulnerable." To the accompaniment of this reiteration of level playing field discourse, the report argued that more investment was necessary to sustain the United States as the protector and manager of the system. The very same argument was then applied to cyberspace.

> The Internet is also playing an increasingly important role in warfare and human political conflict. From the early use of the Internet by Zapatista insurgents in Mexico to the war in Kosovo, communication by computer has added a new dimension to warfare. Moreover,

the use of the Internet to spread computer viruses reveals how easy it can be to disrupt the normal functioning of commercial and even military computer networks. . . . An America incapable of protecting its interests or that of its allies in space or the "infosphere" will find it difficult to exert global political leadership.[95]

In these arguments and others like them a form of geostrategic three-step was articulated that later went on to become a dominant feature of attempts to legitimate the Iraq war. First came the geoeconomic assumption about a level plain being created by globalization; second came the threat assessment concerning unmanaged enemies estranged from the emergent global system; and third came the geopolitical assertion about the need for the United States to play the role of systems manager. Following this logic, the geoeconomic starting place could still lead to a geopolitical argument about the need for American national action, but the starting point also effectively pre-scripted what that action was about: namely, the stately work of systemic oversight, protection, and incorporation. Even so ardent a unilateralist as Kagan ultimately followed this three-step at a basic level in his book *Of Paradise and Power*.[96]

On the surface of it Kagan's book was all about trumpeting the integrity and realism of geopolitical unilateralism (embodied for Kagan in American policy) over the idealism of multilateralism (embodied in E.U. policy).[97] But, as he battled on about these banal binaries, Kagan ultimately gave the game away when he cited with approval the advocacy of a new liberal imperialism by the senior British diplomat Robert Cooper. An advisor to Tony Blair, Cooper had earlier argued in the Spring of 2002 that the time was right for a postmodern liberal imperialism that would work just like traditional liberal imperialism by fostering a deliberate double standard.[98] "The postmodern world has to start to get used to double standards," Cooper said.

> Among ourselves, we operate on the basis of laws and open cooperative security. But, when dealing with old-fashioned states outside the postmodern continent of Europe, we need to revert to the rougher methods of an earlier era—force, pre-emptive attack, deception, whatever is necessary to deal with those who still live in the nineteenth century world of every state for itself.[99]

Such a view not only helps explain Blair's own subsequent support for the preemptive Iraqi campaign, but also gives a clue as to how an avowed unilateralist such as Kagan was drawing on assumptions about globalization.[100] Kagan basically accepted Cooper's global vision, quibbling only that it described America's present rather than Europe's future. "The United States," he claimed, "is already operating according to Cooper's double standard. . . . American leaders too believe that global security and a liberal order—as well as Europe's postmodern paradise—cannot long survive unless the United States uses its power in the dangerous Hobbesian world that still flourishes outside Europe."[101] Kagan's assertion was that the United States was the guardian of the global system, struggling manfully to protect the postmodern paradise of pooled sovereignty and expand a global liberal order without ever fully capitulating to its multilateral rules. America, he thus concluded, "mans the walls but cannot walk through the gate. The United States, with all its vast power, remains stuck in history, left to deal with the Saddams and the ayatollahs, the Kim Jong Ils and the Jiang Zemins, leaving most of the benefits to the others."[102]

Kagan's vision of manning the walls was ultimately not so different from that of the Clinton-era geostrategicians that he and his PNAC associates occupationally railed against. There was certainly what Perry Anderson called "a sharp contrast in atmospherics": the nationalist stridency of the Bush primacy and preemption doctrines versus the "wonderful opportunity" rhetoric of "Bill the Benign."[103] But both approaches to American foreign policy basically shared notions of the United States acting alone on the outskirts of the level playing field to deal with its misfits. Perhaps more aggressive about engagement with these unmanaged outskirts, and veering still further from the cold war geopolitics of containment and exclusion, Kagan's vision still looked a lot like that of Clinton's first term national security advisor. As Lake had himself once put it: "The successor doctrine of containment must be a strategy of enlargement—enlargement of the world's free community of market democracies."[104] Moreover, as Madeleine Albright emphasized in her "indispensable nation" arguments, the reason the United States could be construed as the systems manager of the global process of enlargement lay in a kind of guard-on-the-wall perspective. "We stand tall. We *see* further into the future," she said.[105] Indispensability, in these terms, would seem to have been simultaneously enabled and legitimized by a geoeconomic worldview that not only envisioned an expanding global plain but envisioned it from commanding and specifically American heights.

The similarity with Kagan's image of the United States manning the walls is clear.

It might be protested that the wider PNAC optic was more narrowly nationalistic and not really as geoeconomic as that of the Clinton-era visionaries. Certainly, that was the insinuation in much of the muscular posturing about American traditions of "leadership" by the neoconservatives themselves. For example, in recalling Theodore Roosevelt's call for "warlike intervention by the civilized powers," and remembering Franklin Roosevelt's Atlantic charter, Kagan and Kristol sought to distinguish their vision in precisely this way in 2000 when they set about criticizing what they saw as the overly economic concerns of Clinton's foreign policy. They complained that "[i]n recent years, many American foreign policy thinkers, and some politicians, have come to define the 'national interest' as consisting of plots of ground, sea lanes, industrial centers, strategic chokepoints and the like."[106] Against this definition, they argued that "Americans should once again embrace a broad understanding of the 'national interest,' one in keeping with Roosevelt's vision."[107] However, the very same historical period can equally be reviewed— just like the *Strategy*, PNAC's reports, and Kagan's vision—in terms of the underlying geoeconomic premises that the great historical heroes of the national interest themselves once shared. Indeed, without ever using the term, this is exactly what two of the most recent and most successful historical surveys of American empire have done.

In his much-acclaimed *American Empire,* the retired U.S. military officer Andrew Bacevich argues against the simplistic binary oppositions of multilateralism versus unilateralism to suggest that a much more continuous worldview has shaped American foreign policy. Long before the Clinton era, and reaching back to the leadership of those lionized by Kagan and Kristol, he maintains that American internationalism has been underpinned at a fundamental level by concerns with coordinating and expanding free-market capitalism.[108] Republican and Democrat administrations alike, Bacevich argues, have effectively held to this common global purpose throughout most of the twentieth century.

> That purpose is to preserve and, where both feasible and conducive to US interests, to expand an American imperium. Central to this strategy is a commitment to global openness—removing barriers that inhibit the movement of goods, capital, ideas and people. Its ultimate

objective is the creation of an open and integrated international order based on the principles of democractic capitalism, with the United States as the ultimate guarantor of order and enforcer of norms.[109]

Although much more critical and historically sophisticated, this is also an argument elaborated by the Marxist geographer Neil Smith in another *American Empire* text published amid the buildup to the Iraq war. Examining the period between the Roosevelts in detail, Smith shows how American leaders repeatedly imagined their postcolonial imperium as "a quintessentially liberal victory *over* geography."[110] This "deracination of geography in the liberal globalist vision," argues Smith, "abetted a broad ideological self justification for the American Empire." Moreover it did so, Smith says, because of its economically smoothed worldview. "[This] flattened geography," he concludes, "enabled a politics flattened to the lowest common denominator of American globalism."[111] What Smith calls a "flattened geography" is what I have been calling here geoeconomics, the smooth-world vision that elides the very American dominance that it helps biopolitically to reproduce. And just like Bacevich, Smith sees powerful historical continuities in the American ordering of this open and deterritorialized global space from the early part of the twentieth century right through to today.

Beyond noting the symptoms of geoeconomic vision in the neo-conservatives' prowar geopolitical assertions, and beyond charting historical precedents of geoeconomic discourse in moments of American history that they prefer to script geopolitically, it is also possible to point to some more immediate ways in which geoeconomic assumption also played a direct role in making the war make sense to those who planned and executed it. In this regard I am drawing on another essay I coauthored with Sue Roberts and Anna Secor in which we argued that a key legitimation of the Iraq war rested on a form of "neoliberal geopolitics."[112] Here my additional suggestion is that what made the geopolitical legitimations of preemptive war and American primacy "neoliberal" was the whole way in which they were enframed by an underlying geoeconomic worldview. They reserved a special place for America the systems manager, but the basic system that America was scripted as upholding and the basic system to which the war promoters remained themselves unquestioningly committed was that of globalized free-market capitalism. Again Rumsfeld's regime at the Pentagon provides an example, this time in the shape of an aspiring Department of Defense assistant for "strategic futures," Thomas Barnett.

In March 2003, just as the official war was beginning, Barnett published an article in *Esquire* magazine entitled "The Pentagon's New Map." A primary goal of the article, it seems, was that of legitimation. "Let me tell you why military engagement with Saddam Hussein's regime in Baghdad is not only necessary and inevitable, but good," Barnett enthused.[113] His explanation commenced in the form of a new global cartography that, much like Albright's indispensability axiom and Kagan's picture of America manning the gates of free-market paradise, was premised on the masculinist assumption of a god's eye view. From this perspective, Barnett surveyed the whole world charting the progress (supposedly) of globalization. Those parts of the world seen as fully integrated into the networked world he labeled "the Functioning Core"; those parts deemed disconnected from the global system he described as "the Non-integrating Gap." Asked later in an interview in 2003 about what the "Gap" was, Barnett elaborated as follows:

> The Non-integrating Gap began as a simple set of observations. First, you plot out on a map all the places where we've sent U.S. military forces since the end of the Cold War. Through 2002 that was 132 cases. Then you simply draw a line around roughly 95 percent of them, which, outliers aside, is basically the Caribbean Rim, the Andes portion of South America, most of Africa, the Balkans, the Caucasus, the Middle East, much of Southeast Asia, and interior China. The question I was looking to answer was, "what is it about these countries that continues to demand attention from U.S. military forces?" Basically, these are the countries that are having trouble with globalization.[114]

With this neat retroactive explanation of U.S. intervention, Barnett proceeded to propose a post–cold war security axiom: namely that *"disconnection defines danger."*[115] Only by forcibly reconnecting the countries of the Gap into the globalized system, Barnett argued, could the dangers of terrorism and instability threatening the Core be defused. As he explained to Wolf Blitzer on CNN,

> We've got to shrink these parts of the world that are not integrating with the global economy, and the way you integrate a Middle East in a broadband fashion . . . is to remove the security impediments that create such a security deficit in that part of the world.[116]

It scarcely needs noting that Barnett's "we" here is a distinctly American one. Practically parroting Thomas Friedman, who insists that "America truly is the ultimate benign hegemon and reluctant enforcer,"[117] Barnett's picture of his country evinces innocent pride. On America falls the task of "integrating in broadband fashion"; on the U.S. military falls the responsibility of removing "security impediments"; and only America can in these terms presume to play the role—as Barnett likes to put it—of "Systems Administrator." Moreover, following the same dualistic logic about double standards that Kagan articulated in his vision of America guarding the gates of the liberal global order, Barnett suggests it is entirely appropriate for America to employ other, less liberal, rule sets when acting in the Gap.[118]

> To accomplish this task we must be explicit with both friends and foes alike about how we will necessarily differentiate between our security role within the Core's burgeoning security community and the one we assume whenever we intervene militarily in the Gap. Seeking two sets of rules for these different security roles is not being hypocritical but honest and realistic.[119]

In other words, America can act multilaterally vis-à-vis the Core and unilaterally vis-à-vis the Gap without fundamentally contradicting the overall global system. America can have its illiberal outposts and aggressions on the global plain, but these, everyone must understand, are only about securing and expanding the functioning Core: doing so, moreover, not by containing and excluding the Gap, but by forcibly integrating it into the Core. Here we see the biopolitical force of geoeconomics in embodied geopolitical action. The business school vocabulary and arrogant global vision all combined with the nationalist affect of an up-and-coming officer's assumption that it is the manifest destiny of his country alone to be the systems administrator of the globe. Underneath it all, the deterritorializing dynamics of globalization are assumed to be rendering older geopolitical boundaries irrelevant, but America coded as systems manager can persist in integrating "in a broadband fashion," imposing with force what the "Bush doctrine" asserts is the single, sustainable model for national success: "freedom, democracy and free enterprise."

As an assistant in Rumsfeld's Office for Force Transformation as well as a professor at the Naval War College, Barnett no doubt remains an influential voice. But his ideas are more interesting here as symptoms of a much wider complicity between geopolitics and geoeconomics in the discourses shaping the justification, acceptance, and prosecution of the war.[120] As such, it is worthwhile reflecting on his own assessment of the unique American place in globalization. "We live a very good life under globalization," Barnett told one interviewer, summing up the American situation. "In effect, it allows us to live beyond our means. We export sovereign debt and we import far more than we normally would."[121] This very candid portrait of global financial asymmetry is followed by one more military finesse from Barnett, for he concludes in turn that America effectively pays back to the global system through its work as systems manager. "One of the reasons why countries put up with th[is] arrangement is because we export security," he argued.[122] Thus, even as the mapping of Core and Gap enframes a globalizing world in which American geopolitical aggression is cartographically obscured (by being used to outline the Gap that is then blamed on poor integration with globalization), Barnett nevertheless makes explicit much more widely shared assumptions about American intervention serving at once as premise and protector of the global system.

It should now be clear that to argue that geoeconomic assumptions underpin arguments such as Barnett's is not to deny the coactive force of national geopolitical imperatives. The Iraq war was undoubtedly about American national retribution, and it was also—albeit in a more attenuated way—about reordering the geopolitical matrix of the Middle East along lines long outlined by Israeli right-wingers and their American allies. Moreover, as we shall examine in the next section, the war was also fundamentally about America's access to oil. All of these concerns meant that the "challenge of Iraq" was indeed, as Henry Kissinger himself put it, "geopolitical."[123] But equally all of these concerns could also still be made to coincide with the reproduction of an underlying geoeconomic worldview. As Bush told reporters even in the first flush of his post-9/11 chauvinism: "The terrorists attacked the World Trade Center, and we will defeat them by expanding and encouraging world trade."[124] And, as the war plans took shape in 2003, the same vision remained of American force making free trade and democracy flower in Iraq, precipitating a wider leveling of the Middle Eastern playing field and a geoeconomic domino effect of cascading capitalist opportunity. This admittedly precarious ideological articulation worked, I think, because it was more than just an ideology about the globalizing world that was in play. It worked and remained stable through the prosecution of the war because of the ways in which the geoeconomic assumptions were interlinked into the wider biopolitical organization of American informal imperialism at home.

In the early months of 2003 as the military buildup proceeded apace, Americans were barraged with news about economic anticipations of war. Futures markets had already hedged a spring spike in oil prices; stock and bond markets were factoring in a war "bounce"; television producers were agreeing contracts to fill overseas staffing requirements; reporters were being embedded with the military; the protocols of news censorship were being finalized with media legal departments; satellite time was being purchased in advance; children's war games were being stockpiled in toy shops; flags were selling fast and furious; and large advertising billboards announced in corporate style but without any corporate insignia that "United We Stand." The list went on and on, but considered in its overall mind-numbing banality it appeared as an effective and affective administrative machine: a machine that, like Hardt and Negri's, was intimately tied to the production (and destruction) of political-economic subjects globally, but a machine too that, through the banalities of consumerism, sutured the paradoxical and distinctly American business-class subjectivity of the patriot-globalist. These banalities of the machine at home often belied its uncanny global interdependency: Stars and Stripes regalia with "Made in China" small print, high fashion nationalist clothing colors from French designers, and so on. However, it was the passing comments in the business pages that best illustrated how the whole overarching network of ideas and interdependencies was being reproduced in the core of the core. Here, the geoeconomic arrogance of seeing the whole world as one could be seen to be working on a daily basis to reframe the risks of the geopolitical adventurism in the quotidian vernacular of corporate risk management.

> Extreme Times, Extreme Portfolios: In an era of war and oil shocks, an unconventional mix of risky stocks and cold hard cash may be the prudent strategy.[125]

> The dollar was flat against the euro after some traders speculated a message from Osama bin Laden would make an attack on Iraq more likely.[126]

To some, resolution in Iraq—assuming a swift U.S. military victory and peace within the country—could lead to more uncertainty elsewhere. "If you get Iraq past you, do you think about reprisals, Iran, North Korea?" asks David Cooley, a portfolio manager at J & W Seligman & Co in New York. He worries about the high level of consumer debt in the U.S. and how these unresolved geopolitical issues might weigh on Americans' willingness to keep spending.[127]

The dollar dropped against the euro after Secretary of State Colin L. Powell said the possibility of an attack on Iraq was increasing. In New York, the euro settled at 1.1045.[128]

It's the waiting that makes you nuts, isn't it? The waiting for the war we know is going to happen. . . . It'll start on T.V., and we all know the drill: One reporter in Kuwait City, those bulbous towers glowing in the night sky behind him. Perhaps another in Baghdad with some night-vision tape of anti-aircraft fire leaping into the green sky. Then the speech from the Oval Office we know by heart: U.N. resolutions, defiance, failure to disarm, liberation.[129]

Such a list of news bites from the business pages not only illustrates the normalization of the war, but also captures something of the aura of inevitability that thereby seemed to pass from the usual business-page master-narrative about globalization to the geopolitical master-narratives of American primacy and preemptive strikes. Clearly this was hardly the fashioning of the global multitude, and yet, borrowing from Hardt and Negri, it can still be argued that a certain military-capitalist administrative machine biopolitically secured in such ways the willing geopolitical coalition for war, and it did so, moreover, on fundamentally geoeconomic grounds. This argument is in effect a bigger claim about biopolitics and war than Hardt and Negri themselves tried to make in *Empire*. There they reinterpreted the first Gulf War as a global imperial police action rather than an imperialist American aggression. They acknowledged that the earlier war was led by the United States. However, they claimed that this was *"not as a function of its own national motives but in the name of global right"* (*Empire*, 180; italics in the original). This distinction is what allowed them to suggest in a signature gesture of imperial denial that "[t]he United States is the peace police, but only in the final instance, when the supranational organizations of peace call for an organizational activity and an articulated complex of juridical and organizational initiatives" (181).

More unfortunate than its resonances with Barnett's vision of the United States as systems manager, the weakness of this whole argument was that it ultimately rested on a reading of only the *rhetoric* attending the first Gulf War. It is "the name of global right" on which Hardt and Negri based their case that the war was a police action. By contrast, my suggestion is that more than rhetoric was involved in the promotion of the Iraq war as an act of global management. The war plans were also partly developed, processed, and legitimated through the political-economic practices and neoliberal risk management ideas—including the geoeconomic worldviews— that have emerged in concert with the development of neoliberal globalization. Not only was this more than rhetoric, it was also obviously quite often *different* from the dominant prowar rhetoric (at least in the United States). None of the globalist assumptions and mediations I have been discussing precluded the simultaneous representation of the war in the most jingoistic of geopolitical and nationalist ideological formats. The Murdoch media empire and Fox News were certainly part of the administrative military-capitalist complex, but the last thing it was broadcasting were pastoral views of America as the peace police. The politics were more contradictory than this. If we instead see the war planning and resulting talk as a complicit mix of geopolitical affect and geoeconomic assumption, such contradictions become comprehensible as the contradictions of an informal American imperialism being pushed in the direction of formality and force amid globalized capitalist interdependency. In the next section, I consider in turn how—understood as such—the contradictions became more explicit during the war and yet further strained in its aftermath.

THE CONTRADICTIONS OF WAR: GEOPOLITICAL AFFECT AND GEOECONOMIC ASSUMPTION IN ACTION

It was scripted as "Shock and Awe": the bombing of Baghdad told as a simple orientalist story of an angry America metaphorized by its military hitting back at an evil Arab despot in the only way oriental terrorist types understand.[130] The resulting spectacle involved satellite-guided volleys of thousands of the most expensive armaments in the world, most of them directed from across the planet using global positioning systems to multiple targets the length and breadth of Iraq. But all the dependency on globe-spanning (and often commercially developed) technology aside, and all the benefits to the corporate suppliers of the U.S. military noted, the war remained a mediatized enactment of the old American Western sheriff story. The nation was riding into town again, and though it was doing so by proxy on cruise missiles and drones, it still had the singular shotgun purpose of removing a bad guy who was messing up the expansion of capitalist order in the desert. These affect-freighted geopolitics, shocking and awful and nationally narrated as they were, were also underpinned by less belligerent geoeconomic assumptions. These, like the globe-girdling technologies that enabled them, appeared to do the important background work of legitimating the war for the American and (though, as we shall see, much less successfully) foreign business-class elites who, like Tony Blair, supported the war even though they did not really believe the tall tales about Iraq's weapons of mass destruction.[131] The colonialist romance of executing a degenerate tyrant was twinned in this way with the more comforting globalist idea that the intervention was all about bringing freedom, private property, democracy, and free markets to the middle of the Middle East; that it was therefore ultimately about establishing a beachhead in an olive tree world that would soon thereafter be incorporated into the expanding level plain of globalization. The complicity and combined ideological articulation of these geopolitical and geoeconomic visions only worked, of course, on the assumption that American interests coincided with the good of global capitalism: that the seizure and privatization of Iraqi oil production would defang OPEC and cheapen the price of oil for the engines of business everywhere; and that the anticipated boost to the American economy from the military Keynesianism would create a Ronald Reagan–style recovery and thus the necessary consumptive demand in America to lift other economies out of recession too. This was what business magazines referred to as the "benign war" scenario: not very convincing for the thousands upon thousands of dead Iraqis, to be sure, but comforting all the same for the transnational capitalist class.[132] However, as the war and its aftermath hit more and more obstacles, the contradictions that had been obvious to foreign critics from the beginning started to also become more obvious to the business classes, first abroad and then increasingly in America too.

The problem for the long-term endurance of the geopolitics-geoeconomics articulation was that the war and its economic affects were real events with material consequences. Beneath the "bullets are bullish" shock and awe people were dying and learning to resist, and not just in Iraq. The war catalyzed global resistance, and while much of it was fleeting and, in the case of German and French leadership, minimized by being neoliberalized, wider arguments against the war allowed more and more critics to see the links between neoliberalism and American imperialism. The war effectively concretized the contradictions of a global system purporting to be level while remaining fundamentally asymmetric and American-dominated. In this sense what happened in Iraq represented a performative destabilization of the globalization metanarrative. If, as Pierre Bourdieu and Loïc Wacqant argue, one effect of the big neoliberal globalization story "is to dress up the effects of American imperialism in the trappings of cultural oecumenicism [and] economic fatalism,"[133] the war became a sustained dressing down. And it did so in part, I want to suggest here, because of the impossibility of containing the contradictions of geopolitics and geoeconomics in the context of the American assault and occupation. These contradictions became especially evident in the three main ways through which economic dynamics mediated the violence: namely, the commodity economics, the oil economics, and the financial economics. In all three arenas the intertwining of geopolitics and geoeconomics in the vision of benign war began to unravel.

Were the Bullets Bullish?

In an immediate sense the bullets were indeed bullish. The stocks and bombs story was a happy one, and not just for defense contractors. Despite some early dips as the northern advance of American forces slowed, equity markets ultimately tended upward. The calculus on Wall Street, it seemed, was that the death and destruction in Iraq was preempting deflation and a double-dip recession whether or not there was a terrorist threat from Saddam Hussein to be preempted too. "With United States troops closing on Baghdad," ran one typical report, "investors bid up stocks yesterday, sending markets worldwide strongly higher. More than any economic or corporate profit news, the war is driving stock, bond and oil prices, investors and Wall Street analysts said."[134] Though they did not use Harvey's term, and though more superficial commentary focused merely on rising U.S. consumer confidence, Iraq was thus treated as one more spatial fix for the lingering overcapacity problems of the late 1990s bubble economy.[135] In America itself, the business pages were full of hopeful predictions that the war spending combined with the tax cuts would stimulate a recovery like the one engineered by Reagan's administration in the late 1980s.[136]

As well as boosting equity prices, the war was itself fully commodified. It was produced, packaged, and sold through diverse market mediations, and like a big Hollywood movie, it had all kinds of commercial spin-offs too. Having boasted that it would "be a campaign unlike any other in history," the American general in charge of the attack, Tommy Franks, proceeded to give his press announcements of the war's progress from a $250,000 stage set in Qatar that was designed by the same designer that builds sets for Disney, MGM, and the *Good Morning America* show.[137] The embedded-with-the-military reporting likewise built on the unreal television genre of so-called reality shows, and the war show, in this sense, reached its season finale when President Bush touched down onto a giant "Mission Accomplished" stage set on a real aircraft carrier (moored safely just off the U.S. coast) with the president fully wardrobed for the role of commander and fighter in chief. American viewers should have known all this was coming, though, given that the White House had earlier explained its approach to the planning of the war in crassly commercial terms. In August 2002, before the pantomime in the United Nations, before the vote in Congress, and even before the release of the *National Security Strategy*, Andrew Card, the White House chief of staff, had let slip to reporters asking about Iraq that "From a marketing point of view, you don't introduce new products in August."[138] A critical Frank Rich writing later in the *New York Times* suggested this was a refreshing moment of honesty in the war. "Mr. Card has taken some heat for talking about the war as if it were the roll-out of a new S.U.V," wrote Rich. "But he wasn't lying, and history has already proved him right. This campaign has been so well timed and executed that the new product already owns the market."[139]

Part of the product's success, it seems, was branding. The Bush administration had learned from the fiasco over the Operation Infinite Justice name for the Afghanistan war (which had apparently alienated Muslim believers in the idea that only Allah can promise infinite justice). That war had been rebranded as Operation Enduring Freedom, and the Iraq campaign simply built on the resulting brand recognition with the new name Operation Iraqi Freedom. But it wasn't just the branding that sold the war, it was also the fashioning of the war's appeal to consumers through tried and tested commercial tactics: human interest stories (Jessica Lynch), glossy logos (Showdown with Iraq), sports-style commentating ("kicked-off with cruise missiles," "special forces scored a touchdown," "infantry stepping up to the plate"), and as had also been the case with the first Gulf War, the inevitable appeals to the god-tricks of boyish war games ("the map shows American advances in bold"). Thomas de Zengotita described the allure of the latter well.

> What about those graphics in the papers—the beige-and-gray foldout maps of Iraq, crisscrossed with thrusting arrows showing the progress of columns and with cool symbols for various deployments and engagements? A powerful aura emanated from those pages; it was as if the field commanders were consulting maps just like this one. It was horrifying, if you thought about what was represented—a crushing application of tremendous force against a virtually helpless enemy— but weirdly innocent too, evocative somehow of hobbies.[140]

De Zengotita's point in highlighting this aura was to suggest that it contributed to the romance of American empire, and it clearly did have this sort of geopolitical affect. But again this was consolidated by the convenient convergence of the hobbyist interest in the instruments of intervention with wider and more prosaic capitalist commodity chains, including the production and marketing of war games themselves. Indeed, as a telling example of the wider pattern, toy manufacturers would seem to have at once profited from and contributed to the Iraq war both materially and ideologically.

"The United States' $US20.3 billion toy industry is closely watching the Iraq war with an eye towards new products for Christmas," noted one report.[141] The reporter proceeded to note the mutually enabling and market-mediated relationship between the industry and the military. All kinds of new action figures were brought out to coincide with the appearance of particular military units in the media coverage of the war. As special forces were being sent in, Hasbro produced a desert Tactical Adviser figure, modeled after the army's Delta Forces, and later, a large toy retailer called Small Blue

Planet promoted a lineup of "Special Forces: Showdown with Iraq" figures. "We started work when the 'Showdown' buzzword hit the airwaves," the company's president explained. "There's fierce competition among manufacturers to get the new things out first."[142] At the other end of the war, Blue Box Toys of Hong Kong rushed in the same way to produce a model of Bush in the aviator gear he wore when landing on the USS *Abraham Lincoln* to declare the war over.[143] Meanwhile, a Pentagon spokesman explained that, far from being just commercial emulators of the military, the toy makers were also innovators who made important contributions to the war machine. "The M-16 rifle is based on something Mattel did," he said, before describing the more recent ways in which the Pentagon was researching ideas in little boys' toys. "Inspiration has come from model aircraft (reconnaissance drones), 'supersoaker' water guns (quick loading assault weapons), cheap cellular phones for teenagers (video capable walkie-talkies) and gaming control panels (for unmanned robotic vehicles)."[144] Many other indications of the two-way ties emerged, but perhaps the most remarkable and obscene indication of the interdependency was the Sony corporation's patenting of the term "Shock and Awe" for a new computing game.[145]

The kinds of commercial ties illustrated by the toy business between the war and commodity production were just a small sample of the much bigger networks constituting the industrial-military complex of the war making. Another notable feature of this complex that also underlined the complicity of neoliberal ideology was the role Private Military Companies (PMCs) played in the war. The trend toward outsourcing and thereby privatizing military "work" to such corporatized mercenaries had already accelerated in the early 1990s when Dick Cheney was Defense secretary.[146] Despite endless conflicts of interest (most notably with Cheney subsequently becoming the CEO of Halliburton whose Kellog, Brown and Root unit is one of the largest PMCs in the United States), they captured increasing numbers of Pentagon contracts during the 1990s and, like any other burgeoning business keen to foster support in Washington, formed a trade group, the International Peace Operations Association. The euphemism might once perhaps have seemed to affirm *Empire*'s picture of a global peace police, but it was really much more resonant with Barnett's double-edged depiction of the United States as a systems manager exporting violence and using the tools and techniques of the capitalist system—such as outsourcing—to manage the geoeconomic margins with geopolitical intervention.

The Iraq war created a whole new set of opportunities for the privatized but distinctly American "Peace Operations" of the PMCs. Asked about whether U.N. peacekeeping troops would help with policing in postwar Iraq, one Pentagon official gave a telling answer. "We know we want something a little more corporate and more efficient," he said, while back in the United States a PMC called Dyncorp—which had previously held Pentagon contracts to fly coca eradication missions in Columbia—began to run advertisements on its Web site offering jobs to "individuals with appropriate experience and expertise to participate in an international effort to re-establish police, justice and prison functions in post-conflict Iraq."[147] This was the administrative machine of Hardt and Negri's peace police in action, and yet, of course, it was a distinctly American operation.[148] The working assumption throughout was that Americans and, specifically, American private companies do neoliberalism best. In practice, though, as Paul Krugman bemoaned in a *New York Times* opinion column, the assumptions did not hold up. The privatized system serviced by U.S. PMCs proved anything but efficient and accountable. The cases of American troops torturing Iraqis under instruction from private contractors working for army intelligence were only the most egregious cases of unaccountability.[149] Citing a Newhouse News Service report, Krugman also described how instead "US troops suffered through months of unnecessarily poor living conditions because some civilian contractors hired by the Army for logistics support failed to show up."[150] Subsequently, two senior Democratic congressmen raised other concerns over the extremely inflated price Kellog, Brown and Root was charging the U.S. government for providing, of all things, imported gasoline in Iraq.[151] But mind-boggling as this was—especially so given that Halliburton's other assignments in Iraq included the rebuilding of the oil production infrastructure—it was significant that the congressional critics, like Krugman, effectively issued their criticisms on economic grounds. The greatest leverage for their arguments, it seemed, was not so much outrage at the whole war-making–profit-taking machine, nor even the insider deals for particular PMCs (although Krugman was a stalwart critic of these ties throughout the war), but rather the poor product delivery, bad accounting, and cost overruns of the outsourcing system. Potential worries about unpatriotic privateering (a geopolitical framing) were thus displaced by concerns about accountability and transparency (a geoeconomic framing). In this sense, the PMCs and their political allies (many of them, like Cheney and Richard Perle, in the PNAC patriot circuit) had preemptively neutralized criticism by moving their business onto geoeconomic ground.

The geoeconomic assumptions used by and made manifest in the treatment of PMCs reflected not legalistic ploys but rather their basic economic outlook as private for-profit companies. Halliburton is especially notable in this regard because through its oil and gas business it has regularly infringed geopolitically framed U.S. laws against doing business in countries such as Iran, Libya, and, of course, Iraq (where two companies in which Haliburton held stakes sold Saddam Hussein over $73 million of production equipment during the post–Gulf War period when Cheney was CEO and sanctions were in force).[152] Against the seeming contradictions, Cheney took the god's eye view: "The good Lord didn't see fit to put oil and gas only where there are democratic regimes friendly to the United States."[153] This economic calculus of global opportunity, it needs remembering, here came from the same man who did perhaps the most to promote the Bush doctrines of primacy and preemption. For him and Halliburton, it seemed, the charmed complicity of geoeconomic assumption and geopolitical assertion was complete. The same remains true for a limited number of other military contractors (such as the Bechtel corporation) that have been major recipients of postwar reconstruction contracts in Iraq. For this charmed community of capitalists the links between the global bottom line and American unilateral assertiveness are clear and not at all contradictory. Indeed, while busily profiting from the huge costs being passed on to future U.S. taxpayers and future generations of Iraqis, Bechtel and Halliburton meanwhile continued to fund the costs of neoconservative politicking in Washington, paying for events such as a gala tribute to Wolfowitz as a "Keeper of the Flame" at the right-wing Center for Security Policy.[154] Wolfowitz won that honor (following others such as Reagan, Gingrich, and Rumsfeld) as the policy architect of the war. However, the flame of patriotic leadership he was thereby supposedly keeping was increasingly only visible to the charmed circles funded and guarded by the likes of Bechtel and Halliburton. Elsewhere, among growing numbers of the transnational business class, the heightened contradictions of U.S. informal imperialism (including the crony capitalism of the military contractors) were buffeting the flame of American "leadership" on all sides.

Already extremely fragile in the aftermath of the 1990s bubble, facing huge problems of overcapacity around the world, and experiencing heightened vulnerabilities of global interdependency in commodity production as well as in finance, the representatives of business classes from outside the United States saw their geoeconomic world of boundless opportunity imperiled by the unilateralist war.[155] One indication of this disruption was the changing reception American representatives were greeted to at various corporate gatherings in Europe. At the annual meeting of the World Economic Forum in Davos, for example, John Ashcroft (Bush's Christian conservative attorney general) was looked at askance by global business leaders more accustomed to American leadership from the likes of Bill Gates. They were worried by the prospect of a new American Davos man inclined more toward prayer breakfasts and warmongering than to "friction free" capitalism.[156] As a result, reporters noted that anti-American feeling ran as high inside the conference as outside on the streets where global justice and environmentalist groups also turned their critical ire on America and distributed fake dollar bills with tanks on them. Likewise, the *Financial Times* reported that when Alan Larson, the U.S. undersecretary of state for economic, business, and agricultural affairs, went to Brussels to ask for support in the postwar reconstruction efforts he "met a barrage of criticism" from business leaders.[157] It was not as if all these concerns were about the abstract idea of sustaining global capitalism. Some complainants such as George Brodach from ABB, the Swedish industrial group, were simply worried about why U.S. companies were being awarded all the contracts for postwar reconstruction. But even at this level of critiquing Washington's crony capitalism, foreign corporate criticism worried away at the contradictions in the American position.

At the same time as American emissaries were hearing the criticisms of non-American neoliberals, American commodities were suffering boycotts in foreign stores. The *Washington Post* ran an article that noted in this way that

> While America has won the war in Iraq in less than four weeks and with astonishingly few casualties, it has been suffering collateral damage in another theater of conflict—its trade relations. In the Arab

world, and more seriously in the rich markets of Europe, American companies and their famous brands have been at the receiving end of a small but highly visible boycott movement. In ordinary times this might be shrugged off; in today's fevered atmosphere it is further tinder on the fire—and has all the potential, if unchecked, to have ugly economic consequences.[158]

The actual examples of threats to American exporters were idiosyncratic and dispersed. In Germany:

[a] restaurant chain in Hamburg no longer sells Budweiser, Marlboro or Coca-Cola. An antiwar Web site, www.consumers-against-the-war.de, lists 27 American companies, including American Express and Walt Disney, whose products German consumers should avoid. It has received some 100,000 hits since it was launched a month ago. Bicycle maker Riese and Mueller GmbH has stopped taking supplies from its American contractor.[159]

Meanwhile, in France, the reporter noted,

the spread of "Mecca Cola," a Coca-Cola substitute developed by French entrepreneur Tawfik Mathlouthi, is ominous for what it represents: Tagged with the slogan "No more drinking stupid, drink with commitment," it was launched last November and first sold only in Muslim districts of France. Now it is available in the larger supermarkets in Belgium, France and Germany; and Mathlouthi describes advance orders as "phenomenal." And of course, almost ritually, a McDonald's in Paris has been attacked.[160]

Disparate as they might have been, the attacks on American brands were worrying for the business elites. Back in America itself, leaders of TNCs such as Howard Schulz of Starbucks braced for trouble.[161] More generally, business opinion leaders amplified a concern they had begun to raise at the start of the war. Michael Sesit writing in the *Wall Street Journal* had lamented that the war "unleashed forces that could impact the global economy and financial markets for years." As the war proceeded, Jeff Madrick of the *New York Times* argued that "American unilateral bravado regarding the war would be misplaced and could be costly to the economy." And as the war went from bombing to an unstable occupation with looting and multiple civilian casualties, *Business Week*'s Christopher Farrell worried about how "collateral damage from the war to the global economy is also all too possible."[162] Summarizing these concerns about disruption and underlining the threat they posed to the smooth-world vision of globalization, Stephen Roach of Morgan Stanley stated that "[t]his postwar period is the real challenge for the world and globalization as we know it."[163]

Against the backcloth of these concerns the Bush administration nevertheless pressed ahead with its own geoeconomic expansion plan for the Middle East, a plan centered on converting Iraq into an embodiment of neoliberal doctrine and an anchor of a new Middle East Free Trade Area (MEFTA). In the damning words of free trade critic Naomi Klein, Iraq was thus being "treated as a blank state on which the most ideological Washington neoliberals can design their dream economy: fully privatized, foreign-owned and open for business."[164] "Some argue that it's too simplistic to say this war is about oil," she went on. "They're right. It's about oil, water, roads, trains, phones, ports and drugs. And if this process isn't halted 'free Iraq' will be the most sold country on earth." Just as with the old Washington Consensus, the plan still allowed for all kinds of monopolistic privileges for American corporations, but the overweening ideology remained the geoeconomic one. The fact that the leveling of this blank state had required an asymmetric assault carried out by the most powerful military machine in history, and the fact that the so-called postwar peace demanded an extraordinarily costly military occupation, did not mean that the neoliberal nostrums were all wrong. This, after all, was just the visible fist coming to the aid of the invisible hand, or in Barnett's terminology, the work of systems administration. Against such complicit assumptions, Klein asked two sharply critical questions:

> So what is a recessionary, growth addicted superpower to do? How about upgrading Free Trade Lite, which wrestles market access through backroom bullying, to Free Trade Supercharged, which seizes new markets on the battlefields of pre-emptive wars?

This critique of the geopolitical formalization of American informal imperialism was extremely astute, and Klein's subsequent debunking of the new Washington Consensus was brilliant. "Bush hasn't abandoned free trade," she wrote, noting the neoliberal worries in Europe and elsewhere, "he just has a new doctrine: 'Bomb before you buy.'"

In a subsequent article Klein quoted British journalist Robert Fisk as arguing that the uniform of Paul Bremer, the American administrator of Iraq, said it all: "a business suit and combat boots."[165] This business suit, it might be added, was not just for show. Just before heading off to an economic forum on the MEFTA in Jordan in the summer of 2003, Bremmer announced that his administration would be radically cutting funding for Iraqi state enterprises. "Short term sacrifices," the *Economist* reported him as saying, "would create 'a level playing field' with the private sector. Inefficient industries would close down, or like oil, be privatized."[166] With this symptomatic announcement of yet one more level playing field vision there also came, however, a gigantic catch, a catch that no amount of geoeconomic smoothing could assume away. This was the problem of oil and specifically the economics of postwar oil production, and lack thereof, in Iraq. These, as the *Economist* noted, completely overshadowed the deliberations over the MEFTA and the hopes for the entrenchment of neoliberalism across the Middle East. Moreover, the oil economics, as we shall now see, also comprised a still more contested condensation point for the contradictions in the precarious American articulation of geopolitics and geoeconomics.

Was It a War for Oil?

The geopolitical interpretations of the war by both critics and advocates not only focused on the doctrines of primacy and preemption, they also stressed the issue of American access to Iraqi oil. "No war for oil," critics shouted in street protests around the world. And, in the big antiwar march in Seattle, one of the more ironic protest signs underlined the imperial outlook of the energy grab: "Who put our oil under their sand?" This oil geopolitics interpretation of the war was buttressed in many critics' minds by the close relationship between the Bush administration and Texan oil companies, as well as by the whole history of American oil companies using the U.S. government to secure access to Persian Gulf oil.[167] This was also how it must have seemed to some enterprising soldiers from the 101st Airborne Division in Iraq when they named one forward operating base "Shell" and another "Exxon."[168] More senior military personnel acknowledged the point too, and later on, in June 2003 when still no weapons of mass destruction had been found, Wolfowitz himself explained to reporters that the protesters had basically been right. "Let's look at it simply," he said. "The most important difference between North Korea and Iraq is that economically, we just had no choice in Iraq. The country swims on a sea of oil."[169]

The admission from Wolfowitz was doubly telling because as well as acknowledging the oil imperative he also coded it as an economic one. Here a certain set of geoeconomic assumptions also came into play about the global supply of oil and the smooth functioning of global capitalism. The hope of the neoconservatives, it seems, was to rapidly increase Iraqi oil production, flood the world market with oil, and push the price of oil per barrel down to $15 or less. Such transformations were expected to at once reinvigorate the global economy and destroy OPEC's price-setting capabilities, while also disciplining states such as Iran, Syria, and Libya. Larry Lindsey, one of President Bush's top economic advisors, argued in these ways that "When there is regime change in Iraq, you could add 3 million to 5 million barrels of production to world supply . . . successful prosecution of the war would be good for the economy."[170] On the surface of it such possibilities must have appeared compelling, allowing American geopolitical aggrandizement to again be imagined in terms of improving the global economy and making the world safe for liberal capitalism. The appeal of Iraq's oil in this respect was not just its plenty (the second largest reserves in the world), but its relatively low production costs. According to Thomas Ferguson and Robert Johnson, this meant that (at least in theory) controlling Iraq's supply of oil to the global economy would not only help cap and bring down world oil prices, but also, and just as significantly, serve to prevent global price-gouging by the other main low-cost producer, Saudi Arabia. They explained thus that

> if the Saudis decide, as they have twice done in recent years, to wage a ruinous price war, lowering prices sharply in order to deter other cartel members from overproducing, then Iraq's role is again key. With another low-cost gas station open for business, the Saudis cannot count on maintaining total revenues as prices fall, because they will now have to split the take with the Iraqis. This downward price deterrence will be welcome news to marginal producers [i.e., high-cost producers] around the world, including those in Texas, and it is very important in assessing the long-run impact of the American move.[171]

This picture of Iraqi oil as a regulator on both the upward and downward movement of global oil prices seems much more resonant with a vision of maintaining the smooth operations of global capitalism as a whole. To be sure, there is still the direct American interest in preserving the viability of high-cost production out of the Gulf of Mexico—where Halliburton as an oil production logistics firm has a lot to lose. But, by the same token, the price-capping effect of releasing Iraqi supply would reduce the likelihood of companies like Halliburton benefiting from developing new high-cost facilities in the Arctic National Wildlife Refuge in Alaska. Moreover, it was clear in these prewar economic analyses that the release of Iraqi oil also cut both ways for big American oil companies such as Exxon-Mobil and Chevron. They might gain advantage in Iraq over France's Total-Elf-Fina and Russia's Lukoil, but profiting very well from the preceding system and their business in the rest of the Gulf, their economic interest in the war was counterbalanced by the prospects of adjustment costs and the mid- to long-term likelihood of lower prices. In these anticipations of the impact of the war on oil economics, therefore, the immediately American benefits were less than clear. The expected long-term advantage was imagined instead in terms of the balancing of world supply and predictable prices in a deterritorialized global marketplace.

The big problem with the idea of turning Iraq into a global oil price regulator was that in reality it depended on more than just regime change. Huge infrastructural investments were necessary in order for Iraqi oil to flow in the requisite amounts onto the global market. Before the war Daniel Yergin of Cambridge Energy Research Associates had predicted that the grand vision of flooding the world market and disciplining OPEC was extremely hard to imagine happening in these more practical terms. "[A] 'new' Iraq," he said, "is unlikely to do any flooding, even if it wanted to. The first task of a new regime would be to get production capacity, damaged by the war and poor operating practices, back into gear. Fixing the immediate problems would take time and money. It would take even more time—as well as a great deal of investment and a lot of technology—to get capacity back to where it was in 1979."[172] According to Yahya Sadowski, a growing awareness of these realities also "finally rebutted the neoconservative plan" when PNAC associate Douglas Feith led a Pentagon study in January 2003 that

> learned just enough about oil economics to retreat in horror from the neoconservatives' earlier proposals. Initially, officials at the Pentagon and the White House assumed that they would be able to recoup the costs of the war by dipping into Iraq's oil revenues. . . . But when they did the maths, they made unpleasant discoveries. Expanding Iraq's production will not only take time, it will also be very expensive.[173]

It appeared that at least $58 billion would have to be spent to reach the production goals originally thought possible. The geoeconomic concept of Iraq being reintegrated into the global system as a price regulator (with America simply controlling the geopolitical levers) was not going to be as easy to bring about in practice as it was in the economic graphs of Larry Lindsey. In the context of the postwar occupation these sobering economic realities began to sink in. Oil prices in July 2003 did not go down—staying around $30 a barrel—because of the slow pickup in Iraqi production caused by looting, sabotage, and the legacies of all the years of sanctions and disinvestment. Instead of the 2.5 million barrels a day being produced just before the war started, instead of the 3.5 million barrels a day when Iraqi production was at its height in 1979, and far from the 6 million barrels a day originally anticipated by the neoconservatives, Iraq was only able to produce 8 million barrels in the whole of July.[174]

If the difficulties of restarting Iraq's creaking oil production infrastructure upset ideas of quickly turning the country into a global price and supply regulator, they also indicated a significant chink in the vision of an all-powerful America intervening geopolitically on imperial impulse. To be sure, the Iraqi adventure enabled the United States to establish a long-term base for its military in the Middle East, it destroyed a regime that might one day have threatened Israel and other U.S. client states in the region (had Hussein's military ever recovered from the sanctions), and combined with the bases in central Asia secured by the Afghanistan campaign (including key footholds in Pakistan and the old Soviet satellite states), it also allowed the United States to surround much of Iran. These were more than geopolitical fantasies. They were practical military achievements that not only secured long-term access to Iraqi oil, but also a strong U.S. presence in the whole Caspian oil and gas basin.[175] In Christian Parenti's critical terms, all this established the United States as an "oil gendarme" for the world: a military (not peace) police with a powerful weapon to wield over both East Asia and Europe at once.[176] However, just as Iraq had once been imagined as the geopolitical centerpiece of this sweeping empire, its postwar experience and, in particular, the problems of restarting its oil production began to reveal the economic unsustainability of the overall imperial project. With the costs of occupation spiraling and with scarcely any oil profits to pay for them, a humbled President Bush was forced to return to the United Nations to plead for multilateral financial and military support.[177] However, a senior official from the Bush administration said, "We expect billions of dollars out of the rest of the world. Billions." Meanwhile, an additional $87 billion had to be requested in the form of a supplemental spending appropriation from Congress.[178] Primacy and preemption, it seemed, had found their match in looted pumping stations, sabotaged pipelines, and a degraded oil-production network.

It might be protested that one geopolitical-geoeconomic complicity concerning the global oil supply system nevertheless remained intact and, indeed, resecured in the aftermath of the war. In this view America's war could be understood as having successfully preempted the possibility of switching the currency in which oil is globally traded from dollars to euros. In November 2000 Iraq had switched to only receiving payments for its oil in euros. At first blush it was an accounting shift, hardly a weapon of mass destruction. But its implications for American global influence might well have been huge had other oil producers, particularly those in OPEC, followed suit. It would have led to huge transfers of funds out of dollars into euros as oil purchasers bought euros to pay for oil and oil sellers moved their dollar assets into euros to protect them from a falling dollar. This would have removed one (though, by no means all) of the structural asymmetries elevating the value of the dollar in the global economy, and the result would well have been devastating to a U.S. economy completely dependent on foreign capital investments to fund its monumental current account deficit. By thereby weakening the ability of the United States to borrow in its own currency—an exceptional privilege that, as Gowan and others have long pointed out, lies at the contradictory heart of America's fragile financial dominance—a transfer in oil pricing to euros may well have expedited American hegemonic decline.[179]

The way in which the war preempted a wider switch in oil pricing was by no means just the focus of leftist debate. Mainstream newspaper accounts articulated the same calculus quite directly. The *Boston Globe* published an article suggesting that at minimum a coordinated move to trading oil in euros would decrease America's gross national product by as much as one percent permanently.[180] And in the *Los Angeles Times* business section Ferguson and Johnson explained both the problem and the solution:

> A major prop for the dollar has long been the simple fact that oil is priced in U.S. dollars. If the new Iraqi petroleum authorities announce that they will accept checks only in dollars, invest their sur-

plus in dollars, and swell U.S. exports by contracting principally with American firms for services and goods, the dollar's prospects will brighten.[181]

Not surprisingly, postwar Iraqi petroleum authorities (i.e., the Americans) did make the change back to dollars. But the prospects for the dollar did not brighten as a result. Instead, the lack of meaningful oil exports and the high costs of occupation came together, as we shall now see, with the more chronic and systemic problems facing the U.S. economy to dim dollar prospects and, with them, the long-term viability of the vision of American global systems management. Both the assertion of geopolitical ambition and the assumption of a geoeconomic playing field were in financial jeopardy, and the war had only made things worse.

What Has Been the Financial Fallout?

The day-to-day reporting in the American business pages depicted the end of the war as the "end of uncertainty" and thus, combined with the stimuli of tax cuts and war spending, a good reason to expect a Reagan-style recovery and renewed economic growth. In the third quarter of 2003 this sanguine view saw a certain amount of vindication in rising stock-market indices and increased corporate profits. But the grim news from Iraq of the rising costs of the occupation brought into focus a much more unsettling economic outlook, a future promising little but increasing indebtedness, financial turmoil, and crisis. It was this outlook that threatened both the vision of American geopolitical omnipotence and the enframing geoeconomic assumption of a global level playing field at the very same time.

Well before the war the progressive American economist William Greider summarized the financial threats to the geopolitical vision of primacy in an article suitably entitled "The End of Empire." "The imperial ambitions of the Bush administration," he said,

> are founded on quicksand and are eventually sure to founder. Bush's open-ended claims for U.S. power—including the unilateral right to invade and occupy "failed states" to execute "regime change"—offend international law and are prerogatives associated only with empire. But Bush's great vulnerability is about money. You can't sustain an empire from a debtor's weakening position: sooner or later the creditors pull the plug. That humiliating lesson was learned by Great Britain early in the last century, and the United States faces a similar reckoning ahead.[182]

Greider emphasized that the United States would be unable to keep ignoring the worldviews of its foreign creditors when its debts to them increasingly represented such a large percentage of such a rapidly expanding overall debt load. During the war, the French economist Frédéric Clairmont noted in the same way that, while busily sending thousands of missiles and troops overseas, the United States was simultaneously importing over $2 billion in new foreign capital *per day*. This meant that foreign investors were now holding more than 18 percent of long-term U.S. equity securities and 42 percent of U.S. Treasury bills.[183] As the veteran *New York Times* business commentator Floyd Norris put it in a headline "Foreigners May Not Have Liked the War, but They Financed It."[184] Norris's point was hardly celebratory. He acknowledged that the "flood of foreign money helps to keep interest rates low while supporting the dollar." He also accepted that the war could "be financed relatively cheaply at those low rates." But he returned at the close to the basic point about interdependency: "borrowers may eventually need to pay attention to the views of the lenders. It would not be fun if foreigners began to invest the way they talk."

At the end of the war there were still foreign investors (the Japanese and Chinese in particular were both still buying dollars with a view to keeping their own currencies down and the spending power of American consumers up). However, the short-term economic fun of a "victory" bull market was overshadowed by declines in the value of the dollar and widening concern about whether U.S. interest rates could continue to remain low and growth steady while government borrowing ballooned to pay for the war and Bush's tax cuts. The occupation of Iraq was also starting to look like an increasingly expensive proposition, especially given the lack of oil export receipts. In addition to the $1 billion a week in military expenses and all the investment needed to repair and improve the oil production system, other bills were piling up fast: $5 billion for initial humanitarian aid, $7 billion for repairs to utilities and public services, $3 billion for resettlement costs, and an estimated $200 billion to rebuild all the country's institutions.[185] Moreover, even if the net profits of Iraq's oil exports did reach the unlikely but promised figure of $20 billion a year, much of this money was already spoken for in the form of the $200 billion war reparation debt forced on Iraq after the first Gulf War, $60 billion in contractual debts, and $90 billion in conventional debt to former arms suppliers, most notably the French and Russians.[186] The Bush administration was of course geopolitically inclined to just cancel the latter debts, but the wider economic drain of occupation could not be so arrogantly ignored in light of America's own economic insecurity. It was in this new context that Bush sounded new notes of humility about consensus building, that Colin Powell replaced Donald Rumsfeld as the administration's chief foreign policy spokesman, that Condoleezza Rice's National Security Office took over from the Pentagon in overall Iraqi policy coordination, and that even Wolfowitz talked about how the United States did not "own" the Iraqi situation. Certain cheerleaders of geopolitical imperialism such as the indefatigable Max Boot complained that such changes represented "pragmatism winning out over unilateralism."[187] Nonetheless, the changes began to be more and more marked. Predictions about the limits of a hegemony of force that were made by Perry Anderson before the war now looked correct: "the sputtering of the US economy, where the ultimate foundations of American hegemony lie," he had argued, "does not, in any case, promise the Republican administration a long leash."[188]

Greider's own view had been that the "Bush warriors' reckless American unilateralism [would] only hasten the day when the creditors conclude that they must assert their leverage."[189] While this point about the economic constraints on geopolitical recklessness was well taken, Greider's example of wealthy Saudi investors pulling almost $200 billion out of U.S. financial markets in the buildup to the war represented a much more direct financial tit for tat than was ever likely to happen in the normal course of market movements.[190] In this wider networked world of currency and equity trading America's financial problems had long been acknowledged as well as hedged with all kinds of derivative profit-making. The difference the war and its aftermath made was more in the form of an additional shock to the system. Nevertheless, insofar as the extra costs of the war and occupation coincided with an especially vulnerable moment for global capitalism, they led to increasing deliberations among economists and business elites about the problems of American global economic preeminence. They therefore brought into more explicit focus the defining asymmetries of the not-so-level global financial playing field, and in catalyzing this concern, the economic turmoil exacerbated by the war and its aftermath heralded a crisis in geoeconomic assumptions as much as they humbled the champions of geopolitical primacy.

If the big story in the markets was that the end of the war promised the end of uncertainty, not everyone in the financial world accepted it. "I don't buy that" exclaimed Stephen Roach, the chief economist of Morgan Stanley. Instead, Roach countered, "[t]he big story is the ever-mounting and unsustainable imbalances in our U.S.-centric world."[191] Coming from one of the leaders of global finance, what followed was a clear elaboration of the huge asymmetries and unevenness more normally obscured in geoeconomic flights of fancy about financial deterritorialization.

> In the fourth quarter of 2002, America's current-account deficit surged to an annualized $548 billion, a record 5.2 percent of GDP. Financing such a shortfall requires $2.2 billion of capital inflows each and every business day—hardly a trivial consideration for a postbubble U.S. economy offering low returns. Nor is the situation stable. As the federal budget goes deeper into deficit, the U.S.'s net national savings rate—that of consumers, businesses and the government combined—could easily plunge from late 2002's record low of 1.6 percent toward zero. If that occurs, the U.S. current-account deficit could approach 7 percent of GDP. This would require about $3 billion of foreign financing every business day. History is pretty clear on what would happen next: a classic current-account adjustment. This would entail a very different macro outcome for the U.S.—namely, a weaker dollar, higher real interest rates and a slowdown in domestic demand.[192]

Like other economists focused on the long-term trajectory of the global economy, Roach saw this looming economic crisis as stemming from bigger and broader imbalances than those presented by the geopolitics of war. However, he did see the Iraq war as having two significant effects on the overall macroeconomic situation. First, Roach argued that it threatened to hasten the growth of both the U.S. budget deficit and the current account deficit. This would therefore increase the "adjustment" requirements and, with them, all the attendant dangers of a global economic crash. Second, and still more sweepingly, he suggested that

> the war could spell trouble for globalization. The war threatens to undermine political support for the supranational alliances that have long bound the world together. The possibility, combined with the potential trade frictions arising from a weaker dollar, a supercompetitive

Chinese economy and the outsourcing of white-collar jobs to nations like India, portends tough times ahead for globalization.[193]

Here "globalization" was being used to refer to both the political commitment to a global neoliberal system and the actual economic realities of economic interdependency. In this sense, Roach was also effectively arguing that the war was undermining both the ideological and practical underpinnings of geoeconomics at the same time. The necessary global vision needed to make multilateralism work was becoming harder to muster at the exact same time as the war was unleashing the very economic contradictions that the cant of "multilateral" governance more usually covered up. In the place of a smooth world of deterritorialized financial flows, the war was unmasking the perils of what Roach openly labeled as a dysfunctional U.S.-centric global economy.

Roach's dire predictions from the belly of the global financial beast were not the only cautions on offer to the transnational capitalist class. The *Economist* provided a perhaps still more sobering assessment in September as the bad news from Iraq continued apace. Like Roach it noted that "a dollar crash and a global recession are not the only gloomy possibilities. Equally worrying, and much more likely, is a surge in protectionism . . . [which] would have grave consequences."[194] Again the whole project and vision of globalization was seen as under threat. Ironically, however, having argued at length that the problems stemmed from the world economy "flying on the one engine" of American-centered growth, the magazine concluded that the solution could only lie, once again, in American leadership.

> If America shows the necessary leadership, and others live up to their responsibilities, there is still time to replace the one-engined global economy with a safer model. But if nothing changes, get ready for a crash landing.[195]

Having noted that the Bush administration was not even admitting there was a problem, having argued that the Plaza accords (in which James Baker as U.S. Treasury secretary in 1985 orchestrated a controlled descent for the dollar) would be extremely difficult to restage in the context of globally reduced governmental controls over monetary policy, and having emphasized that American policy priorities were a big part of the problem, this ritual call for American systems administration was contradictory in the extreme. How American "leadership" could do anything but worsen the crisis tendencies was unclear. Indeed, as Roach suggested, the most likely scenario was yet one more attempt to manipulate the global financial system enough to create another speculative credit-binge-cum-consumption-boom in America ahead of the 2004 elections. This hardly augured well for the project to geopolitically engineer a "new" American century. In this sense, Peter Gowan's predictions of unfolding tragedy for *Pax Americana* (in his review of Mearsheimer's *The Tragedy of Great Power Politics*) appeared especially apposite: "The commanding vision of the architects of the American century, from Elihu Root through Stimson and Acheson to the Rockefellers, who believed America's surplus capital could transform and knit the world together, risks turning into something approaching its opposite: A US economy requiring manipulation of global monetary and financial, as well as political relationships to suck in capital to sustain its domestic consumer booms and speculative bubbles."[196] After Iraq, these risks were turning into realities. The days of American arrogance containing and profiting from the imbalances of global finance seemed numbered.

If transnational capitalist-class commentaries about the dysfunctional, one-engined, American-centric global economy represented symptoms (albeit especially influential symptoms) of the failure to hold geopolitical appeals for American dominance and geoeconomic assumptions about globalization coherently together, there were many others. Beyond the mournful predictions of a global economic crash-landing, perhaps the most obvious of all the more immediate symptoms of contradiction was the notable absence of a democracy and free enterprise ripple effect through the Middle East. Tensions only rose as the level-the-playing-field-with-bombs strategy created its entirely predictable blowback of resistance in Iraq and across the region (not to mention a related upsurge in increasingly violent and authoritarian attacks on Palestinians by Israel). Far from igniting a "new era of global economic growth through free markets and free trade" as the *National Security Strategy* had promised, the systems administration of Bush et al. had brought only a growing free trade in violence.

All this is not to deny that at a more micro level American administration in Iraq was attempting in various ways to interpellate and incorporate a new generation of neoliberal visionaries. However, accounts of their faltering attempts to reimagine Iraq along the lines of a neoliberal smooth world order only seemed to make plainer the contradictions of geopolitical and geoeconomic complicity. Take for example the case of Wathiq Hindo, a would-be Iraqi tourism entrepreneur whose vision was described in the *New York Times*. The journalist writing the article approached Mr. Hindo's neoliberal vision with a mix of admiration and disbelief at the absurdity of it all in the midst of the postwar violence.

> At first glance, Iraq may not seem like an ideal place for a holiday in the sun. Terrorists and bandits roam through a bomb-scarred landscape, and gun battles rage by night in the capital. But to Wathiq Hindo, this is the world's next great tourist destination. "You've got all the ingredients," Mr. Hindo said, pointing excitedly at a large map of Iraq on the wall in his spacious offices off Karrada Street. "People still think of this as the birthplace of civilization. You've got Babylon and Nineveh, and near Ur you've got the site of the garden of Eden." Mr. Hindo, a 55-year-old entrepreneur, does not just want to lure history buffs. He envisions package tours, four-star hotels and resorts, American families cruising in minivans down new superhighways, water skiing, maybe even a Disneyland on Lake Habbaniya. Religious tourists will flock to see where Job and Jonas died, or to the Muslim holy cities Najaf and Karbala.[197]

Here, it seems, the whole Iraqi landscape was being reimagined in neoliberal terms and, as such, appeared as inserted (like a tourism promotion pamphlet in the Sunday paper travel section) into the larger geoeconomic space of global competition for touristic consumption spending. The nationalist violence of geopolitical orientalism seemed replaced in this way by the bland but still violently abstracting and homogenizing imperatives of commercial orientalism. Iraq was being imaginatively inducted into the smooth space of the functioning core, a smooth space where the marketplace remakes lived-place in the economistic image of accountancy. Najaf and Karbala were thus to be reimagined yet once more: from holy sites, to terrorism sites, to bomb sights and battle sites, all the way finally to tourism sights, and for the geoeconomic visionary at least, profit sites too perhaps. But at the end of the newspaper account of Mr. Hindo's vision, the incongruity of it all with the quotidian geopolitical struggle over American occupation came violently to the foreground. The reporter was being taken by Mr. Hindo to the site of a potential future attraction when a large boom sounds close by, possibly a grenade. The reporter glanced around warily, but Mr. Hindo scarcely seemed to notice. "You put up a concession here, maybe a tent, people can stop here and have a snack," he said, squinting happily into the setting sun. "It's going to be real nice."

Back in America the contradictions of geopolitics and geoeconomics were also increasingly evident. During the war the PNAC patriot Richard Perle, for example, had been forced to resign from his position as chair of the Pentagon's civilian Defense Policy Board after reporter Seymour Hersh publicized the ways in which Perle was using his influence on the board to enrich himself.[198] Specifically he had been talking geoeconomic talk and lobbying on behalf of a Hong Kong billionaire in order to overcome American opposition to the Chinese buyout of the bankrupt MCI-Worldcom corporation. Perle went back to his geopolitical register immediately and quickly labeled Hersh a "terrorist," but the damage was done and the contradictions of Perle's complicities exposed.[199] Later in 2003 such contradictions also caused problems for Wolfowitz and Rumsfeld themselves when they were obliged to finesse differences between geopolitical Republicans and geoeconomic Republicans over Pentagon outsourcing. The former side wanted a law to oblige the Defense Department to "buy American," but at the risk of not seeming altogether patriotic Rumsfeld felt obliged to declare himself a free trader while Wolfowitz tried to work out language in the buy-American bill that would allow enough freedom (and thus free trade) to keep the office of the U.S. trade representative and other administration neoliberals happy.[200]

To some extent, the brouhaha over the buy-American bill represented another case of successful ideological crisis-management, but the same was not possible for perhaps the best example of a contradictory breakdown in geopolitical-geoeconomic complicity: the public furor over retired Admiral John Poindexter's terrorism futures market plan. Poindexter, infamous to many but not seemingly enough Americans for his role in the Reagan-era Iran-Contra free trade deals, had been working behind the scenes in Rumsfeld's Pentagon where his unit had come up with a creative scheme to establish a futures market that would supposedly predict future terrorism strikes. Examples of the sorts of bets that could be made on this market were given on the project's Web site and included such events as the overthrow of the king of Jordan, a missile strike by North

Korea, and the assassination of Yasir Arafat. It was just another attempt to reframe geopolitics in geoeconomic terms. Speculators from all over the world would have been able to access the market and place bets on the chances of terrorism strikes all over the world. The site would thereby supposedly have provided valuable information to the Pentagon about where it would have to intervene. But given the bizarre implications of how the Pentagon might address future investor complaints that its preemptive geopolitics represented unfair government intrusion into the marketplace, and considering the still more absurd anticipations of what insider trading might look like on this market, the plan quickly became a futures market without a future.[201] Senator John Warner, the powerful Republican chair of the Senate Armed Services Committee called it "a very significant mistake," and with a tacit acknowledgment of the geoeconomic inventiveness of the project, Wolfowitz noted that "[i]t sounds like they got too imaginative in this area."[202]

CONCLUSIONS UNBOUND

The contradictory and, as I have shown, increasingly crisis-bound complicity between geopolitical assertion and geoeconomic assumption by no means describes all of the complexities and brutalities of the Iraq war. However, it does take us beyond the crippling either-or intellectual debates that set up American imperialism as a power structure or project somehow separate from neoliberal globalization. As Thomas Friedman is ever keen to remind us, we need instead to understand how these forces come together.

> The United States can destroy you by dropping bombs and the Supermarkets can destroy you by downgrading your bonds. The United States is the dominant player in maintaining the globalization gameboard, but it is not alone in influencing the moves on that gameboard. This globalization gameboard today is a lot like a Ouija board—sometimes pieces are moved around by the obvious hand of the superpower, and sometimes they are moved around by the hidden hands of the Supermarkets.[203]

Here Friedman's Ouija board is just another metaphor for the level plain of geoeconomics, and as we have seen, his own complicitous discourse (double entendre intended) can thus be seen to reflect the much more widely shared assumptions about the role of the United States as the level game board's player-manager. It is this distinctively double-decked worldview that overdeterminies what I have problematized in this chapter's title as empire's geography. If we want to understand the ongoing transnational graphing of the geo of American state hegemony, I am suggesting that we need to come to terms thus not just with the god-trick of globalist geoeconomics, but also with what might be called a Jesus-trick: a Jesus-trick imagined in the geopolitically incarnate form of the U.S. military coming down to earth (or at least dropping bombs down to earth) and bringing neoliberal apostates and agnostics into order.[204] Perhaps the best intellectual rendering of the resulting double vision came in the midst of the buildup to the Iraq war with the publication of Phillip Bobbitt's symptomatic *The Shield of Achilles*.[205] Even the anachronistic Christian rhetoric of the book's dedication—"To those by whose love God's grace was first made known to me and to those whose loving-kindness has ever since sustained me in His care"—alludes to the godly imaginations that follow for readers who can bear to go beyond the Baptist unction. If they do they are exposed to an argument of enormous arrogance (as well as eloquence) that builds on its author's god's eye view as a powerful Washington intellectual: a nephew of Lyndon Johnson, a law professor in both Texas and Oxford, and a former Director of Intelligence on the National Security Council under Clinton. What makes Bobbitt's vision a double one, though, is that he combines all kinds of geopolitical assertions about the need for American leadership with a remarkably lucid discussion of neoliberal globalization, or what he likes to portray as the rise of "the market-state." He suggests along the way that the market-state's indifference to justice not only relates to the transnational entrenchment of the free market and "the cliché 'level playing field,'" but also stems from the military and technical legacies of the cold war.

> The rocket technology developed to deliver weapons in the Long War has propelled man into a perspective from space; his communications technology, also developed for strategic reasons, has sent back an image from that perspective. I am inclined to think that something of the market-state's indifference to fate and sensitivity to risk is related to this reorientation, where the illusion of limitless opportunity meets the reality of choice.[206]

This is part of his wider argument about how the legacies of one military-cum-constitutional order shape the next, but it also illustrates an uncanny awareness of the illusions that attend the Father and Son god-tricks of geoeconomic and geopolitical perspective. As the war went on, these illusions became clearer to many critics too, critics for whom the "reality of choice" was resistance: not Bobbitt's Achilles Shield so much as American imperialism's Achilles heel. Roy's critique of the illusory military-cum-corporate missionary mandate was one of the best:

So here we are, the people of the world, confronted with an Empire armed with a mandate from heaven (and, as added insurance, the most formidable arsenal of weapons of mass destruction in history). Here we are, confronted with an Empire that has conferred upon itself the right to war at will, and the right to deliver people from corrupting ideologies, from religious fundamentalists, dictators, sexism and poverty by the age-old, tried-and-tested practice of extermination. Empire is on the move, and Democracy is its sly new war cry. Democracy home delivered to your doorstep by daisy cutters. Death is a small price to pay for the privilege of sampling this new product: Instant-Mix Imperial Democracy (bring to a boil, add oil, then bomb).[207]

For Roy such Democracy with a capital D is just "Empire's euphemism for neo-liberal capitalism" because capitalists "have mastered the technique of infiltrating the instruments of democracy—the 'independent' judiciary, the 'free' press, the parliament—and moulding them to their purpose."[208] Yet Roy did not reproduce smooth-world discourse in the course of critiquing this biopolitical machine. Speaking in New York at the height of the war, she told her American audience that they had a special role to play in rejecting the instant-mix imperial democracy. "You have access to the Imperial Palace and the Emperor's chambers," she argued. "Empire's conquests are being carried out in your name, and you have the right to refuse."

Much more might be said about how the complicity of geo-economics and geopolitics relates to the material archipelagoes of American TNCs and American military bases around the world, and how they thereby at once underpin and reflect what the radical historian Bruce Cummings once called a "Global Realm With No Limit, Global Realm With No Name."[209] Here, however, I have been more narrowly focused on how the complicity underpinned the war in Iraq. A much more detailed geographical critique by Derek Gregory of the visioning of the assault has described the mediatized American depiction and projection of the violence in the terms of "Boundless War."[210] Gregory's damning critique of this visioning of the violence highlights with great precision and detail what had to be bounded out—including the horrendous Iraqi injuries and casualties that "embedded" reporting ignored—for the war to be effectively legitimated and thereby pursued without limits and beyond bounds. Here, by contrast, I have focused on how the war depended at the same time on the ideological binding of ideas about American geopolitical destiny to the geoeconomic concept of a boundless smooth world order. In the latter part of the chapter, I have also sought to show how this working complicity has been subject to all kinds of contradictory convulsions in the context of Iraq's occupation. But if understanding the force of geoeconomics, geopolitics, and their articulation helps us unpack empire's geography and increasingly unstable foundations, what do they tell us about the geography of *Empire* the book?

By this point it should be clear that the main concern about Hardt and Negri's project at issue here is the way in which it encrypts a privileged place for America in the midst of a geoeconomic scripting of smooth-world space. It is, I have suggested, this very same gesture that Barnett and so many others repeat in their gung ho arguments about America's constitutional manifest destiny to manage globalization. Insofar as the war has illustrated the practical force of this geoeconomics that encodes and allows for American privilege, it also has a number of theoretical implications for the kinds of arguments advanced in *Empire*. It has revealed first of all the dangers of reproducing discourses of imperial denial in the context of offering critical accounts of globalization. Second, it has obviously also made manifest the need to examine how the ideological encoding of American privilege relates to real but by no means permanent privileges relating to America's long experience with the liberal model of laissez-faire capitalism. And third, by thematizing American dominance it has provided at least a starting point for investigating the likelihood of its decline. In the last part of this chapter I have suggested that a real decline is clearly in the financial offing, but having made this case, I do not want to suggest that imminent hegemonic collapse is certain. Such chiliastic accounts of economic doom are, just like Hardt and Negri's account of the jump from imperialism to empire, ultimately disabling. For one thing, as Gindin and Panitch suggest, such crisis theories of American capitalism risk ignoring the continuing victories of the U.S. capitalist class ranging from their successful extraction of extra work hours from American workers, to the not unrelated production of a docile body politic, to the global entrenchment of neoliberal norms. They note thus that "by focusing on the fragility of American capitalism and searching for data that provide evidence of the next and deeper crisis, the left tends to downplay the significance of the continuing capacity of American capital and the American state to restructure the world 'in its own image.'"[211] One result, they argue, is that the Left has frequently failed "to come to terms with the reconstitution of American Empire that followed the crisis of the early seventies."[212] This is the point I have repeated here by arguing that we need to examine how the globalization dynamics that supposedly eclipsed American hegemony in the 1970s instead generated a biopolitically productive regime that has actually worked to legitimize and consolidate ongoing and generally informal forms of American imperialism right up to the present. The fact that this work of legitimation now appears threatened by all the extra geopolitical affect it has been obliged to carry is hardly cause for great celebration.

It would be comforting to end like Hardt and Negri do with an affirmative appeal to the spirit of the multitude to resistance, but instead of genuflecting before Saint Francis of Assisi the protocommunist, I am arguing against god-tricks of all kinds, including faith in some ineffable global resistance. There were of course many concrete examples of resistance to this latest war. Some like that of Gerhard Schröder, the German leader, were quickly and predictably revoked afterwards.[213] But the more globally networked antiwar movement was more persistent, and partly so because of its articulation—as in Roy's arguments—of a simultaneous critique of neoliberalism too.[214] This is not to invoke a global community of the multitude at all. If anything, the war has taught us that the worn-out fictions of global community, global village, and global level playing field have been used in the interests of American dominance once too often. But understood as overburdening geoeconomics with a geopolitical project that cannot last, the war has revealed the critical importance of examining and critiquing how American imperialism works in conjunction with neoliberal globalization. Such a critique, I have argued, can only really begin when imperialism and globalization are no longer posed as binary opposites, and no longer seen as the exact same thing. To avoid these parallel pitfalls of compartmentalization and homogenization, studying the complicity of geoeconomics and geopolitics seems a useful first step.

After all the pages of this chapter and after all the argument of this book as a whole it may seem strange to end with talk about making first steps. However, if there is one clear conclusion of *In the Space of Theory* it is that the geographies of displacement and disjuncture disclosed by deconstructive graphings of the geo in geography can never be fully finalized. This is not to deny the political, economic, and cultural geographic forces that remake social life in powerful, sometimes lethally, finalizing ways. American military force contradicts such inane arguments on a daily and panglobal basis. It is rather to make the critical intellectual point that our work of charting such forces is never done, and that we must persistently examine our own complicities with dominant discourse in the process of attempting to produce such charts. One strategy for such persistent critique, the one that I have offered in the preceding chapters, has been to focus on the ways in which critical postfoundational work, however deterritorializing it may be vis-à-vis certain cherished political categories, can often end up reterritorializing the dominant spatial rubrics of the nation-state along the way. Against this I have suggested that the heterogeneous geographies disclosed by the displacements and disjunctures of North American nation-states demand another, more geographically critical kind of approach. In attempting to chart this approach my own mappings have no doubt foreclosed diverse political struggles. My own concluding hope therefore is that others can turn the force of persistent critique on my own arguments and disclose other critical geographies that I have left obscured. From Justice McEachern's B.C. courtroom to Cascadia's boardrooms to NAFTA's negotiations to the divergent citizenship reforms relating to welfare in the United States and the constitution in Canada, I have introduced spaces of such diversity that the elisions have also been many. Other geographical struggles continue aplenty: or at least they should, so long as geopolitical and geoeconomic complicities charted in this chapter do not smooth them out. Persistent critique, in this sense, is not just about the heterogeneity of human geography, but about the continuing viability of life itself.

Notes

INTRODUCTION

1. Gayatri Chakravorty Spivak, "Translator's Preface," in Jacques Derrida, *Of Grammatology*, trans. G. C. Spivak (Baltimore: Johns Hopkins University Press, 1976), lxxxii.

2. Other scholars have read Derrida's deconstructions of the center and margin as operating "geographically as well as conceptually, articulating the power relationships between the metropolitan and colonial cultures at their geographical peripheries." Robert Young, *White Mythologies: Writing History and the West* (New York: Routledge, 1990), 22. Noticing these interarticulations, however, does not adequately answer Spivak's concern that, "[P]aradoxically, and almost by reverse ethnocentrism, Derrida insists that logocentrism is a property of the West." "My final question . . . is plaintive and predictable: what about us? . . . The multiple, oppressive, and more than millennial polytheistic tradition of India has to be written out of the *Indo*-European picture in order that the difference [in this case between the white masculine West and the rest] may stand." These quotations are taken from two different places: Spivak, "Translator's Preface," lxxxii, and Gayatri Chakravorty Spivak, *In Other Worlds: Essays in Cultural Politics* (New York: Routledge, 1988), 140.

3. See Jacques Derrida, "White Mythologies," in *Margins of Philosophy*, trans. Alan Bass (Chicago: University of Chicago Press, 1982). Derrida makes his own argument by blurring the meaning of the words of Polyphilos in Anatole France's *Garden of Epicurus*. He is thus able to move from the cynic's claim that the output of philosophy is only a bloodless form

of analogy, that it is an "anemic mythology," to the idea that the concepts of Western Reason have come in part from elsewhere, their non-West, metaphorical past glossed as such as nonwhite by a superseding "white mythology." Thus, claims Derrida, "[w]hite mythology—metaphysics has erased within itself the fabulous scene that has produced it, the scene that nevertheless remains active and stirring, inscribed in white ink, an invisible design covered over in the palimpsest" ("White Mythologies," 213). It is here, with this description of "an invisible design covered over in the palimpsest," that Derrida's argument suggests a way of problematizing the anemic geography of the "historico problematic terrain" of white mythology and its discontents. In this context, the philosopher does not pursue directly questions relating to the racialization of "the West" as such, and, as Spivak argues with respect to his more general argument, he still more problematically treats logocentrism (although not phonocentrism) as "a property of the West." Yet with these limits noted, the notion of a dissembling palimpsest he introduces in this context remains, as we shall see, instructive.

4. Toni Morrison, *Playing in the Dark: Whiteness and the Literary Imagination* (New York: Vintage Books, 1992), 3.

5. See Uday Mehta, *Liberalism and Empire: A Study in Nineteenth Century British Liberal Thought* (Chicago: University of Chicago Press, 1999). For a further discussion of the continuities between liberalism and neoliberalism, see Katharyne Mitchell, *Crossing the Neo-Liberal Line: Pacific Rim Migration and the Metropolis* (Philadelphia: Temple University Press, 2004).

6. Michel Foucault, "Questions of Geography," in *Power/Knowledge: Selected Interviews and Other Writings, 1972–1979,* ed. Colin Gordon (New York: Pantheon, 1980).

7. Gayatri Chakravorty Spivak, "Can the Subaltern Speak?" in *Marxism and the Interpretation of Culture,* ed. Lawrence Grossberg and Cary Nelson (Urbana: University of Illinois Press, 1988), 291. An updated version of this essay subsequently appeared as the second part of her chapter on History in Gayatri Chakravorty Spivak, *A Critique of Postcolonial Reason: Toward a History of the Vanishing Present* (Calcutta: Seagull Books, 1999). In this version, Spivak connects the critique of Foucault still more directly to an engagement with the globality of neoliberal globalization and the Bretton Woods organizations.

8. Spivak, "Can the Subaltern Speak?" 290. In both the 1988 and 1999 versions of the argument Spivak suggests that the critique of Foucault's screen allegories could also be extended to "the ferocious motif of 'deterritorialization' in Deleuze and Guattari." Ibid., 279.

9. Gayatri Chakravorty Spivak, "Subaltern Studies: Deconstructing Historiography," in *The Spivak Reader,* ed. Donna Landry and Gerlad Maclean

(New York: Routledge, 1996), 229–30. Her point as I understand it is that while the historians explored the ways in which peasant systems of territoriality underpinned (and thus ultimately obstructed) subaltern agency and while they addressed the ways actual women contributed to subaltern struggle, they ignored the role the discourse of women played in securing the consanguinal systems of communal power. The resulting "tension between consanguinal and spatial accounts" that Spivak reads as being "shared by subaltern and historian alike" is thereby explained as a product of discourses in which the figure of woman serves as "the neglected syntagm of the semiosis of subalternity or insurgency." Ibid., 230 and 228.

10. Gayatri Chakravorty Spivak, "Woman in Difference: Mahasweta Devi's *Douloti the Bountiful*," in *Nationalisms and Sexualities,* ed. Andrew Parker, Mary Russo, Doris Sommer, and Patricia Yaeger (New York: Routledge, 1992), 96–117.

11. Spivak, *In Other Worlds,* 244–45.

12. See Jacques Derrida, "Signature, Event, Context," in *Margins of Philosophy,* 307–30.

13. Ibid., 316.

14. Gayatri Chakravorty Spivak, *The Post-Colonial Critic: Interviews, Strategies, Dialogues,* ed. Sarah Harasym (New York: Routledge, 1990), 120.

15. Spivak suggests something similar herself in her Derridean/Heideggerian meditation on responsibility and the ecologies of the grounds of Development discourse. In a scientized discussion of flood control she thus reads "only half fancifully, that the grounding of the ground is evident . . . as one thinks from the worlded world." Gayatri Chakravorty Spivak, "Responsibility," in *Gendered Agents: Women and Institutional Knowledge,* ed. Silvestra Marinello and Paul A. Bove (Durham: Duke University Press, 1998), 43.

16. See Jonathan Culler, *On Deconstruction: Theory and Criticism after Structuralism* (Ithaca, NY: Cornell University Press, 1982), 97.

17. Derrida, *Of Grammatology,* 69.

18. See also Jacques Derrida, "Freud and the Scene of Writing," in *Writing and Difference,* trans. Alan Bass (Chicago: University of Chicago Press, 1978).

19. Spivak, "Translator's Preface," xlv.

20. Derrida's later essay on the production and delivery of truth in psychoanalysis goes further in this regard, notably with its brilliant critique of Lacan's triangulations of truth in the anemic space of the mirror stage and its imaginary reflections. See Jacques Derrida, *The Post Card: From Socrates to Freud and Beyond,* trans. Alan Bass (Chicago: University of Chicago Press, 1988). Nevertheless, he remains even here more preoccupied with the linguistic as opposed to the geographic writing of consciousness. For a

more extended discussion of Derrida, Freud, and the spatiality of *fort-da*, see Matthew Sparke, "Writing on Patriarchal Missiles: The Chauvinism of the Gulf War and the Limits of Critique," *Environment and Planning A* 26 (1995): 1061–89.

21. In Raoul Mortley, *French Philosophers in Conversation* (New York: Routledge, 1991), 100.

22. For a debunking of such gloomy relativism, see Spivak, "Translator's Preface," xiii.

23. See Jacques Derrida, "The Ends of Man," in *Margins of Philosophy*, 109–36.

24. On how deconstruction is not a liquidation of "the subject," see Jacques Derrida, "'Eating Well' or the Calculation of the Subject," in *Who Comes After the Subject?* ed. Eduardo Cadava, Peter Connor, and Jean-Luc Nancy (New York: Routledge, 1991), 96–115.

25. Jacques Derrida, *Specters of Marx: The State of the Debt, the Work of Mourning, and the New International,* trans. Peggy Kamuf (New York: Routledge, 1994), xix. The italics are in the original.

26. Ibid.

27. Gayatri Chakravorty Spivak, *Thinking Academic Freedom in Gendered Postcoloniality* (Cape Town: University of Cape Town Press, 1992).

28. Spivak, "Can the Subaltern Speak?" 280.

29. Gayatri Chakravorty Spivak, "Ghostwriting," *diacritics* 25, no. 2 (1995): 82.

30. Derrida, *Specters of Marx,* 32.

31. Quoted in Leslie Sklair, *The Transnational Capitalist Class* (Oxford: Blackwell, 2001), 149.

32. Gayatri Chakravorty Spivak, "Feminism and Deconstruction, Again: Negotiating with Unacknowledged Masculinism," in *Between Feminism and Psychoanalysis,* ed. Teresa Brennan (New York: Routledge, 1989), 206.

33. Spivak, *Post-Colonial Critic,* 40.

34. Wolfgang Natter and John Paul Jones III, "Signposts towards a Poststructuralist Geography," in *Postmodern Contentions: Epochs, Politics, Space,* ed. John Paul Jones III, Wolfgang Natter, and Theodore R. Schatzki (London: Guildford Press, 1993), 193.

35. David Campbell, *Writing Security: United States Foreign Policy and the Politics of Identity* (Minneapolis: University of Minnesota Press, 1998).

36. Gearoid Ó Tuathail, "(Dis)placing Geopolitics: Writing on the Maps of Global Politics," *Environment and Planning D: Society and Space* 12 (1994): 332.

37. Miranda Joseph, *Against the Romance of Community* (Minneapolis: University of Minnesota Press, 2002); Michael Shapiro, *Violent Cartographies: Mapping Cultures of War* (Minneapolis: University of Minne-

sota Press, 1997); and Donald S. Moore, Jake Kosek, and Anand Pandian, *Race, Nature, and the Politics of Difference* (Durham: Duke University Press, 2003).

38. Cindi Katz and Neil Smith, "Grounding Metaphor: Towards a Spatialized Politics," in *Place and the Politics of Identity*, ed. Michael Keith and Steve Pile (New York: Routledge, 1993), 67–83.

39. Geraldine Pratt, "Spatial Metaphors and Speaking Positions," *Environment and Planning D: Society and Space* 10 (1992): 241–44.

1. TERRITORIES OF TRADITION

1. Quoted in Don Monet and Skanu'u (Ardythe Wilson), *Colonialism on Trial: Indigenous Land Rights and the Gitksan and Wet'suwet'en Sovereignty Case* (Philadelphia, PA: New Society Publishers, 1992). At the time of the trial the spelling for Gitxsan that was used was Gitksan. Throughout this chapter, including in quotations such as the one used here, I have amended these spellings to "Gitxsan" with an "x," the now more widely used alternative.

2. M. Smith, *Our Home or Native Land? What Governments' Aboriginal Policy is Doing to Canada* (Toronto: Stoddart, 1995).

3. *Delgamuukw v. the Queen*, Supreme Court of British Columbia, Action No. 0843, Smithers Registry, June 2, 1988, 6871.

4. R. Cole Harris, ed., Geoffrey J. Matthews, cartographic designer, *Historical Atlas of Canada*, vol. 1, *From the Beginning to 1800* (Toronto: University of Toronto Press, 1987), unpaginated. Hereafter, this volume will be referred to as *Historical Atlas*, vol. 1.

5. Some of this was from the Ontario government, but most came in the form of a succession of Social Sciences and Humanities Research Council grants beginning in 1979. See Anne B. Piternick, "The Historical Atlas of Canada / The Project Behind the Product," *Cartographica* 30, no. 4 (1993): 21.

6. Jean-Pierre Wallot, "Foreword II," in *Historical Atlas*, vol. 1, unpaginated.

7. J. M. Bumstead, "Putting It on the Map," *The Beaver* 68 (1988): 53.

8. William Westfall, review of *Historical Atlas*, vol. 1, *Ontario History* 80, no. 3 (1988): 261.

9. Piternick, "Historical Atlas of Canada," 21.

10. Benedict Anderson, *Imagined Communities: Reflections on the Origin and Spread of Nationalism*, rev. ed. (London: Verso, 1991).

11. Edward Said, *Culture and Imperialism* (New York: Alfred A. Knopf, 1993).

12. Ibid., 51.

13. Ibid., 226.

14. Wallot, "Foreword II."

15. Homi Bhabha, "DissemiNation: Time, Narrative and the Margins of the Modern Nation," in *The Location of Culture* (New York: Routledge, 1994), 148. Hereafter referred to in the text as "DissemiNation." An earlier version of the essay with some slightly different formulations of the same basic argument was published as Homi K. Bhabha, "DissemiNation: Time, Narrative and the Margins of the Modern Nation," in *Nation and Narration,* ed. Homi K. Bhabha (New York: Routledge, 1990), 319–42.

16. *Delgamuukw v. the Queen,* 6871.

17. Alan McEachern, "Reasons for Judgement: Delgamuukw et al. v. The Queen in right of British Columbia et al.," *Dominion Law Reports,* 4th series, 79 (1991): 185–640.

18. Appeal Transcripts, *Delgamuukw, also known as Earl Muldoe, suing on his own behalf and on behalf of the members of the Houses of Delgamuukw and Haaxw (and others suing on their own behalf and on behalf of thirty-eight Gitksan Houses and twelve Wet'suwet'en Houses v. Her Majesty the Queen in Right of the province of British Columbia* (Ottawa: Supreme Court of Canada, 1997).

19. S. Bell, "In Historic Judgement, Top Court Strengthens Indian Land Claims," *Vancouver Sun,* December 12, 1997, A1–A2; Anthony dePalma, "Canadian Indians Celebrate Vindication of Their History," *New York Times,* February 9, 1998, A1 and A8.

20. See the official Gitxsan and Wet'suwet'en Web pages at http://www .gitxsan.com/html/treaty.htm and http://www.wetsuweten.com/home.htm. The Wet'suwet'en pages addressing the aftermath of the trial note that "The Supreme Court decision strongly reinforces what our Chiefs and Elders have always told us and taught us. The decision itself outlines the legal principles of Aboriginal title, outlines how Aboriginal title is constitutionally protected, and stated the nature of proving Aboriginal title. The decision clearly left the possibility for us to go back to trial and prove our Aboriginal Title but prefers that First Nations and the government sit down and negotiate in good faith." From http://www.wetsuweten.com/dpts/tn/ court/decision.htm (accessed December 11, 2003). The Gitxsan treaty chiefs note that in 1999 "[s]mall progress was made and a bilateral Reconciliation Agreement was signed with the province." The then left-of-center New Democratic Party government in British Columbia agreed to come back to the treaty table with the Gitxsan and Canada under the B.C. Treaty Process. However, the chiefs note that these treaty "[t]alks have been slow due to the B.C. Liberal government's decisions to refuse to discuss governance issues and to hold a provincial vote on minority rights described as

a treaty referendum." From http://www.gitxsan.com/html/treaty.htm (accessed December 11, 2003).

21. Although according to Aijaz Ahmad, Bhabha's work also essays a defense of the nation from the postmodern relativist abyss. "[It comprises] a very considerable effort, albeit in very arcane ways, to pre-empt other kinds of critiques of nationalism by offering plays on 'poststructuralist theories.'" Aijaz Ahmad, *In Theory: Classes, Nations, Literatures* (London: Verso, 1992), 69.

22. For another critical geographical supplementation of Bhabha's wider argument about hybridity, see Katharyne Mitchell, "Different Diasporas and the Hype of Hybridity," *Environment and Planning D: Society and Space* 15 (1997): 533–53.

23. See J. B. Harley, "Deconstructing the Map," in *Writing Worlds: Discourse, Text and Metaphor in the Representation of Landscape*, ed. Trevor J. Barnes and James S. Duncan (New York: Routledge, 1992), 231–47; Harley, "Silences and Secrecy: The Hidden Agenda of Cartography in Early Modern Europe," *Imago Mundi* 40 (1988): 57–76; Harley, "Maps, Knowledge, and Power," in *The Iconography of Landscape*, ed. Denis Cosgrove and Stephen Daniels (Cambridge: Cambridge University Press, 1988), 277–312; and Harley, "Re-reading the Maps of the Columbian Encounter," *Annals of the Association of American Geographers* 82, no. 3 (1992): 522–42.

24. Harley, "Silences and Secrecy," 61.

25. Mark Monmonier, "The Rise of the National Atlas," *Cartographica* 31, no. 1 (1994): 1.

26. Ibid.

27. Henri Lefebvre, *The Production of Space,* trans. Donald Nicholson-Smith (Cambridge, MA: Blackwell, 1991), 86.

28. For a full discussion of his argument to this effect, see Derek Gregory, *Geographical Imaginations* (Cambridge, MA: Blackwell, 1994), especially 382–406.

29. Lefebvre, *Production of Space,* 194.

30. Michel Foucault, "Two Lectures," in *Power/Knowledge: Selected Interviews and Other Writings, 1972–1979,* ed. Colin Gordon (New York: Pantheon, 1980), 98.

31. This is an argument I have made more extensively elsewhere; see Matthew Sparke, "Between Demythologizing and Deconstructing the Map: Shawnadithit's New-Found-Land and the Alienation Of Canada," *Cartographica* 32, no. 1 (1995): 1–21. See also Barbara Belyea, "Images of Power: Derrida/Foucault/Harley," *Cartographica* 29, no. 2 (1992): 1–9.

32. Timothy Mitchell, "The Limits of the State: Beyond Statist Approaches and Their Critics," *American Political Science Review* 85, no. 1 (1991): 77–96.

33. Michel Foucault, *The History of Sexuality*, trans. Robert Hurley (New York: Pantheon, 1978), 85.

34. Denis Wood and John Fels, "Designs on Signs: Myth and Meaning in Maps," *Cartographica* 23, no. 1 (1986): 64.

35. Timothy Mitchell, *Colonising Egypt* (Cambridge: Cambridge University Press, 1988), 44.

36. Mitchell's work on enframing follows at least two philosophical precedents. On the one hand his account of the enframing effect creating the abstract "world as exhibition" harks back to Heidegger's description of modernity as "the age of the world picture." See, in this respect, Timothy Mitchell, "The World as Exhibition," *Comparative Studies in Society and History* 31 (1989): 217–36. This is the aspect of enframing that Derek Gregory explores in *Geographical Imaginations*, 34–42. However, Mitchell's account in *Colonising Egypt* seems also very much informed by Jacques Derrida's tracings of the dissembling dynamics of modern picturing. It is this Derridean attention to the construction of *Truth in Painting* (trans. Geoffrey Bennington [Chicago: University of Chicago Press, 1985]) that also informs my discussion here of the dissembled role of cartography in lending linearity and cohesion to abstract state space.

37. The way in which cartography was involved in the creation of the abstract effect of the modern state in Elizabethan England has been usefully disclosed by Richard Helgerson, *Forms of Nationhood: The Elizabethan Writing of England* (Chicago: University of Chicago Press, 1992). Attending to the recursive proleptic effects of mapping—the way maps contribute to the construction of spaces that later they seem only to represent—he highlights how the new national maps of Saxton, Camden, and others were part and parcel of a civil and conceptual revolution in which it was made to seem as if the land itself spoke of the kingdom as a single state.

38. On the notion of a "Third Space of enunciation," which, he says, "makes the structure of meaning and reference an ambivalent process," see Bhabha's essay, "The Commitment to Theory," in *Location of Culture*, 19–39. In this essay he characterizes it as the disruptive opposite to the homogeneous, serial time Benedict Anderson described as the organizing assumption of the modern nation. Such a focus on space as the site of enunciation seems to me to foreclose analysis of how the production of space can itself serve to generate the abstract terrain on which homogenization is secured.

39. Robert Young, *White Mythologies: Writing History and the West* (New York: Routledge, 1990), 146.

40. Although as Medig'm (Neil Sterritt) has emphasized, it was only one strategy among others; see his "It Doesn't Matter What the Judge Said," in *Aboriginal Title in British Columbia: Delgamuukw v. the Queen*, ed.

Frank Cassidy (Lantzville, BC: Oolichan Books, 1992), 303–7. On the more general difficulties of negotiating with the structure of colonial violence (and white patriarchy) in Canadian law, see Mary Ellen Turpel, "Home/Land," *Canadian Journal of Family Law* 10 (1991): 17–40; and Turpel, "Aboriginal Peoples and the Canadian Charter: Interpretive Monopolies and Cultural Differences," *Canadian Human Rights Yearbook* (Ottawa: Les Presses de l'Université d'Ottawa, 1989/90), 249–95. Having written about the violence of Canadian law, Turpel has nevertheless also taken up the challenge of working within its structures as a judge in Saskatchewan. See Mary Ellen Turpel-Lafond's Web page on the Web site of "Aboriginal Faces of Saskatchewan," http://collections.ic.gc.ca/faces/wturpma.htm.

41. Satsan, "The Fire within Us," in Cassidy, *Aboriginal Title,* 54.

42. For a discussion of the limits of Canadian law exposed by this process when the case finally reach the Supreme Court of Canada, see John Borrows, "Sovereignty's Alchemy: An Anlysis of Delgamuukw v. British Columbia," *Osgoode Hall Law Journal* 37 (1999): 537–96.

43. Satsan, "Fire within Us," 55.

44. James Clifford, "Identity in Mashpee," in *The Predicament of Culture: Twentieth-Century Ethnography, Literature, and Art* (Cambridge: Harvard University Press, 1988), 288–89.

45. Timothy Solnick, "Power, Resistance and the Law in a British Columbia Land Title Trial" (master's thesis, University of British Columbia, 1992).

46. Cited in Monet and Skanu'u, *Colonialism on Trial,* 50.

47. Ibid., 42.

48. Allan McEachern, *In the Supreme Court of British Columbia, between: Delgamuukw, also known as Ken Muldoe, suing on his own behalf and on behalf of all the members of the House of Delgamuukw, and others, plaintiffs, and Her Majesty the Queen in right of the Province of British Columbia and the Attorney General of Canada, defendants: reasons for judgment of the Honourable Chief Justice* (Vancouver: Supreme Court of British Columbia, 1991), 259. Hereafter cited in the text as *Reasons for Judgment.*

49. Monet and Skanu'u, *Colonialism on Trial,* 98.

50. Neil Sterritt's testimony in *Delgamuukw v. the Queen,* 7036.

51. Hugh Brody, *Maps and Dreams* (Vancouver: Douglas and McIntyre, 1988). The first edition of the book was published in 1981.

52. Ibid., especially 148–49 and 266–67. For a useful discussion of Brody's treatment of this complex overlap, see Graham Huggan, "Maps, Dreams and the Presentation of Ethnographic Narrative: Hugh Brody's 'Maps and Dreams' and Bruce Chatwin's 'The Songlines,'" *Ariel* 22, no. 1 (1991): 57–69.

53. In addition to Brody's *Maps and Dreams,* a further discussion of "map biographies" is available in Peter J. Usher, Frank J. Tough, and Robert M. Galois, "Reclaiming the Land: Aboriginal Title, Treaty Rights and Land Claims in Canada," *Applied Geography* 12 (1992): 109–32. They note (p. 125) how the Gitxsan and Wet'suwet'en attempt to prove title by ownership and House territories worked with the notion of fee simple ownership rather than the more common *profit à prendre* appeal to use and occupancy charted with map biographies.

54. Describing the Inuit's cartographic resistance, Robert Rundstrom ends his discussion of the strategy's success with a note of concern about the dangers. "The Inuit have resituated themselves as part of the cartographic establishment. Working from an early position as victims whose cartography was co-opted for colonial purposes, they have recently burst through with a kind of map insurrection. . . . [But b]y going public and inscribing their maps now, they have dangerously exposed their knowledge to Quallunaat." In Robert A. Rundstrom, "Mapping, Postmodernism, Indigenous People and the Changing Direction of North American Cartography," *Cartographica* 28, no. 2 (1991): 3.

55. *Delgamuukw v. the Queen,* 279.

56. See Cole Harris, *Making Native Space: Colonialism, Resistance, and Reserves in British Columbia* (Vancouver: University of British Columbia Press, 2002).

57. Quoted in J. S. Murray, "The Map-Makers," *The Beaver* 69 (1989): 24.

58. For a more extended analysis of how space is reduced to a stage by the epistemic imperialism of conventional Western perspectives such as McEachern's, see Paul Carter, *The Road to Botany Bay: An Exploration of Landscape and History* (New York: Knopf, 1988), especially xvi–xviii.

59. Harley, "Re-reading the Maps," 531.

60. For an alternative, and infinitely more nuanced, postcolonial analysis of the uneven emergence of British Columbia on the horizon of imperial knowledge production, see Daniel Clayton, *Islands of Truth: The Imperial Fashioning of Vancouver Island* (Vancouver: University of British Columbia Press, 2002).

61. Cited in Monet and Skanu'u, *Colonialism on Trial,* 154.

62. Ibid.

63. Ibid.

64. Boyce Richardson, *People of Terra Nullius: Betrayal and Rebirth in Aboriginal Canada* (Vancouver: Douglas and McIntyre, 1993), 303.

65. Audre Lorde, "The Master's Tools Will Never Dismantle the Master's House," in *Sister Outsider: Essays and Speeches* (New York: Crossing Press, 1984), 98–105.

66. José Rabasa, "Allegories of the Atlas," in *Europe and Its Others,* vol. 2, ed. Francis Barker et al. (Colchester: University of Essex, 1985), 3.

67. R. C. Harris (Directeur-Director), L. Dechêne (Directeur-Director), M. Paré (Traduction-Translations), and G. J. Matthews (Cartographe-Cartographer), *Atlas Historique du Canada,* vol. 1, *Des origines à 1800* (Montréal: Les Presses de l'Université de Montréal, 1987).

68. I have focused almost entirely on volume 1 of the *Atlas* partly because it marks the start of the three-volume origin story but mainly because, unlike the other volumes in the series, its content reflects a concerted editorial effort to recognize native historical geographies.

69. G. Fremlin and L. M. Sebert, "National Atlases," in *Cartographica,* monograph 4 (Toronto: University of Toronto Press, 1972), 30. They continue: "By presenting clear concepts about the nature of a country and its population, economy, culture and its various achievements, the national atlas cultivates a love of one's country and a feeling of national pride."

70. Wm. G. Dean, "Sic enim est traditum," *Mapping History/L'Histoire Par les Cartes* 1 (1980): 12.

71. Wm. G. Dean and James Walker, "The Project," *Mapping History/ L'Histoire Par les Cartes* 1 (1980): 3.

72. Cited in Piternick, "Historical Atlas of Canada," 21.

73. Wm. G. Dean, "Foreword I," in *Historical Atlas,* vol. 1, unpaginated.

74. Westfall, review of *Historical Atlas,* vol. 1, 261.

75. Ibid.

76. Roger Hall, "A Country with 'Too Much Geography,'" *Globe and Mail,* December 1, 1990, C20.

77. Paul Robinson, "Mapping Canada's Early Years," *Atlantic Provinces Book Review* 14, no. 4 (1987): 5.

78. Wanda Quoika Stanka, review of *Historical Atlas,* vol. 1, *Canadian Library Journal* 46, no. 1 (1989): 55.

79. James Reaney, "Swimming in the Past," *Saturday Night* 103, no. 3 (1987): 59.

80. Yvon Lamonde, "Le Temps dans l'espace," *Le Devoir* (Montréal), October 17, 1987, B1. Translated, he thus said that the *Atlas* was "a pleasure for both the eye and the intellect."

81. Jean-Pierre Bonhomme, "Le Premier Tome d'un atlas du Canada," *La Presse,* October 24, 1987, 16. Translated, he thus said that "the specificity of the French-Canadian regime and Jacques Cartier's epic are not given a very long treatment."

82. J. V. Wright, "Mapping Canada's Prehistory," *Transactions of the Royal Society of Canada,* 5th series, 1 (1986): 203.

83. Claude Tessier, "Le Peuplement du Canada, une vielle histoire," *Le Soleil,* November 22, 1987. Translated: "Who are these hunters with their

fluted points? Who are the Planoans? And the Martimiens? And the Boucleriens? And the Laurentiens? There is an answer. They are all the first true Canadians."

84. Carter, *Road to Botany Bay*, xviii.

85. Bruce G. Trigger, *Natives and Newcomers: Canada's "Heroic Age" Reconsidered* (Kingston and Montreal: McGill–Queen's University Press, 1985), 6–7.

86. Fabida Jara and Edmundo Magana, "Rules of Imperialist Method," *Dialectical Anthropology* 7 (1982): 117.

87. Allan Greer, review of *Historical Atlas*, vol. 1, *Labour/Le Travail* (Ottawa) 22 (1988): 274.

88. Most notable among these critiques is Johannes Fabian's argument that the evolutionary time deployed by modern disciplines like anthropology amounts to a systematic denial of coevalness. See Johannes Fabian, *Time and the Other: How Anthropology Makes Its Object* (New York: Columbia University Press, 1983).

89. Johannes Fabian, "Of Dogs Alive, Birds Dead, and Time to Tell a Story," in *Chronotypes: The Construction of Time,* ed. John Bender and David Weelberry (Stanford: Stanford University Press, 1991), 193.

90. See Sparke, "Between Demythologizing and Deconstructing the Map."

91. Cole Harris, "Preface," in *Historical Atlas,* vol. 1, unpaginated.

92. As one review highlighted, such a visual gesture of nationalization would seem especially potent in a visual age. Liam Lacey, "Lush Atlas Caters to a 'Visual Age,'" *Globe and Mail,* November 5, 1987, C1.

93. Donald Kerr and Deryck Holdsworth, eds., *Historical Atlas of Canada,* vol. 3, *Addressing the Twentieth Century, 1891–1961* (Toronto: University of Toronto Press, 1990).

94. Harris, "Preface."

95. Ged Martin, "Cartography, Teleology and an Antipodean Contrast," *British Journal of Canadian Studies* 3, no. 1 (1988): 84.

96. Ibid., 86, and Harris, "Preface."

97. Martin, "Cartography," 86.

98. Lacey, "Lush Atlas," A15.

99. Joe C. W. Armstrong, review of *Historical Atlas*, vol. 1, *Quill and Quire* 53, no. 11 (1987): 23.

100. J. M. S. Careless, "'Limited Identities' in Canada," *Canadian Historical Review* 50, no. 1 (1969): 1–10.

101. As Priscilla Wald argues, the plural American "We" of "We the People" has proven incredibly plastic and expandable in the service of national crisis-management. See *Constituting Americans: Cultural Anxiety and Narrative Form* (Durham: Duke University Press, 1995).

102. Robert J. C. Young, *Colonial Desire: Hybridity in Theory, Culture and Race* (New York: Routledge, 1995), especially chapter 3.

103. Gregory, *Geographical Imaginations,* 39–40.

104. Roland Barthes, *Michelet,* trans. Richard Howard (New York: Hill and Wang, 1987), 29.

105. Gregory, *Geographical Imaginations,* 44.

106. Jacques Derrida, *Dissemination,* trans. Barbara Johnson (Chicago: University of Chicago Press, 1981).

107. Ibid., 10.

108. Claude Lefort, *The Political Forms of Modern Society: Bureaucracy, Democracy, Totalitarianism* (Cambridge, MA: MIT Press, 1986).

109. Ibid., 227.

110. *Delgamuukw v. the Queen,* 16408. The date is a typo. It should read "1981" as on the earlier transcript p. 16356.

111. Ibid., 16408.

2. RETERRITORIALIZING LOCALITY IN GLOBALITY

1. Kenichi Ohmae, *The End of the Nation-State: The Rise of Regional Economies* (New York: Free Press, 1995), 129.

2. Arjun Appadurai, *Modernity at Large: Cultural Dimensions of Globalization* (Minneapolis: University of Minnesota Press, 1996), 19 and 33. Hereafter referred to in the text as *Modernity.*

3. Arjun Appadurai, "Globalization and the Research Imagination," *International Social Science Journal* 160 (June 1999): 231.

4. Paul Schell and John Hamer, "Cascadia: The New Binationalism of Western Canada and the U.S. Pacific Northwest," in *Identities in North America: The Search for Community,* ed. Robert Earle and John Wirth (Palo Alto, CA: Stanford University Press, 1995), 141.

5. Paul Schell and John Hamer, "What is the Future of Cascadia?" *Discovery Institute Inquiry,* 1993, 12.

6. Martin Albrow, "Traveling beyond Local Cultures: Socioscapes in a Global City," in *Living the Global City: Globalization as a Local Process,* ed. John Eade (New York: Routledge, 1997), 54.

7. Gilles Deleuze and Felix Guattari, *Anti-Oedipus: Capitalism and Schizophrenia,* trans. R. Hurley and H. R. Lane (London: Athlone Press, 1977).

8. Aiwha Ong, *Flexible Citizenship: The Cultural Logics of Transnationality* (Durham: Duke University Press, 1999), 11.

9. Other scholars of transnational migration itself have also expressed doubt about the scope of Appadurai's deterritorialization narrative in this

regard. In a section of their book, entitled "Grounding Transnationalism," Michael Peter Smith and Luis Guarnizo point out that among transmigrants there remain embodied and localized spatial practices that anchor and limit the kinds of circulatory possibilities celebrated by Appadurai. "Transnational practices," they say, "while connecting collectivities located in more than one national territory, are embodied in specific social relations established between specific people, situated in unequivocal localities, at historically determined times." As I am also arguing here, Smith and Guarnizo conclude that "'locality' thus needs to be further conceptualized." Michael Peter Smith and Luis Guarnizo, eds., *Transnationalism from Below* (New Brunswick, NJ: Transaction Publishers, 1998), 11.

10. Ong, *Flexible Citizenship,* 11.

11. In attempting to theorize and understand such efforts at fashioning locality in globality, I also wholly agree with Anna Tsing's reflections on the limits of traditional anthropological (and, it can certainly be added, traditional regional geography) approaches. "[O]ur tools for thinking about the big picture are still rudimentary," she notes. "Holding on, as I think we should, to a disciplinary heritage of close-up detail, we find ourselves with data about how a few people somewhere react, resist, translate, and consume. From here it is an easy step to invoke distinctions between local reactions and global forces, local consumption and global circulation, local resistance and global structures of capitalism, local translation and global imagination. I find myself doing it. Yet we know that these dichotomies are unhelpful. They draw us into an imagery in which the global is homogenous precisely because we oppose it to the heterogeneity we identify as locality." Anna Tsing, "Inside the Economy of Appearances," *Public Culture* 12 (2000): 119.

12. See Ohmae, *End of the Nation-State,* 143.

13. Ibid., 7.

14. Ernest Callenbach, *Ecotopia: The Notebooks and Reports of William Weston* (Berkeley: Banyan Tree Books, 1975).

15. Joel Garreau, *The Nine Nations of North America* (Boston: Houghton Mifflin, 1981).

16. David McCloskey, "On Ecoregional Boundaries," *Trumpeter* 6, no. 4 (1989): 127–31; and McCloskey, "Cascadia," in *Futures by Design: The Practice of Ecological Planning,* ed. Doug Aberley (Gabriola Island, BC: New Society Publishers, 1994), 98.

17. See P. Schoonmaker, B. von Hagen, and E. Wolf, *The Rain Forests of Home: Profile of a North American Bioregion* (Washington, DC: Island Press, 1997).

18. William Henkel, "Cascadia: A State of (Various) Mind(s)," *Chicago Review* 39 (1993): 112–13.

19. McCloskey, "On Ecoregional Boundaries."

20. Michael A. Goldberg and Maurice D. Levi, "The Evolving Experience along the Pacific Northwest Corridor Called Cascadia," *New Pacific*, Winter 1993/94, 28. It might be noted that Goldberg and Levi include Alaska in their definition of Cascadia, hence the reference to two oceans.

21. Quoted in Vincent Schodolski, "Northwest's Economy Defies National Borders: History, Trade, Climate Define Vibrant Region," *Chicago Tribune*, August 1, 1994, 1.

22. Alan Artibise, "Cascadian Adventures: Shared Visions, Strategic Alliances, and Ingrained Barriers in a Transborder Region" (paper presented at the symposium "On Brotherly Terms: Canadian American Relations West of the Rockies," University of Washington, Seattle, 1996), 13.

23. Quoted in J. Francis, "Cascadia Isn't Just for Dreamers Anymore," *Sunday Oregonian*, September 20, 1992, R4.

24. McCloskey, "Cascadia," 102.

25. James N. Gardner, "The Competitive Advantage of Cascadia," *New Pacific*, Winter 1992/93, 12.

26. Charles Kelly, "Rallying Around the Flag," *New Pacific*, Winter 1992/93, 7.

27. Kelly quoted in Robert Gilbert, "Erasing National Borders to Build a Trade Region," *Christian Science Monitor*, July 20, 1992, A9.

28. Alan Artibise, *Opportunities for Achieving Sustainability in Cascadia* (Vancouver: International Centre for Sustainable Cities, 1994), 2.

29. For an extended critique of Artibise's complicity with the progrowth agenda in Vancouver itself, see Katharyne Mitchell, "Visions of Vancouver: Ideology, Democracy and the Future of Urban Development," *Urban Geography* 17, no. 6 (1996): 478–501.

30. World Commission on Environment and Development (Bruntland Report), *Our Common Future* (Oxford: Oxford University Press, 1987). See also P. McManus, "Contested Terrains: Politics, Stories and Discourses of Sustainability," *Environmental Politics* 5 (1996): 48–53.

31. David Harvey, "What's Green and Makes the World Go Round?" in *The Cultures of Globalization*, ed. Fredric Jameson and Masao Miyoshi (Durham: Duke University Press, 1998), 337.

32. Ibid., 342.

33. Artibise, *Opportunities*, 5.

34. Ibid.

35. Ibid., 6.

36. Ibid., 6 and 7.

37. Ibid., 4.

38. It obviously does a disservice to this literature to recapitulate it so briefly in passing, but it is such an important backcloth to my analysis and represents work that is so often ignored or left uncited by nongeographers

(who then often busy themselves with reinventing the spatial wheels of their arguments) that I feel obliged to note it here. For a typical gloss that barely mentions any work by geographers, see Saskia Sassen's treatment of the geography of centrality in *Globalization and Its Discontents* (New York: New Press, 1998).

39. David Harvey, *The Limits to Capital* (London: Verso, 2000).

40. David Harvey, *Consciousness and the Urban Experience* (Oxford: Blackwell, 1985).

41. David Harvey, *The Urbanization of Capital* (Oxford: Blackwell, 1985), 213.

42. David Harvey, "From Managerialism to Entrepreneurialism: The Transformation of Urban Governance in Late Capitalism," *Geografiska Annale* 71B (1989): 3–17.

43. See also Erik Swyngedouw, "The Mammon Quest. Glocalization, Interspatial Competition and the Monetary Order: The Construction of New Scales," in *Cities and Regions in the New Europe: The Global-Local Interplay and Spatial Development Strategies,* ed. M. Dunford and G. Kafkalas (New York: Wiley, 1992), 39–67; Swyngedouw, "Neither Global Nor Local: 'Glocalization' and the Politics of Scale," in *Spaces of Globalization: Reasserting the Power of the Local,* ed. Kevin Cox (New York: Guildford Press, 1997), 137–66; and Clare Newstead, Carolina Reid, and Matthew Sparke, "The Cultural Geography of Scale," in *The Handbook of Cultural Geography,* ed. Kay Anderson, Mona Domosh, Steve Pile, and Nigel Thrift (London: Sage, 2003), 485–97.

44. Doris Jones Yang, "Magic Mountains: Attracted by Pristine Mountain Beauty, the Pacific Northwest's High-Tech Wizards Are Aiming at Conquering World Markets," *New Pacific,* Autumn 1992, 19.

45. Ibid., 19.

46. G. Halverson, "Regional Road Maps Guide Some Mutual Funds," *Christian Science Monitor,* October 8, 1996, A9.

47. Artibise, "Cascadian Adventures," 12.

48. Alan Artibise, Anne Vernez Moudon, and E. Seltzer, "Cascadia: An Emerging Regional Model," in *Cities in Our Future,* ed. Robert Geddes (Washington, DC: Island Press, 1997), 149.

49. Paul Schell, "Bulldozing Borders," *New Pacific,* Summer 1990, 10.

50. Graham Fysh, "A Head for Heights," *New Pacific,* Autumn 1992, 11.

51. Jim Sutherland, "Natural Selection," in *Cascadia: A Tale of Two Cities, Seattle and Vancouver, B.C.,* ed. Morton Beebe (New York: Harry Abrams, 1996), 42.

52. This similarity with the gated-community phenomena runs far deeper than Sutherland's seemingly offhand allusions. As Evan McKenzie points out in his analysis of privatized residential communities, contemporary American

forms of gated community have their roots—much like Cascadia—in a form of ecotopian planning discourse: namely Ebenezer Howard's "Garden City" ideas. These roots, McKenzie argues, have effectively been corrupted into the privatized vision of spatial control that we see today. McKenzie critically calls this vision "Privatopia," a name that seems equally well suited to the neoliberal ideoscapes and financescapes of Cascadia. See Evan McKenzie, *Privatopia: Homeowner Associations and the Rise of Residential Private Government* (New Haven: Yale University Press, 1994), chapter 1.

53. Charles Kelly, "Midwifing the New Regional Order," *New Pacific,* Spring 1994, 6.

54. This information was given to the author in an interview with Alan Artibise in Vancouver, July 1998.

55. These regions have not only been the focus of Ohmae, but have also been researched far more rigorously by the economic geographers studying agglomeration. See Michael Storper's work for an overview: "The Resurgence of Regional Economies, Ten Years Later: The Region as a Nexus of Untraded Interdependencies," *European Urban and Regional Studies* 2–3 (1995): 191–221.

56. Although Microsoft did purchase British Columbia's Consumers Software in order to acquire its network management systems.

57. Goldberg and Levi, "Evolving Experience," 30.

58. Howard Wall, "How Important is the US-Canada Border?" *International Economic Trends,* August 1999, 1.

59. These findings are also borne out in a book-length study by the Vancouver-based economist John Helliwell who shows again in great detail what he calls a significant "border effect" in the interprovince/-state trade data. John Helliwell, *How Much Do National Borders Matter?* (Washington, DC: Brookings Institution Press, 1998). Helliwell concludes (p. 4) that "even after accounting for the expansion of trade between the United States and Canada in the wake of the Free Trade Agreement . . ., interprovincial trade linkages are still twelve times tighter than those between provinces and states."

60. Bruce Chapman, "Cooperation Not Competition, Key to Cascadia Region Success," *Seattle Post-Intelligencer,* June 14, 1996, A16.

61. "The Power of One," *New Pacific,* Summer 1992, 7.

62. Artibise, *Opportunities,* 4.

63. Schodolski, "Northwest's Economy Defies National Borders," 1.

64. Cascadia Planning Group, "British Columbia – Washington Corridor Task Force" (mimeo, January 1999), 3–4.

65. Schodolski, "Northwest's Economy Defies National Borders," 1.

66. Quoted in A. Webb, "Promoting the Two Nation Vacation," *Puget Sound Business Journal,* November 1995, 5A.

67. *The Cascadian Traveler* (undated and unpaginated pamphlet).

68. Jim Miller, "Transportation Key to Cascadia Regionalism and Pacific Trade," *Pacific Economic Review,* Fall 1993, 36.

69. Schell, "Bulldozing Borders," 5.

70. Artibise, *Opportunities,* 11.

71. *IMTC News,* 2000, 1: 1.

72. Schell and Hamer, "Cascadia," 148.

73. For a more extended discussion on the vision of neoliberal "citizenship" instantiated in the PACE lane and its successors, see Matthew Sparke, "Passports into Credit Cards: On the Borders and Spaces of Neoliberal Citizenship," in *Boundaries and Belonging,* ed. Joel Migdal (Cambridge: Cambridge University Press, 2004), 251–83. On the problematic of neoliberal citizenship more generally, see Katharyne Mitchell and Sallie Marston, "Citizens and the State: Contextualizing Citizenship Formation in Space and Time," in *Spaces of Democracy,* ed. Murray Low and Clive Barnett (Thousand Oaks, CA: Sage, 2004).

74. For example, Jack Metcalf, the Republican House Representative from Everett, who voted for the bill told a local reporter that "he believed it wasn't supposed to touch Canadians." Quoted in Steve Wilhelm, "Future Border Procedures Concern Trade Advocates," *Puget Sound Business Journal,* October 16, 1997, 1. Whether or not Metcalf thought this because he considered Canada part of the United States or because he thought of "aliens" as a name only applying to people crossing from Mexico was not specified.

75. A useful overview of the controversy is provided by Theodore Cohn, "Cross-border Travel in North America: The Challenge of U.S. Section 110 Legislation," *Canadian American Public Policy* 40 (October 1999): 1–70.

76. Quoted in L. Pynn, "Without Politicians, Cascadia Is Just a Dream," *Vancouver Sun,* November 12, 1997, A1.

77. Schell and Hamer, "Cascadia," 148.

78. Quoted in Jon Frandsen, "Tighter Entry Rules Could Snarl the Border," *Seattle Times,* November 25, 1997, A1.

79. *Illegal Immigrant Reform and Immigrant Responsibility Act of 1996,* Public Law 104, 104th Congress, 2nd session, *United States Code Congressional and Administrative News,* 3:208–325.

80. Ronald J. Hays, "INSPASS: INS Passenger Accelerated Service System" (paper authored January 4, 1996, that was published on a now inactive Web page of the Department of Justice).

81. Ibid. For reasons that are no doubt connected to the argument for public-private partnerships put forward here by Hays, his paper was later made available on the Web at the time of revising this chapter (August 12, 2002) on the site of the Biometric Consortium at http://www.biometrics .org/REPORTS/INSPASS.html. For a useful exploration of the wider devel-

opment of biometric passenger-management practices at airports, see Richard Adey, "Surveillance at the Airport: Surveilling Mobility/Mobilising," in *Ecumene,* forthcoming.

82. See Joel Connelly and Michael Paulson, "U.S., Canada Say Border Law Would Create Havoc," *Seattle Post-Intelligencer,* May 19, 1999, A3. Mayors from north and south of the border are noted to have written a letter to Congress stating that "all Cascadia cities would be negatively impacted."

83. Anthony dePalma, "Slow Crawl at the Border," *New York Times,* October 21, 2001, A1.

84. Meg Olson, "PACE Reopening Unlikely," *Northern Light,* November 1, 2001, 1.

85. Canada–United States Smart Border Declaration, http://webapps.dfait-maeci.gc.ca/minipub/Publication.asp?Filespec=/Min_Pub_Docs/104780.htm (accessed December 12, 2001).

86. Ibid.

87. Ibid.

88. See the White House Web-site records at http://www.whitehouse.gov/news/releases/2002/05/20020514-4.html (accessed August 13, 2002).

89. The application materials for NEXUS were at the time of writing available on a Canadian customs Web site at http://www.ccra-adrc.gc.ca/customs/individuals/nexus/menu-e.html (accessed August 13, 2002).

90. Quoted in Meg Olson, "Nexus Tweaking Should Speed-up Enrollment Process," *Northern Light,* July 4, 2002, 1.

91. Erwin L. Weber, *In the Zone of Filtered Sunshine: Why the Pacific Northwest Is Destined to Dominate the Commercial World* (Seattle: Seattle Chamber of Commerce, 1924).

92. Ibid., 30.

93. Ibid., 2.

94. Ibid.

95. Even the title of a recent journalistic overview of local groups is illustrative of this kind of rationale for regionalism. See David A. Neiwert, *In God's Country: The Patriot Movement and the Pacific Northwest* (Pullman: Washington State University Press, 1999).

96. The Web page of the Northwest Kinsmen was available at http://www.concentric.net/~Nwk/ (last accessed June 1999).

97. Northwest Kinsmen, http://www.concentric.net/~nwk/dedication.htm.

98. See James Ridway, *Blood in the Face: The Ku Klux Klan, Aryan Nations, Nazi Skinheads and the Rise of a New White Culture* (New York: Thunders Mouth Press, 1990); and James A. Aho, *The Politics of Righteousness: Idaho Christian Patriotism* (Seattle: University of Washington Press, 1990).

99. See Corinne Jackson, "Klan's B.C. Boss Fired by Top Security Firm," *The Province,* August 10, 1997, A1 and A3; and also Warren Kinsella, *Web of Hate: Inside Canada's Far Right Network* (Toronto: HarperCollins, 1994).

100. Reported in Martin Schuldhaus, "Arms and Survival Gear Seized from U.S. Militia in B.C.," *Seattle Post-Intelligencer,* October 26, 1996, A2.

101. Neiwert, *In God's Country,* 265.

102. Schell and Hamer, "Cascadia," 144.

103. Quoted in Robert Kaplan, "Travels Into America's Future," *Atlantic Monthly,* August 1998, 54.

104. Schell and Hamer, "Cascadia," 152.

105. Ibid., 144.

106. William Sturgis, *The Oregon Question: Substance of a Lecture before the Mecantile Library Association* (Boston: Jordan, Swift and Wiley, 1845), 32.

107. *The Cascadian Traveler* pamphlet.

108. These remarks and those that follow were recorded by the author who was there as an observer at the conference in June 1996.

109. It might be noted in this regard that a group from the Colville Reservation in northeast Washington actually ran a small advertising campaign for a so-called Three Nation Vacation during the mid-1990s that included visits to the Reservation.

110. Jan Halliday and Gail Chehak, *Native Peoples of the Northwest: A Traveller's Guide to Land, Art and Culture* (Seattle: Sasquatch Books, 1996).

111. Reported by Joel Connelly, "Tribes Put Kinship above Boundaries," *Seattle Post-Intelligencer,* July 24, 1999, A1.

112. Robert D. Kaplan, *An Empire Wilderness: Travels into America's Future* (New York: Vintage Books, 1999), 327–28.

3. AN ALMOST TRANSCENDENTAL LEVEL PLAYING FIELD

1. Quoted in Fernando Coronil, "Towards a Critique of Globalcentrism: Speculations on Capitalism's Nature," *Public Culture* 12 (2000): 351–74, at 351.

2. Mulroney quoted in Judith Darcy, "Introduction," in *Crossing the Line: Canada and Free Trade with Mexico,* ed. Jim Sinclair (Vancouver, BC: New Star Books, 1992), xi; Bush quoted in Frederick W. Mayer, *Interpreting NAFTA: The Science and Art of Political Analysis* (New York: Columbia University Press, 1998), 143; and Carlos Salinas de Gotari, "North American Free Trade: Mexico's Route to Upward Mobility," *New Perspectives Quarterly* 8, no. 1 (1991): 4.

3. See Stephen Clarkson, "Constitutionalising the Canadian-American

Relationship," in *Canada Under Free Trade,* ed. Duncan Cameron and Mel Watkins (Toronto: James Lorimer, 1993), 3–20.

4. Timothy Mitchell, "The Limits of the State: Beyond Statist Approaches and Their Critics," *American Political Science Review* 85, no. 1 (1991), 94. Hereafter referred to in the text as "Limits."

5. Bertell Ollman, "Going beyond the State? Comment," *American Political Science Review* 86, no. 4 (1992): 1016. Ollman is best known for his emphasis on reading Marx as a theorist of internal relations. See Bertell Ollman, *Alienation: Marx's Conception of Man in Capitalist Society* (London: Verso, 1971).

6. "Limits," 94. In this respect, Mitchell's account shares something with Michael Mann's widely heralded historical sociology of modern state formation as a process of "polymorphous crystallization." Michael Mann, *The Sources of Social Power,* vol. 2, *The Rise of Classes and the Nation-State* (Cambridge: Cambridge University Press, 1991).

7. See the assessment of the three main types of models used—partial equilibrium analyses using regressions of national data aggregates; single country computable general equilibrium models; and multiple country computable general equilibrium models—in Raúl Hinojosa-Ojeda and Sherman Robinson, "Labor Issues in a North American Free Trade Area," in *North American Free Trade: Assessing the Impact,* ed. N. Lustig, B. P. Bosworth, and Z. Lawrence (Washington, DC: Brookings Institution Press, 1992), 69–98.

8. Timothy Mitchell, *The Rule of Experts: Egypt, Techno-Politics, Modernity* (Berkeley: University of California Press, 2002).

9. For an account of what the negotiations excluded, and for a critique of how free trade "belies the exclusivity of its remapping of those other, dominant, North American continental divides—class, gender, and ethnicity," see Barbara Harlow, "Negotiating Treaties: Maastricht and NAFTA," in *Marxism in the Postmodern Age: Confronting the New World Order,* ed. Antonio Callari, Stephen Cullenberg, and Carole Biewener (New York: Guildford Press, 1995), 515.

10. Critical scholars also joined the debate in this way. See, for example, Stephen McBride and John Shields, *Dismantling a Nation: Canada and the New World Order* (Halifax: Fernwood Publishing, 1993). The cover of this book replayed a common theme of critique and depicted a U.S. hand dipping broken-up parts of the Canadian national map into tomato ketchup as if they were fries.

11. Timothy Mitchell, "Fixing the Economy," *Cultural Studies* 12, no. 1 (1998): 82–101, at 92.

12. See Sylvia Bashevkin, *True Patriot Love: The Politics of Canadian Nationalism* (Toronto: Oxford University Press, 1991), 100–101.

13. Government of Canada, *Report of the Royal Commission on the Economic Union and Development Prospects of Canada,* vol. 1 (Ottawa: Minister of Supply and Services, 1985).

14. For a summary of the report, see Rod McQueen, *Leap of Faith: The Macdonald Report* (Toronto: Cown, 1985).

15. Ibid., 6.

16. Ibid., 38.

17. Ibid., 41.

18. See Dave Langille, "The BCNI Calls the Shots," *The Facts* 10, no. 2 (1988): 102–7; and Clarkson, "Constitutionalising the Canadian-American Relationship," 11.

19. See Bashevkin, *True Patriot Love,* 100–105.

20. Michael J. Twomey, *Multinational Corporations and the North American Free Trade Agreement* (Westpoint, CT: Praeger, 1993).

21. Leo Panitch, "Dependency and Class in Canadian Political Economy," *Studies in Political Economy* 6 (1981): 7–33.

22. William Burgess, "Planning Implications of Foreign Ownership in the Canadian Economy" (master's thesis, University of British Columbia, 1994); and Burgess, "Foreign Direct Investment: Facts and Perceptions about Canada," *Canadian Geographer* 44, no. 7 (2000): 98–113.

23. Frederick Engels, "Preface," in Karl Marx, *Free Trade: A Speech Delivered before the Democratic Club of Brussels, Belgium, Jan. 9, 1848,* trans. F. K. Wischrewetszky (Boston: Leo and Shepard, 1888), 13.

24. Following Janine Brodie, it should also be noted that free trade cannot rightly be seen as a crisis of Canadian Fordism since liberalized trading relations with the United States were a part of Canada's whole postwar development policy. See Janine Brodie, *The Political Economy of Canadian Regionalism* (Toronto: Harcourt Brace Jovanovich, 1990).

25. For a review of how that actual promotion of free trade tended to be done in a masculinist language that downplayed the gendered implications of the agreements, see Marianne Marchand, "Selling NAFTA: Metaphors and Implications," in *Globalization: Theory and Practice,* ed. Eleonore Kofman and Gillian Youngs (London: Pinter, 1996), 253–70.

26. National Action Committee on the Status of Women, *What Every Woman Needs to Know about Free Trade* (Toronto: NAC, 1988). For a retrospect on NAC's campaign against free trade, see Marjorie Griffin Cohen, "Macho Economics: Canadian Women Confront Free Trade," *dollars and sense,* November/December 1995, 18–21. Another critic who caught the masculinism was Reg Whitaker who argued that the subtext of Bay Street boosterism "was macho: free trade will give us big balls like the yanks." In Reg Whitaker, "No Laments for the Nation: Free Trade and the Election of 1988," *Canadian Forum,* 1989, 9–13.

27. David McNally, "Beyond Nationalism, Beyond Protectionism: Labour and the Canada-U.S. Free Trade Agreement," *Capital and Class* 43 (1991), 233–52.

28. See Whitaker, "No Laments for the Nation," 10.

29. For a sustained discussion of such effects, see John B. Thompson, *The Media and Modernity* (Stanford, CA: Stanford University Press, 1995).

30. Anthony Smith, *Nationalism in the Twentieth Century* (Oxford: Martin Robertson, 1979), 191.

31. Earle Gray, *Free Trade, Free Canada: How Free Trade Will Make Canada Stronger* (Woodville, ON: Canadian Speeches, 1987).

32. Philip Resnick argues that, at least in English Canada, the state predates the development of a Canadian nationality and was the major force fostering its growth. In *The Masks of Proteus: Canadian Reflections on the State* (Montreal and Kingston: McGill-Queen's University Press, 1990), especially 207.

33. See Mildred Schwartz, "NAFTA and the Fragmentation of Canada," *American Review of Canadian Studies,* Spring 1998, 11–28.

34. Narrating Canadian nationality by othering Americans as, in Semour Martin Lipset's words, more "classically liberal, Whig, individualistic, anti-statist, [and] populist" is so widespread and profound that it even plays a role in containing and giving order to the work of sociologists and political scientists who, like Lipset, discipline the dynamic as a historical artifact. In *Continental Divide* (New York: Routledge, 1990), 212 and passim.

35. Cited by Fred Gudmundson, "Free Trade: The Real Agenda," *Canadian Dimension* 20, no. 5 (1985): 1–15 of the special supplement.

36. Mitchell, "Fixing the Economy," 89. Mitchell also argues here that one of the results of this common sense has historically been to suspend analysis of the spatial practices and politics that actually constitute the borders of nation-states. "Thinking of the national economy as simply 'the macro level,'" he says, addressing the formal disciplinary treatment of national economies in Economics, "provided a substitute for a theoretical analysis of its geopolitical construction." Ibid., 89.

37. See, for example, Duncan Cameron, ed., *The Free Trade Deal* (Toronto: Lorimer, 1988); Ed Finn, Duncan Cameron, and John Calvert, eds., *The Facts on Free Trade* (Toronto: Lorimer, 1988); Gudmundson, "Free Trade: The Real Agenda"; Whitaker, "No Laments for the Nation"; and the varied contributions to Laurier La Pierre, ed., *If You Love This Country: Facts and Feelings on Free Trade* (Toronto: McClelland and Stewart, 1987). For subsequent critiques from similar positions, see Mel Hurtig, *The Betrayal of Canada* (Toronto: Stoddard, 1991); and Maude Barlow, *Parcel of Rogues: How Free Trade Is Failing Canada* (Toronto: Key Porter Books, 1991).

38. Canadian Auto Workers, *Canada Does Not Belong to These Two Men* (Willowdale, ON: CAW, 1987), 6.

39. Canadian Labour Congress, *Full Employment and Fairness: The Workers' Agenda for Canada* (Ottawa: CLC, 1986), 3.

40. Canadian Labour Congress, *Our Canada or Theirs? Workers Confront the Corporate Blueprint* (Ottawa: CLC, 1986), 1.

41. GATT-Fly, *Building Self-Reliance in Canada* (Toronto: GATT-Fly, 1987).

42. Anticipating Ross Perot, Mel Hurtig and Duncan Cameron referred to the job-stealing Mexican worker in their election time op-ed piece: "No Longer Will Canada Make Economic Sense," *Globe and Mail,* November 14, 1988, A7.

43. See Bryan Palmer, *Working Class Experience: The Rise and Reconstitution of Canadian Labour, 1800–1980* (Toronto: Butterworth, 1983), especially chapter 6.

44. Alain Gagnon and Mary Beth Montcalm, *Québec: Beyond the Quiet Revolution* (Scarborough, ON: Nelson Canada, 1990).

45. Marjorie Cohen, *Free Trade and the Future of Women's Work: Manufacturing and Service Industries* (Toronto: Garamond Press, 1987), 21.

46. Ibid., 49–65.

47. Ibid., 38.

48. Victoria Burstyn and Judy Rebick, "How 'Women Against Free Trade' Came to Write Its Manifesto," *Resources for Feminist Research* 17, no. 3 (1988): 140.

49. Ibid., 140.

50. NAC, *What Every Woman Needs to Know about Free Trade.*

51. Margaret Atwood, "About the Only Position," in La Pierre, *If You Love This Country,* 20.

52. Susan Tomc, "'The Missionary Position': Feminism and Nationalism in Margaret Atwood's *The Handmaid's Tale,*" *Canadian Literature* 138/39 (1993): 73–87.

53. See "Questions for NAC," *Montreal Gazette,* June 7, 1992, A7.

54. See "Canadian Threat Fades," *New York Times,* November 19, 1993, A10.

55. Perot initially used the phrase in the course of running as a presidential candidate against Clinton and Bush in 1992. "Let's go to the center of the bull's eye—the core problem," he said. "You implement that NAFTA—that Mexican trade agreement where they pay people $1 an hour, have no health care, no retirement, no pollution controls etc., etc., etc.—and you are going to hear a *giant sucking sound* of jobs being pulled out of this country." Quoted in Mayer, *Interpreting NAFTA,* 229.

56. Chip Roh, an assistant U.S. trade representative for North America, quoted in ibid., 42.

57. Quoted in ibid., 309.

58. Gary Hufbauer, "More Exports, More Jobs," *New York Times,* November 15, 1993, A16.

59. See Bob Herbert, "NAFTA's Bubble Bursts," *New York Times,* September 11, 1995, A13.

60. Louis Uchitelle, "In a Numbers War No One Can Count," *New York Times,* November 14, 1993, D1.

61. Ibid., 1. This form of argument had also been affirmed by more comprehensive academic surveys, including Jaime Ros's examination of the negligible and highly uncertain results produced by general equilibrium models; see Jaime Ros, "Mexico and NAFTA: Economic Effects and the Bargaining Process," in *Mexico and the North American Free Trade Agreement: Who Will Benefit?* ed. Victor Bulmer-Thomas, Nikki Craske, and Monica Serrano (London: Macmillan, 1994), 11–28.

62. Revealingly, the split in intranational labor organizing was already emerging prior to CUFTA's implementation as a result of the new continentalist "flexibility"-focused restructuring, a form of restructuring that pitted workers in Canada and the United States against each other. See John Holmes, "The Continental Integration of the North American Automobile Industry: From the Auto-Pact to the FTA and Beyond," *Environment and Planning A* 24 (1992): 95–119.

63. Thomas Friedman, "Adamant Unions Zero in on Clinton," *New York Times,* November 16, 1993, A9.

64. George [H. W.] Bush, *North American Free Trade Agreement with Mexico and Canada: Communication from the President of the United States Transmitting Notification of his intent to enter into a North American Free Trade Agreement with the governments of Mexico and Canada, pursuant to section 1103 (a) (1) of the Omnibus Trade and Competitiveness Act of 1988* (Washington, DC: GPO, 1992).

65. See Geoffrey Faux and William Spriggs, *U.S. Jobs and the Mexico Trade Proposal* (Washington, DC: Economic Policy Institute, 1991); and Timothy Koechlin, Mehrene Larudee, Samual Bowles, and Gerald Epstein, *Effect of the North American Free Trade Agreement on Investment, Employment and Wages in Mexico and the U.S.* (Amherst: University of Massachusetts, 1992).

66. International Brotherhood of Electrical Workers, *Examples of IBEW Job Losses to Mexico* (undated pamphlet).

67. *AFL-CIO News* 8 (1992): 3.

68. Quoted in Mayer, *Interpreting NAFTA,* 294.

69. Quoted in ibid., 253.

70. Ross Perot with Pat Choate, *Save Your Job, Save Your Country: Why NAFTA Must Be Stopped Now!* (New York: Hyperion, 1993). Pat Choate, a well-known protectionist critic of U.S. trade policy with Japan and Europe, later became a leader in the Perot-founded Reform Party.

71. Ibid. See especially chapter 4, "A Giant Sucking Sound," which begins "One million Mexicans enter the work force each year. They need jobs," at p. 41.

72. *The Economist,* July 10, 1993, 27.

73. See David Rosenbaum, "Gore and Perot Duel on T.V. Over the Trade Pact," *New York Times,* November 10, 1993, A1.

74. To be sure, the CNN duel appeared to many commentators as less than serious. Political scientists such as Martin Wattenberg worried that it was in fact a threat to the executive branch of the state and "demeaning to the White House" (quoted in David Rosenbaum, "White House Tactic to Debate Perot on Trade Pact," *New York Times,* November 8, 1993, A9), while columnist Maureen Dowd described it as "[m]ore like Punch and Judy—with charts instead of bats" ("More Like Wrestling Than Debating," *New York Times,* November 10, 1993, A12).

75. The lawsuit filed against the U.S. trade representative by these groups resulted in a federal district judge issuing an order that an environmental impact assessment be conducted on NAFTA's implications. After this embarrassment for Clinton's new Environmental Protection Agency, the order was overturned by a higher court. See *Public Citizen v. Office of the US Trade Representative,* 822 F. Supp. 21 (D.D.C. 1993) rev'd 5 F.3d 549 (1993).

76. David Rosenbaum, "House Backs Free Trade Pact in Major Victory for Clinton After a Long Hunt for Votes," *New York Times,* November 18, 1993, A1 and A14. More critical commentators also saw it as a political victory for the president, a victory, in Gordon Clark's words, coincident with "organized labor's loss." See Gordon Clark, "NAFTA – Clinton's Victory, Organized Labor's Loss," *Political Geography* 13 (1994): 377–84.

77. Rosenbaum, "House Backs Free Trade Pact," A1 and A14.

78. Ibid., A1.

79. For a useful analysis and critique of the labor side accord, the North American Agreement on Labor Cooperation, see Leonard Bierman, "The North American Agreement on Labor Cooperation: A New Frontier in North American Labor Relations," *Connecticut Journal of International Law* 10 (1995): 533–69.

80. Ross Perot, "Keep Wealth in the North," *New Perspectives Quarterly* 10, no. 4 (1993): 30–32.

81. Ibid., 31.

82. Ibid.

83. Perot with Choate, *Save Your Job, Save Your Country*, 29.

84. Ibid.

85. Ibid.

86. Ibid., i.

87. Ibid., 66.

88. See especially the first page in which Perot attempts to persuade readers of the high stakes involved by comparing Mexico to a U.S. state revoking constitutionally guaranteed rights and rules. Ibid., i.

89. Ibid.

90. Ibid., 77.

91. Mitchell, "Fixing the Economy."

92. Mitchell, *Rule of Experts*, 9.

93. Ibid., 292.

94. In some 1996 comments to interviewers Mitchell did note that the fixity of "the economy" was being undone by new economic developments. However, as he thereby complemented his intellectual unpacking of representations of "the economy" with a more practical economic argument, he nevertheless turned the latter into a thesis about new modes of representation. "What has happened is that the multiplication and intensification of the processes of representation (such as the growth of the service sector, as commodified representations are called, and the globalization of finance), has made it increasingly difficult to sustain the effect that economic discourse refers to a real, self-contained space that one can identify and map as the economy." Timothy Mitchell, "The Represented and the 'Real': Economy, Postmodernity and PostOrientalist Research," *disClosure* 5 (1996): 104.

95. This is the terminology of John Ruggie who has argued that the new world economy "is disembedded in several key dimensions." The first of these, he says, "is in its policy templates: the mental maps of spaces and structures with which policy-makers visualise the basic contours of their world." John Gerard Ruggie, "At Home Abroad, Abroad at Home: International Liberalisation and Domestic Stability in the New World Economy," *Millennium* 24, no. 3 (1994): 525.

96. I am quoting Michael Mann here who notes that the "territoriality of the state has created forces with a life of their own." See Michael Mann, "The Autonomous Power of the State: Its Origins, Mechanisms, and Results," *European Journal of Sociology* 25 (1984): 210.

97. Stephen Gill, "Globalisation, Market Civilisation, and Disciplinary Neoliberalism," *Millennium* 24, no. 3 (1995): 412. See also Stephen Clarkson, "A Continental Constitution Without a Referendum," *Canadian Forum*, 1992, 15–16.

98. Antonio Gramsci, *The Gramsci Reader: Selected Writings 1916–1935*, ed. David Forgacs (New York: New York University Press, 1989), 210.

99. For another theoretical account that also opens the door to such suggestions, see John Holloway, "Global Capital and the Nation State," *Capital and Class* 52 (1994): 23–43. See also Neil Fligstein's more Weberian account, which makes the case that markets are part of state formation. Neil Fligstein, *The Architecture of Markets: An Economic Sociology of Twenty-First Century Capitalist Societies* (Princeton: Princeton University Press, 2001).

100. Meric Gertler and Erica Schoenberger, "Industrial Restructuring and Continental Trade Blocs: The European Community and North America," *Environment and Planning A* 24 (1992): 2–10. See also Roger Rouse, "Thinking through Transnationalism: Notes on the Cultural Politics of Class Relations in the Contemporary United States," *Public Culture* 7 (1995): 357.

101. Sidney Weintraub, "A Vote against Free Trade Is a Vote for Protectionism," *New Perspectives Quarterly* 8, no. 1 (1991): 26–28.

102. Quoted in Stephen Blank, Stephen Krajewski, and Henry Yu, "Responding to a New Political and Economic Architecture in North America: Corporate Structure and Strategy," *Northwest Journal of Business and Economics,* Spring 1994, 17–18.

103. For one of the most cogent and concise critiques of North American free trade, see Ricardo Grinspun and Maxwell Cameron, "The Political Economy of North American Integration: Diverse Perspectives, Converging Criticisms," in *The Political Economy of North American Free Trade,* ed. Ricardo Grinspun and Maxwell Cameron (New York: St. Martin's Press, 1993), 3–25. For a more sanguine but still subtle analysis, see Robert A. Pastor, "NAFTA as the Center of an Integration Process: The Non-Trade Issues," *Brookings Review* 11, no. 1 (1993): 40–45.

104. See June Nash and Christine Kovic, "The Reconstitution of Hegemony: The Free Trade Act and the Transformation of Rural Mexico," in *Globalization: Critical Reflections,* ed. James H. Mittelman (Boulder, CO: Lynn Rienner, 1996), 165–85.

105. Viewing this process as illustrative of the "internationalization of the state," Panitch concludes that interstate treaties such as CUFTA and NAFTA thereby serve "to legally enforce upon future governments general adherence to the discipline of the capital market." Leo Panitch, "Rethinking the Role of the State," in Mittelman, *Globalization: Critical Reflections,* 96.

106. Keith Bradsher, "Clinton's Shopping List for Votes Has Ring of Grocery Buyer's List," *New York Times,* November 17, 1993, A11.

107. Ibid.

108. Ibid.

109. *North American Free Trade Agreement between the Government of the United States of America, the Government of Canada, and the Govern-*

ment of the United Mexican States (Washington, DC: GPO, 1993), vol. 1, Article 402, p. 4 - 2 - 43. Henceforth this text is referred to as *NAFTA*.

110. Allen Myerson, "Under the Free Trade Pact, Snarls on the Mexican Border," *New York Times*, June 21, 1994, A1 and C2.

111. Ibid., C2.

112. Darcy, "Introduction," xi.

113. Attorney General of Ontario, *The Impact of the Canada/U.S. Free Trade Agreement: A Legal Analysis,* Toronto, May 1988, 9.

114. Bruce Campbell, "Continental Corporate Economics," in Cameron and Watkins, *Canada under Free Trade,* 24.

115. See Scott Sinclair, "Trade Law," in Cameron and Watkins, *Canada under Free Trade,* 173–84, especially 177; and Sinclair, "NAFTA and US Trade Policy: Implications for Canada and Mexico," in Grinspun and Cameron, *Political Economy of North American Free Trade,* 219–33.

116. On employment, see especially Andrew Jackson, "Manufacturing," in Cameron and Watkins, *Canada under Free Trade,* 101–24. On the environment, see Steven Shrybman, "Trading Away the Environment," in Grinspun and Cameron, *Political Economy of North American Free Trade,* 271–94.

117. Jesús Silva Herzog, "Introduction," in Bulmer-Thomas et al., *Mexico and the North American Free Trade Agreement,* 3.

118. Quoted in Panitch, "Rethinking the Role of the State," 97.

119. David Sanger, "Rescue Package Tightens Restrictions on Mexico's Economic Policies," *New York Times,* February 22, 1995, A6.

120. For platitudes from Salinas about preserving Mexican sovereignty, see Carlos Salinas de Gotari, "NAFTA Is a Building Block, Not a Trade Bloc," *New Perspectives Quarterly* 10, no. 2 (1993): 14–18.

121. William Connolly, *Identity\Difference: Democratic Negotiations of Political Paradox* (Minneapolis: University of Minnesota Press, 1991), 201. See also David Held, "Democracy and Globalization," *Alternatives* 16, no. 2 (1991): 161–200.

122. Connolly, *Identity\Difference,* 200–201.

123. Robert B. Reich, *The Work of Nations: Preparing Ourselves for 21st-Century Capitalism* (New York: Vintage, 1992).

124. Ibid., 59.

125. Stephen Cullenberg and George Demartino, "The Competitiveness Debate: Toward an Internationalist Critique," in Callari, Cullenberg, and Biewener, *Marxism in the Postmodern Age,* 482–92.

126. See Robert B. Reich, *Locked in the Cabinet* (New York: Alfred Knopf, 1997).

127. See especially Timothy Mitchell, "The World as Exhibition," *Comparative Studies in Society and History* 31 (1989): 217–36.

128. Kathryn Kopinak, "The Maquiladorization of the Mexican Economy," in Grinspun and Cameron, *Political Economy of North American Free Trade*, 141–61.

129. Most notably Paul Hirst and Grahame Thompson translate the NAFTA acronym as referring to an "Area" in their widely cited critique of globalization exaggeration. Paul Hirst and Grahame Thompson, *Globalization in Question: The International Economy and the Possibilities of Governance* (Cambridge: Polity Press, 1996), 11.

130. Quoted in Ralph Nader, "Introduction: Free Trade and the Decline of Democracy," in *The Case against Free Trade: GATT, NAFTA, and the Globalization of Corporate Power*, ed. Ralph Nader et al. (San Francisco: Earth Island Press, 1991), 1–12.

131. See Denise Nadeau, "Women Fight Back," in Sinclair, *Crossing the Line*, 162.

132. Christina Gabriel and Laura Macdonald, "NAFTA, Women and Organising in Canada and Mexico: Forging a Feminist Internationality," *Millennium* 23, no. 3 (1994): 535–62.

133. Ibid., 559.

134. Kim Moody and Mary McGinn, *Unions and Free Trade: Solidarity vs. Competition* (Detroit: Labor Notes, 1992), 1.

135. Quoted in Matt Witt, "Labor and NAFTA," *Latin American Labor News* 5 (1992): 7 and 13.

136. Quoted in "Mexican Leader Joins Teamster Caravan," *New Teamster*, December 1992, 6.

137. See Tom Laney, "Step by Step," in *Free Trade Organizer's Packet* (Detroit: Labor Notes, n.d.); Barry Carr, "Globalization from Below: Labour Internationalism under NAFTA," *International Social Science Journal* 159 (March 1999): 49–60; and Robin Alexander and Peter Gilmore, "The Emergence of Cross-Border Labor Solidarity," *NACLA Report on the Americas* 28, no. 1 (1994): 42–49.

138. Carr, "Globalization from Below," 53.

139. See Rachel Hays, "AFL-CIO Restructuring Favors Cross-Border Solidarity," *BorderLines* 4, no. 9 (October 1996): 28.

140. Rebecca Johns, "Bridging the Gap between Class and Space: US Worker Solidarity with Guatemala," *Economic Geography* 74, no. 3 (1998): 252–71. Johns draws a useful distinction between this kind of progressive international solidarity and what she calls "accomodationist" solidarity, intervening abroad only with a view to reducing the competitive pressures represented by cheaper labor and less regulated foreign workplaces.

141. Carr, "Globalization from Below," 57.

142. See Kim Moody, *Workers in a Lean World: Unions in the International Economy* (London: Verso, 1997), 241.

143. Moody's book, *Workers in a Lean World,* finally ends with a manifesto for international social-movement unionism, having built up to it with richly detailed discussion of the successes, failures, and challenges to such developments on the ground right around the world.

144. Quoted in Gabriel and Macdonald, "NAFTA," 556.

145. Manuel Castells, for example, speaks of the disjuncture between what he calls spaces of flows and spaces of places in exactly this way. He concludes with depressing fatalism that "in the end, even democracies become powerless confronted with the ability of capital to circulate globally, of information to be transferred secretly, of markets to be penetrated or neglected, of planetary strategies of political-military power to be decided without the knowledge of nations" and so on. Manuel Castells, *The Informational City: Information Technology, Economic Restructuring and the Urban-Regional Process* (Oxford: Blackwell, 1989), 349. For a useful discussion of the nostalgia for the national that often animates these sorts of narratives, see Murray Low, "Representation Unbound: Globalization and Democracy," in *Spaces of Globalization: Reasserting the Power of the Local,* ed. Kevin Cox (New York: Guildford Press, 1997), 240–80. Low also effectively addresses here the more general problem of noncongruence between politics and economics, advocating the development of a less area-bound understanding of democracy.

146. Most of the emerging textbooks on globalization address this question in detail, most especially Jan Aart Scholte, *Globalization: A Critical Introduction* (New York: Palgrave, 2000), chapter 6; and David Held, Anthony McGrew, David Goldblatt, and Jonathan Perraton, *Global Transformations: Politics, Economics and Culture* (Stanford, CA: Stanford University Press, 1999), chapter 1.

147. See David Harvey, *The Limits to Capital* (London: Verso, 1999), especially chapter 13; and Neil Smith, *Uneven Development: Nature, Capital and the Production of Space* (Oxford: Blackwell, 1984).

148. Mitchell, "Fixing the Economy," 92.

149. See especially chapter 7 on "The Object of Development" in Mitchell, *Rule of Experts*. In this brilliant and detailed account of how U.S. development interests construct Egypt as an object of their so-called aid, Mitchell writes at length about the geographical fashioning of the country. "By portraying the country and its problems as a picture laid for the mind's eye like a map," he notes, "the image presents Egypt itself as something natural. The particular extent of space and population denoted by the name 'Egypt' is represented as an empirical object" (228). This chapter revised arguments from Timothy Mitchell, "America's Egypt: Discourse of the Development Industry," *Middle East Report,* March–April 1991, 18–34.

4. THE HAUNTING GROUND OF THE HYPHEN

1. Ernesto Laclau and Chantal Mouffe, *Hegemony and Socialist Strategy: Towards a Radical Democratic Politics* (New York: Verso, 1985). Hereafter referred to in the text as *Hegemony*.

2. The significance of this manifesto for wider work was made clear during the late 1980s by the development of arguments by other theorists, particularly antiracists such as Stuart Hall and Paul Gilroy, who were attempting to make room on the Left for accounts of the politics of race, racism, and antiracism. See Stuart Hall, *The Hard Road to Renewal: Thatcherism and the Crisis of the Left* (London: Verso, 1988); and Paul Gilroy, *"There Ain't No Black in the Union Jack": The Cultural Politics of Race and Nation* (London: Hutchinson, 1987). Notably, these writers were far more attentive than Laclau and Mouffe themselves to the inclusions and violent exclusions of nation-state boundaries. The British development of a New Times manifesto in the pages of *Marxism Today* was especially reflexive and valuable in this regard. See Stuart Hall and Martin Jacques, *New Times: The Changing Face of Politics in the 1990s* (London: Lawrence and Wishart, 1989).

3. Quoted in David Hollinger, *Postethnic America: Beyond Multculturalism* (New York: Basic Books, 1995), 141.

4. B. W. Powe, *A Tremendous Canada of Light* (Toronto: Coach House Press, 1993), 68. In another more subtle version of this Canadian national diversity discourse, the literary critic Linda Hutcheon has argued that it is the basis of a distinct cultural genre she calls "Canadian irony." Canadian culture, Hutcheon submits "is not yet a closed book. The historical anomalies that Canada has grown from make contradictions visible. Uniform national identity is challenged by a pride in heterogeneity and difference." See Linda Hutcheon, *Splitting Images: Contemporary Canadian Ironies* (Toronto: Oxford University Press, 1991), 39. A theorist of postmodernism, Hutcheon happily concludes thus that Canada actually encapsulates the ironies of postmodernity in the heterogeneity of the nation.

5. Richard Rorty, *Contingency, Irony and Solidarity* (Cambridge: Cambridge University Press, 1989), 191.

6. Critiques of Rorty's position are numerous, but of these, Terry Eagleton's stands out as the most witty and Bruce Robbins's as one of the most sophisticated. See Terry Eagleton, "Defending the Free World," in *Socialist Register, 1990*, ed. Ralph Miliband, Leo Panitch, and John Saville (London: Merlin Press, 1990), 85–93; and Bruce Robbins, *Feeling Global: Internationalism in Distress* (New York: New York University Press, 1999), chapter 7.

7. James Tully, "Diversity's Gambit Declined," in *Constitutional Predicament: Canada after the Referendum of 1992,* ed. Curtis Cook (Montreal and Kingston: McGill-Queen's University Press, 1994), 161.

8. Hollinger, *Postethnic America,* 162. Hereafter referred to in the text as *Postethnic.*

9. James Tully, *Strange Multiplicity: Constitutionalism in an Age of Diversity* (Cambridge: Cambridge University Press, 1995). Hereafter referred to in the text as *Multiplicity.*

10. In effect I will be showing how Laclau and Mouffe's reworking of the concept of citizenship leaves unexamined the national space of citizenship in liberal theory. Ironically, this liberal inheritance in their work therefore illustrates Hobsbawm's point that "much of the liberal theory of nations emerges only, as it were, on the margins of the discourse of liberal writers." In Eric Hobsbawm, *Nations and Nationalism since 1780: Programme, Myth, Reality,* 2nd ed. (Cambridge: Cambridge University Press, 1992), 24.

11. It should be emphasized that this does not mean that the concepts of hegemony and hegemonic formation are somehow redundant in the context of transnationalism. Far from it, as Katharyne Mitchell has documented at great length, the morphing transborder movements of migrants, capital, and ideas help make the geography of hegemony that much more apparent and therefore available for various forms of rearticulation. See Katharyne Mitchell, *Crossing the Neoliberal Line: Pacific Rim Migration and the Metropolis* (Philadelphia: Temple University Press, 2004).

12. This is not, however, to deny that Laclau and Mouffe's work has supported some rather similar, depoliticizing claims in the humanities. In 1988 Gayatri Chakravorty Spivak went so far as to describe such claims as reactionary. "Laclau and Mouffe's work," she commented in an interview, "to an extent, is supporting the kind of very reactionary pluralism that most humanities students are into anyway. [This] anti-essentialist metaphysics is in fact giving support to the politics of overdetermination: 'we are all overdetermined' sort of multiplicity of agents, which is really rather a reactionary position." In Gayatri Chakravorty Spivak with Ellen Rooney, "In a Word: Interview," *differences* 1, no. 2 (1988): 129. More recently, Chantal Mouffe herself has taken aim at Third Way rhetoric itself, criticizing the ways in which it negates the ground of politics altogether by presuming to transcend the agonism of Left/Right political conflict. See Chantal Mouffe, "A Politics Without Adversary?" in *The Democratic Paradox* (London: Verso, 2000), chapter 5.

13. See, for the most notable example, Norman Geras, "Post-Marxism?" *New Left Review* I/163 (1987): 42–79. Subsequently these same criticisms were rehearsed by others coming from less predictable quarters. Christopher Norris, for example, a writer of numerous handbooks and articles on deconstruction and poststructuralism, seemed born again as a materialist when he criticized the New Times theory of Stuart Hall and others that

drew on *Hegemony*. Such work, argued Norris, made manifest an "elective affinity" between a historicist approach to postmodernism and "that strain of ultra-nominalist skeptical thought for which the sublime figures as limit-point of language and representation." Christopher Norris, "Old Themes for New Times: Postmodernism, Theory and Cultural Politics," in *Principled Positions: Postmodernism and the Rediscovery of Value,* ed. Judith Squires (London: Lawrence and Wishart, 1993), 167. I do not want to revisit these torturous debates here, and will only note that Laclau and Mouffe's unfortunate reliance on axiomatic stipulations—such as "no object is given outside every discursive condition of emergence"—only exacerbated the problem. Not only did such statements complicate their own later appeals to the "given" in the book. It also meant that critics could easily overlook their less sweeping, if still axiomatic, elucidation of the fundamentally political nature of the "objects" they were discussing: "What is denied is not that such objects exist externally to thought, but the rather different assertion that they could constitute themselves as objects outside any discursive condition of emergence." *Hegemony,* 107–8.

14. Bob Jessop, *State Theory: Putting Capitalist States in Their Place* (Cambridge: Polity Press, 1990), 294.

15. Nicos Mouzelis, "Marxism or Post-Marxism?" *New Left Review* I/167 (1988): 116.

16. Donna Landry and Gerald MacLean, "Rereading Laclau and Mouffe," *Rethinking Marxism* 4, no. 4 (1991): 41–60.

17. It should be noted nonetheless that Laclau and Mouffe deploy the classic gesture of Western historicism to claim that contemporary Third World politics take the form of simplified, two-camp popular struggles. See *Hegemony,* 131, and Landry and MacLean, "Rereading Laclau and Mouffe."

18. In these particular lines it seems we are asked to forget all the earlier pronouncements upon how such "structural limits" are but part of the wider discursive flux of politically mediated social life, we are asked to forget all the authors' critiques of struturalism, and we are left, I think, with the worst of both worlds: namely, a theoreticist vision of politics supported at the end by the final deus ex machina of a particularly anonymous, untheorized, and therefore overly totalized picture of a structure proceeding from the outside. It is the haunting hyphen in nation-state that seems to consolidate this awkward resolution. Presumably it is part of such "structural limits." But as a meeting point of politics, economics, and culture its redefinition must clearly be considered part of the struggle for radical democracy. Certainly, that was what the U.K. theorists of New Times suggested when, following Laclau and Mouffe, they also made the question of the nation and citizenship a focal point of the new debate about hegemony. See Stuart Hall and David Held,

"Citizens and Citizenship," in *New Times,* ed. Stuart Hall and David Held (London: Verso, 1990), 173–88. However, in *Hegemony* itself, the nation-state only ever returns as a suppressed specter haunting the argument with abstract spatial metaphors.

19. As the comprehensive rereading of *Hegemony* and Laclau and Mouffe's more recent work by Anna Marie Smith valuably underlines, their conception of a radical and plural democracy continues to invoke the creation and defense of a "space of contestation." Anna Marie Smith, *Laclau and Mouffe: The Radical Democratic Imaginary* (New York: Routledge, 1998), 185. Smith herself suggests that this space need not always coincide with the nation-state when she notes that "radical democratization would ultimately require economic transformations and progressive forms of political solidarity on a transnational level" (31). However, her Derridean attention to the recitative aspect of Laclau and Mouffe's own argument—the way they suggest "that every moment of democratic struggle to some extent stands on historically prepared ground" (7)—helps explain why this lonely hour of the transnational never comes in *Hegemony.* As I have sought to detail at length here, it never comes because the text, its historicist genealogy of hegemony, and its resulting investment in the terrain of liberal democracy, along with all the attendant vocabularies of state, civil society, and citizenship, remain haunted by the hyphen in nation-state.

20. This incarceration figure is for 1994, the year Hollinger wrote the preface to *Postethnic America.* Cited in Katherine Beckett and Bruce Western, "Governing Social Marginality: Welfare, Incarceration and the Transformation of State Policy," *Punishment and Society* 3, no. 1 (2000): 43.

21. It is no wonder, then, that *Postethnic America* is praised in such lofty terms on the back cover. "Reading this book," says one high-minded reviewer, "is like breathing pure mountain air when one has been long in the suffocating valleys of struggles over identity." Tully, by contrast, is keen to keep breathing the valley air, which is to say he attempts repeatedly to make his audience consider what the peaks of liberal normativity look like from the position of the colonized and marginalized. As well as citing Said, Paula Allen Gunn, bell hooks, Carlos Fuentes, Bhikhu Parekh, Iris Marion Young, and Mary Ellen Turpel in this regard, Tully also draws attention to the work of Ronald Takaki who, he notes, "expose[s] the bias of the dominant traditions of interpretation and the unlikelihood of a fair hearing within their conventions." *Multiplicity,* 54.

22. Quoted and examined in detail in *Postethnic,* 67–75.

23. Tully, "Diversity's Gambit Declined," 161.

24. James Tully, "Struggles over Recognition and Distribution," *Constellations* 7, no. 4 (2000): 475.

25. Patchen Markell, a commentator on Tully's writing on recognition,

makes this clear when he notes that Tully "puts politics back into the 'politics of recognition.'" Patchen Markell, "The Recognition of Politics: A Comment on Emcke and Tully," *Constellations* 7, no. 4 (2000): 501.

26. See Jeremy Webber, *Reimagining Canada: Language Culture, Community and the Canadian Constitution* (Kingston and Montreal: McGill-Queen's University Press, 1994), especially 319.

27. Janet Azjenstat, "Constitution Making and the Myth of the People," in Cook, *Constitutional Predicament*, 121.

28. Tully, "Diversity's Gambit Declined," 162.

29. It is never fully fixed, Laclau and Mouffe argue, because the actual establishment of the relationship simultaneously transforms the conjoined identities in the new identity. "[W]e call articulation any practice establishing a relation among elements such that their identity is modified as a result of the articulatory practice." *Hegemony*, 105. Later they elaborate how the "practice of articulation, therefore, consists in the construction of nodal points which partially fix meaning; and the partial character of this fixation proceeds from the openness of the social, a result in its turn, of the constant overflowing of every discourse by the infinitude of the field of discursivity" (113).

30. Insofar as this transnational neoliberal regime severely curtails options for democratic action and change, I am suggesting an affirmative answer to the question posed by Markell in his sympathetic critique of Tully. "Does the relationship between citizens and the state come to be figured as a relationship of recognition," he asks, "precisely in response to the felt difficulty of locating spaces for meaningful democratic action and participation in contemporary public spheres?" Markell, "Recognition of Politics," 504.

31. For a particularly useful survey of these trends that is well attuned to their geographical ramifications, see Janine Brodie, *The Political Economy of Canadian Regionalism* (Toronto: Harcourt Brace Jovanovich, 1990).

32. Jane Jenson, "'Different' But Not 'Exceptional': Canada's Permeable Fordism," *Canadian Review of Sociology and Anthropology* 26, no. 1 (1989): 69–94.

33. For what remains one of the best accounts of the differences between Fordism and its timing of onset and decline in the wealthy Western countries, see Scott Lash and John Urry, *The End of Organized Capitalism* (Madison: University of Wisconsin Press, 1987).

34. For example, the political economists Stephen McBride and John Shields outline quite clearly how this represented a hegemonic articulation of constitutional politics with commitments to deregulatory, laissez-faire political-economic reform. "The Mulroney government," they note (albeit using the word *neo-conservative* in place of *neo-liberal*), "made efforts to take advantage of the 'openness' of Canada's constitutional arrangements,

largely the result of territorial and national cleavages, to constitutionalize neo-conservative principles concerning the respective spheres of governments and markets." Stephen McBride and John Shields, *Dismantling a Nation: Canada and the New World Order* (Halifax: Fernwood Publishing, 1993), 164.

35. Most canonically, for example, Peter Russell, *Constitutional Odyssey: Can Canadians Become a Sovereign People?* (Toronto: University of Toronto, Press, 1993), especially chapter 5.

36. In an interesting article about what he calls the "three equalities," Alan Cairns suggests that much of the constitutional crisis can be read in the terms of a clash between three discourses of equality: "the equality of citizens" (symbolized by the Charter itself), "the equality of the provinces" (symbolized by the amending formula), and "the equality of the two national peoples" (symbolized by bilingualism). In Alan C. Cairns, "Constitutional Change and the Three Equalities," in *Options for a New Canada,* ed. Ronald Watts and Douglas M. Brown (Toronto: University of Toronto Press, 1991), 69. My own account is different insofar as I am linking the equality of both citizens and provinces to the logic of democratic equivalence inaugurated by the Charter. I regard these as brought into crisis by the multinational nature of the negotiations, which, including the politics of First Nations excluded by Cairns, seems irreducible to the logic of equivalence.

37. See Michael Mandel, *The Charter of Rights and the Legalization of Politics in Canada* (Toronto: Wall and Thompson, 1989).

38. However, to do so was to negotiate in what was in many ways a legal recoding of structural violence. Native judge and legal scholar Mary Ellen Turpel captured this very well when she described how the Charter had a colonizing effect for First Nations, an effect that (similar to Laclau and Mouffe's own Eurocentric narrative of democracy) infringed rights to collective self-government while it operated in the name of democracy. See M. E. Turpel, "Aboriginal Peoples and the Canadian Charter: Interpretative Monopolies and Cultural Differences," *Canadian Human Rights Yearbook* (Ottawa: Les Presses de l'Université d'Ottawa, 1989–90), 249–95.

39. Cited in F. L. Morton, "The Living Constitution," in *Introductory Readings in Canadian Government and Politics,* ed. Robert M. Krause and R. H. Wagenberg (Toronto: Copp Clark Pitman, 1991), 60.

40. See also Webber, *Reimagining Canada,* 157.

41. For a more extensive account, see J. Vickers, P. Rankin, and C. Appelle, *Politics as if Women Mattered: A Political Analysis of the National Action Committee on the Status of Women* (Toronto: University of Toronto Press, 1993), as well as Matthew Sparke, "Negotiating National Action: Free Trade, Constitutional Debate and the Gendered Geopolitics of Canada," *Political Geography* 15 (1996): 615–39.

42. Webber, *Reimagining Canada,* 152.

43. The consultation process was launched with much fanfare by the government under the banner of a Citizens' Forum on Canada's Future. This supposed "forum," organized formally as a Royal Commission and led by Keith Spicer, became known as the Spicer Commission. See the *Citizens' Forum on Canada's Future: Report to the People and Government of Canada* (Ottawa: Minister of Supply and Services, 1991).

44. Keith Spicer, "Chairman's Foreword," in *Citizens' Forum on Canada's Future,* 5.

45. See *Shaping Canada's Future Together: Proposals* (Ottawa: Minister of Supply and Services, 1991), 3.

46. Ibid., 29.

47. See ibid., 32.

48. See ibid., 38–39.

49. Gérald Beaudoin and Dorothy Dobbie, *Report of the Special Joint Committee on a Renewed Canada* (Ottawa: Minister of Supply and Services, 1992), 3.

50. The proposals for greater harmonization of fiscal polices (in a monetarist direction) were rejected, as was the proposed restriction of the Bank of Canada's mandate to the narrowed issue of price stability (ibid., 9).

51. Ibid., 22.

52. *Consensus Report on the Constitution: Charlottetown, August 28, 1992, Final Text/Rapport du Consensus sur la Constitution: Charlottetown, Le 28 août 1992, Texte définitif* (Ottawa: Government of Canada, 1992), § III, ¶¶29–35.

53. Ibid., § III, ¶25.

54. Ibid., § IB, ¶4.

55. Ibid., § IA, ¶1, Amendment 2, (1) b.

56. Rosemary J. Coombe, "Tactics of Appropriation and the Politics of Recognition in Late Modern Democracies," *Political Theory* 21, no. 3 (1988): 419.

57. George Sánchez, "Creating the Multicultural Nation: Adventures in Post-Nationalist American Studies in the 1990s," in *Postnationalist American Studies,* ed. John Carlos Rowe (Berkeley: University of California Press, 2001), 40.

58. Quoted in ibid., 40.

59. Ibid., 41.

60. Ibid.

61. Nikhil Pal Singh, "Culture/Wars: Recoding Empire in an Age of Democracy," *American Quarterly* 50, no. 3 (1998): 506.

62. Nancy Fraser, *Unruly Practices: Power, Discourse, and Gender in*

Contemporary Social Theory (Minneapolis: University of Minnesota Press, 1989).

63. Section 101 Findings, *The Personal Responsibility and Work Opportunity Reconciliation Act of 1996* (henceforth PRWORA), Public Law 104-193, U.S. Statutes at Large 110 (1996): 2110.

64. Gwendolyn Mink, "Aren't Poor Single Mothers Women? Feminists, Welfare Reform and Welfare Justice," in *Whose Welfare?* ed. Gwendolyn Mink (Ithaca, NY: Cornell University Press, 1999), 171.

65. Ibid., 173.

66. David Hollinger, "Authority, Solidarity, and the Political Economy of Identity: The Case of the United States," *diacritics* 29, no. 4 (1999): 117.

67. Ibid.

68. See Jamie Peck, *Workfare States* (New York: Guildford Press, 2001), 68.

69. Ed Gillespie and Bob Schellhas, eds., *Contract with America: The Bold Plan by Rep. Newt Gingrich, Rep. Dick Armey and the House Republicans to Change the Nation* (New York: Random House, 1994), 70.

70. Dan Carter, *From George Wallace to Newt Gingrich: Race in the Conservative Counterrevolution, 1963–1994* (Baton Rouge: Louisiana State University Press, 1996), especially 110–11.

71. Orrin Hatch quoted in Rickie Solinger, "Dependency and Choice: The Two Faces of Eve," in Mink, *Whose Welfare?* 7.

72. Eileen Boris, "When Work Is Slavery," in Mink, *Whose Welfare?* 37.

73. Robert Pear, "Welfare Spending Shows Huge Shift," *New York Times,* October 13, 2003, A1.

74. Jason deParle, "Shrinking Welfare Rolls Leave Record High Share of Minorities," *New York Times,* July 27, 1998, A1.

75. One of the most sophisticated accounts of this peculiarly restrictionist aspect of the devolution offered in PRWORA is provided in Sanford F. Schram, *After Welfare: The Culture of Postindustrial Social Policy* (New York: New York University Press, 2000), 92 and 96.

76. See Gillespie and Schellhas, *Contract with America,* 19 and 66. Other expressions of this quotidian kind of federalist common sense are, of course, common. See, for example, Sam Brownback, "A New Contract with America," *Policy Review* 76 (1996): 16–21.

77. Schram, *After Welfare,* chapter 4.

78. Schram notes: "If we adjust benefit levels for the variation in the cost of housing, we find there is very little variation across states, thus making welfare migration economically irrational in most instances." Ibid., 102.

79. Ibid., 106.

80. The links between states' rights discourse and racism go back, of course, to the Civil War. But thanks to the hegemonic rearticulation work

of southerners such as George Wallace, that heritage has overshadowed late twentieth-century American politics very powerfully. See Carter, *From George Wallace to Newt Gingrich.*

81. Joe Soss, Sanford Schram, Thomas Vartanian, and Erin O'Brien, "Setting the Terms of Relief: Explaining State Policy Choices in the Devolution Revolution," *American Journal of Political Science* 45, no. 2 (April 2001): 390.

82. Schram, *After Welfare,* 18.

83. *Postethnic,* 156. Specifically, Hollinger's critique is aimed at scholars such as Nancy Fraser and Arjun Appadurai whom he describes as "celebrants of multiple publics and of diasporic solidarities" (156).

84. Schram, *After Welfare,* 7.

85. Newt Gingrich, *Lessons Learned the Hard Way: A Personal Report* (New York: HarperCollins, 1998), 7.

86. See Beckett and Western, "Governing Social Marginality."

87. See Peter Edelman, "The True Purpose of Welfare Reform," *New York Times,* May 29, 2002, A18.

88. Robert B. Reich, *Locked in the Cabinet* (New York: Alfred Knopf, 1997).

89. Peck, *Workfare States,* 6.

90. Schram, *After Welfare,* 33 and 34.

91. Peck, *Workfare States,* 361.

92. Audrey Singer, "Immigrants, Their Families and Their Communities in the Aftermath of Welfare Reform," *Research Perspectives on Migration* 3, no. 1 (2001): 1.

93. Jaqueline Hagan and Nestor Rodriguez, "Resurrecting Exclusion: The Impact of Legislative Reforms in Texas and Mexico," *Research Perspectives on Migration* 3, no. 1 (2001): 15.

94. Singh, "Culture/Wars," 510.

95. William E. Connolly, "Democracy and Territoriality," *Millennium* 20, no. 3 (1991): 463.

5. EMPIRE'S GEOGRAPHY

1. Michael Hardt and Antonio Negri, *Empire* (Cambridge, MA: Harvard University Press, 2000). Hereafter referred to in the text as *Empire.*

2. Robert Kagan and William Kristol, "The Present Danger," *National Interest,* Spring 2000, http://www.nationalinterest.org/ (accessed August 17, 2003).

3. For a typical newspaper article registering the increasing and often positive uses of the term "American empire," see Julia Keller and Marja

Mills, "Going Global Many Are Now Resigned to the New American Empire," *Times Union,* May 4, 2003, B1.

4. Michael Ignatieff, "The Burden? With a Military of Unrivaled Might, the United States Rules a New Kind of Empire," *New York Times Magazine,* January 5, 2003, 22.

5. Max Boot, "American Imperialism? No Need to Run Away from Label," *USA Today,* May 6, 2003, 15A.

6. "The former American Secretary of State Dean Acheson famously said that Britain had lost an empire but failed to find a role. Perhaps," Ferguson concludes his glossy imperial apologia, "the reality is that the Americans have taken our old role without yet facing that an empire comes with it." Niall Ferguson, *Empire: The Rise and Demise of the British World Order and the Lessons for Global Power* (New York: Basic Books, 2003), 370.

7. Maureen Dowd, "Lemon Fizzes on the Banks of the Euphrates," *New York Times,* September 18, 2002, A16. Dowd later went on to describe the Bush team's occupation of Iraq as an "Empire of Novices." "The Bush foreign policy team always had contempt for Bill Clinton's herky-jerky, improvised interventions around the world," she noted. "But now the Bush 'dream team' is making the impetuous Clinton look like Rommel." Maureen Dowd, "Empire of Novices," *New York Times,* September 3, 2003, A19.

8. "War Lite Is All Very Well. Empire Lite Is a Mistake," *The Economist,* August 16, 2003, 9–10.

9. "America and Empire," *The Economist,* August 16, 2003, 19–22.

10. Vladimir Lenin, "Imperialism, the Highest Stage of Capitalism: A Popular Outline," in *Selected Works in Three Volumes,* vol. 1 (Moscow: Progress Publishers, 1963), 634–731. Although Lenin is most often read as an economistic theorist of imperialism who was overly wedded to a stagist model of monopolization and financialization leading to interimperial rivalry, it needs noting that, beneath all these politically instrumental arguments, Lenin still wanted to theorize the contradictions of imperialism as contradictions emerging from the conjunctural grounds of capitalism.

11. Perry Anderson, "Force and Consent," *New Left Review* 17 (2002): 5–30.

12. Arundhati Roy, "Mesopotamia. Babylon. The Tigris and Euphrates," *Critical Geopolitics,* 2003, http://www.criticalgeopolitics.com/Web/Roy.htm (accessed June 27, 2003).

13. Thomas de Zengotita, "The Romance of Empire and the Politics of Self-Love," *Harper's Magazine* 307 (July 2003): 31.

14. For a suggestive but rather different attempt to chart two opposing imagined geographies of the contemporary moment, see Tariq Ali, *The Clash of Fundamentalisms: Crusades, Jihads and Modernity* (London: Verso, 2000).

15. Richard O' Brien's *Global Financial Integration: The End of Geography* (London: Pinter, 1992) remains a classic statement of the genre. For some suggestive but all too abbreviated explorations of the imagined geographies attending globalization discourse, see Peter Bratsis, "Over, Under, Sideways, Down: Globalization, Spatial Metaphors, and the Question of State Power," in *Implicating Empire: Globalization and Resistance in the Twenty-first Century*, ed. Stanley Aronowitz and Heather Gautney (New York: Basic Books, 2003), 123–31.

16. I have adapted the term "geoeconomics" from its initial usage by the Washington, D.C., foreign policy pundit Edward Luttwak who uses it in a statecentric and representationally realist way to describe interstate conflict over economic issues in the context of intensified economic globalization. In the 1990s, Luttwak thus depicted conflicts such as those over technological espionage as becoming the dominant successor paradigm of international tension after the geopolitical rivalries of the cold war. See Edward Luttwak, "The Coming Global War for Economic Power: There Are No Nice Guys on the Battlefield of Geo-Economics," *International Economy* 7, no. 5 (1993): 18–67. My approach, by contrast, draws on all the work in critical geopolitics examining the cultural scripting of geopolitical discourse. In Gerard Toal's own words, this work has shown that, "[r]ather than being an objective recording of the realities of world power, *geopolitics is an interpretative cultural practice.*" Gerard Toal, "Geopolitical Structures and Geopolitical Cultures: Towards Conceptual Clarity in the Critical Study of Geopolitics" (unpublished mimeo, 2004). Geoeconomics needs to be seen as a subspecies of such interpretative, but powerfully consequential cultural practices. Like geopolitics, therefore, it needs also to be seen as being interarticulated with structural political-economic changes that it both reflects and, through the strategic discourse of political and business leaders, affects. Elsewhere I have argued in this way that the case of Cascadia (discussed here in chapter 2) can be understood as both a kind of *promotional* geoeconomics that reflects real economic shifts (including CUFTA and NAFTA) and a representational strategy aimed to attract global investment into the stylized cross-border region. See Matthew Sparke "From Geopolitics to Geoeconomics: Transnational State Effects in the Borderlands," *Geopolitics* 3, no. 2 (1998): 61–97; and Matthew Sparke and Victoria Lawson, "Entrepreneurial Political Geographies of the Global-Local Nexus," in *A Companion to Political Geography*, ed. J. Agnew, K. Mitchell, and G. Ó Tuathail (London: Sage, 2002), 315–34. Here, by contrast, I am addressing the more sweeping planetary discourse of globalist geoeconomics, a discourse that simultaneously reflects and contributes to the expansion of free-market relations globally. I take the term "globalist" in this sense from Manfred Steger's useful critique of the ways

in which promoters of laissez-faire neoliberal reforms have ideologically instrumentalized accounts of globalization as inevitable and unchangeable. Manfred Steger, *Globalism: The New Market Ideology* (New York: Rowman and Littletree, 2001). As feminist geographers have shown, such globalism also involves accepting and reproducing the simple ideologically interested master narrative of globalization as unstoppable penetration. See J.-K. Gibson-Graham, *The End of Capitalism (As We Knew It): A Feminist Critique of Political Economy* (Oxford: Blackwell, 1996). It is this same sense of penetrative mastery that I argue here also enables the masculinist geoeconomic vision of a global level plain of smooth space.

17. This is also often an argument on the Left. See, for example, Carl Parrini, "The Age of Ultraimperialism," *Radical History Review* 57 (1993): 7–20.

18. The historical case for this was made with aplomb by Eric Hobsbawm in the immediate aftermath of the Iraq War. Eric Hobsbawm, "Empire on Which the Sun Will Set," *Le Monde Diplomatique,* June 2003, 1–2.

19. For a useful summary of the various versions of hegemonic decline thesis, see John Agnew and Stuart Corbridge, *Mastering Space: Hegemony, Territory and International Political Economy* (New York: Routledge, 1995), especially 106–14. Some of the most articulate statements of the thesis continue to come from Immanuel Wallerstein himself, most recently in his book *The Decline of American Power: The U.S. in a Chaotic World* (New York: New Press, 2003). Wallerstein usefully discusses the ways in which the unilateralist visions of the hawks in the Bush administration are based on faulty assumptions about absolute American power that the Left has too commonly just reproduced, albeit in inverted ethical evaluations. He also makes a compelling case about why the move toward more militaristic intervention will only hasten the decline of American influence. But when he argues that the military option is the "only card" that the United States can play (24), he misses the ongoing influence of American state practices through the mediated networks of international finance, currency policies, and world trade arrangements. He also therefore misses the ways in which the exercise of military force needs to be understood in relationship to the ideologies—including geoeconomic discourse—attending the entrenchment of neoliberalism worldwide. In addition to Anderson's argument about a new hegemony of force, another very useful antidote to the declinist thesis is provided by Peter Gowan, "The American Campaign for Global Sovereignty," *Socialist Register,* 2003, 1–27.

20. Quoted in Ignatieff, "The Burden?" 22.

21. This was ultimately the *Economist*'s position in "War Lite Is All Very Well," but see also Joseph Nye, "Ill-Suited for Empire," *Washington Post,* May 25, 2003, B7.

22. Quoted in Ignatieff, "The Burden?" 22.

23. In this sense the chapter follows up on the suspicions of Rob Walker. "[W]hile the term empire has many interesting resonances under contemporary circumstances," he notes, "both the narrative of a modernising process of internalisation [Empire] and the competing narratives of great power hegemony and American imperialism that rise up every time Bush the Younger opens his mouth will quickly seem fairly threadbare as ways of making sense of contemporary political life." R. B. J. Walker, "On the Immanence/Imminence of Empire," *Millennium* 31, no. 2 (2002): 344.

24. Quotations from *Empire,* 307. Geographer John Agnew, for example, suggests thus that the argument of *Empire* addresses the reorganization of world hegemony in a useful way even if the term Empire itself is inadequate to the task. "Their choice of the word 'empire' to describe this phenomenon," he says, "is misleading if attention getting." John Agnew, "American Hegemony into American Empire? Lessons from the Invasion of Iraq," *Antipode* 35, no. 3 (2003): 871–85.

25. Italics in the original. The italics in *Empire* function in various ways: sometimes just to mark an emphatic point, as here, and sometimes to register Hardt and Negri's uncanny but ultimately arrogant experiments with a more prophetic, quasi-spiritual voice.

26. The reference to the example of Francis of Assisi comes as part of the buildup to *Empire*'s final, oracular appeal to "the irrepressible lightness and joy of being communist" (413). The political theology of the multitude's spirit, though, shines from many other tabernacles throughout the book. We are invited in this way, for example, to genuflect before a notably fetishized ontology of labor mobility. It is in workers' movements that Hardt and Negri expect us to see the most hopeful expressions of the smoothing of the striae of national tradition. And yet it is precisely in the brutally unsmooth and often deadly experience of borders by migrant workers that we see the nation-state living on. "Ultimately," as Kalyvas argues, "by dissolving the distinction between factum (migration as a socio-economic category) and jus (migration as an anti-capitalist, communist desire), Hardt and Negri's ontology of labor mobility flees from its own radicalism, gesturing towards a labor metaphysics and a political theology." Andreas Kalyvas, "Feet of Clay? Reflections on Hardt and Negri's *Empire*," *Constellations* 10, no. 2 (2003): 272.

27. Stuart Corbridge, "Countering Empire," *Antipode* 35, no. 1 (2003): 188.

28. Reprinted as Karl Kautsky, "Ultra-imperialism," *New Left Review* I/59 (1970): 46.

29. Nor are Lenin's competing theses about interimperial rivalry, monopolization and financialization, directly relevant to today's global con-

juncture. While the Clinton years might be interpreted retroactively to have been about proving Kautsky right and while Bush seems more interested in vindicating Lenin's view, neither account is really adequate to a moment in which older forms of imperialism have morphed into more integrated but still yet contested and far from unified networks of global order. Perry Anderson puts it enigmatically but suggestively when he says that "we live in a world which is inseparably—in a way that neither of them could foresee— both the past described by Lenin and the future anticipated by Kautsky." Anderson, "Force and Consent," 21.

30. Leo Panitch and Sam Gindin, "Gems and Baubles in *Empire*," *Historical Materialism* 10, no. 2 (2002): 17–43, at 30.

31. Tarak Barkawi and Mark Laffey, "Retrieving the Imperial: Empire and International Relations," *Millennium* 31, no. 1 (2002): 124.

32. Alex Callinicos has protested this reframing saying that the idea of an international state dominated by the United States is "false." Strangely, he prefers to call on the more realist formulations of interstate rivalry offered by Kenneth Waltz and Samuel Huntington in order to buttress his abstract argument that "The world of imperialism, as it was portrayed by Lenin and Bukharin during the First World War—an anarchic struggle of unequal rivals—still exists, with the United States as first among unequals." Alex Callinicos, "The Actuality of Imperialism," *Millennium* 31, no. 2 (2002): 319–26. This alternative argument unfortunately downplays the ways in which interstate relations are powerfully mediated by both neoliberal governmentality and U.S. state intervention at the same time.

33. They even note that "Hegel had already perceived something very similar," and then proceed to quote from him: "America is . . . the country of the future, and its world-historical importance has yet to be revealed in the ages which lie ahead. . . . It is a land of desire for all those who are weary of the historical arsenal of old Europe." *Empire,* 375. Rumsfeld's fondness for so-called New Europe is also in some senses anticipated here.

34. Leslie Sklair, *The Transnational Capitalist Class* (Oxford: Blackwell, 2001). For an earlier anticipation of these sorts of arguments, see also Richard Sklar, "Postimperialism: A Class Analysis of Multinational Corporate Expansion," *Comparative Politics* 9, no. 1 (1976): 75–92.

35. Peter Dicken, "Placing Firms – Firming Places: Grounding the Debate on the Global Corporation" (unpublished paper presented at the conference on "Responding to Globalization" at the University of Colorado, Boulder, 2002). See also his book-length treatment of the same issues: Peter Dicken, *Global Shift: Reshaping the Global Economic Map of the 21st Century* (New York: Guildford Press, 2003).

36. Ibid., 4.

37. See Lisa Rofel, "Discrepant Modernities and Their Discontents,"

positions 9, no. 3 (2001): 637–49. I have elsewhere sought to build myself on Spivak's rearticulation of value theory in an empirical study of the temping industry that also draws on Diane Elson's arguments about the value theory of labor. See Matthew Sparke, "A Prism for Contemporary Capitalism: Temporary Work as Displaced Labor as Value," *Antipode* 26, no. 4 (1994): 295–321.

38. Sue Roberts, "Global Strategic Vision, Managing the World," in *Globalization under Construction: Governmentality, Law and Identity*, ed. B. Maurer and R. W. Perry (Minneapolis: University of Minnesota Press, 2004), 1–22; and Nigel Thrift, "Performing Cultures in the New Economy," *Annals of the Association of American Geographers* 90, no. 4 (2000): 674–92.

39. Of course, as other scholars of corporate governmentality have pointed out, the resulting global imaginaries are often worked out in very place-specific ways. See Erica Schoenberger, "Corporate Strategy and Corporate Strategists: Power, Identity and Knowledge within the Firm," *Environment and Planning A* 16 (1994): 435–51; and Wendy Larner and Richard Le Heron, "The Spaces and Subjects of a Globalizing Economy: A Situated Exploration of Method," *Environment and Planning D: Society and Space* 20 (2003): 753–74.

40. Examples of the influence of these sorts of collaborations on the geo-economic plain are valuably documented in Y. Dezalay and B. G. Garth, *The Internationalization of Palace Wars: Lawyers, Economists and the Contest to Transform Latin American States* (Chicago: University of Chicago Press, 2002).

41. Leo Panitch and Sam Gindin, "Global Capitalism and American Empire," *Socialist Register*, 2004, http://www.yorku.ca/socreg/Panitch%20 and%20Gindin%2004.html (accessed February 3, 2005).

42. Thomas L. Friedman, *Longitudes and Attitudes: Exploring the World after September 11* (New York: Farrar, Strauss and Giroux, 2002), 49.

43. The Project for the New American Century, *Rebuilding America's Defenses: Strategies, Forces and Resources for a New Century* (Washington, DC: PNAC, 2000), 51. At http://www.newamericancentury.org/ (accessed September 26, 2003).

44. Neil Mackay, "Bush Planned Iraq 'Regime Change' before Becoming President," *Sunday Herald* (Glasgow), September 15, 2002, 1.

45. PNAC, *Rebuilding America's Defenses*, 14.

46. At http://www.newamericancentury.org/iraqclintonletter.htm (accessed September 26, 2003).

47. Available on the PNAC Web site at http://www.newamericancentury .org/statementofprinciples.htm (accessed September 26, 2003).

48. See, in particular, Nicholas Lemann, "The Next World Order," *New*

Yorker, April 1, 2002, 42–48; and Joseph Cirincione, "Origins of Regime Change in Iraq," *Carnegie Endowment for International Peace: Issue Brief 6,* no. 5 (2003), 1–3.

49. Quoted in Jane Perlez, "America Talks and (Some) Others Listen. (Madeleine Albright Sees the U.S. as the 'Indispensable Nation')," *New York Times,* September 12, 1999, WK 1.

50. Quoted in Gowan, "American Campaign," 9.

51. See the valuable genealogy offered by Alain Frachon and Daniel Vernet, "The Strategist and the Philosopher," *Le Monde,* http://www.lemonde.fr/article/0,5987,3230—316921-,00.html (accessed April 18, 2003); and Sam Tanenhaus, "Bush's Brain Trust," *Vanity Fair,* July 2003, 114–35; as well as the very useful interview between Danny Postel and the Canadian philosophical critic of Strauss, Sadia Drury: Danny Postel, "Noble Lies and Perpetual War: Leo Strauss, the Neo-Cons, and Iraq," http://www.opendemocracy.net/debates/article-3-77-1542.jsp (accessed November 24, 2003). From the perspective of the argument I develop later in the chapter about a complicity between the geopolitics and globalist geoeconomic assumptions, Drury interestingly underlines the ambivalence that the Straussian neoconservatives have had toward the modern concept of nationalism. Irving Kristol, having at one point denounced nationalism, later went on to explain in 1993 that a neoconservative nationalism was much more worldly. "Neoconservatives believe," he said, " that the goals of American foreign policy must go well beyond a narrow, too literal definition of 'national security.' It is the national interest of a world power, as this is defined by a sense of national destiny . . . not a myopic national security." Quoted by Drury in ibid.

52. Paul Wolfowitz, "Excerpts from 1992 Draft 'Defense Planning Guidance,'" http://www.pbs.org/wgbh/pages/frontline/shows/iraq/etc/wolf.html (accessed September 26, 2003).

53. Byrd quoted in Bernard Weiner, "How We Got into This Imperial Pickle: A PNAC primer," Information Clearing House, May 27, 2003, http://www.informationclearinghouse.info/article3544.htm (accessed September 29, 2003).

54. Quoted on CBSNews.com, "Plans For Iraq Attack Began on 9/11," http://www.cbsnews.com/stories/2002/09/04/September 11/main520830.shtml (accessed September 29, 2003).

55. D'Arcy Doran, "Many Americans Say Saddam Was Behind Attacks," *Seattle Post-Intelligencer,* September 9, 2003, A13. See also Paul Krugman, "Pattern of Corruption," *New York Times,* July 15, 2003, A13.

56. Gerard Toal, "Just Looking for a Fight: American Affect and the Invasion of Iraq," *Antipode* 35, no. 3 (2003): 856–70.

57. Drawing on feminist critiques, I have written elsewhere at length on

the dangers of using psychoanalytic hypotheses to analyze war culture at a societal level; see Matthew Sparke, "Writing on Patriarchal Missiles: The Chauvinism of the Gulf War and the Limits of Critique," *Environment and Planning A* 26 (1995): 1061–89.

58. Michael J. Shapiro, "Wanted, Dead or Alive," *Theory and Event* 5, no. 4 (2002): 1–9. See also Richard Slotkin, *Gunfighter Nation* (New York: Atheneum, 1992).

59. Toal, "Just Looking for a Fight," 859.

60. Quoted in Maureen Dowd, "Culture War with B-2's," *New York Times,* September 22, 2002, A13.

61. Ibid.

62. Ibid. Thomas de Zengotita also usefully highlighted how the masculinist affect mediated through Bush connected 9/11 firefighters with U.S. troops in a single fell swoop of manly "sweet revenge." See de Zengotita, "Romance of Empire."

63. On the subsequent influence of Cheney in controlling Bush's overall foreign policy (and the ways this control was questioned by both Republicans and Democrats in Congress), see Jim Lobe, "Cheney's Grip Tight on Foreign Policy Reins," *Asia Times Online,* October 23, 2003, http://www.atimes .com/atimes/Front_Page/EJ23Aa01.html (accessed October 25, 2003).

64. See Weiner, "How We Got into This Imperial Pickle."

65. Michael Lind, "The Weird Men behind George W. Bush's War," *New Statesman,* April 7, 2003, http://www.newstatesman.com/ (accessed April 18, 2003).

66. Ibid.

67. Back in 1996 Richard Perle and Douglas Feith coauthored a paper with other Israeli-linked strategists for the Jerusalem- and D.C.-based Institute for Advanced Strategic and Political Studies. Entitled "A Clean Break: A New Strategy for Securing the Realm," the paper presented a master plan for Israeli regional dominance and called for "the removal of Saddam Hussein and the installation of a Hashemite monarchy in Baghdad" as well as Israel's abandonment of the Oslo accords and the reestablishment of the principle of preemption. See Kurt Nimmo, "Bush and the Neo-Con Pharisees," *Counterpunch,* December 14, 2002, http://www.counterpunch.org/ nimmo1216.html (accessed October 1, 2003); "The Rise of the Washington 'Neo-Cons,'" *The Guardian,* April 14, 2003, http://www.guardian .co.uk/usa/story/0,12271,936393,00.html (accessed October 1, 2003); and William Hughes, "Where Is Iraq War Instigator, Richard Perle?" *Palestine Chronicle,* July 9, 2003, http://globalresearch.ca/articles/HUG307B .html (accessed October 1, 2003). During the buildup to the Iraq war Perle reportedly made a presentation to senior military officers at the Pentagon that depicted Israel as permanently in control of the West Bank, Jordan as

Palestine, and Iraq again as the seat of the Hashemite Kingdom. See Jim Lobe, "When the Where Conveys More Than the Words," *Foreign Policy in Focus,* February 28, 2003, http://www.fpif.org/commentary/2003/0302neocon_body.html (accessed October 1, 2003).

68. Melanie McAlister, *Epic Encounters: Culture, Media and U.S. Interests in the Middle East, 1945–2000* (Berkeley: University of California Press, 2001).

69. See also Matthew Engel, "Meet the New Zionists," *Guardian Weekly,* November 21–27, 2002, 23.

70. "The Naked Empire," *The Progressive,* November 2002, 7.

71. *The National Security Strategy of the United States of America* (Washington, DC: The White House, 2002), 1.

72. Ibid., preface.

73. Ibid., 14.

74. Ibid., 15.

75. Maureen Dowd, "The Empire Strikes First," *New York Times,* January 29, 2003, A14.

76. He also, of course, claimed following the PNAC script that "The people of the United States and our friends and allies will not live at the mercy of an outlaw regime that threatens the peace with weapons of mass murder." CNN, "Bush Declares War," http://www.cnn.com/2003/US/03/19/sprj.irq.int.bush.transcript/ (accessed July 7, 2003).

77. Joseph Cirincione, "The New American Colonialism," *San Francisco Chronicle,* February 23, 2003, http://www.ceip.org/files/nonprolif/templates/Publications.asp?p=8&PublicationID=1220 (accessed September 29, 2003).

78. Gopal Balakrishnan, "Algorithms of War," *New Left Review* 23 (2003): 5.

79. Anderson, "Force and Consent."

80. Ibid., 13.

81. Lemann, "Next World Order," 42.

82. *National Security Strategy,* preface.

83. Robert Wright, "Contradictions of a Superpower," *New York Times,* September 29, 2002, A17.

84. *National Security Strategy,* 1.

85. Scott Kirsch, for example, did not use the term geoeconomics I am using here, but he argued that the emergent "Bush doctrine" could be directly interpreted, in the terms of *Empire,* as an "expansion of . . . 'imperial sovereignty.'" See Scott Kirsch, "Empire and the Bush Doctrine," *Environment and Planning D: Society and Space* 21 (2003): 2.

86. See Gowan, "American Campaign," 21.

87. Robert Kagan, "Multilateralism, American Style," *Washington Post,*

September 13, 2002, http://www.newamericancentury.org/global-091302 .htm (accessed October 7, 2003).

88. See Maureen Dowd , "Latter-Day Gladiators Reach for Empire," *Times-Picayune* (New Orleans), March 8, 2003, B7; and Dana Priest, *The Mission: Waging War and Keeping Peace with America's Military* (New York: Norton, 2003), 30 and 399. Priest notes that Rumsfeld's concern at the time of entering office was on cutting the Pentagon's more independent global agenda that had been nurtured during the Clinton years, an agenda that was very geoeconomic in outlook. Ironically, his own post-9/11 investments in the project of national retribution may well have brought Rumsfeld back round to see the value of what Priest describes as the CinC system's global mission.

89. *Empire,* 347. Hardt and Negri, it needs noting, make much of the structural resonance between the Roman Empire, Empire, and American constitutionalism before proceeding to their denial that the United States is a new Rome.

90. Quoted in Priest, *The Mission*, 30.

91. On the fantasies and failures of Lewis as a historian, see Edward Said, "Impossible Histories," *Harper's Magazine* 305 (2002): 69–74.

92. A. Toffler and H. Toffler, *War and Anti-War: Survival at the Dawn of the Twentieth-First Century* (Boston: Little Brown, 1993).

93. See Priest, *The Mission*; and Richard Ek, "A Revolution in Military Geopolitics?" *Political Geography* 19 (2000): 841–74.

94. PNAC, *Rebuilding America's Defenses,* 63.

95. Ibid., 69 and 63.

96. Robert Kagan, *Of Paradise and Power: America and Europe in the New World Order* (New York: Knopf, 2003).

97. The simple argument of the book is that Europeans are building an idealistic vision of cosmopolitan capitalist peace and order, whereas Americans are still engaged in a Hobbesian battle for primacy. "The problem today," Kagan summed up, "is that America can go it alone. . . . Geopolitical logic dictates that Americans have a less compelling interest than Europeans in upholding multilateralism as a universal principle." Ibid., 39.

98. See Robert Cooper, "Why We Still Need Empires," *The Observer,* April 7, 2002, http://observer.guardian.co.uk/worldview/story/ 0,11581,680117,00.html (accessed July 7, 2002). It is hardly surprising that a British foreign policy guru was advising imperial double standards given the long history of authoritarian and exceptionalist assumptions by British liberals about the need for brute force in the colonies. See Uday Mehta, *Liberalism and Empire: A Study in Nineteenth-Century British Liberal Thought* (Chicago: University of Chicago Press, 1999).

99. Cooper, "Why We Still Need Empires."

100. A defensive Blair later explained that if the skeptical British public would only listen to President Bush for longer than thirty seconds they would understand too "that what we have to construct is a complete global agenda which gives us a multilateralism that works, multilateralism that is effective." From Blair's perspective, American leadership was going to be effective in this way because it was "correctly identifying on behalf of the world the key security threats of the 21st century and dealing with it in a balanced, measured and just way, so that advantages like Britain and America have are extended to other countries in the world." Quoted in Warren Hodge, "Blair Urges War Dissenters to Look Beyond Their Objections," *International Herald Tribune*, November 12, 2003, 4.

101. Kagan, *Of Paradise and Power*, 75.

102. Ibid., 75–76.

103. Anderson, "Force and Consent," 13.

104. Quoted in Gowan, "American Campaign," 9.

105. Quoted in Perlez, "America Talks," emphasis added.

106. Kagan and Kristol, "The Present Danger."

107. Ibid.

108. Andrew Bacevich, *American Empire: The Realities and Consequences of U.S. Diplomacy* (Cambridge, MA: Harvard University Press, 2002). Of course, other retired U.S. military officers have come to comment on the capitalist complicities of U.S. military engagements. Most famously, Major General Smedley Butler came to write in this way about the early twentieth-century period in extremely critical terms. "I served in all commissioned ranks from Second Lieutenant to Major General," Butler wrote in his retirement, "[a]nd during that period, I spent most of that time being a high-class muscle-man for Big Business, for Wall Street and for the Bankers. In short I was a racketeer, a gangster for capitalism. I suspected I was part of a racket at the time. Now I am sure of it. I helped make Honduras 'right' for American fruit companies in 1903. I helped make Mexico, especially Tampico, safe for American oil interests in 1914. I helped make Haiti and Cuba a decent place for the National City Bank boys to collect revenues in. I helped in the raping of half a dozen Central American republics for the benefit of Wall Street. The record of racketeering is long. I helped purify Nicaragua for the international banking house of Brown Brothers in 1909–1912. I brought light to the Dominican Republic for American sugar interests in 1916. In China I helped to see to it that Standard Oil went its way unmolested." Quoted in Ali, *Clash of Fundamentalisms*, 260. Bacevich's assessment is no less telling, but his tone is—perhaps a sign of today's amoral and nonjudgmental business outlook on the world—much less scandalized. Instead, like Friedman in his comments about globalization, Bacevich presumes merely to be delivering a factual accounting.

"America today is Rome, committed irreversibly to the maintenance and, where feasible, expansion of an empire that differs from every other empire in history. This is hardly a matter for celebration; but neither is there any purpose served by denying the facts." *American Empire,* 244.

109. Ibid., 3. Gowan describes Bacevich's book as a "tonic to read" against much of the hype about globalization. Peter Gowan, "Instruments of Empire," *New Left Review* 21 (2003): 31–36. It is that, but as such, its comfort with the vision of America as the enduring systems manager is as problematic as *Empire's* picture of an entirely unmanaged system.

110. Neil Smith, *American Empire: Roosevelt's Geographer and the Prelude to Globalization* (Berkeley: University of California Press, 2003), xviii.

111. Ibid.

112. Sue Roberts, Anna Secor, and Matthew Sparke, "Neoliberal Geopolitics," *Antipode* 35, no. 3 (2003): 886–97.

113. Thomas Barnett, "The Pentagon's New Map," *Esquire,* March 2003, http://www.nwc.navy.mil/newrulesets/ThePentagonsNewMap.htm (accessed April 5, 2003).

114. Quoted in Daniel Kennelly, "Q & A . . . Thomas P. M. Barnett," *Doublethink,* Summer 2003, 17.

115. Ibid., 18.

116. Thomas Barnett, interview by Wolf Blitzer, *Wolf Blitzer Reports,* CNN, February 26, 2003.

117. Thomas L. Friedman, *The Lexus and the Olive Tree: Understanding Globalization* (New York: Farrar, Straus and Giroux, 1999), 375.

118. It needs noting that the whole approach clearly relies upon a wide array of orientalist assumptions in order to justify the double standard. Ignacio Ramonet described how these worked in concert with the globalization metanarrative quite well in the context of the Iraq war. "The neo-imperialism of the US revives the Roman concept of moral domination, based on the conviction that free trade, globalization and the diffusion of Western civilization are good for the world. But it is also a military and media domination exercised over peoples considered inferior." Ignacio Ramonet, "Transition to Empire," *Le Monde Diplomatique,* May 2003, 1.

119. Thomas Barnett, "The 'Core' and the 'Gap,'" *Providence Journal-Bulletin,* November 7, 2002, 4.

120. The particular parallels with Friedman's outlook could be explored at much greater length. The complicity between geopolitics and geoeconomics in Barnett's discourse is, for example, reproduced in Friedman's poetic coupling of "America Onduty" and "America Online." "America Onduty believes that U.S. foreign policy has been, and continues to be, about defending, erecting and bringing down walls. . . . America Online by contrast,

sees America at the center of an increasingly integrated global web—a web of trade, telecommunications, finance, and environment. For America Online, U.S. foreign policy is about protecting the web from those who would disrupt it, strengthening that web, and expanding it to others—because, after all, America is now the biggest beneficiary of the web, since American products, technologies, values, ideas, movies, and foods are the most widely distributed through it." Friedman, *Longitudes and Attitudes,* 19.

121. Barnett, "Pentagon's New Map," 20.

122. Ibid., 20.

123. Quoted in George Monbiot, "America's Imperial War," *Counterpunch,* February 12, 2002, http://www.counterpunch.org/monbiotimperial.html (accessed April 19, 2003).

124. Quoted in William Finnegan, "The Economics of Empire," *Harper's Magazine,* May 2003, 41.

125. Christopher Farrell, "Extreme Times, Extreme Portfolios," *Business Week,* March 7, 2003, http://www.businessweek.com/ (accessed April 22, 2003).

126. "Currencies," *New York Times,* February 12, 2003, B4.

127. Michael Sesit, "Uncertainty Is Only Certainty Today," *Wall Street Journal,* March 24, 2003, B8.

128. "Currencies," *New York Times,* March 11, 2003, B4.

129. James Lileks, "The Waiting Isn't Really the Hardest Part," *Times-Picayune* (New Orleans), March 6, 2003, B7.

130. Following the pattern charted by Melanie McAlister, this orientalist American script was, as Derek Gregory has also shown in enormous detail, animated by a host of Israeli influences and inspirations. Derek Gregory, *The Colonial Present* (New York: Blackwell, 2004), especially chapter 6 "Boundless War." For a much shorter commentary on how Israeli antiterrorism and U.S. antiterrorism rhetorics and policies were drawing on a common repertoire of orientalist tropes at the time of the Iraq war, see Barbara Piett, "US and Israel's Common Cause," *BBC News,* March 15, 2003, http://news.bbc.co.uk/2/hi/middle_east/2852299.stm (accessed March 17, 2003).

131. While appeals to "British intelligence" provided cover for the White House from time to time in its claims about Iraq's weapons of mass destruction, Tony Blair himself acknowledged to Robin Cook (the former British foreign secretary who subsequently resigned) that he did not believe Saddam's weapons posed a real and present danger to Britain. Cook's own interpretation of Blair's real reason for going to war was "that he found it easier to resist public opinion of Britain than the request of the US president." Quoted in Gaby Hinsliff, "Cook's WMD claims spark No 10 fury," *Guardian Weekly,* October 9–15, 2003, 11. Yet more than just a poodle's

instinct or, in Perry Anderson's terms, an equerry mentality, it is more use-ful to reflect on Blair's support for Bush in terms of his overarching ideo-logical commitment to globalist neoliberalism.

132. On the "benign war" scenario and the argument that "the no war scenario is not necessarily the best for the economy," see "The Economics of War: Calculating the Consequences," *The Economist,* November 30, 2002, 63–64. On Iraqi deaths (and in the face of Tommy Franks, the Ameri-can general who said "we don't do body counts"), see the Web site of the Iraq Body Count Project, http://www.iraqbodycount.net/, which attempt-ed to produce the most rigorous maximum and minimum figures of *civilian* Iraqi casualties from the war. As of October 17, 2003, they were reporting 9,193 as the maximum estimate and 7,390 as the minimum. They were also reporting over 20,000 civilian injuries from the war. Military casualties have remained much harder to assess.

133. Pierre Bourdieu and Loïc Wacquant, "NewLiberal Speak," *Radi-cal Philosophy* 105 (2001): 4.

134. "Stocks Rally as Hopes Rise for Brief War," *New York Times,* April 3, 2003, C1.

135. In the British press, however, George Monbiot of the *Guardian* devoted a whole column to summarizing Harvey's analysis of the over-accumulation imperatives behind the war. George Monbiot, "Too Much of a Good Thing," *The Guardian,* February 18, 2003, 17.

136. As we shall see, though, more sober commentators nevertheless worried out loud about how the phenomenal government borrowing that Bush's policies necessitated would exacerbate wider systemic problems by eventually forcing up interest rates, weakening the dollar, and triggering a long-awaited shock to global capitalism. See William Neikirk, "Tax Cuts Face Maze of Doubts," *Chicago Tribune,* May 5, 2003, 1.

137. John M. Broder, "General Stays on Message at Media Briefing," *Se-attle Times,* March 23, 2003, A5. "This will be a campaign unlike any other in history," Franks said, "characterized by shock, by surprise, by flexibility and by the employment of precise munitions on a scale never before seen, and by the application of overwhelming force."

138. "Quotation of the Day," *New York Times,* September 7, 2002, A1.

139. Frank Rich, "Never Forget What?" *New York Times,* September 14, 2002, A25.

140. De Zengotita, "Romance of Empire," 34.

141. "Toymakers and Troops Play the Same Game," *Sidney Morning Her-ald,* April 19, 2003, http://www.smh.com.au/ (accessed April 22, 2003).

142. Quoted in ibid. See also John Cristoffersen, "Iraq War Action Fig-ures Become Hot Items," *Salon,* April 19, 2003, http://www.salon.com/ (accessed April 22, 2003).

143. D. Parvaz, "He's a Real Doll," *Seattle Post-Intelligencer,* October 20, 2003, E1.

144. Ibid.

145. Julia Day, "Sony to Cash in on Iraq with 'Shock and Awe' Game," *The Guardian,* April 9, 2003, http://www.mediagarden.co.uk/ (accessed April 15, 2003).

146. "Business on the Battlefield: The Role of Private Military Companies," *Corporate Research E-Letter,* http://www.corp-research.org/ archives.htm (accessed March 10, 2003).

147. Quoted in Pratap Chatterjee, "Dyncorp Rent-a-Cops May Head to Post-Saddam Iraq," *Corpwatch,* April 9, 2003, http://www.corpwatch .org/ (accessed April 15, 2003).

148. Subsequently, during the occupation, British and even South African mercenaries became involved in providing so-called security; see Robert Fisk and Severin Carrell, "Occupiers Spend Millions on Private Army of Security Men," originally published in the *Independent,* March 28, 2004; also available at http://www.robert-fisk.com/ (accessed April 6, 2004). However, these groups—with their neoliberal names like "Global Risk Strategies"— remained vastly outnumbered by the American PMCs. The mercenaries fighting for these companies, moreover, increasingly became a legal, political, and economic concern back in the United States. See David Barstow, "Security Companies: Shadow Soldiers in Iraq," *New York Times,* April 19, 2004, http://www.nytimes.com/2004/04/19/international/middleeast/19SECU .html?pagewanted=1&ei=1&en=225b06cf99f005a1&ex=1083382063 (accessed April 19, 2004).

149. Paul Krugman, "Privatization in Iraq Is Out of Control," *International Herald Tribune,* May 5, 2004, 7. Krugman noted that employees from CACI and Titan—two private military contractors—were operating as interrogators at Abu Ghraib prison. Illustrating their built-in unaccountability, Donald Rumsfeld refused to answer Senator McCain's questions about these same private interrogators at the Senate Armed Services Committee meeting in May 2004. David Stout, "Rumsfeld Offers an Apology," *International Herald Tribune,* May 8–9, 2004, 1.

150. Paul Krugman, "Thanks for the MREs," *New York Times,* August 12, 2003, A23.

151. Neela Banerjee, "2 in House Question Halliburton's Iraq Fuel Prices," *New York Times,* October 16, 2003, C1.

152. Lee Drutman and Charlie Cray, "Cheney, Halliburton and the Spoils of War," *Corpwatch,* April 4, 2003, http://www.corpwatch.org/ (accessed April 15, 2003).

153. Quoted in ibid.

154. Julian Borger, "Wolfowitz Preaches to Hawkish Choir," *Guardian Weekly*, October 16–22, 2003, 6.

155. The *Economist* magazine while supportive of the war issued increasingly worried assessments through 2002 and 2003 about the fragile state of the global economy, the failure to really devalue the overaccumulations of the 1990s, the dependency of global demand on the U.S. housing market bubble, mortgage refinancing, and an overvalued dollar, and the reduced ability of multilateral capitalist meetings such as the Cancun WTO talks to generate forward momentum for the expansion of the neoliberal playing field. See especially, "Is It at Risk? Globalization," *The Economist*, February 2, 2002, 65–68; and "Capitalism and Democracy: Special Report," *The Economist*, June 28, 2003, 1–18. The latter special report made a particular point of criticizing America's crony capitalism and the problems of executive influence and overpay. The destabilization caused by the war itself was elsewhere the concern of many real economists; see Paul Blustein, "War Spurs Fears of Another Recession Some Economists Discount Worries," *Washington Post*, March 28, 2003, B15.

156. See Mark Landler, "Meet the New Davos Man," *New York Times*, February 21, 2003, W2.

157. Judy Dempsey, "US Mission to Rally European Support Runs into Criticism," *Financial Times* (London), March 28, 2003, 6.

158. Will Hutton, "Goodbye, Coke. Hello, Mecca Cola; This Boycott of U.S. Products Could Really Do Some Damage," *Washington Post*, April 20, 2003, B4.

159. Ibid.

160. Ibid.

161. See Joseph Weber, "The Postwar Stakes for Business," *Business Week*, April 10, 2003, http://www.businessweek.com/ (accessed April 22, 2003).

162. Jeff Madrick, "Economic Scene," *New York Times*, March 20, 2003, C2; and Christopher Farrell, "Slash Taxes? No, Heal the World," *Business Week*, April 14, 2003, http://www.businessweek.com/ (accessed April 22, 2003). Sesit's concerns were quoted alongside other corporate as well as leftist criticisms in Bob Burnett, "Note to Bush: We Need the World," *Alternet*, April 21, 2003, http://www.alternet.org/story.html?StoryID=15695 (accessed April 22, 2003).

163. Quoted in Weber, "Postwar Stakes for Business."

164. Naomi Klein, "Privatization in Disguise," *The Nation*, April 15, 2003, http://www.alternet.org/ (accessed April 15, 2003). The following quotations from Klein are all from this article.

165. Naomi Klein, "Free Trade Is War," *The Nation*, September 29, 2003, http://www.thenation.com/ (accessed September 29, 2003).

166. "But It All Depends on Iraq," *The Economist,* June 28, 2003, 41.

167. Robert Fisk, "Will Bush's Carve-Up of Iraq Include Getting Hands on Its Oil?" *The Independent* (London), October 12, 2002, 7.

168. Neela Banerjee, "Iraq: US Army Depots Named After Oil Giants," *New York Times,* March 27, 2003, A6.

169. Quoted in George Wright, "Wolfowitz: Iraq War Was About Oil," *The Guardian,* June 4, 2003, 1.

170. Quoted in "Economics of War."

171. Thomas Ferguson and Robert A. Johnson, "Oil Economics Lubricates Push for War," *Los Angeles Times,* October 13, 2002, 4.

172. Daniel Yergin, "Oil Prices Won't Depend on Iraq, but on Its Neighbors," *New York Times,* August 22, 2002, B5.

173. Yahya Sadowski, "No War for Whose Oil?" *Le Monde Diplomatique,* April 2003, 4–5.

174. See Neela Banerjee, "Just a Dribble of Oil Exports as Iraq Struggles," *New York Times,* July 17, 2003, C1–C7. There were still surprises here, and the article quotes a Mr. Alkadiri as saying that "[t]he looting came as a surprise to the Americans. . . . And the Americans' inability to deal with it came as a surprise to the Iraqis."

175. See Michael Klare, "United States: Energy and Strategy," *Le Monde Diplomatique,* November 2002, 2.

176. Christian Parenti, "Mapping Planet America," *Alternet,* April 7, 2003, http://www.alternet.org/ (accessed May 10, 2003).

177. Steven Weisman, "Bush Foreign Policy and Harsh Reality," *New York Times,* September 5, 2003, A9. Apparently the United States asked potential donor country diplomats for $20 billion in September 2003 to pay for the costs of administration in 2004. These diplomats were in turn apparently stunned. "Think of it this way" said one official. "You'd be putting more than a third of the world's development assistance in 2004 into a country with the second largest oil reserves in the world. Imagine what that does to the rest of the poor countries in the world. All of Africa doesn't get that much money."

178. Oliver Burkeman and Suzanne Goldenberg, "Bush Changes Strategy with $87bn Gamble," *Guardian Weekly,* September 11–17, 2003, 1.

179. "Dollars, the Euro and War in Iraq," *Foundation for the Economics of Sustainability,* February 10, 2003, http://www.indymedia.ie/cgi-bin/newswire.cgi?id=28334 (accessed March 27, 2003).

180. Robert Page, "The World Pushes Back," *Boston Globe,* March 23, 2003, 1.

181. Ferguson and Johnson, "Oil Economics Lubricates Push for War."

182. William Greider, "The End of Empire," *The Nation,* September 23, 2002, 13–15.

183. Frédéric Clairmont, "United States: Unsecured Dollars," *Le Monde Diplomatique*, April 2003, 2.

184. Floyd Norris, "Foreigners May Not Have Liked the War, but They Financed It," *New York Times*, September 12, 2003, C1.

185. Donald Hepburn, "Nice War. Here's the Bill," *New York Times*, September 3, 2003, A19.

186. Ibid.

187. Max Boot quoted in Sonya Ross, "U.N. Support Will Cost More Than a Slice of Humble Pie," *Seattle Post-Intelligencer*, September 5, 2003, A10.

188. Anderson, "Force and Consent," 29.

189. Greider, "End of Empire."

190. Some of these more systemic market ties were clearly spelled out in James K. Galbraith, "Don't Turn the World Over to the Bankers," *Le Monde Diplomatique*, May 2003, 6–7. "Should international wealth even begin to depart US shores, the deteriorated ability of the US to provide for its own needs will be exposed. There could be a big effect on US demand. This would soon be transmitted to the exports of countries that rely on the US market, and that will affect their ability to pay their debts. That in turn would affect their credit and reputation of US financial institutions, the bulwarks of international finance and the dollar system. The risk of a crisis arising from such a sequence is perhaps not imminent. But it's not negligible either" (7).

191. Stephen Roach, "The Perils of a Dysfunctional Economy," *Institutional Investor*, April 1, 2003, 1–7.

192. Ibid.

193. Ibid.

194. "Leadership and Luck: The World Economy Needs Both," *The Economist*, September 20, 2003, 31.

195. Ibid., 32.

196. Peter Gowan, "A Calculus of Power," *New Left Review* 16 (2002): 63.

197. Robert Worth, "Iraqi Businessman Sees War-Ravaged Country as a Potential Tourist Attraction," *New York Times*, September 8, 2003, A11.

198. Seymour Hersh, "Lunch with the Chairman," *New Yorker*, March 17, 2003, http://newyorker.com/printable/?fact/030317fa_fact (accessed October 27, 2003).

199. Ibrahim Warde, "It's the Economy Stupid," *Le Monde Diplomatique*, April 2003, 5.

200. Sharon Weinberger, "Administration Weighs Latest Cut to 'Buy America,'" *Defense Daily* 219, no. 12 (October 17, 2003): 1; and Stephen Barr, "Pentagon Plan Would Shift 10,000 Military Jobs to Civilians," *Washington Post*, October 7, 2003, A4.

201. See Carl Hulse, "Swiftly, Terror Futures Market Is a Concept Without a Future," *New York Times,* July 30, 2003, A1 and A10.

202. Quoted in Hulse, "Terror Futures Market," A10.

203. Friedman, *The Lexus and the Olive Tree,* 12.

204. The Christian metaphor seems to me doubly relevant. At the time of writing, General Boykin of the U.S. military was hitting the headlines with his claims that the U.S. battle against Islamic militants was part of a war against Satan. Bradley Graham, "Pentagon to Probe Remarks Made by General Boykin," *Washington Post,* October 22, 2003, A2.

205. Philip Bobbitt, *The Shield of Achilles: War, Peace and the Course of History* (New York: Knopf, 2003).

206. Ibid., 232.

207. Arundhati Roy, "Instant-Mix Imperial Democracy (Buy One, Get One Free)" (paper presented at the Riverside Church, New York City, May 13, 2003, permission from arnove@igc.org).

208. Ibid.

209. Bruce Cummings, "Global Realm With No Limit, Global Realm With No Name," *Radical History Review* 57 (1993): 46–59. Cummings asks, "How might we specify the territory of this empire?" and answers, "It is in the first instance an archipelago of military bases" (52).

210. Gregory, *Colonial Present,* chapter 6.

211. Sam Gindin and Leo Panitch, "Rethinking Crisis," *Monthly Review* 54, no. 6 (2002): 34. See also James B. Rule, "Dissenting from the American Empire," *Dissent,* Fall 2002, 45–49.

212. Gindin and Panitch, "Rethinking Crisis."

213. Gerhard Schröder, "Germany Will Share the Burden in Iraq," *New York Times,* September 19, 2003, A23. Schröder expressed support for the pacification of Iraq and merely lectured in his op-ed piece "that security in today's world cannot be guaranteed by one country going it alone; it can be achieved only through international cooperation." It was a position that bore out Gowan's earlier scathing critique: "The various West European states would all prefer the US to proceed with less unilateralism. But their conception for what passes for 'multi-lateral'—essentially a matter of style rather than substance—remains sufficiently minimal not to represent any threat to American hegemony. . . . The anxiety with which the incoming Bush administration was greeted in European capitals was a sign of dependence rather than distance." Peter Gowan, "Neoliberal Cosmopolitanism," *New Left Review* 11 (2001): 6.

214. See Ruth Rosen, "A Global Antiwar Movement," *Alternet,* February 13, 2003, http:/www.alternet.org/story.html?StoryID=15182 (accessed May 20, 2003).

Index

Abrams, Elliot, 265
abstract national state space, 13,
320n37; and Appadurai, 61,
63–64; and Bhabha, 13, 47–48,
320n38; and cartography, 10–13,
320nn37–38; and *Delgamuukw
v. the Queen,* 15–16, 20–21,
48–49; and emptiness, 22–23;
and financescapes, 75–77; and
free trade, 117, 149; and *Historical Atlas of Canada,* 41–43;
and official names, 20–21; and
property rights, 21–22; and state
practices, xiii. *See also* nation-
state enframing
Acheson, Dean, 353n6
Action Canada Network, 128
affect, 248, 257, 263–64
AFL-CIO (American Federation
of Labor and Confederation
of Industrial Organizations),
136–38, 159–60, 162
agglomeration, 83, 329n55
Agnew, Bruce, 70

Agnew, John, 356n24
Ahmad, Aijaz, 319n21
Alaska, 327n20
Albright, Madeleine, 261, 275,
278
Albrow, Martin, 60
ambivalence, 8–9; in Appadurai,
61–62; Bhabha on, 8, 12–13;
and cartography, 4, 19–20, 50
American Empire (Bacevich),
276–77
American Empire (Smith), 277
American Enterprise Institute, 261
Americans for Better Borders, 99
American studies, xvii–xviii
Anderson, Benedict, 3, 88, 320n38
Anderson, Perry, 243, 244, 269,
271, 275, 357n29, 366n131; on
U.S. budgetary shortages, 301
anemic geographies, xvii, xxix,
xxxiv; and Appadurai, 57; and
Derrida, xvi, 314n3; in *Histori-
cal Atlas of Canada,* 35; and
Laclau and Mouffe, 176–77,

nies, 290; *Rebuilding America's Defenses*, 259–62, 267, 273–74; and war declaration, 268, 361n76
property rights, 21–22

Québécois independence: and Canadian constitutional politics, 203, 205, 206, 207, 208, 210–11; and free trade, 129–30; and *Historical Atlas of Canada*, 33–34

Rabasa, José, 29–30
racism: and Cascadia, 103–5, 107; and free trade, 141–42; and geopolitical basis for Iraq war buildup, 263; and Hollinger, 192–93, 347nn20–21; Morrison on, xvii; and states' rights, 226–27, 351–52n80; and welfare reform, 216–17, 223–25, 227, 228. *See also* white supremacism
Ramonet, Ignacio, 364n118
Rawls, John, 194
Reagan, Ronald, 114, 145, 157, 216, 242, 261, 286
Reaney, James, 32–33
Rebuilding America's Defenses (PNAC), 259–62, 267, 273–74
redistributive practices. *See* Fordist state practices
Red Mexicana de Acción frente al Libre Comercio (RMALC), 163
regional value content, 148–50
Reich, Robert, 156, 229
Reid, Bill, 190–91, 195–96
resistance. *See* counterhegemonic struggle; transnational solidarity
Resnick, Philip, 335n32
responsibility: Derrida on,

xxxi–xxxii; and graphing the geo, xxix, xxx–xxxi, 315n15; and postfoundational theory, xxxiv; and Spivak, xxiv–xxvii, xxxiv, 315n15
reterritorialization, xvii, xviii; and Appadurai, 59–60; and Canadian constitutional politics, 188; and "end of the nation-state" rhetoric, 54; and First Nations, 108–11; and free trade, 120, 144; and globalization, 79–80; and ideoscapes, 67, 74; and mediascapes, 92; and national economy concept, 144, 339n95; and neoliberalism, 112. *See also* Cascadia
Rice, Condoleezza, 267, 301
Rich, Frank, 286
Ridge, Tom, 100
RMALC (Red Mexicana de Acción frente al Libre Comercio), 163
Roach, Stephen, 293, 302–3, 304
Robbins, Bruce, 344n6
Roberts, Sue, 256–57, 277
Robinson, Paul, 32
Rodriguez, Nestor, 231–32
Rofel, Lisa, 256
Roosevelt, Franklin, 276
Roosevelt, Theodore, 276
Rorty, Richard, 173, 188, 194, 344n6
Ros, Jaime, 337n61
Roy, Arundhati, 243, 244, 309
Ruggie, John, 339n95
Rule of Experts (Mitchell), 143, 168, 343n149
Rumsfeld, Donald: and buy-American bill, 306; and geo-economic underpinning of Iraq war, 272, 273, 277–78, 362n88; and geopolitical basis for Iraq

MATTHEW SPARKE is associate professor of geography and international studies at the University of Washington in Seattle. He is the author of numerous articles on topics ranging from globalization, geopolitics, and borderlands to Marxist, feminist, and postcolonial theory. His research and teaching on the political geographies of globalization are funded by a U.S. National Science Foundation CAREER award.